The Longest War

Sex Differences in Perspective

Under the Series Editorship of
Irving L. Janis, Yale University

The Longest War #6

Sex Differences in Perspective

CAROL TAVRIS

CAROLE OFFIR
San Diego Mesa College

HARCOURT BRACE JOVANOVICH, INC.
New York Chicago San Francisco Atlanta

ISBN: 0-15-551182-3
Library of Congress Catalog Card Number: 76-54484
Printed in the United States of America

Interior and cover art by Saul Bass & Associates, Inc.

Credits and Acknowledgments

The authors are grateful to the following publishers and copyright holders for
permission to use reprinted material in the book:

ACTA SOCIOLOGICA for·**Table 14,** p. 283, from Elina Haavio-Mannila, "Convergences Between
East and West," *Acta Sociologica,* Vol. 14, nos. 1–2 (1971). Reprinted by permission.

AMERICAN ANTHROPOLOGICAL ASSOCIATION for **Table 11,** p. 243, from William Divale and Marvin
Harris, "Population, Warfare, and the Male Supremacist Complex." Reproduced by permission
of the American Anthropological Association from the *American Anthropologist* 78:527, 1976.

AMERICAN JOURNAL OF PSYCHIATRY for **Table 9,** p. 221, from Genevieve Knupfer, Walter Clark,
and Robin Room, "The Mental Health of the Unmarried," *American Journal of Psychiatry,* Vol.
122 (February 1966), p. 842. Copyright 1966, the American Psychiatric Association. Reprinted
by permission.

AMERICAN PSYCHOLOGICAL ASSOCIATION for **Table 7,** p. 196, from Sandra L. Bem, "The Measure
of Psychological Androgyny," *Journal of Consulting and Clinical Psychology,* Vol. 42 (1974).
Copyright 1974 by the American Psychological Association. Reprinted by permission.

AMERICAN SOCIOLOGICAL ASSOCIATION for **Table 12,** p. 250, from Karen E. Paige and Jeffery M.
Paige, "The Politics of Birth Practices: A Strategic Analysis," *American Sociological Review,*
Vol. 38, 1973. Reprinted by permission.

BASIC BOOKS, INC., for various quotations from *Collected Papers,* by Sigmund Freud, edited by
Ernest Jones, M.D., Volume 2, authorized translation under the supervision of Joan Riviere,
published by Basic Books, Inc., by arrangement with The Hogarth Press Ltd. and The Institute
of Psycho-Analysis, London. And from *Collected Papers* by Sigmund Freud, edited by Ernest
Jones, M.D., Volume 5, edited by James Strachey, published by Basic Books, Inc., by
arrangement with The Hogarth Press Ltd. and The Institute of Psycho-Analysis, London. And
for 40 words from *Three Essays on the Theory of Sexuality,* by Sigmund Freud, translated and
newly edited by James Strachey, with an Introductory Essay by Steven Marcus, © 1962 by
Sigmund Freud Copyrights Ltd., London. Introductory Essay © 1975 by Steven Marcus, Basic
Books, Inc., Publishers, New York. And for 320 words from *Letters of Sigmund Freud,* selected
and edited by Ernst L. Freud, translated by Tania and James Stern, © 1960 by Sigmund
Freud Copyrights Ltd., London, Basic Books, Inc., Publishers, New York. All material reprinted
by permission.

Pages 332–33 represent a continuation of the copyright page.

With love to my mother, who taught me to want to become something, and to the memory of my father, who believed I could become anything I wanted.

Carol Tavris

To my children, Jessica and Jason, whose generation is a step closer to the truce.

Carole Offir

Preface

The battle of the sexes is not only the longest war but the oldest mystery. There are many puzzles in the relationship of the sexes: Why isn't "man's best friend" woman? Why has male supremacy rather than status equality been the norm? Why is men's work everywhere more valued than women's work? Why have women not achieved as much as men in science, business, politics, the arts? Why, when so many men and women love each other, is there so much distrust and animosity between them as well? Why are people inclined to emphasize the sexual differences between men and women, instead of their human similarities?

Such questions clearly transcend the concerns of any one scholarly discipline. Researchers who study sex differences are like archeologists: each marks an area for excavation and digs independently, hoping to unearth the city that lies beneath them all. Each finds fragments—a tool here, a potsherd there—but the complete city has yet to be revealed. The problem is not that one field is searching in the right way while another is trying to shovel dirt with teaspoons. It is that each discipline raises questions specific to its interests, defines goals and problems in its own way, and uses its particular methods to get answers.

For example, in psychology the study of sex differences (and, occasionally, similarities) tends to produce descriptions of how women and men do on various tests, or how they act in certain situations. The nature of psychological inquiry, by definition, focuses on the individual, usually at a specific moment in history. Psychological explanations often overlook cultural relativity and changes over time. On the other hand, sociologists, whose central business is to study groups, organizations, and societies, tend to minimize the role of the brain and the body in explaining human behavior. Although our own professional degrees and research have been primarily in psychology—one of us is a social psychologist, the other an experimental psychologist—we are interdisciplinary by training and inclination, and saw this book as a good chance to find out what each social science is doing at its excavation site.

We begin with an introductory chapter that describes the historical tendency to see the female sex as the different one, the one to be explained. Throughout the ages, most writers (of both sexes) have placed woman either above man, on a pedestal, or below him, in the gutter. The next two chapters (Part One) explore the gap between stereotype and reality, reporting what research has found about the actual differences between women and men in ability, personality, and sexuality.

To account for the strength of sexual stereotypes and the survival of status differences between men and women, Part Two examines sex differences from five perspectives, beginning with the smallest unit of analysis, the individual, and moving outward to larger social units. Each perspective has a different emphasis. The biological perspective (Chapter 4) regards sex differences in behavior and status as a result of hormonal, genetic, and reproductive differences. The psychoanalytic perspective (Chapter 5) emphasizes unconscious processes and the way anatomy influences the feelings and sexual development of women and men. The learning perspective (Chapter 6) considers the ways children learn the culture's standards of masculinity and femininity. The sociological perspective (Chapter 7) stresses the influence of organizations and social roles on people's attitudes and behavior, particularly through the institutions of work and the family. The evolutionary perspective (Chapter 8) looks at the adaptive value of social customs for the survival of societies. It explains sex roles in terms of the material needs, ecology, and technology of a culture. The final chapter describes twentieth-century efforts to achieve sexual equality, concentrating on China, the Soviet Union, Sweden, and Israel, and speculates on how fast the winds of change are blowing.

Because the book focuses on differences between the sexes, we had to sacrifice important questions of class and race differences within each sex. The life of a Roman slave had little in common with that of a wealthy Roman. In our own society, the gap between rich and poor, of whatever sex and race, creates enormous differences in people's attitudes and behavior. Further, the lives of many black women, who endure the double prejudice of color and sex, are not wholly comparable to the lives of many white women. For instance, studies on achievement motivation, socialization, family life, and economic discrimination find differences between black women and white. But to summarize these findings without space to discuss them would be more confusing than helpful, we thought, and would deflect attention from our main topic: the chasm between women and men of all classes, cultures, and races.

We called the book *The Longest War* even though the title created controversy. Some people thought it sounded too militant; others feared it might seem unserious. But it captures an important paradox. Men and women, though engaged in an endless love affair, have often regarded each other as "the other side," and sometimes as the enemy. Further, it takes two to disagree, and this book tries to understand the situation of both sexes. Because women have been regarded as "the problem," most of the research on sex differences focuses on why women are not more like men. But rigid sex roles, myths, and stereotypes have caused problems for men as well as women—too many problems, we believe, to offer much hope for "male conspiracy" theories of history.

The subject of sex and status differences is both personally immediate and politically explosive. Questions about sex and the sexes are not mere intellectual puzzles. They affect real human lives and have consequences for all of us. In this book, we have tried to follow a fine line between the bland neutrality that feigns fairness and the polemical commitment that obscures divergent points of view. In addition to evaluating studies and theories in scientific terms, we discuss their social and political implications, pointing out bias at both ends of the political spectrum. When our search for scientific answers led to data-less dead ends (a not uncommon occurrence), we occasionally turned to personal experience and hunches, which most scientists publicly discount but privately admit inform their most inspired work. We do not apologize for our anecdotes and hunches. They are clearly labeled and cannot be mistaken for scientific truths. Besides, from little hunches mighty theories grow.

The book can be used as a core text or supplement in courses on women's studies, sex differences, women and men, and gender. It will also fit into broader courses that include a unit on sex differences or male–female relations, such as human development, personality, social psychology, social problems, and marriage and the family. Some instructors in cultural anthropology, political science, and biology also deal with male–female issues in enough detail to make the book useful. Finally, it may find a place in interdisciplinary courses, since it demonstrates how various groups of scientists formulate and try to answer the same basic questions. Because the book was written mainly for undergraduates, we have kept technical terminology to a minimum and tried to make underlying concepts explicit. Our goal was for readers of all backgrounds and disciplines to be able to understand and evaluate the material. Most of all, we have tried to retain the sense of humor that keeps human beings sane in the face of serious issues.

Many people helped us finish *The Longest War*. We are especially grateful to our editor, Catherine Caldwell Brown. She razors through complex issues with a sharp mind and clear knowledge of the material, and her skill with the written word is matched only by her wit and good sense. She has added immeasurably to this book, in both substance and style, and we have been enriched by the experience of working with her.

Judith Greissman of Harcourt Brace Jovanovich is an author's dream. Her extraordinary clarity of mind aided us from the inception of the book to its execution. She has a rare ability to see to the heart of a problem, articulate solutions, rouse flagging energy, and hasten delayed chapters. We also profited from the skills of Susan Joseph, our copy editor; Nancy Kirsh, who designed the book; Kenzi Sugihara, who supervised its production; and John Holland, who managed the in-house course of the book. Laurie R. Abramson read the manuscript with a student's eye and was consistently enthusiastic and supportive. Our special thanks to Saul Bass, of Saul Bass & Associates, Inc., whose cover drawing and illustrations for this volume were a labor of love and provide just the right blend of insight and humor.

Our academic reviewers did their job with sensitivity and care, criticizing the hardest way—constructively. Our warm appreciation goes to Karen E. Paige, University of California, Davis; Phillip Shaver, New York University; Letitia Anne Peplau, University of California, Los Angeles; Sandra Scarr, University of Minnesota; Cynthia Fuchs Epstein, Queens College of the City University of New York; Irving L. Janis, Yale University; Brian Weiss; Constance L. Hammen, University of California, Los Angeles; Rebecca Stafford, University of Nevada, Reno; Julia R. Heiman, State University of New York at Stony Brook; Anne C. Petersen, Michael Reese Medical Center; and Rose L. Coser, State University of New York at Stony Brook. Thanks go also to Carol Roberts, San Diego Mesa College, for making unpublished data available to us and for her helpful comments. Professionals, of course, evaluate a book from the perspective of their own training and knowledge. But we were also greatly helped by those for whom the book was written—students—whose questions, reactions, and complaints in our courses helped us identify and analyze the issues that most concerned them.

Not least, our love to the men who love us, who have taught us that the bond between the sexes offers the sweetest hope for ending the longest war.

Carol Tavris
Carole Offir

Contents

6

Getting the message: The learning perspective   161

7

Earning the bread vs. baking it:
The sociological perspective   201

8

The origins of roles and rituals: The evolutionary perspective 237

9

Conclusion: The age of alliance? 271

The Longest War

Sex Differences in Perspective

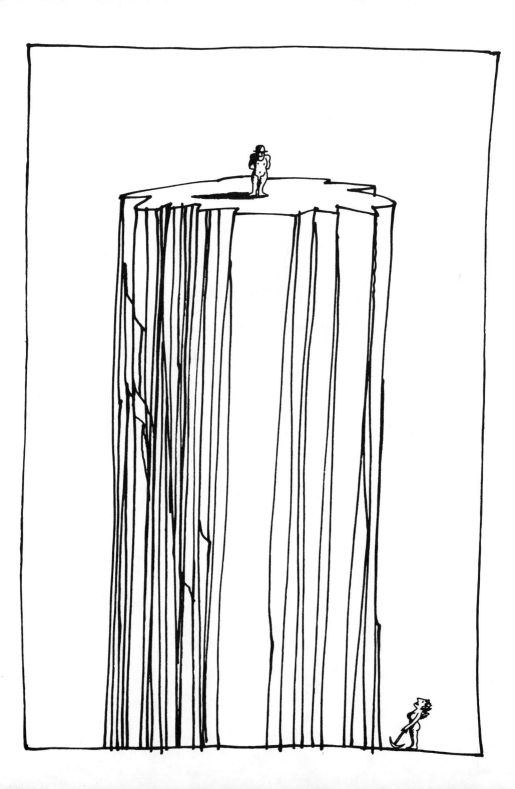

1

Introduction: The longest war

Men and women are two halves of the same species, so one might expect them to fit together like two sides of a coin. Yet throughout history the sexes have regarded each other less as fellow human beings than as alien and exotic creatures—to be loved, feared, cherished, or confined. In every society, in every century, people have assumed that males and females are different not merely in basic anatomy but in elusive qualities of spirit, soul, and ability. They are not supposed to do the same things, think the same way, or share the same dreams and desires.

Men and women have wooed each other with lustful abandon and ritual restraint, but they have also fought—if not with military weapons then with psychological, economic, and sexual ones. The battle of the sexes began in the sleepy dawn of prehistory and has continued to the present. There have been countless alliances and dalliances across enemy lines, but the peace treaties never seem to last. It is truly the longest war.

It is also the longest love affair, of course, and the great love stories in history still thrill us: Abélard and Héloïse, Beatrice and Dante, Robert Browning and Elizabeth Barrett, Antony and Cleopatra, the Duke and Duchess of Windsor. But love does not guarantee equal, or even kind, treatment. Periander of Corinth married Melissa of Epidaurus for love, six centuries before Christ, but that didn't keep him from murdering her in a jealous rage—and it was his legal right to do so. The puzzle is why history sometimes records more affinity between man and dog (or horse, or even camel) than between man and woman. Misogyny, the hatred of women, has enjoyed a long and robust tradition, and for some reason the enmity on the male side of the sexual barrier has been more openly expressed than that on the female side. Although the Greeks wrote of the Amazons as a "man-hating, man-killing" group, there are few accounts of women who were fervently antimale, and we have no single word for a woman's hatred of men. Woman-hating is an established custom, with articulate and eminent spokesmen. Man-hating is too new, or too newly out of the closet, even to have its own label.

Nonsense, some readers will say, most men *love* women, and vice versa. It is not fair to pick out a few surly males and label the whole lot misogynists. Woman has been esteemed, worshipped, and protected as often as she has been loathed, ignored, and reviled. True. We call these apparently opposite attitudes the pedestal-gutter syndrome. Woman is goddess and devil, virgin and whore, sweet madonna and malevolent mom. She can bring a man up to salvation or drag him down with her to hell. On the face of it, the pedestal-gutter syndrome appears to reflect views that are diametrically opposed: woman is good, woman is bad. But in fact these views represent a single attitude: woman is different. After all, whether you are looking up to women or stooping down to them, you don't have to look them in the eye.

Differences by themselves need not cause animosity. It is only when one group considers the other to be immoral, deficient, or dangerous that conflict arises. In the relationship between the sexes, women have been regarded as deficient males, insatiable sexpots, and incarnations of evil. They are the second sex, the weaker sex, the inferior sex, the sex to be explained. The "woman problem" has proved so obsessive to men that we emerged from our reading with a new sense of appreciation for ourselves. Our sex has been the object of a 10,000-year worry.

Man's concern about woman is marked by passion and paradox. As long as man sees woman as the opposite sex, the mysterious one, he can never explain her satisfactorily. She will shift and change as he does, like a reflection in a pool. The poet Semonides of Amorgos summarized male ambivalence in the seventh century B.C.: "For Zeus designed [woman] as the greatest of all evils—and bound us to it in unbreakable fetters." The fetters are need and desire, but in spite of (or perhaps because of) these powerful motivations, men and women have never faced each other as equals. No culture anywhere has said, "OK, women, who have wombs, will bear the children. Men, who are strong, will fight the wars. Now we can divvy up control of the gods, the arts, the politics, and the McDonald's franchises." Men and women have never shared power, privilege, and status on an equal basis.

Instead, every society has distinguished men's work from women's work and created barriers between the sexes. Sometimes men and women have had so little to do with one another that one wonders how the population explosion ever managed to take place. Sarah Pomeroy (1975), a historian, reports that in classical Athens, which people usually regard as a highly civilized city, the segregation of the sexes was so complete that husbands had to be directed by law to consort with their wives three times a month. That was more than enough, the law supposed, to produce the required number of heirs and, added Plutarch, to reduce marital tensions.

Even today, men and women in some cultures work, sleep, and eat apart from each other, getting together on only a few critical occasions for the sake of the species.

The basic questions this book tries to answer are: Why are the sexes so alien to each other? Why are lovers not more often friends? Why has an equal society never existed on this planet? In the first part of this chapter we review three prominent and recurrent themes that seem to characterize men's reflections on women: how to control women's sexuality, assure their obedience, and justify their inferior status. We chose these themes in order to illustrate how attitudes can legitimize inequality, *not* in an effort to argue that a male conspiracy has caused it. These pervasive male concerns about women provide a background for later chapters, for the themes change in shape but never in substance across the centuries.[1]

In the second part of the chapter we contrast what men think about women with the realities. What men say women do frequently bears little resemblance to what women actually have done, and this is a fascinating discrepancy. Finally we describe the organization of the rest of the book, which examines the riddle of female "otherness" from various perspectives.

the bitter half: themes of misogyny

controlling female sexuality

Woman is a pitfall—a pitfall, a hole, a ditch,
Woman is a sharp iron dagger that cuts a man's throat.

—*Babylonian poet*

Woman as a treacherous, seductive manipulator of sexual wiles appears in the earliest recorded literature. In the Gilgamesh epic, a Babylon-

---

[1] Originally we wanted to include the other half of the picture—how women have regarded men. We had to abandon this plan, because there is not enough material available written by women. Those who did have something to say on the subject, such as the eleventh-century historian Anna Comnena or the second-century writer Lady Pan Chao, usually mirrored the prevailing male view, that the best of woman was a lesser man. This fact in itself is important, because it indicates that both sexes accepted the dominant values of their societies. Those values specified who was taught to write, what sort of thing was allowed to be written, and which writers were heeded. "In the war of the sexes, as in other wars," says Morton Hunt (1967), "history is written by the victors."

ian classic, the gods create Enkidu from clay to fight Gilgamesh and save the city of Erech. Gilgamesh sends a harlot to distract Enkidu. She does.

She put aside her robe and he lay upon her.
She used on him, the savage, a woman's wiles,
His passion responded to her.

For six days and seven nights Enkidu approached and coupled with the prostitute.
After he was sated with her charms,
He set his face toward his game

(Quoted in Bullough 1973, p. 28.)

Enkidu, innocence lost, is now in trouble: his knees wobble, he weakens, he loses speed. He has learned what Samson will learn from Delilah, Marc Antony from Cleopatra, and a generation—a past one, we hope—of football players from their coaches: sex saps your strength.

Every great religion and almost all regional ones warn men about women's seductiveness. The Manu code of India, a set of laws dating from about A.D. 100, explains that "it is in the nature of women to seduce men [and] for that reason the wise are never unguarded [in the company of] females. For women are able to lead astray in this world not only a fool, but even a learned man, and to make him a slave of desire and anger."

In the Judeo-Christian tradition, the story of Adam and Eve warns of the tragedy that awaits the man who yields to the temptation of woman: he must lose paradise. Actually, according to the ancient Hebrews, God tried three times to make a suitable partner for the first man. The first woman, Lilith, was made of "filth and sediment" instead of Adam's pure dust, and she behaved accordingly. She even had the gall to say, "Why must I lie beneath you? I also was made from dust, and am therefore your equal" (quoted in Figes 1970). Naturally Adam was offended and tried to force her into obedience. Lilith, furious, took off and populated the world with evil demons. God then tried a second time to give Adam a mate he could tolerate, but this attempt also failed. Finally God came up with Eve, and we all know what she did.

The story of Lilith associates the sexual mysteries of women with reproductive ones. Men have thought of women as not only seductive but unclean. For example, throughout history men have reacted to menstruation with a mixture of awe, pity, disgust, and fear. The early Siberians made menstruating women sit in a special hut and wear a special hat so they would not contaminate the heavens, much less the men. Segregated menstrual huts are still common in many parts of the world. The Australian aborigines feared the menstrual flow so much that a man who found his menstruating wife on his blanket might be moved to kill her. The Roman writer Pliny published a long list of the "virulent effects" of the menstrual discharge. He warned that menstruating women could cause bees to abandon their hives, pregnant mares to miscarry, and fruit to fall from the tree. Further, they could blunt the edge of a good razor, sour new wine, and make green grass wither. Religions have reinforced such fears. The Old Testament forbade men to touch a menstruating woman lest they too become "unclean," and Orthodox Jewish women today must still take a ritual bath, the mikvah, following their periods. Hindu law decreed that a menstruating woman should not look at anyone, even her own children. Zoroaster wrote that a menstruating woman was the work of the devil, and during her "periodical illness" she was not to gaze upon the sacred fire, behold the sun, or talk to a man. The Koran, the holy book of the Muslims, called the menstruating woman a "pollution."

Many cultures warned men about the horrible things that may happen to those who yield to female sexual mysteries and lures: they turn weak, they die, their penises fall off, they lose magic powers. Because sex was so powerful and mysterious, it was taboo on many occasions. As analyst Wolfgang Lederer noted, "A man about to go to war, or to the hunt, a man aiming to do some serious fishing or to conduct some serious business, had better not touch a woman, neither to sleep with her nor to eat with her."

The harder men tried to suppress their own sexuality, the more anxious their descriptions of female sexuality became. The most intense reaction probably occurred in that heyday of celibacy, the Middle Ages. Monks and priests, striving to adhere to the Christian ideal of sexual abstinence in thought as well as deed, found an outlet in eloquent name-calling. Salimbene, a thirteenth-century Franciscan monk, collected some of his colleagues' thoughts on the matter:

> Wouldst thou define or know what a woman is? She is glittering mud, a stinking rose, sweet poison, ever leaning toward that which is forbidden her.

> Woman is adamant, pitch, buckthorn, a rough thistle, a clinging burr, a stinging wasp, a burning nettle.

> Lo, woman is the head of sin, a weapon of the devil, expulsion from paradise, mother of guilt, corruption of the ancient law.

> (Quoted in Bullough 1973, p. 173.)

Male anxiety is also revealed in an inflammatory book written by two Dominican theologians in the fifteenth century, Heinrich Kramer and Jacob Sprenger. They issued the *Malleus Maleficarum* (Witches' Hammer), a sort of "Everything You Always Wanted to Know" about the black arts. The two monks had been appointed by Pope Innocent VII as inquisitors and told to wipe out witchcraft in Germany. Their book explained, among other things, why there were fewer male witches than females. Women, they concluded, are more superstitious than men, weaker in mind and body, and insatiable in their sexuality—vices that make them particularly susceptible to the devil. Men, themselves tainted by original sin, had better be on guard lest these voluptuous vessels of lust entice them to the devil's work (van Vuuren 1973).

Few male writers in any age considered the possibility that a man might stray because *he* is weak or sexually insatiable. The blame always went to the woman. (This still happens today, as when rapists protest that they didn't do anything wrong—the victim provoked them by looking seductive.) A fourteenth-century English preacher warned his congregation about the startling power of a provocative woman:

> In the woman wantonly adorned to capture souls, the garland upon her head is as a single coal or firebrand of Hell to kindle men with that fire. . . . In a single day, she inflames with the fire of her lust perhaps twenty of those who behold her, damning the souls God has created and redeemed at such a cost (quoted in Hunt 1967, p. 147).

If a simple garland on the head could so inflame a man, drastic action was called for. Throughout history, regulations appeared on the proper dress for women; they typically recommended covering up completely and denounced perfume and paint. For instance, an old Athenian treatise had advised that the ideal woman would not "cover herself with gold, nor braid her hair with artful device, nor anoint herself with Arabian perfume, nor will she put white makeup on her face or rouge her cheeks or darken her brows and lashes or artfully dye her graying hair; nor will she bathe a lot" (quoted in Pomeroy 1975). Obviously, some Greek man knew exactly what aroused him.

Not *every* culture had a negative view of sexuality. But even in societies that had a positive view of sex, a good woman-bad woman distinction was often made and the rules for being good were clearly drawn. Thus, the ideal Islamic woman, unlike the Athenian, "is always elegantly attired; she perfumes herself with scents, uses antimony for her toilets, and cleans her teeth with souak [the bark of the walnut tree]." But she must never "surrender herself to anybody but her husband, even if abstinence would kill her" (quoted in Bullough 1973).

The point is that female sexuality has always been subject to rituals and taboos that define when a woman can make love and with whom.

Standards of sexual attractiveness and performance change frequently, as fashions do, and styles of sexuality vary from Renaissance plump to Virginia slim. Some cultures regard sex as furtive, dirty, and secret; others elevate it to high art. Historically and cross-culturally, nonetheless, male efforts to control the female's sexuality and reproductive ability have lingered. They are not the idiosyncratic maunderings of a few fanatics.

keeping women in their place

How bitter it is to be a woman. Nothing on earth is held so cheap.

—Fu Hsuan

Any two groups that are unequal in resources, opportunities, and access to the political process—whether by virtue of age, class, race, education, or sex—confront each other from different positions of power. In the case of women, the difference in power has had a specific economic function; they have served as a currency of exchange and negotiation. Often, like slaves, they have been regarded as men's property, to be bought and sold, punished and raped, traded or married off in political allegiances. The thirteenth-century Franks knew exactly what their property was worth. If a man killed a mature woman, he had to pay 500 solidi to her owner; but if he killed a young, unskilled girl, he had to pay only 200 solidi. The law said that any man could beat his wife, but being an advanced law it added, "provided death does not ensue" (Hunt 1967).

Susan Brownmiller argues in *Against Our Will* (1975) that rape, which has been and still is astonishingly prevalent, is much less a sexual act than an act of power and dominance, an assertion of man's control over his property—or his neighbor's property. Even the rules of chivalry during the era of courtly love, when rich women were virtually worshipped, permitted rape now and then. The woman, however adored by her knight, was little more than a pawn in an elaborate chess game, a prize for the best player. Brownmiller quotes an explanation of chivalric rules by Chrétien de Troyes:

> If a knight found a damsel or wench alone, he would, if he wished to preserve his good name, sooner think of cutting his own throat than of offering her dishonor; if he forced her against her will, he would have been scorned in every court. But, on the other hand, if the damsel were accompanied by another knight, and if it pleased him to give combat to that knight and win the lady by arms, then he might do his will with her just as he pleased, and no shame or blame whatsoever would be held to attach to him (quoted in Brownmiller 1975, p. 291).

Obviously, if women were to be used as objects of barter and liaison, as tests of courage and symbols of conquest, they must learn to be obedient. "The courage of a man is shown in commanding, of a woman in obeying," wrote Aristotle, who thought men were superior to women in all ways, and even had more teeth. Throughout history, women's duties were carefully spelled out by anyone who could spell (usually a man). The basic rule, as the Roman historian Livy noted, was that "women's servitude is never terminated while their males survive." The Manu code of India and China's principle of the "three dependencies" stated that a woman was first subject to her father, then to her husband, finally to her sons. (In most American wedding ceremonies, the father still "gives away" the bride, though the expression is no longer taken as literally as it once was.) The Book of Proverbs tells us precisely how the perfect wife should behave, and it's no wonder that her price is above rubies, because she works constantly with nary a moment's rest. "She riseth also while it is yet night. . . . Her candle goeth not out by night [and] she eateth not the bread of idleness."

Such pronouncements clearly express male fantasies about the perfect woman, but they also raise the question: Why have there been so few fantasies of an intellectual partner, an equal, a friend? Women who stepped out of line, or who tried to step up, were generally greeted by emotional outbursts. Juvenal, a famous misogynist who wrote in the second century A.D., held a special grudge against women who fancied themselves intellectually equal to men. "I hate a woman who observes all the rules and laws of language," he muttered, "who quotes verses I never heard of."

Scholarly debate from Plato to the eighteenth-century French *philosophes* has pondered the problem of female education. One didn't want them to become too smart, for then they might get out of hand, but one didn't want wives who were mentally feeble, either. The question was how to educate them to the point where they would be knowledgeable but not disobedient. A French Catholic archbishop and writer of the seventeenth century, Fénelon, offered one approach:

> A woman's intellect is normally more feeble and her curiosity greater than those of a man; also it is undesirable to set her to studies which may turn her head. Women should not govern the state or make war or enter the sacred ministry. Thus they can dispense with some of the more difficult branches of knowledge which deal with politics, the military art, jurisprudence, philosophy, and theology (quoted in Bullough 1973, p. 272).

What is left, you ask? Fénelon recommended that women learn a little arithmetic for purposes of household economics, reading, writing, and a dash of reasoning: to make them less susceptible to flattery.

After the French Revolution even the *philosophes,* who had hoped that education would cure women's defects, were reluctant to advocate full political equality for women. Eva Figes (1970) analyzes this inconsistency in the philosophy of Jean Jacques Rousseau, whose ringing call for freedom—"Man is born free, and everywhere he is in chains"—inspired a generation. The trouble is, says Figes, that Rousseau literally meant man, not woman; in *The Social Contract,* Rousseau described an exclusively male bond. Females, he said, "must be trained to bear the yoke from the first, so that they may not feel it, to master their own caprices and to submit themselves to the will of others." In *Emile,* Rousseau explained in more detail how this training was to be accomplished. A woman must learn to be passive and docile, modest and chaste, "to submit to injustice and to suffer the wrongs inflicted on her by her husband without complaint." Suffer injustice in silence—strange advice from one who wrote so passionately of man's right to overthrow tyranny. When it came to women, Rousseau the modern emancipator was no different from the ancient Greek male who admonished wives to endure their husband's "temper, stinginess, complaining, jealousy, abuse, and anything else peculiar to [their] nature" (quoted in Pomeroy 1975).

Probably the first recorded protest on the part of women (Lilith's was an individual resistance) occurred in 195 B.C., when Roman women gathered to demand repeal of the Oppian Law, which had confiscated much of their wealth and forbade them to display the remainder in dress or carriage. The women won, but they provoked dire warnings from certain senators about the consequences of giving in to women. Livy reported one such speech, attributed to Cato:

> Give loose rein to their uncontrollable nature and to this untainted creature and [you cannot] expect that they will themselves set bounds to their license. . . . It is complete liberty or, rather, complete license they desire. If they win in this, what will they not attempt? . . . The moment they begin to be your equals, they will be your superiors."

It's the old foot-in-the-door theory: give 'em the vote and they'll run for Congress, give 'em a book and they'll want college, give 'em a job and they'll want yours. Two thousand years after Cato, men were still chastising women who stepped out of line, as in this nineteenth-century reaction to the fledgling feminist movement: "There is no deformity of human character from which we turn with deeper loathing than from a woman forgetful of her nature, and clamourous for the vocation and rights of men" (quoted in Myrdal 1944). Again we must ask what prompted such a worried reaction: why loathing instead of loving?

The reaction is not altogether universal. Some men have been strong allies of women, especially during the last hundred years, when women themselves began to speak up in organized efforts for equality. John Stuart Mill, who wrote "The Subjection of Women" in 1861, was an ardent feminist who believed that marriage conferred excessive power on the husband, that women were conditioned to roles that made them servants of men, and that no biological destiny fitted women to be subordinates. George Bernard Shaw skewered antiwoman mores in his plays and essays, coming out strongly in favor of the independent woman who refused to obliterate herself in the service of the family. "If we have come to think that the nursery and the kitchen are the natural sphere of a woman," he wrote in an 1891 essay on the role of women, "we have done so exactly as English children come to think that a cage is the natural sphere of a parrot—because they have never seen one anywhere else."[2] And sex researcher Havelock Ellis, battling Victorian waves of sexual repression, wrote that women were sexual beings too, and entitled to full sexual pleasure. It is an interesting question in itself, however, why male feminists—and female feminists, for that matter—should arrive so late on the historical scene, and why movements for sexual equality have figured so insignificantly in human history.

justifying female inferiority

What inspires respect for woman, and often enough even fear, is her *nature,* which is more "natural" than man's, the genuine, cunning suppleness of a beast of prey, the tiger's claw under the glove, the naiveté of her egoism, her uneducability and inner wildness, the incomprehensibility, scope, and movement of her desires and virtues. . . .

—*Friedrich Nietzsche*

---

[2] "No doubt," Shaw continued, "there are Philistine parrots who agree with their owners that it is better to be in a cage than out, so long as there is plenty of hempseed and Indian corn there. There may even be idealist parrots who persuade themselves that the mission of a parrot is to minister to the happiness of a private family by whistling and saying 'Pretty Polly.' . . . Still, the only parrot a free-souled person can sympathize with is the one that insists on being let out as the first condition of its making itself agreeable."

Historically, men's perception that women were easily overcome by lust, vanity, and greed fit their general view that females were animal-like by nature. Men, who after all had been created in the image and likeness of God, were more noble and intellectual. Plato, when forced to the philosophic wall, stated that "the gifts of nature are alike diffused in both [sexes]; all the pursuits of men are the pursuits of women also"—but then he couldn't help adding, "but in all of them a woman is inferior to a man." The problem for women, according to Plato, is that they are governed by their wombs, not their brains.

> The womb is an animal which longs to generate children. When it remains barren too long after puberty, it is distressed and sorely disturbed, and straying about the body and cutting off the passages of the breath, it impedes respiration and brings the sufferer into extreme anguish and provokes all manner of diseases, besides.

Plato's cure for the "wandering uterus" syndrome was for the woman to get pregnant immediately. He never suggested, however, that any male ills occur because the prostate gland detaches itself and floats up to chat with the lungs.

Some writers, in their effort to show that women were more like animals than human beings, got carried away. Think about the slang words that refer to women and you will have enough animals to populate a small zoo: bitch, bird, cow, pig, cat, dog, hen, chick, mule, filly. But your list will be nothing compared to the catalog that Semonides detailed in the seventh century B.C.:

> From the beginning God made the mind of woman
> A thing apart. One he made from the long-haired sow;
> While she wallows in the mud and rolls about on the ground,
> Everything at home lies in a mess.
> The god made another from the evil fox,
> A woman crafty in all matters—she doesn't miss a thing. . . .
> The next one was made from a dog, nimble, a bitch like its mother,
> And she wants to be in on everything that's said or done.
> Another woman is from the stumbling and obstinate donkey. . . .
> [She will] welcome any male friend
> Who comes around with sex on his mind.
>
> (Quoted in Pomeroy 1975, pp. 49—50.)

Semonides compared women to all manner of beasts, concluding that the only woman who is worth anything at all is like the bee: she bustles about busily and serves her husband, and she "does not take pleasure in sitting among the women when they are discussing sex."

Although the Greeks made the first effort to explain women's inferiority on an empirical basis, it was not until the eighteenth and nineteenth centuries—the Age of Enlightenment—that science took from theology the responsibility for explaining the deficiencies of women. To the rational mind, Eve's fall could no longer be used to explain female frailty, but physiology could. Science did not dispel the prevailing concept of female inferiority; instead, the conviction of inferiority directed much of the research. The conclusions that scientists reached about women were similar to those they drew about blacks: women and Negroes, the white men agreed, had smaller brains and larger instincts, which accounted for and justified their subordinate position in society.

Thus, when the infant science of psychology took up the matter of sex differences in the late nineteenth century, it sought to identify the precise deficiency in the female brain that accounted for her weak intellect and strong emotions. As Stephanie Shields (1975) reports in her review of early psychological research on women, much effort was expended to show that men had larger heads and larger brains and were therefore more intelligent. But this explanation did not hold up, because the males' greater height and weight offset their brain-size advantage. Undaunted, some researchers pointed out that the ratio of brain surface to body surface favors men. Others found that the ratio of brain weight to body weight favors women. Eventually, this general line of reasoning was dropped.[3]

Another attack tried to identify which sections of the brain were different enough in men and women to account for male superiority. When scientists discovered that the frontal lobes were responsible for intellectual ability, several neuroanatomists found that women's frontal lobes were less ample than men's, while female parietal lobes were larger. Then, at the turn of the century, some scientists argued that the parietal lobes, not the frontal lobes, were responsible for intellect. This change in the concept of brain functions, Shields wryly observes, "involved a bit of revisionism." Neuroanatomists hastened to their laboratories and discovered that parietal lobes were actually smaller in women and the frontal lobes larger. This scientific about-face, along with findings of other supposed anatomical deficiencies in females, required a remarkable lack of objectivity. It didn't

[3] But not by everyone. Bkaktivedanta Swami Prabhupada, founder of the International Society of Krishna Consciousness, explains the shortage of women in his movement as follows: "Woman is not equal in intelligence to man. Man's brain weighs sixty-four ounces. Woman's weighs thirty-six ounces. It is just a fact. . . . Women are meant to assist man and that is all." (*Arizona Daily Star*, July 27, 1975).

help that in many studies the researchers knew the sex of the brain they were dissecting; they could see the differences they wanted and expected to see.

Other scientists accounted for the "woman problem" by studying women's bodies rather than their brains. Like Plato, they concluded that it was the female reproductive system that made women so irrational. Because women are built to bear children, their drives and desires are biologically determined, controlled by their fluctuating hormones and the maternal instinct. In 1890, Shields reports, P. Geddes and J. A. Thomson explained that the sexes have fundamentally different metabolisms: men are active, creative, and "catabolic," while women are passive, conservative, and "anabolic." Physically, intellectually, and emotionally, the sexes are complementary, not equal: "Man thinks more, woman feels more. He discovers more but remembers less; she is more receptive and less forgetful."

Efforts to find sex differences in the brain continue today, because the similarity between hemisphere function and sexual stereotype is too tempting to let go. The two halves of the brain, like yin and yang, have complementary qualities: the right hemisphere has been associated with the "feminine" activities of emotion, inspiration, intuition, and passion, while the left hemisphere has been associated with the "masculine" abilities of analytic thinking, logic, and reason. So scientists are studying the brain-wave patterns of men and women doing various tasks, to see which half of the brain is more active. Others study "split-brain" patients, people whose cerebral hemispheres have been surgically separated to reduce the severity of epileptic seizures. The results of such research, however, are contradictory and inconclusive. Female traits do not fall neatly into one side of the brain while male traits bunch up in the other. So far, researchers have not found out much more about sex differences by splitting brains than by weighing them.

the female paradox: attitudes vs. reality

To judge from the writings of men, women have never been able to do anything right. They are supposed to be sexy and seductive, but then men complain that they are insatiable and immodest. Women are excluded from direct participation in the political machinery of society, but then men complain that they are sneaky, manipulative, and indirect in getting what they want. Women are often deprived of education and professional training, but then men complain that they are dumb. Women are disparaged as inferior, weak, and passive, yet when women seek equality in a strong and active manner, men panic.

It would be easy to suppose that men's attitudes toward women are somehow the cause of male supremacy: "Most Athenians in ancient Greece hated women, so they shut them up in solitude and took away their rights." But attitudes do not spring forth randomly like wildflowers; they reflect and perpetuate the social order. It is just as possible to argue that misogynistic attitudes were the *result* of a system of male supremacy rather than the cause: "Because women in Athens were walled up and isolated from men, men learned that they were supposed to hate women."

If female inferiority were obvious to everyone, if there were in fact basic personality differences between the sexes that insured the higher status of one sex, controls on female behavior would not be necessary. No law states that dogs and four-year-olds may not run for public office; when we find such laws against women, who some men *say* have the mental capacity of dogs and four-year-olds, we must ask what they accomplish. Human beings erect rules when they are faced with temptations and alternate possibilities, not when everything is obvious and easy.

We must avoid, therefore, the common tendency to attribute conscious plots to the course of evolution. Primitive men did not gang together one languid afternoon and decide to keep women forever barefoot and pregnant. Nor did primitive women, after a gossipy day down at the river washing clothes, decide that they would rather do the weaving and leave the warfare to men. We cannot explain the tenacity of sex differences by name-calling; the double standard has not persisted because men are "male chauvinist pigs" and women are "insatiable dumb broads." When we find a custom that is as widespread as polygyny (one husband with several wives) and one that is as rare as polyandry (one wife with several husbands), we can't simply grumble that men are unfair and greedy. When male adultery is regarded as an amusing peccadillo or a God-given right but female adultery brings society's wrath and sometimes the woman's death, we're better off looking for explanations that go beyond group attitudes. When we find cultural universals, patterns that recur in places as disparate as Egypt and China, India and Indiana, we must seek the powerful evolutionary forces behind them.

cultural consistencies

Anthropologists have identified some of those cultural universals, which are impressive in view of the extraordinary diversity of human ritual and social organization. There are notable consistencies, for example, in the tasks that men and women have done throughout history. If a society's economy includes fishing, hunting large game, farming a long way from home, making weapons, or metal-working, men have always handled these activities. Men have always been primarily responsible for fighting the wars, women for tending the children (D'Andrade 1966). Similarly, there are some consistencies to the personality traits that are supposed to mark each sex. A cross-cultural study of 110 societies found that boys are typically trained to be self-reliant and to achieve, while girls learn to be nurturant, responsible, and, as we saw, obedient (Barry, Bacon, and Child 1957).

Apart from these patterns, most of the personality traits and specific activities that cultures assign to men and women vary widely. But everywhere in the world masculinity is considered the opposite of femininity, even when the traits and jobs associated with males in one culture are those associated with females in another. In the United States, for example, people tend to think that women are emotional and irrational compared to men, but in Iran women are considered the cold and logical sex. The Manus, according to Margaret Mead, are convinced that only men enjoy playing with babies, and a Philippine tribe is certain that it is the men who cannot keep secrets. In some tribes men weave and women do not, and in others women weave and men do not.

Further, men's work is universally regarded as more valuable than women's work, no matter how arbitrary the division of labor. In many cultures, including our own, women do the shopping and marketing, and those activities are considered unintellectual tasks for the unintelligent sex. But in ancient Greece, marketing was men's work, because buying and selling were complicated financial transactions too difficult for the female mind (Pomeroy 1975). Among the Toda of India, men do the domestic chores; such work is too sacred for a mere female. If the women of a tribe grow sweet potatoes and men grow yams, yams will be the tribe's prestige food, the food distributed at feasts (Rosaldo 1974). And if women take over a formerly all-male occupation, it loses status, as happened to the professions of typing and teaching in the United States, medicine in the Soviet Union, and cultivating cassavas in Nigeria.

Surely, in all the myriad forms of social organization that have existed in this world, somewhere women have ruled? The search for matriarchies began in the mid-nineteenth century, when Johann Jakob Bachofen wrote *Das Mutterrecht.* Drawing on myth, poetic epics, and dubious historical tracts, Bachofen concluded that "mother-right" was the first form of human society, that women originally controlled the family and the state. (In the same year, 1861, Henry Sumner Maine published *Ancient Law,* using Scripture and Roman law to argue that patriarchy was the basic human model.) Bachofen's theories won him strong supporters, such as the American anthropologist Lewis Henry Morgan. Morgan in turn influenced Friedrich Engels, who thought that the subordination of women had not begun until the emergence of class hierarchies and private property.

It is true that *myths* of matriarchy have flourished (Webster 1975). In stories and folklore around the world, women are often described as the original creators and rulers of the world; men eventually organized and rebelled, seizing power and banishing women from the men's inner sanctums. But myths cannot be taken as reality. Although a horde of archaeologists and social anthropologists have sought evidence to support Bachofen, they have found not one single undisputed case of matriarchy —not one culture in which women *as a class,* not as exceptions, controlled the resources and the men (Bamberger 1974). In some societies, such as the Iroquois, some women could achieve a measure of power and influence (Brown 1975), but even Iroquois women, who played an important role in village politics and lineage, could not join the Council of Elders, the ruling body.

Within each society, in other words, males have held the most prized offices, controlled the basic resources, and extolled the superiority of their sex. Although women in some countries had more advantages and opportunities than women in other places, and although "male dominance" has not always meant female suppression, the relative position of the sexes in each culture is always the same. The women of ancient Egypt had more rights than Mesopotamian women, but Egyptian men believed that a woman's place was in the home, even though both sexes worked in the fields. Spartan women were far better off than Athenian women: the girls of Sparta were as well-fed as the boys, got as much exercise, and could wear the Dorian peplos, a predecessor of the miniskirt. In contrast, Athenian women were confined to their houses and wore a cumbersome, voluminous garment called a chiton. But the relatively liberated Spartan women did not have the vote, and Spartan men regarded them as decidedly inferior to themselves.

Similarly, the upper-class Roman wife of the late Empire had considerably more rights and choices than her foremothers in Rome or her contemporaries in Greece. She could go to parties, plays, and the temple, and she was even allowed to eat with her husband. But Roman men thought their women were licentious and incompetent, and no Roman female ever got into the Senate. American women today are far better off, legally and economically, than women in India, Japan, or Turkey, but most American men still do not regard them as equals.

Some people think that men have higher status because they do the "important" productive work while women handle the menial chores. This theory derives from the assumption that men, by virtue of their greater strength, took on the more strenuous tasks in the course of evolution, while women, weakened by the physiological burdens of pregnancy and nursing, did the simpler tasks. Many anthropologists are challenging this assumption. Women may not have held the power, but they have always participated fully in the economic and cultural lives of their societies. Joel Aronoff and William D. Crano (1975), for example, studied a sample of 862 societies from around the world. They found that the supposed universal division of family labor—men handle the economy, women handle the children—was simply not so. Women add significantly to the subsistence economy of their societies, contributing, over the whole sample, 44 percent of the food. In most hunting-and-gathering societies, women, the gatherers, provide fully two-thirds of the tribe's food. Men, the hunters, get the necessary but sporadically available protein. Males, in short, are not the only sex that brings home the bread.

Nor are women the weaker sex. On the contrary, they often work harder and longer than men. Among the Dobe Bushmen of the Kalahari Desert in Africa, women provide two-thirds of the food for their camps. The men spend a few hours a day hunting, and the women gather vegetables, carrying loads of fifteen to thirty-three pounds back to camp along with small children and water (Friedl 1975). It's rarely been children *or* work for women; more commonly they have done both.

Nor are women the incompetent sex. When countries are at war and the men go off to fight, women customarily manage the economy. They have directed the household, run the shop, superintended the farming, collected taxes for the castle, staffed the factories. Some women have governed countries that were otherwise entirely partriarchal in structure and philosophy: Hatshepsut and Cleopatra in Egypt, Nee Lu in China, the queens of England and France, Indira Gandhi in India. When women had the leisure of court or convent, many became artists and poets; in the eleventh century, a Japanese court woman, Murasaki Shikibu, wrote the first novel, *The Tale of Genji*.

So there are some curious discrepancies between man's vision of woman and the reality, between her participation in society and her subordinate status, between beliefs and behavior. This puzzle is fascinating, because our society and many others around the world seem to be on the verge of a genuine revolution in sex roles. During the transition, if such it is, people need to know which differences between women and men are basic and useful and which have outlived their usefulness to the culture and to individuals.

an American dilemma

American women have come a long way from the days in which they were traded like cows or supervised like sheep, but the historically contradictory image of woman lives on in the modern mind. If you think that equality is just around the corner, consider the evidence:

1. *Salary.* Women earn, overall, only 58 percent of what men do, even when the sexes are matched for age, education, experience, skill, and tenure on the job (Levitin, Quinn, and Staines 1973; Treiman and Terrell 1975). In some occupations women earn as much as 80 percent of the average salary of men; on the other hand, the 1970 census found that while male physicians earn an average of $25,000 a year, female physicians earn $9,788. Men outdistance women even on women's home turfs, such as nursing, teaching, and typing. The only occupation in which women earn more than men is kindergarten teaching (Sommers 1974).

2. *Politics.* Women are running for and winning political office in increasing numbers, but there are, at this writing, only eighteen women in Congress and none in the Senate.

3. *Business.* It is still unusual to see women in the bastions of financial power and in high corporate echelons. Virtually all the wealthiest women in the country got their money by marrying it or inheriting it, not by earning it (Robertson 1973).

4. *Law.* In many states, when a woman marries she trades the rights of a "person" for the duties of a wife. Husbands no longer have total command of their spouses, but many inequities remain. Alabama and Kentucky prohibit a wife from selling or leasing her own property without her husband's written approval. (He does not need her approval to sell his property, though.) In most states a married woman may legally keep her maiden name, but usually not without struggling through red tape. Census-takers, doctors' offices, local businesses, and relatives all assume that the man is the head of the household and carries financial responsibility for the family, even if the wife earns as much as he does or more. A married woman's legal domicile is defined as the domicile of her husband, which means that a husband who deserts his wife, takes a temporary job in another state, or goes to school in another state can seriously affect his wife's right to vote, serve on juries, run for office, and so on.[4]

5. *Physical abuse.* Even the notion that a wife is her husband's property lingers, both in law and in practice. In almost every state in the union, men have the legal right to rape their wives and to administer an unspecified amount of physical punishment. The laws define rape as "an act of sexual intercourse with a female, *not one's wife,* against her will and consent" (Brownmiller 1975).

Perhaps the most compelling evidence that a "war" between the sexes still exists comes from the data on wife-beating and rape. The incidence of both is increasing. In 1973, according to the FBI, 51,000 rapes were reported, a rise of 62 percent in five years. The FBI estimates that ten times that many actually occurred. In 1973 in New York State, 14,000 wife-abuse cases were taken to family court; Boston police get over 16,000 wife-beating calls a year. The FBI thinks that wife-abuse occurs three times as often as rape—that is, about 1.5 million times a year. Even that figure may be low. Stewart Oneglia, a female attorney who counsels victims of wife-abuse, thinks half of all American marriages may involve some physical abuse of the wife, and she doesn't mean light slaps. "My worst case," she told *People* magazine (May 3, 1976), "was the wife of a physician in Montgomery County, Maryland, the richest county in the nation, whose husband jumped on her spine, causing paralysis, because she left the door open and the cool air-conditioned air escaped." That case was one of 650 incidents of assaults by husbands in one year in Montgomery County (Gingold 1976). The phenomenon, in short, crosses all economic and racial lines, though most cases of wife-abuse and rape never reach the courts. Allan Rogers, director of the Massachusetts Law Reform Center, says that people don't consider wife-beating a serious matter. "They say every man has the right to beat his wife once in a while."

6. *Attitudes.* Stereotypes, like laws, usually persist even after the realities have changed. If you believe that misogyny is anachronistic, ask some people to tell you the traits they think are typical of women and men. You

---

[4] In many places married women confront indignities that single women do not. Sometimes they are trivial but have psychological consequences. One woman we know applied for a library card and was told she could have one only in her husband's name. "But it's for *me,*" she said. "My daughter, age fourteen, even has her own card." The librarian was adamant; who would pay for the book if it were lost? "I will, damn it," our friend bellowed. "Oh?" said the librarian. "And just what do you do?" "I," she lied calmly, "am a prostitute." She got the card.

will probably hear that women are dependent, talkative, timid, weepy, vain, and bad at numbers, and that men are strong, self-reliant, courageous, dominant, athletic, and good at math. Psychologists have demonstrated in the laboratory that the two sexes agree on the "typical" traits of men and women (Broverman et al. 1972), as shown in Table 1. Male and female raters alike assign positive value to more masculine qualities than feminine ones. Also, the valued qualities associated with women tend to be the reverse of those associated with men. Women may "express tender feelings"; men should "hide emotions." Women "do not use harsh language"; men may "talk freely about sex with other men." Women "appreciate art and literature"; men "like math and science." Women need security; men are independent and adventurous.

Since masculine traits are so highly regarded, it's no wonder that most prospective parents prefer boys. Two decades ago, Simon Dinitz and his colleagues (1954) asked young adults what sex they would like their first-born to be and what sex they would prefer if they could have only one child. Two-thirds of the men and women cared about the sex of their first child—and almost 92 percent of these wanted a boy. As for an only child, 91 percent of the men and 66 percent of the women preferred a boy. The times haven't changed these attitudes much. In a recent rerun of Dinitz's study, the one significant difference was that "only" 81 percent of the men wanted their only child to be male (Peterson and Peterson 1973).

Attitudes about the sexes often are coated in humor. A joke is not supposed to be taken seriously, and of course anyone who criticizes jokes can be accused of lacking a sense of humor. Philip Zimbardo and Wendy Meadow (1974) looked at the sexes in American humor as revealed in the pages of the *Reader's Digest*. They chose the *Digest* because of its huge circulation, because it draws material from many media, and also because it has been around for decades and they could compare jokes from the 1940s, 1950s, and 1960s. Zimbardo and Meadow went through 1,000 jokes, counting as antifemale those that portrayed women in derogatory ways, depended on the target being female instead of male, and contained a punch line that characterized women negatively. They used parallel criteria to identify antimale jokes.

The researchers found six times as many antifemale as antimale jokes. Most typically, women were depicted as stupid or foolish: "Sweet young thing to husband: 'Of course I know what's going on in the world! I just don't understand any of it, that's all.'" Other categories of antiwoman jokes included women who dominate men, exploit men for their money, are jealous of other women and catty, are irresponsible with money, gossip and nag, and are overanxious to marry. Antifemale humor was especially prevalent in the 1940s, right after World War II; such jokes made up nearly one-third of the total. (This high percentage may have reflected the social and economic insecurities of the times, when women left wartime jobs to make room for returning soldiers.) After the 40s, the percentage of antifemale jokes declined, but even in the late 60s they were 12 percent of the total, and the ratio of antifemale to antimale jokes had not changed.

Table 1. Stereotypic traits

Masculine pole is more desirable	
Feminine	Masculine
Not at all aggressive	Very aggressive
Not at all independent	Very independent
Very emotional	Not at all emotional
Does not hide emotions at all	Almost always hides emotions
Very subjective	Very objective
Very easily influenced	Not at all easily influenced
Very submissive	Very dominant
Dislikes math and science very much	Likes math and science very much
Very excitable in a minor crisis	Not at all excitable in a minor crisis
Very passive	Very active
Not at all competitive	Very competitive
Very illogical	Very logical
Very home oriented	Very worldly
Not at all skilled in business	Very skilled in business
Very sneaky	Very direct
Does not know the way of the world	Knows the way of the world
Feelings easily hurt	Feelings not easily hurt
Not at all adventurous	Very adventurous
Has difficulty making decisions	Can make decisions easily
Cries very easily	Never cries
Almost never acts as a leader	Almost always acts as a leader
Not at all self-confident	Very self-confident
Very uncomfortable about being aggressive	Not at all uncomfortable about being aggressive
Not at all ambitious	Very ambitious
Unable to separate feelings from ideas	Easily able to separate feelings from ideas
Very dependent	Not at all dependent
Very conceited about appearance	Never conceited about appearance
Thinks women are always superior to men	Thinks men are always superior to women
Does not talk freely about sex with men	Talks freely about sex with men

Feminine pole is more desirable	
Feminine	Masculine
Doesn't use harsh language at all	Uses very harsh language
Very talkative	Not at all talkative
Very tactful	Very blunt
Very gentle	Very rough
Very aware of feelings of others	Not at all aware of feelings of others
Very religious	Not at all religious
Very interested in own appearance	Not at all interested in own appearance
Very neat in habits	Very sloppy in habits
Very quiet	Very loud
Very strong need for security	Very little need for security
Enjoys art and literature	Does not enjoy art and literature at all
Easily expresses tender feelings	Does not express tender feelings at all easily

SOURCE: Broverman et al. 1972. The table shows the extreme poles of 7-point rating scales. Average ratings of the typical male fall toward one pole; of the typical female, toward the other pole.

For all our awareness and sophistication, then, relations between the sexes in America are not that different from sexual relationships all over the world. Men's work has the prestige and brings in more income, even when it is neither intrinsically more interesting nor socially more valuable than women's work. Men and women still think men are the better, smarter sex. Men still want a first-born son, though they won't strangle a first-born daughter, as the Yanomamo Indians of South America do.

Why?

perspectives on female "otherness"

For the sake of argument, let us for the moment draw two opposing hypotheses about the nature of sex differences. The first suggests that the human condition is such that the bliss and the agony of sexual attraction depend on power and mystery. Perhaps we are dealing with paradoxical but inevitable attraction and antagonism between opposites, a natural polarity in body and mind. When all is said and done, perhaps men will always reserve part of themselves for other men and women will share some things only with other women. Perhaps neither sex can understand the experience of the other: male and female may indeed be like the two sides of a coin, in that the bond between them requires them to face in opposite directions.

Or it might be that sex differences in power and personality are archaic, decaying leftovers from old systems. The mystery of the opposite sex, in this view, is a result of ignorance and is hardly inevitable. As soon as economic and social conditions change to allow women equal participation in politics and work, equality in sexual relationships will follow.

In the following chapters we consider the questions raised in this chapter from a set of widening perspectives, beginning with the biology and psychology of the individual and ending with the evolution and anthropology of societies. The two chapters of Part I deal with the basics: which differences between the sexes are real, as far as the research shows, and which are imagined. Chapter 2 takes up differences in abilities and personality, the stuff of stereotypes, and Chapter 3 deals with differences in sexual behavior and attitudes. Although people persist in believing that the sexes differ in style, substance, and sex drive, the evidence confirms more similarities than differences.

Part II describes and evaluates various explanations that have been offered for the prevalence of sex stereotypes and sexual inequalities:

—The biological perspective (Chapter 4) argues that women have been subordinate to men because they are internally programed for their roles as wives and mothers: their hormones, genes, and reproductive instincts channel and limit their skills and personalities.

—The psychoanalytic perspective (Chapter 5) takes as its starting point the anatomical differences between the sexes as represented in the unconscious mind. It states that each sex regards the other's reproductive and sexual abilities with elements of fear and envy, and that these emotions help account for both the attraction and the animosity between the sexes. Male supremacy and misogyny, in this view, derive either from the anatomical superiority of the male or from the ultimate mystery of motherhood.

—The learning perspective (Chapter 6) argues that sex differences in behavior and personality are learned and socially prescribed. Boys and girls are not "naturally" different, but they are treated differently from childhood and taught to play different roles. This chapter discusses not only how learning occurs but what is learned—the messages about sex roles that fill our books, media, and minds.

—The sociological perspective (Chapter 7) says that roles themselves determine how people act and feel. Sociologists are less interested in why people with certain personality traits choose certain roles than in the reverse: how roles shape personality. Thus, they regard sex differences as created and perpetuated by institutions, especially work and marriage; by patterns of power and discrimination; and by the economic needs of societies.

—The evolutionary perspective (Chapter 8) explores the economic and ecological forces that have supported sexual inequalities and that have produced the apparently irrational attitudes and rituals described in Chapter 1. This view looks for the origins of rules and roles in a culture's subsistence economy, history, and social structure.

Some perspectives will suit you and others you will dislike. It is not easy to separate the strengths and weaknesses of an approach from its subjective appeal. Because the topic of sex differences is immediate and personal, it is hard for women and men to regard themselves as products of time and culture, specks in a system that has come a long way and will go a long way hence. But distance from the problem may make its contours clearer, as it does the forms in an impressionistic painting.

Naturally, the perspectives overlap; there are many ways to illuminate a dark room, and they are not mutually exclusive. Probably no perspective, considered alone, is either completely right or totally wrong. Our intent in presenting the perspectives one at a time is not to minimize the overlap but to clarify each perspective's contribution.

Finally, in Chapter 9, we consider the prospect for sexual equality in the future, looking at some imaginative twentieth-century social experiments being tried in Israel, Russia, China, and Sweden. Many people say that these efforts to eradicate sexual inequalities have failed, and that the reason must be that they run counter to woman's biological destiny. Others say the right experiment has yet to be done. The last chapter reviews some barriers to equality and each perspective's answer to the question so aptly put by Henry Higgins: "Why can't a woman be more like a man?"

I

The sexes: Defining the qualities

2

Sex differences, real and imagined

The stereotypes people hold about men and women are easy to identify; you merely have to go out, questionnaire in hand, and ask people about them. You soon find out that the Archie Bunkers of this world, who yearn for the days when "girls were girls and men were men," and the Maude Findlays, who would like to see the Archies stifled forever, can at least agree on what the stereotypes are. If only it were as easy to find out which of the supposed sex differences are real.

But it is not. In an area as controversial as sex differences, personal beliefs can easily affect research results. In the nineteenth century, biased assumptions caused scientists to flip-flop in a suspicious manner when they were looking for sex differences in the brain. Scientists nowadays are more enlightened about how their own expectations can influence their experiments, but it is still difficult to run objective studies. A few years ago Robert Rosenthal and his colleagues demonstrated in a dramatic way how belief can become reality. They asked some student-experimenters to train rats to run a maze. Half of the experimenters believed their rats had been specially bred to learn maze-running rapidly, while the other half thought the rats had been bred for dullness. Although there was no real genetic difference between the two groups of rodents, the supposedly bright rats did, in fact, learn faster. If an experimenter's expectations can influence rats, Rosenthal concluded, they surely can influence human beings, and this he demonstrated in many other studies (Rosenthal 1966; 1968).

The manner in which an experimenter produces a self-fulfilling prophecy is usually nonverbal and, like the abominable snowman, hard to track down. For example, Rosenthal observed that male experimenters gave instructions to the men and women in their studies rather differently. Only 12 percent of the researchers smiled at the men, but 70 percent smiled at the women. "It may be a heartening finding to know that chivalry is not dead," says Rosenthal, "but as far as methodology is concerned it is a disconcerting finding." It's easy to imagine how an experimenter's facial expression might affect his results. For instance, if his smile made people feel friendly and rewarded and his study happened to concern people's need for affiliation (their desire to be with others), he might find a sex difference that he himself had unwittingly caused.

Another methodological problem arises in studies that rely on self-reports. Suppose you believe that males are more independent than females, and you want to prove it. If you merely ask people how independent or dependent they are, your interviewees may slant their answers toward what they believe is socially desirable: a man may try to sound more self-reliant than he feels; a woman, less so. Or your interviewees may have distorted perceptions of themselves that have little to do with the way they behave in daily life. One solution is to question a second party. Many child psychologists use this method; they ask teachers and parents to describe the children in their care. Here again, though, one risks collecting biases instead of objective observations.

Another approach is for the researcher personally to observe the behavior of children or adults in a natural setting, such as home or school. This method allows you to deal with actual behavior, but you still have the problem of your own implicit assumptions. As a psychologist interested in assertiveness, how would you distinguish "passive" behavior from that which is merely "easy-going"? How would you distinguish submissiveness, which is the opposite of assertiveness, from cooperation, which is not? The danger is that you might label the same bit of behavior differently when a girl did it than when a boy did.

In addition to assigning different labels to the same act, an observer may simply fail to notice certain kinds of behavior. Someone who claims that housewives are passive and submissive may be overlooking many situations in which housewives are active. (Caring for children and organizing and maintaining a home require considerable assertiveness and initiative.) Similarly, if someone tells you that men tend to be unemotional and insensitive, it may be because she or he has ignored situations that allow men to be expressive.

As if all this were not bad enough, there is another obstacle that impedes the pursuit of scientific truth. Studies that identify sex differences are much more likely to be published in professional journals than those that do not. Nonfindings don't have much drama and, besides, scientific convention dictates that it is impossible to prove that a difference between groups does *not* exist. All a researcher can say is that there is no evidence a difference does exist, which is pretty dull compared to proclaiming: "Eureka! Men do X and women do Y." For that reason, studies identifying even small sex differences often have exaggerated clout.

In recent years there have been attempts to review the scientific literature on sex differences and to come up with some reliable generalizations. The reviews have tended to give more weight to studies that find differences than to those that don't, and to accept results uncritically. A good example is a 1968 monograph, "Sex Differences in Mental and Behavioral Traits," by Josef E. Garai and Amram Scheinfeld. The authors cited 474 studies but did not explain how they had selected them, nor did they discuss the quality of the procedures used in the studies. Most of the conclusions they reached conformed to popular stereotype. For example, the review found that females have greater social needs than males, and that males are superior to females in abstract reasoning and conceptualizing—which, the authors believed, helps explain "the outstanding achievements of men in science, philosophy, and the construction of theories." Garai and Scheinfeld suggested that the talent gap between the sexes might be bridged by encouraging girls to achieve and by giving them a bit of compensatory education, such as special training in creativity and problem-solving.

In 1974, Eleanor Maccoby and Carol Jacklin, two Stanford psychologists, published *The Psychology of Sex Differences,* which quickly became a classic text. In preparing their book, Maccoby and Jacklin carefully examined a larger body of research than any of their predecessors—over 2,000 articles and books, most of them published after 1966. Unlike other reviewers, they made a special effort to locate and include studies that might have found differences but did not. They even reanalyzed data when they thought it was necessary. So that readers could follow their analysis, they included a 233-page annotated bibliography and eighty-three summary tables. Maccoby and Jacklin concluded that many common assumptions about sex differences, including some that Garai and Scheinfeld maintained were proven, were completely unfounded; they were simply myths posing as facts. But they also found that males and females do differ in some interesting ways.

The Maccoby and Jacklin review is not without some serious weaknesses. Although the authors discussed methodological problems at length, when it came to evaluating hypotheses their approach was to tally all the studies pro or con, usually without counting the better research more heavily. Sometimes they reached conclusions mainly on the basis of studies with young children, a serious error because some sex differences do not emerge clearly until adolescence. So Maccoby and Jacklin's book is not the final word on sex differences, but it is far and away the most complete and thoughtful summary to date.

In the following sections we will review the findings most relevant to the issue of sex roles and status differences, as summarized in Table 2. The discussion frequently draws on Maccoby and Jacklin's information, (1974a and b), but we also question some of their conclusions and bring in other studies. Keep two things in mind as you read. First, when we speak of differences we mean group differences, or average differences. To say that one sex outdoes the other on some test does not mean that all members of that sex do better than all members of the opposite sex. Men and women overlap in abilities and personality traits, as they overlap in physical attributes. Men on the average are taller than women, but some women are taller than most men. Second, in this chapter we confine ourselves mainly

Table 2. Sex Differences and Similarities

Abilities

General intelligence	No difference on most tests.
Verbal ability	Females excel after age 10 or 11.
Quantitative ability	Males excel from the start of adolescence.
Creativity	Females excel on verbal creativity tests; otherwise, no difference.
Cognitive style	No general difference.
Visual-spatial ability	Males excel from adolescence on.
Physical abilities	Males more muscular; males more vulnerable to illness, disease; females excel on manual dexterity tests when speed important, but findings ambiguous.

Personality Characteristics

Sociability and love	No overall difference; at some ages, boys play in larger groups; some evidence that young men fall in love more easily, out of love with more difficulty.
Empathy	Conflicting evidence.
Emotionality	Self-reports and observations conflict.
Dependence	Conflicting findings; dependence probably not a unitary concept.
Nurturance	Little evidence available on adult male reactions to infants; issue of maternal vs. paternal behavior remains open; no overall difference in altruism.
Aggressiveness	Males more aggressive from preschool age on.

to describing research findings on sex differences in twentieth-century American society, with only brief detours to offer explanations. In later chapters we will analyze in more detail the factors that may account for actual sex differences and help perpetuate beliefs about mythical ones.

sex differences in ability

Women's intuition is the result of millions of years of not thinking.

—Rupert Hughes

Women are only children of a larger growth; they have an entertaining tattle, and sometimes wit; but for solid, reasoning good sense, I never in my life knew one that had it.

—Earl of Chesterfield

Women, as everyone knows, have not achieved fame in the arts, sciences, and professions as often as men; the Madame Curies and Margaret Meads stand out as exceptions. Part of the problem is that many notable women have been lost to history, unrecognized for their achievements. Regardless, a popular explanation for women's relative lack of public success is that females are not as bright as males. Although girls get better grades in school than boys, it is assumed they lack the genius necessary for oustanding achievement.

Tests of general intelligence do not show differences in the average IQs of males and females. This is not surprising, because the most widely used IQ tests were designed to minimize sex differences. If a question happened to differentiate between males and females, the test-maker would throw it out, or carefully balance an item favoring one sex with an item favoring the other. So we must turn to tests of specific abilities, not to IQ scores, in the search for sex differences.

verbal ability

If a woman could talk out of the two sides of her mouth at the same time, a great deal would be said on both sides.

—George Prentice

When both husband and wife wear pants it is not difficult to tell them apart—he is the one who is listening.

—Anonymous

Pediatricians, parents, and comedians credit females with having the gift of gab from infancy on. They are not necessarily paying women a compliment, though. As we all know, quantity does not guarantee quality: the politician who gives long, windy speeches and the party-goer who tells interminable stories are bores. According to the stereotype, women talk a lot but often have nothing worthwhile to say. So the stereotype has more to do with gossip and chit-chat than with intellectual skill.

When psychologists speak of verbal ability, however, they refer to specific abilities measurable in specific ways. These include simple measures of articulation, spelling, punctuation, sentence complexity, vocabulary size, the ability to name objects, and fluency, and also more sophisticated, higher-level measures of reading comprehension, creative writing, and the use of language in logical reasoning. Until recently, most psychologists believed that girls, from the time they first learned to talk, were superior on at least the simple measures. They based this assumption on several large studies from the 1930s and 1940s, which found that girls start to talk earlier than boys, use longer sentences, and excel verbally in other ways (McCarthy 1954). But Maccoby and Jacklin argue that psychologists need to reevaluate these findings. They observe that many of the early studies showed only small sex differences, some not even statistically significant. Although there are few recent studies comparable in scope to the early ones, some smaller ones do not find a sex difference in children younger than two or three. The safest conclusion seems to be that we do not yet know for sure whether girls talk sooner or more, or are more skilled with words, than boys during the first few years of life.

From age two to age ten, boys are far more likely than girls to have reading problems, but otherwise they do not lag behind girls in linguistic competence. At the age of ten or eleven, however, girls edge ahead. Though not every study reports a sex difference, those that do find that girls perform better on verbal tasks than boys. Girls maintain this superiority, or even increase it slightly, during high school, even though low-achieving boys drop out of school in larger numbers, leaving a rather select comparison group (Droege 1967).

In their 1968 monograph, Garai and Scheinfeld said that girls were better at simple verbal tasks but claimed that they were inferior on the higher-level ones. Perhaps, they speculated, that is the reason men do better in science and engineering. The Maccoby and Jacklin review finds no evidence for this distinction. After the age of ten or eleven, girls do better on both "lower" and "higher" measures of verbal skill. Apparently it is not for want of a golden tongue that most girls fail to become scientists and engineers—or courtroom lawyers, political orators, and auctioneers.

quantitive ability

She is like the rest of the women—thinks two and two'll come to make five, if she cries and bothers enough about it.

—George Eliot (Mary Ann Evans)

In our culture, women are not supposed to worry about such things as facts and numbers, which supposedly suit the male mind better. But young children do not differ in quantitative ability. Two-year-old girls are as good as two-year-old boys at counting (which is to say, not very), and in the early grades the two sexes are equally able to master numerical operations and concepts. There is one qualification: large studies with disadvantaged children have found that girls outperform boys.

Around puberty the picture changes. Although most studies of children aged nine to thirteen report no sex differences in math ability, a few show that boys do better than girls. By adolescence, boys usually do better, though the magnitude of the difference varies. Boys take more math courses, which might improve their performance on standardized tests, but Maccoby and Jacklin report that the male advantage also showed up in a study that compared the scores of male and female high-school seniors who had taken the same number of math courses. Males also score higher on the mathematical aptitude section of the college boards, and the math gap seems to survive into adulthood.

Many people believe that the sex difference in math ability is due to conditioned anxiety and cultural norms rather than to an inborn male advantage. They say, for example, that girls learn early that math is men's work and that they will be unpopular if they do well with numbers. As Sheila Tobias, assistant provost at Wesleyan University, notes, "Once a person has become frightened of math, she or he begins to fear all manner of computations, any quantitative data, and words like 'proportion,' 'percentage,' 'variance,' 'curve,' 'exponential.' " Women are especially likely to suffer from "mathophobia" and to go out of their way to avoid classes that require any mathematics (Tobias 1976).

For girls, "math anxiety" is a double-decker issue: they worry about mastering the concepts, and they worry about seeming unfeminine if they do. We think this explanation has merit in terms of the average male and female learning math but we do not know whether it explains the greater frequency of male geniuses in the field. Genius in math appears very early and may have, in either sex, a genetic component.

creativity

Very learned women are to be found in the same manner as female warriors; but they are seldom or never inventors.

—*Voltaire*

Women have more imagination than men. They need it to tell us how wonderful we are.

—*Arnold H. Glasgow*

The stereotype alleges that women are emotionally sensitive, aesthetic, and intuitive. It also creates an enigma: why do these qualities not assure that women will become leading artists, musicians, novelists, poets, and creative scientists? Garai and Scheinfeld seem to think the problem lies partly in the different ways the sexes relate to the outer world. The male, they claim, "has an innate drive to act upon and transform the environment, and consequently to engage in exciting and challenging investigation of the numerous unfamiliar objects, shapes, and machines. Thus, in his search for control over the world of things, the young boy is led toward more challenging, farther removed, and more difficult goals than the more sedentary girls." This claim is without merit. There is no basis for assuming that boys are born with a greater urge to transform the environment than girls; little girls are far from sedentary; and, most important, it is not true that males are more creative than females.

Most psychologists define creativity as the ability to produce unique and novel ideas. Psychologists themselves have been very creative in their attempts to assess creativity in the laboratory. One measure, called the Alternate Uses Test, asks people to list as many uses as they can for various common objects, such as a brick. Some people give obvious answers: "You use a brick when you build a house." Others, more creative, go on listing until forced to stop. (Our favorite response, offered by a colleague, was to use a brick as a bug-hider: "You leave it on the ground for a few days, then pick it up and see all the bugs that have been hiding.") The Alternate Uses Test has the advantage of yielding scores that do not correlate closely with IQ; it is a fairly direct measure of the ability to generate novel ideas. The Remote Associates Test, which yields scores that do correlate with IQ, measures flexible thinking in a different way. A person is given three words and must come up with a fourth word that links the first three. For example, for the triplet *stool, powder,* and *ball,* the answer is *foot*; for *house, village,* and *golf* the answer is *green.* People who are widely acknowledged to be creative in real life tend to score higher on such tests than other people.

The research reviewed by Maccoby and Jacklin shows that on creativity tests like these, which involve a degree of verbal fluency, there is indeed a sex difference among children older than seven: females do better. On nonverbal tests of creativity, neither sex does better than the other. They conclude that girls and women "are at least as able as boys and men to generate a variety of hypotheses and produce unusual ideas." Thus the data do no more than the stereotype to explain why most inventors and artists are men.

cognitive style and spatial ability

The sagacity of women, like the sagacity of saints, or that of donkeys, is something outside all questions of ordinary cleverness and ambition.

—G. K. Chesterton

Women have a wonderful sense of right and wrong, but little sense of right and left.

—Don Herold

We hear all the time that men and women think differently, although most people would be hard-pressed to say exactly how. David Wechsler, who developed the widely used Wechsler intelligence scales for adults and children, writes that "women seemingly call upon different resources or different degrees of like abilities in exercising whatever it is we call intelligence. . . . Our findings do confirm what poets and novelists have often asserted, and the average layman long believed, namely, that men not only behave but 'think' differently from women" (Wechsler 1958).

Some psychologists have suggested that females are more "global" in the way they perceive and solve problems, whereas males are more "analytic." By this they mean that males find it easier to ignore aspects of a problem that are irrelevant to its solution, to restructure the elements of a problem, and to shut out impulsive, incorrect answers. In 1968 Donald Broverman and his colleagues wrote that this difference between the sexes was well established. Females, they said, are better than males at tasks that require "simple perceptual-motor associations" and at producing fast, accurate, repetitive responses, as in color naming. Males are better than females at "inhibitory perceptual-restructuring tasks" and at producing solutions to novel tasks or situations. In short, "the behaviors [at which men excel] seem to involve extensive mediation of higher processes as opposed to automatic or reflexive stimulus-response connections," while those at which women excel involve "minimal mediation by higher cognitive processes."

Freely translated, what this jargon means is that women are better at dicing celery and men are better at what we think of as thinking. Broverman et al. gave some examples of the tasks at which women supposedly do better—reading fast, writing fast, typing, doing simple calculations, walking—and explained the alleged sex difference in terms of the way sex

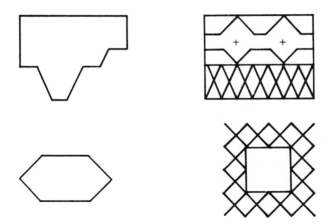

Figure 1. Examples of drawings used in the embedded-figures test. The object is to identify the simple figures in the more complex ones.

hormones affect the nervous system.[1] Although they spoke of each sex as "superior" in one mode of cognitive performance, the fact is that our culture does not regard tasks like typing and simple arithmetic as highly as tasks that require more thought. Imagine the implications if this hypothesis about cognitive differences is correct. If the average woman cannot inhibit automatic reactions as well as the average man can, and if she does better at simple rote tasks, then is it any wonder we find her in the outer office busily typing letters while he sits in the inner office busily writing them?

A sex difference in thinking is a legitimate possibility. The strongest evidence for such a difference comes from studies of field independence ("decontextualization"), which measure the ability to respond to a stimulus without being distracted by its context. Much of this work uses drawings like those shown in Figure 1, in which a person must identify figures that are embedded in a larger whole. In order to find the hidden items you must suppress your response to the drawing as a whole (the "global" response) and restructure the parts of the picture. For this reason, the ability to disembed has been equated with general analytic ability.

[1] In a critique of this article, Mary Parlee (1972) points out that Broverman et al. ignored women's superiority on linguistic tasks, which certainly involve more than simple perceptual-motor associations. See her paper also for a critique of their neurophysiological argument.

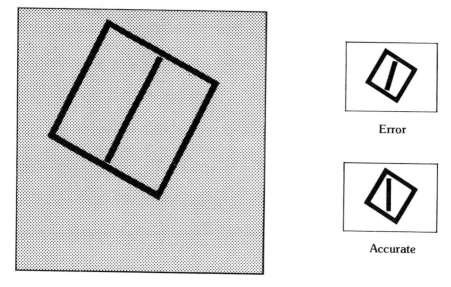

Error

Accurate

Figure 2. The object of the rod-and-frame test is to move the rod into a true vertical position inside the tilted rectangular frame. To do the task accurately, the test-taker must ignore the distracting context of the frame.

The rod-and-frame test (see Figure 2) is also used to measure field independence. In a typical experiment, a person sits in a darkened room where all that is visible is the illuminated outline of a rectangle and, suspended inside the rectangle, a rod. A lever or other device is used to adjust the rod to a true vertical position. The experimenter can make the task difficult by tilting the rectangular frame; in order to judge the position of the rod accurately, you must ignore the frame and attend to subtler cues, such as the angle of your body relative to the floor and the pull of gravity. Again, you must concentrate on the problem and ignore the confusing distractions of its context. Though it is widely believed that males at all ages do better than females on such tasks as embedded figures and the rod-and-frame test, the large body of evidence that Maccoby and Jacklin examined (one table summarizes forty-seven studies) indicates no consistent trend in early childhood. A male advantage does emerge at the beginning of adolescence and continues into adulthood. Though many studies find no difference, whenever a difference is found it favors males, which would seem to support the idea that a sex difference does exist in the way people analyze problems.

Or does it? Julia Sherman (1967) has pointed out that tests of disembedding are usually visual-spatial in nature. That is, they require a person to manipulate objects in space, mentally or physically. Perhaps, says Sherman, the sex difference after puberty is spatial and has nothing to do with analytic ability in general. In other words, people may have misinterpreted what is basically a simple perceptual difference. There are good reasons to think that Sherman is right. First, from adolescence on, males do better at other tasks that involve spatial relations but not disembedding or field dependence—solving mazes, for instance, or playing chess. Second, males do not seem to excel on nonvisual tasks that require disembedding. The sexes do not differ on an embedded figures test that asks them to touch the stimulus instead of looking at it (Witkin et al. 1968), or on a sort of auditory disembedding test that asks them to attend to one voice and block out another (reported in Maccoby and Jacklin 1974a).

As for the claim that women are more impulsive when solving problems, Maccoby and Jacklin review many studies in which an impulsive response leads to error, and they find no reliable sex difference. When all is said and done, there is little reason to believe that males inhibit impulsive responses while females act on them, or that males use higher mediating processes and women lower ones, or that there is any other simple distinction between the mental styles of the two sexes. There *is* reason to believe that males are better, on the average, at visual-spatial tasks. Sherman and others believe this finding can be accounted for by differences in experience. It may also have something to do with a genetically determined brain difference, a topic discussed in Chapter 4.

physical abilities

Her weakness is her strength, and her true art is to cultivate and improve that weakness.

—George Fitzhugh

The intention of your being taught needlework, knitting, and such like is not on account of the intrinsic value of all you can do with your hands, which is trifling, but . . . to enable you to fill up in a tolerably agreeable way some of the many solitary hours you must necessarily pass at home.

—Dr. John Gregory
(to his daughters)

As a group males are stronger, heavier, and taller than females, at least after puberty. How much of the sex difference in muscular strength is innate and how much is due to better athletic training for boys than girls is not known. Studies find that girls finish developing athletically by the time they reach adolescence, while boys continue to improve for several more years; but increased emphasis on athletic programs for girls may change this pattern.

The sex difference in physical strength is of more than passing interest to social scientists because of its possible implications. Garai and Schein-feld argued that the greater height and weight of males gives them an advantage not only in sports but in "all those occupational and recreational domains which require height, weight, physical strength, and vigorous exertion as prerequisites for success." They did not list those domains, though. In many parts of the world women do backbreaking physical labor, carrying heavy baskets on their heads, plows in their hands, and children on their hips for many years. Still, physical strength may help account for certain sex-role distinctions that have prevailed both cross-culturally and historically (see Chapter 8).

The stronger sex does not start life more sturdily than the weaker one. On the contrary, males are more apt to suffer from prenatal problems, birth injuries, and childhood diseases of all types, including pneumonia, influenza, measles, diphtheria, polio, and whooping cough. Throughout life, males are more vulnerable to a wide range of disorders and infections, and the death rate for American women is lower than that for men in every decade of life (Sherman 1971). One unforeseen consequence of sex-role equality may be that women's health will decline to male levels. Lung cancer and heart disease are on the increase among women, possibly due to the rising numbers who smoke and work in high-stress jobs (Horn 1975).

Although men are credited with stronger shoulders, women are credited with faster fingers—with a superiority in manual dexterity, or the ability to perform tasks that require fine, quick finger movements. Among those interested in sex roles, manual dexterity is a controversial, emotionally charged issue. When someone says that women are better than men with their hands, antifeminists cheer while feminists bristle or guffaw. The reason for these reactions is that the assertion has been used to justify the work that women do: typing, sewing, routine factory assignments. The argument that women's nimble fingers equip them for certain jobs crosses all political borders. When one of us (C.T.) visited a silk factory in the People's Republic of China, her host told her that young women did the spinning and worked the looms because of their superior manual skills.

Recent studies do show that women perform better on finger dexterity tasks when speed is important. But it is hard to interpret this finding, because the tasks used to measure dexterity are repetitive and boring and it may be that women are more willing than men to stick out such a task. Even if the difference is real, few people have suggested that it means women are better suited than men to become surgeons and pickpockets. And back in the days when typing was a high-status occupation, no one protested that the great clumsy paws of men should be kept off the keyboard. Even today, all the typists at Lloyds of London are male, and they seem to be doing all right.

sex differences in personality

The sorts of mental and physical abilities we've looked at so far can usually be measured in straightforward ways, though there can be problems in interpreting the results. When it comes to qualities of personality, it is less clear how one should go about measuring them in the first place. Accordingly, sex differences in personality have been much more difficult to study, and firm results have been more elusive.

For example, a psychologist who studies emotionality (or any other personality trait) must keep in mind that people do not behave consistently. They play different roles on different occasions. Suppose you were doing an observational study of timidity, following a young mother through a typical day. At 9:00 A.M. the woman's child injures herself on a jagged rock. Does the mother scream hysterically at the sight of blood? Does she faint dead away? If she is like most mothers of our acquaintance, she scoops up the child, administers first aid, and drives quickly but carefully to the nearest hospital. No fear or timidity there. But that evening the same woman is standing on a chair calling frantically to her husband because a little grey creature with a long tail has appeared. Same woman, different behaviors. Which is she—brave or timid? The same difficulty of attaching one label to a person over many situations applies to men too, of course. A man who is a mouse with his mother may show tremendous courage when battle demands. Which is he—timid or brave?

sociability and love

[Women] no longer engage in spinning and weaving, they do not like any longer to make cap-tassels, they do not make hemp, but they love to gad about on the market place. They neglect the supervision of the kitchen and devote themselves to frivolous pleasures. . . . These ladies indulge in unseemly jokes and pranks. . . .

—*Ko Hung, third century*

A woman either loves or hates; there is no third course.

—*Latin proverb*

Psychologists have long thought girls to be more social than boys. Garai and Scheinfeld's summary is typical. "In psychological development, from earliest infancy on, males exhibit a greater interest in objects and their manipulation, whereas females show a greater interest in people and a greater capacity for the establishment of interpersonal relations." They go on to say that a woman's greater interest in people predestines her to seek satisfaction in life primarily in an intimate relationship "with the man of her choice."

Many studies of sociability begin with babies who have had little time to be influenced by learning and environment. The psychologist presents a drawing, photograph, or model of a human face (or sometimes a real face) to the infant and measures how much time the child spends looking at it. Sometimes the attention that the infant gives to faces, which in such studies are called social stimuli, is compared to the attention he or she directs to other stimuli, such as geometrical forms. Sherman (1971) writes: "By the age of six months, girls notice faces more than boys . . . and they are more interested in other people by the age of two." Bardwick (1971) says: "The preference of six-month-old girls for faces . . . is more marked than in boys of the same age and is consistent with findings for older children; this suggests that infant girls have a greater sensitivity to social stimuli."

Maccoby and Jacklin counter stereotype, arguing that these conclusions are premature. When they reviewed thirty-three studies of visual perception during the first year of life, they found no sex difference in most cases. Ten studies did show a significant sex difference in a baby's attention to visual stimuli, but sometimes the difference favored girls, sometimes boys, and the direction of the difference could not be accounted for by whether the stimuli were social or not. Occasionally, male and female infants show a different pattern of preferences. For example, Michael Lewis and his colleagues (1966) found that six-month-old girls spent more time gazing at faces than at other objects, while boys distributed their attention fairly evenly. But R. C. Bernstein and Jacklin (1973) found no sex differences among three-and-a-half-month-old infants in attention to social versus nonsocial stimuli that were equally complex.

Many people believe that little girls are friendlier, or more concerned with having playmates, than boys. This is not true. If anything, boys are more gregarious. A number of studies have shown that boys interact socially with their peers and play with their same-sex age-mates more often than girls do. At certain ages, boys seem to run in packs, while girls prefer to play in pairs or small groups that Maccoby and Jacklin call "chumships." In addition, boys seem more susceptible than girls to social pressure from peers. In a study by Edwin Hollander and James Marcia (1970), fifth-grade children filled out a questionnaire in which they had to choose between alternate hypothetical activities. Three items required them to choose between what they wanted to do and what their friends wanted. For instance, they had to decide whether to go to a summer camp featuring activities they particularly enjoyed or one that their friends wanted them to go to. In three other items the problem pitted peers' wishes against those of parents. The boys' answers showed them to be more peer-oriented than girls on both types of choice. Unfortunately, the questionnaire did not have the children choose between their own desires and those of their parents, so we cannot tell whether the girls were less peer-oriented than boys because of greater independence or a greater desire to please grown-ups.

What about sociability in adults? Supposedly, women are the friendlier sex. Psychologists call a concern with liking others and being liked a "need for affiliation." They measure its strength by analyzing the themes in people's fantasies, such as daydreams or stories made up about ambiguous pictures, and by analyzing answers to questions like "What makes you happy?" Some studies find a sex difference. For example, when men and women rate the importance of various aspects of life to their overall happiness, women are more likely than men to place love and family above work (e.g., Shaver and Freedman 1976; Lunneborg and Rosenwood 1972). College women are also more likely than men to fantasize and daydream about love and other affiliation themes (Wagman 1967). But other studies find no sex differences in *behavior*. In their actions, both men and women love to be loved.

The results are muddy partly because the same behavior gets different labels in different studies and from different writers. In *Men in Groups* (1969), for example, Lionel Tiger proposes that men, not women, are the affiliative sex because they form closer relationships with members of their own sex. Women's friendships, he claims, are more superficial. Tiger calls the male need for other men "male bonding," which, he explains, is a biologically based response to the prehistoric need for cooperation in hunting. The male-male link shows up today in business, sports, politics, private clubs, and bars. Tiger's thesis is highly speculative; research with Americans does not show that either sex has a greater need for social contact with members of the same sex, and in some societies women, not men, do the "bonding."

Conventional wisdom has it that women depend more on men for love and fulfillment than men do on women. Even the strong-willed Scarlett O'Hara, in *Gone With the Wind,* wound up begging Rhett Butler to stay. He, of course, didn't give a damn. Psychologist Zick Rubin has studied the question in a straightforward way. In the spring of 1972 he and his colleagues Anne Peplau and Charles Hill recruited 231 college couples who were going together. They gave the students extensive questionnaires and then followed up with further questionnaires and some interviews in late 1972, 1973, and 1974. Unexpectedly, they found that men tended to fall in love more quickly and easily than women, and that men rated the desire to fall in love as a more important reason for having entered the relationship than the women did. When Rubin looked up some earlier studies of love and attraction, he found the same pattern.

At the end of three years, 103 of the couples (45 percent) had split up. The researchers asked these students why their relationship had crumbled and who had been the one to end it. In most instances, there had been a breaker-upper and a broken-up-with, although the two ex-lovers did not always agree on who was which. Women were somewhat more likely to end the relationship; further, men reported feeling more depressed, lonely, and unhappy after the end of the affair than women did (Hill, Rubin, and Peplau 1976). In Rubin's words, "Man proposes, woman disposes."

It's not that women have no emotional investment in romantic liaisons. They do, but they may walk out if their love is not returned. The men in this study ended relationships when they had become relatively uninvolved, but women ended affairs when they were either highly involved or uninvolved. Why would someone who is still in love end a relationship? Perhaps women care more about the quality of an affair, and thus are readier to say "love me or leave me." Hill, Rubin, and Peplau also point out that women traditionally have economic reasons behind their love affairs. If a woman's status and income are going to depend on her husband, she must be careful to whom she gives her heart and not waste time on a relationship that's going nowhere. As sociologist Willard Waller said (1938), "A man, when he marries, chooses a companion and perhaps a helpmate, but a woman chooses a companion and at the same time a standard of living. It is necessary for a woman to be mercenary."

To ask which sex is more dependent on love may not be the proper question at all. It may be that men love as deeply and needfully as women do but talk about it less. It may be that women can be as autonomous and self-reliant as men, but that society labels them deviant if they stay single. Or it may be that the sexes define love differently. Again we must look for answers not solely in what people say about themselves but in how they act (see Chapter 7).

empathy

Women are wiser than men because they know less and understand more.
—James Stephens

The stereotype says that females are more sensitive than males to other people's feelings and to subtle nuances of behavior. Maccoby and Jacklin conclude that this assumption is incorrect. The two sexes, they say, "are equally adept at understanding the emotional reactions and needs of others, although measures of this ability have been narrow" (1974b).

Trying to trap empathy in a laboratory is indeed difficult, and we would call the issue undecided. It may be that while women are not "naturally" more empathetic than men, empathy in this society is associated with the traditional feminine role and therefore encouraged in females. Wendy Martyna and Dorothy Ginsberg, working with Sandra Bem, conducted a study in which they asked students to listen to the apparently spontaneous conversation of another person, who was actually a confederate of the experimenters delivering a memorized script. The confederate spoke about some personal problems, and the researchers recorded how often each student listener nodded or made sympathetic comments. It turned out that the most traditionally feminine women reacted with more concern than did men or less traditional women (Bem 1975).

Robert Rosenthal and his colleagues (1974) found that women excel at decoding nonverbal signs of other people's feelings. Rosenthal developed a test called the Profile of Nonverbal Sensitivity (PONS), which measures sensitivity to tones of voice and movements of the face and body. The test consists of a 45-minute film of a woman portraying different emotions. Sometimes she makes a definite facial expression; sometimes she speaks a few indistinguishable phrases; sometimes she does both. When you take the test, you look at or listen to a scene and then indicate what emotion the woman is acting out. If the woman appears to be upset, for example, you may have to decide whether she is expressing jealous anger or talking about her divorce. There is only one correct answer, determined beforehand by the actress herself and a panel of judges who know her.

In general, people are good at recognizing the emotions being expressed, but females are slightly and reliably better than males from the third grade (the earliest age tested) through adulthood. This result may occur because the sender is a woman, but Rosenthal's group also found that females retain their superiority on an audio-only version of the PONS in which the message-sender is a man.

If these findings hold up, several explanations are possible. Perhaps, Rosenthal et al. suggest, motherhood requires sensitivity to nonverbal cues. After all, babies can't tell you what bothers them, and their caretakers must be able to interpret gurgles, whimpers, and cries. Maybe women have built-in interpretative talents, acquired in the course of evolution, or perhaps they learn them as they grow up. Rosenthal's group has found that mothers of very young children are particularly adept at deciphering speech when words are blurred, sounding "a bit like the speech of children who are learning to talk."

Another possibility is that sensitivity to the feelings of others is related to status: the underdog must be able to read signs and signals of the master's moods. Says Rosenthal, "If women, as well as other oppressed groups, must 'read' the expressions of others with great accuracy in order to advance or even survive, then they could become nonverbally sensitive at an early age. . . . When one is powerless, one must be subtle." Housewife folklore and some women's magazines have long instructed wives on how to read their husbands' moods and keep a step ahead of a fight.

Finally, it is possible that sensitivity to others depends on the kind of work one does, at home or in the office. On the PONS test, men who were training for or working in occupations that required nurturance, expressiveness, or artistic skill did as well as women, or better. These men included actors, artists, college students in visual-studies courses, interior and industrial designers, psychiatrists, clinical psychologists, workers in mental hospitals, and schoolteachers. Unfortunately, we do not know whether such work increases social sensitivity or whether sensitive men are drawn to these professions. Also, men in other lines of work may excel at reading nonverbal cues in situations that have not been tested in the laboratory. Maccoby and Jacklin suggest that "because of their greater work experience, men may be better able to 'read' the reactions of people at various levels of an organizational hierarchy."

emotionality

Women are timid and 'tis well they are—else there would be no dealing with them.
—*Laurence Sterne*

According to the *Random House Dictionary of the English Language,* emotion is "an affective state of consciousness in which joy, sorrow, fear, hate, or the like is experienced." But when people complain that women are "so emotional" they usually are not thinking of joy, sorrow, or hate. They mean that women tend to be easily upset and to overreact in expressing their feelings, and that women therefore are not to be trusted in situations requiring self-control and "maturity." Most studies and casual conversations concerning emotionality use the term in this narrow sense. Thus, studies of aggression are not usually classified under the rubric of emotional expression, although people pummeling each other are clearly showing strong emotion.

One part of the stereotype about female emotionality says that females are more timid and anxious than males. Studies based on direct observations of children's behavior do not find that girls are especially fearful, however. Boys and girls react similarly when a parent leaves the room and they cry equally often. They face new experiences, like going to nursery school, or frightening ones, like crossing a narrow plank, with the same degree of courage or resignation. Yet girls and women are more likely than boys and men to report feelings of anxiety or tension on tests of those emotions, and teachers commonly report that girls in their classes are more timid and anxious than boys.

So there is a conflict in the data, with studies of behavior on one side and self-reports and anecdotal observations on the other. Perhaps the discrepancy occurs because girls and women are more willing to admit fear and anxiety than are males, who are under pressure not to be sissies. Another possibility is that the tests are biased. Maccoby and Jacklin observe that many items on the most commonly used questionnaires are by their nature likely to elicit anxiety from females. For example, do you get scared when you have to walk home alone at night? When you are home alone and someone knocks on the door, do you get a worried feeling? An urban woman who feels some uncertainty and apprehension in such situations is not being irrational or neurotically anxious; her concern is an understandable response to big-city reality.

dependence

Eve would have had no charms had she not recognized Adam as her Lord.
—*Anthony Trollope*

By a girl, by a young woman, or even by an aged one, nothing must be done independently, even in her own house.
—*Manu laws of India*

"Dependence" is as complicated a term as "emotionality" to translate into behavior that can be measured. Those who study dependence in children usually record the amount of touching or eye contact between mother and child, the amount of acting-up a child does to attract adult attention, the extent to which a child complies with what others want, or the amount of help a child seeks. Unfortunately, these measures often do not correlate with each other, so many researchers now doubt that dependence can be studied as a unified, coherent trait. The older a person gets, the harder it becomes to define dependent behavior. There are not many studies of adult dependence, although, as noted earlier, women do not seem to be more dependent on men for love than men are on women.

For the moment, let's define dependence as a need for the protection of other people. If a child clings to his mother all day and wants her near at all times, we'll say he's dependent. Psychologists have studied this sort of attachment-dependence by placing a young child in a room with his or her mother and observing the two together. Less frequently, they observe children at home or as they are being left at nursery school. Maccoby and Jacklin went through thirty-two studies in which observers noted the proximity of children to their mothers (or, rarely, their fathers), the amount of touching, and the degree of emotional upset at separation. In some studies girls turned out to be more dependent, in some boys did, and in some there was no sex difference at all.

The independent person copes with life's big and little frustrations in an active, vigorous manner, exercising personal initiative. The dependent person just stands there, suffering the slings and arrows of outrageous fortune, hoping that help will arrive quickly. In a well-known study, Susan Goldberg and Michael Lewis (1969) observed the birth of these two life strategies in infants. They watched thirteen-month-old children and their mothers in a room stocked with toys. The mother sat in a chair while the child was free to roam about the floor, which was marked with a grid so that the researchers could measure the distance of the child from the mother. In this situation boys were less reluctant to leave their mothers, returned less often to them, wandered farther away, stayed away for longer periods, and touched and talked to them less. After fifteen minutes, the experimenters placed a fence in the middle of the room, between the child and the mother, and noted what the child did. Boys were more likely than girls to attack the fence and try to get around it. Girls were more likely than boys to stand in the middle of the room and cry.

Goldberg and Lewis had observed the same children at home on two prior occasions, once when the babies were twelve weeks old and once when they were six months old. They found that the mothers did not treat male and female babies alike. The mothers of twelve-week-old girls looked at and talked to their infants more than the mothers of boys did, but the boys got more touches and cuddles. By six months, the situation had changed: the girls got not only more visual and verbal attention but more physical contact as well. It was as if infant boys were granted a three-month grace period, after which their mothers expected them to become more independent and exploratory (Lewis 1972).

Goldberg and Lewis concluded that prolonged physical contact between parent and child may lessen the child's drive to explore and become independent. This idea is provocative, because it suggests that boys learn to become more autonomous than girls right from the start. But it is at odds with other studies. Maccoby and Jacklin, the great debunkers, repeated some aspects of the barrier study, also using thirteen-month-old children. They did not find that boys tried harder to cross the barrier (Jacklin, Maccoby, and Dick 1973). Other researchers, too, have failed to find a sex difference in the ways that young children cope with problems or react to separation from the mother.

nurturance

We must start with the realization that, as much as women want to be good scientists or engineers, they want first and foremost to be womanly companions of men and to be mothers.

—*Bruno Bettelheim*

Among the more positive qualities attributed to women are warmth, cheerfulness, and helpfulness toward others. These are supposed to equip women for certain social roles: wife, mother, nurse, babysitter, charity worker, community volunteer. But research provides little evidence that the female sex is the more nurturant, especially when nurturance is broadly defined as a disposition to help others.

In one study of children that did find a difference, Beatrice Whiting and Carolyn Pope Edwards (1973) analyzed data collected during the 1950s in six different cultures: Kenya, India, Okinawa, the Philippines, Mexico, and the United States (New England). The 134 children, aged three to eleven, were observed in natural settings over a period of several months. Whiting and Edwards found no sex difference in nurturance among children aged three to six. But seven- to eleven-year-old girls more often offered help and gave more emotional support to others than boys did. However, the researchers needed to combine data from all six communities in order to eke out the sex difference. In most individual communities boys and girls did not differ markedly in helpfulness or nurturance, and in Okinawa the boys were more helpful.

Whiting and Edwards say that nurturance may be related to the tasks a society assigns to the young. In most cultures, girls babysit and help care for small children more often than boys do. In East African cultures in which boys babysit and have other domestic duties, there are fewer sex differences in nurturance. In the New England community that Whiting and Edwards studied, girls under eleven did little childcare, and they scored lower than girls in the other five countries in offering help and support.

Another popular line of research, on altruism, has concentrated on college students and adults and also reveals no sex difference. In a typical study, a confederate of the researchers pretends to be in some sort of trouble: he or she may feign a stroke and collapse in a crowded subway or, less dramatically, drop a bag of groceries. The experimenter watches to see who goes to the victim's aid. Sometimes men are more altruistic, sometimes women, and sometimes they're equally helpful. Whether a Sir Galahad or a Florence Nightingale rushes to the rescue depends on who the victim is and what sort of help is called for.

Females may not be more helpful than males in a general sense, but surely they are more nurturant and loving toward children and other dependent creatures? Many social scientists would say yes. Harry Harlow, the well-known expert on primate behavior, tells of how he showed a picture of an infant rhesus monkey to groups of undergraduates. He observed "gasps of ecstasy" from all-female audiences, he says, but singular silence from all-male audiences. Harlow concluded that "nature has not only constructed women to produce babies but has also prepared them from the outset to be mothers" (1971).

Phyllis Berman recently showed that the way human beings react to infant monkeys (and presumably to infant human beings) depends on the situation. Berman asked college students to look at pictures of infant and adult monkeys and apes and rate each animal's "immediate emotional appeal" on a five-point scale. She then computed scores that reflected each student's attraction to infants relative to his or her attraction to adults. Some students gave their responses publicly, by voting in view of other participants in the study. Others saw the pictures and made their judgments alone. The men and women differed in their reactions to the infants only when they had to announce their ratings in public. The average score for women who gave group ratings was higher than for women who gave them privately, but for men the opposite was true: their scores were higher when the ratings were private (Berman 1975). Men, it seems, are quite capable of the "ecstasy response" to small fuzzy animals but suppress it in public.

Few researchers have studied the way men and women actually behave with children, probably because they think they know what they will find. One psychologist who has raised the question is Sandra Bem. She found in a series of studies that traditionally masculine men are reluctant to do soft, "feminine" things, such as play with a baby or a kitten, but that nontraditional men are as likely as women to do so (Bem 1975). Bem's work suggests that nurturance may be more closely related to sex roles than to inborn tendencies.

Maccoby and Jacklin describe a study in which Ross Parke and S. E. O'Leary observed the parents of newborn infants as the parents looked at, touched, rocked, held, and smiled at their babies. Fathers are supposed to be lumbering oafs in the baby business, but these dads behaved *more* nurturantly than the mothers did when both parents were present, and they were at least as nurturant as the mothers when they were alone with the child.

If men had more time and opportunity to be with children, we might hear more male "gasps of ecstasy" than is now the case; if they were more often included in studies of nurturance, we would have more evidence against which to judge the stereotypes. In daily life, women and men often behave nurturantly toward each other, as in "How about if you make a fire and pick up a pizza while I put the kids to bed and make us some coffee?" Further, though caring for children, home, and spouse is traditionally the woman's job, protecting them is the man's: he is expected to buy life insurance, investigate night noises in the basement, and go down with the ship if the lifeboats are full. There is no doubt which parent usually spends more time with the children, but we cannot conclude with any confidence at this point that one sex is inherently the more nurturant. The possible influence of hormones on maternal behavior is discussed in Chapter 4.

aggressiveness

[We need men] who love a fight, who when they get up in the morning spit on their hands and ask "Whom will I kill today?"
—Eric Hoffer

Charm is a woman's strength just as strength is a man's charm.
—Havelock Ellis

At last, a clear-cut sex difference. The Maccoby and Jacklin review indicates that in every society in which men and women differ in aggressiveness, men are the more aggressive. Dozens of studies show that males of all ages engage in more physical aggression, fantasy aggression, verbal aggression, and play aggression than females do. The difference shows up as soon as children begin to play with each other, at the age of two or three, and lasts into adulthood.

These findings do not mean that girls are submissive. They are no more likely to yield or withdraw under attack than boys are. And they don't have to, because among children the victims of male aggression are usually male.[2] There are several explanations for the finding that both aggressor and victim are likely to be male. First, in our society girls and boys play in highly sex-segregated groups. This reduces the opportunity to fight, or to interact at all, with the opposite sex. Second, many little boys are told in no uncertain terms not to punch little girls. Perhaps girls also learn signals that say, in effect, "You can't hit me—I'm a girl!" Or perhaps, as Maccoby and Jacklin suggest, girls learn ways to inspire affection and sympathy, to make the aggressor feel guilty, and to divert his attention. Third, aggressiveness among children may be related to their efforts to establish dominance, as is the case with nonhuman primates. In general, dominance seems to be a more important issue in male groups than in female.

Some writers argue that females are just as aggressive as males, but they show it differently. For instance, in a study of first graders, Seymour and Norma Feshbach (1973) found that girls were more unkind and unfriendly toward a newcomer trying to enter a two-member "club" than boys were. The girls would ignore the new child, move away, deny a request for help, or announce directly that the newcomer was not welcome—especially if a boy was trying to join a two-girl club. Boys, on the whole, were nicer. The Feshbachs write:

> The quantitative data do not reflect the quality of the children's reactions, especially the disdain that girls expressed toward the new boy and the readiness with which they isolated him and rejected his efforts to play with them. One of the girls even set out to terrorize the newcomer. She spilled out a box of pick-up sticks and, taking one up, began to stalk the new boy around the room. She rolled her eyes and said something about the "strange feeling"

---

[2] The same seems to be true for adults, at least when murder is involved. In homicide cases, males are more frequently the killers and also more frequently the victims (Wolfgang 1969). But see p. 20 for some statistics on wife-beating.

that came over her at certain times. (We subsequently removed the sticks from the room.)

However, the girls' hostility was short-lived; after four minutes or so the sex difference disappeared. Perhaps the girls' initial aggression was due to the importance girls place on small, exclusive groups.

Finally, the aggressiveness of little boys may be related to higher energy levels. As yet there is little firm evidence that the sexes differ in activity level during infancy. Differences do begin to emerge, though not consistently, during the preschool years, and then boys do turn out to be more active. This may explain why, when boys are left to play with a Bobo doll (a large inflatable doll that rights itself after it is punched), they are more likely than girls to hit the doll repeatedly. In one study, boys struck the doll an average of 28 times during one play period, compared to only 4.5 times for the girls (Feshbach and Feshbach 1973). Punching a Bobo doll may be a good way to work off energy, but energy levels probably do not explain why boys do more verbal sparring and fantasizing about aggression than girls.

The finding that males are more aggressive than females has stirred up controversy, for in our culture people are ambivalent about aggressiveness and violence. For all the lip service paid to peace and love, many people regard aggressiveness as a good thing. They may assume, for instance, that physical aggression in the schoolyard paves the way for psychological aggression in the business world. "Aggressiveness" becomes an umbrella that covers everything from hitting a Bobo doll to standing up for one's rights, from striking a playmate to speaking up at a company meeting. So some psychologists worry that Maccoby and Jacklin's findings may reinforce the stereotype that women are ill-equipped to compete with men in the world of work.

The problem seems to be that semantic issues have been confused with behavioral ones. Whatever the label attached to their actions, men engage in more violent and antisocial acts than women do. They commit more crimes (though female crime is on the increase), have more fatal automobile accidents, get into more brawls and battles. Few would argue that these acts are desirable. Some psychologists think we should distinguish aggression, which is hostile in intent or hurtful in effect, from assertiveness, which is the ability to make one's interests and desires known to others. There is evidence that in some situations women are less assertive than men; for example, in two-person conversations men tend to do more talking (Argyle, Lalljee, and Cook 1968). This area is just beginning to be studied, and it is quite possible that these traits have different origins—

aggressiveness might be biologically based and assertiveness not. We will discuss biological explanations of aggressiveness in Chapter 4, and learning explanations in Chapter 6.

Some of the statements in this chapter will become casualties of future research. The problem with trying to describe how men and women differ is that times change, and people change too. Further, what we now know about sex differences is based mainly on studies of white, middle-class, American children. Within the next few years, social scientists will be learning more about how age, race, socioeconomic status, and sex-role attitudes affect ability and personality.

In general, the differences between the sexes are fewer and less dramatic than most people believe. But let's be cautious about how we interpret that fact. Even if all the evidence were in and all the stereotypes about women and men turned out to be false, it would not mean that being male is no different from being female. Psychological research tends, of necessity, to focus on the more obvious and measurable aspects of behavior and personality. But a person's subjective experience is hard to capture on a paper-and-pencil personality test, and subtleties of behavior and thought may go unnoticed by an observer in a laboratory. Girls and women probably see the world differently from boys and men. They make different plans and have different experiences. Most important, they think of themselves as different—which sets the stage for a self-fulfilling prophecy, because when people think they are different, then in some sense they really are. This is especially true for sexual behavior, the subject of the next chapter.

3

Sexuality

Woman wants monogamy;
Man delights in novelty.
Love is woman's moon and sun;
Man has other forms of fun.
Woman lives but in her lord;
Count to ten, and man is bored.
With this the gist and sum of it,
What earthly good can come of it?

—*Dorothy Parker*

One of the most venerable beliefs about men and women is that they find themselves where they do on the ladder of life because of fundamental, unalterable differences in sexuality. In this chapter we will try to untangle the myths from the realities of male and female sexuality. Both physiologically and psychologically, it turns out that men and women are much more sexually alike than was once thought, yet in certain respects they are dissimilar, too. We will argue that the sexual gap between men and women is not simply a matter of one sex having a stronger sex drive than the other. Rather, it is a matter of the two sexes attaching somewhat different meanings to the sexual act. Sex is one of the most profound, emotionally charged, mysterious experiences we mortals have; it can unite the sexes but it can also divide them. The peculiar fact is that an activity that brings men and women together in order to reproduce the species is often a source of animosity between the participants.

the Victorian heritage

Writers on sexual mores usually trace modern concerns about sex to the Victorian era, which spanned roughly the latter two-thirds of the nineteenth century, when Queen Victoria ruled in England. According to most accounts, the majority of middle-class Victorians (including Europeans and Americans) considered sex dirty, dangerous, and disgusting. Premarital sex was bad. Sexual fantasies were bad. Masturbation was bad. Coitus in marriage was okay, but only if the partners didn't do it too often, used acceptable positions, and avoided "unnatural" practices. The Victorians were not the first people in history to condemn sexual pleasure as evil and sinful, of course; many cultures, eastern as well as western, have done so. Certainly the Judeo-Christian ethic, with which most of us have grown up, consistently discouraged sexual pleasure and promoted a narrow interpretation of normality on religious grounds long before the nineteenth century. The Victorians, however, worried as much about the development of good character, spiritual purity, and physical health as they did about the wrath of God, and the voices of authority that warned them against sex belonged not only to churchmen but to physicians and scientists.

The Victorians divided womankind into two groups, as many people still do today—the good and the sexual. Good women rarely if ever desired sexual intercourse. They regarded it as a marital duty, like cooking, sewing, and entertaining guests. The ideal wife was expected to submit stoically and to remain passive and prone. According to an old English joke, when a Victorian girl asked her mother what to do on her wedding night, the mother replied, "Lie still and close your eyes, dear, and think of England." In contrast, men "needed it," and even—the dirty curs—enjoyed it. The most widely quoted sex-advice book in the English-speaking world at the time, Dr. William Acton's *Functions and Disorders of the Reproductive Organs*, instructed readers that "the majority of women (happily for them) are not very much troubled with sexual feelings of any kind. What men are habitually, women are only exceptionally." The "best" mothers and wives, wrote Acton, "know little or nothing of sexual indulgences. Love of home, children, and domestic duties, are the only passions they feel."

Civilized men were expected to recognize that good women were too fragile physically and too sensitive spiritually to engage in frequent intercourse, and thus to exercise their marital privileges with restraint. In a book with the very Victorian title *Amativeness, or Evils and Remedies of Excessive and Perverted Sexuality, Including Warnings and Advice to the Married and Single,* Orson Fowler cautioned that the woman must always be the "final umpire" on the matter of coital frequency: "A husband who tenderly loves a delicate wife will find no difficulty in being continent, because he loves her too well to subject her to what would be injurious." That man was wrong; many men did have difficulty complying with the umpire's decision, and they turned in frustration to the second kind of woman. In *The Sex Researchers* (1969), Edward Brecher tells how "droves of Victorian males each night saved their wives and sweethearts from pollution by pouring their sexual emissions into London's readily available street women."

Indeed, despite their intention to see no evil, hear no evil, and do no evil, the Victorians saw, heard, and did quite a lot of it. All manner of pornography flourished during the Victorian era. Havelock Ellis, a prodigious documenter of Victorian sexual behavior and one of the first sex researchers to approach his topic open-mindedly, filled his seven-volume *Studies in the Psychology of Sex* with case histories of every kind of sexual experience, from Auto-eroticism (masturbation) to Zoophilia (sex with animals). And for all the admonitions to "nice girls," some historians now say that premarital sex was more common during the Victorian period than it had been in previous, supposedly more liberal times (Shorter 1975). In short, despite all the rules and taboos, people did then all the things they do today, though less frequently and in fewer numbers.

Nor were all Victorian writers as antisexual as Acton was. Historian Carl Degler (1974) reports that some doctors acknowledged that women were sexual beings and boldly advised them to express their sexual impulses without feeling guilty. Degler also discovered a sex survey of forty-five well-educated women, most born before 1870, who were far from the asexual Victorian ideal; they regularly had orgasms, enjoyed intercourse, and thought sex a normal part of life. Thus the traditional picture of Victorian morality is probably overdrawn. People in the Victorian age were not asexual; they were, however, relatively ignorant and prudish about discussing sex. No one knew what anyone else was doing, so everyone worried that only he or she was doing it. This gap between behavior and belief meant that many Victorians paid a large price in guilt and remorse for their sexual pleasures.

During the first half of the twentieth century, attitudes toward sex mellowed somewhat. But despite a proliferation of sex manuals and more open talk about sex, people remained in the dark about what others were doing and uncertain about what was "normal." The growing popularity of psychology, especially Freudian psychoanalysis, made sex a legitimate topic for discussion but at the same time created new insecurities. Those who had abandoned the idea that sex was sinful and caused warts now fretted that their sexual activities might be perverted or immature.

During this period the sexual double standard continued virtually unchallenged. As Joseph LoPiccolo and Julia Heiman (in press) say in a recent historical review of sexual attitudes, the cultural message shifted from the view that "Sex is dangerous to your mortal health and immortal soul" to the idea that "Sex is good, but only for men." The double standard was not an unqualified blessing for men, for they were, and still are, under great pressure to pursue and perform. "Real men" were supposed to have sex frequently—with women who were expected to be only mildly interested. The double standard assured miscommunication between the sexes, with each sex out to prove something different.

the scientific study of sex

In 1938, Indiana University selected Alfred C. Kinsey to teach a new course in sex education and marriage. Kinsey was not an obvious choice for the job. He was a biologist who had devoted his career to the study of gall wasps, which reproduce asexually, without insemination of the female by the male. But Kinsey was an extremely conscientious man, so he set out to rectify his lack of knowledge about people by consulting the library. Surprised at the lack of reliable information there, he decided to gather the data himself. Kinsey had spent twenty years collecting and categorizing several million gall wasps; now he applied the same painstaking approach to collecting sexual statistics. For the next eighteen years, he spent his mornings, noons, and nights talking to people about their sex lives.

Kinsey was not the first sex researcher, but he was the first to gather extensive sexual histories from men and women from many geographic areas, walks of life, religious backgrounds, marital statuses, and ages, and he was the first to use statistics to analyze his data. Whereas most previous researchers had relied on case histories of patients in therapy or people who came for counseling and advice, Kinsey used a standard personal interview containing hundreds of questions on every aspect of sexual behavior. His results provided the first detailed information on who was doing what and how often.

There were inadequacies in Kinsey's approach, though. For one thing, instead of using randomly selected informants representative of the American population as a whole, Kinsey recruited volunteers, and they may have been sexier than average. Fortunately, Kinsey was so good at appealing to people to contribute their histories for the sake of science that he often succeeded in signing up whole groups of people—PTA groups, business offices, lecture audiences—en masse. Therefore his sample was much broader than those in many subsequent studies, which have relied on informants (such as magazine readers or college students) who are younger, better educated, and more affluent than average. Still, in his sample some groups, such as farmers and the poorly educated, were underrepresented, and he interviewed so few blacks that he was unable to include their data in his published report.

Another common criticism of Kinsey's methods is that the people he and his associates interviewed could have lied, either by omitting sex acts they felt guilty about or bragging about things they did not do. This is a problem with all sex surveys. But after conducting thousands of lengthy interviews, Kinsey and his colleagues developed good noses for sniffing out false answers, and they cross-checked each other or reinterviewed respondents whenever it seemed necessary.

In 1948 Kinsey and his associates published *Sexual Behavior in the Human Male,* based on their interviews with 5,300 American men. This volume was followed in 1953 by *Sexual Behavior in the Human Female* (with Wardell B. Pomeroy, Clyde E. Martin, and Paul H. Gebhard) based on data from 5,940 females. The basic conclusion of the two books was that many of the sexual practices and "perversions" prohibited since Victorian times were actually common, and some were nearly universal. The smaller statistical surveys done since Kinsey have on the whole confirmed his findings.

Because of the work of Kinsey and later sex researchers, our knowledge of human sexuality has taken a great leap forward in just a few decades. It turns out that in almost every area of sexual behavior women are far from being as sexless as the Victorians hoped, but neither are they as sexy as the Victorians feared. Men are more active than women by all measures of sexual activity—number of partners, frequency of orgasm, homosexual encounters, sexual fantasies, masturbation. Some people take this to mean that men have a stronger sex drive than women. Others say the reason for the difference is that men have been freer than women to act on their sexual impulses. Before trying to decide between these two explanations, let's take a closer look at the data.

premarital sex

before marriage, boys will be
boys and girls will be virgins

The respectable Victorian girl was expected to "save" herself until marriage, so that she could present the precious gift of virginity to her husband. If he also saved himself for her, so much the better, but it was understood that many young men would not achieve that goal. Today a majority of Americans have a more positive view of premarital sex, especially if the partners feel strong affection for each other (Hunt 1974). Yet approval is far from universal. Recently the Vatican reaffirmed its position that "every genital act must be within the framework of marriage." And when Betty Ford told an interviewer that she would not condemn her daughter for having a premarital affair, her tolerant attitude created something of a furor.

The furor came years too late. Kinsey found that while most women born before 1900 (86 percent) had been virgins on their wedding nights, by the 1950s virginity was honored more in word than in deed. Nearly half of the married women in Kinsey's sample had coitus before they were married. (The figures for men were even higher: 98 percent of those with a grade-school education, 85 percent of high-school graduates, and 68 percent of those with some college had had premarital intercourse.) On the other hand, Kinsey did not find that premarital sex had become a casual matter for women. Over half of the women who had sex before marriage had only one partner, almost always the fiancé. A third had two to five partners, and only 13 percent had more than five. For most of the women Kinsey interviewed, premarital sex occurred in the context of a serious relationship.

During the 1960s discussion flourished about whether premarital sex was still on the increase. Some sociologists argued that since the 1920s behavior had not changed nearly so much as attitudes about sex; people were not acting differently, they were simply talking more openly and tolerantly (Reiss 1960, 1969; Bell 1966). This view eventually gave way before mounting evidence of real behavioral change during the 1960s. Two separate studies revealed a striking increase in premarital sex among college women between 1958 and 1968 (Bell and Chaskes 1970; Christensen and Gregg 1970). A national study of over 4,000 young unmarried women found that by the age of nineteen almost half were no longer virgins (40 percent of the white women and 80 percent of the blacks), compared with 18 or 19 percent in the Kinsey sample (Kantner and Zelnik 1972).

The trend away from female virginity continued into the seventies. A national study commissioned by the Playboy Foundation in 1972 and reported by Morton Hunt (1974) found that among married people, the younger the person, the greater the likelihood that intercourse had occurred before marriage (see Table 3). In the youngest group, 81 percent of the women said they were not virgins when they married.

In a 1974 sex survey of 100,000 *Redbook* readers, nine out of ten

Table 3. Percentage of married men and women who have had premarital coitus, by age

	Ages 18–24	25–34	35–44	45–54	55 and over
Males	95%	92%	86%	89%	84%
Females	81	65	41	36	31

AFTER Hunt 1974.

wives under the age of twenty-five reported having premarital sex (Levin and Levin 1975). Although the sexual behavior of *Redbook* readers is not necessarily representative of the whole country, the inescapable conclusion, from many studies of many different groups of women, is that the virgin bride is following the route of the buffalo and becoming a statistical rarity. Men are still more likely than women to have sex before marriage, but the gap is narrowing.[1]

But merely counting virgins can be misleading. When you go beyond these general numbers, you find that many important differences between men and women are still alive. For example, though fewer women today require engagement before having premarital sex than used to, the majority of women who have sex before marriage still do so with the one, or maybe two, they love; men are more likely to sleep with the many, or any, they like. In the *Playboy* survey, the median number of premarital partners reported by males was six. In contrast, over half of the married women who had premarital sex had only one partner, just as in Kinsey's study. In a national sample of teenagers, Robert Sorensen (1973) found that one quarter of the boys were what he called "sexual adventurers"—they preferred to have many sexual partners, concurrently or in rapid succession. In contrast, only 6 percent of the girls were sexual adventurers. Young black women have somewhat fewer partners than young white women (Kantner and Zelnik 1972).

The first experience with intercourse often has a different meaning for males and females. In a survey of the sexual attitudes and experiences of 20,000 *Psychology Today* readers (Athanasiou, Shaver, and Tavris 1970),

[1] One complication in talking about "premarital" sex is that researchers sometimes combine data from people *now married* with those *still unmarried* (on the assumption, not incorrect, that most of the latter will eventually tie the knot). Among young unmarried people, the gap in sexual experience between men and women is a little larger. In Hunt's recent sample, 97 percent of the unmarried men had had intercourse by age twenty-five, compared to nearly three-fourths of women.

66 percent of the women but only 41 percent of the men said that their first partner had been a spouse, fiancé(e), or steady date. Fifteen percent of the men but only 6 percent of the women reported that their first partner was a casual acquaintance or stranger. Similarly, Harold Christensen and Christina Gregg (1970) found in a 1968 study of midwestern college students that 86 percent of the women but only 53 percent of the men had their first premarital experience with a steady or fiancé(e). Other studies have found similar results.[2]

So more women are having premarital sex than ever before, but they are not necessarily motivated to seek sexual adventure in itself as often as men are. Christensen and Gregg reported that 23 percent of the college women they questioned said that during their first premarital experience they had yielded because of force or a sense of obligation rather than personal desire. Only 2.5 percent of the men questioned said the same. When Judith Bardwick (1971) asked some college women why they made love, she got answers like the following:

> "He'd leave me if I didn't sleep with him."
> "Right now to please him."
> "Well, a great strain not to. Fairly reluctant for a while, but then I realized it had become a great big thing in the relationship and it would disintegrate the relationship . . . I wanted to also."
> "Mostly to see my boyfriend's enjoyment."
> "I gave in to Sidney because I was so lonely."

Few of Bardwick's interviewees said that they made love because *they* wanted to and because they physically enjoyed sex. Bardwick thinks most of them accepted sex as the price of a romantic relationship, or as a way to prove their love. Whereas previous generations of women said no to premarital sex because they feared they would lose the man if they said yes, Bardwick's work suggests that today many young women say yes because they fear they will lose the man if they say no. At any rate, that is what they tell interviewers.

In an effort to discover the sexual concerns of young men and women, psychologist Carol Roberts asked her community college students, most of them unmarried, to list any problems they had with "any aspect of sexual functioning—psychological, physiological, or social." She has been doing this for several years and has a remarkable set of replies.

---

[2] Although men have access to prostitutes and women do not, we don't believe this factor accounts for the greater tendency of women to be emotionally involved with their first partner. Premarital experience with prostitutes has dropped in recent years (Hunt 1974).

The women speak mostly of insecurities, guilts, and fears:

> Fear of pregnancy
> Fear of rape
> Being conquered and of no further use
> Being rejected if one says no
> Masturbation—accepting it
> Fear that one's partner is physically repulsed by you
> Fear of loss of self-respect
> Fear of becoming too attached when the feeling is not mutual
> Guilt feelings about premarital sex
> Pressure to have sex even when one doesn't want to
> Fear of not satisfying one's partner
> Embarrassment or concern over not being orgasmic

But many of the men's comments are complaints about women rather than expressions of their own conflicts or worries:

> Finding a partner who is open to varying sexual experiences
> Having to be always on the hunt
> Not being able to have sexual relations when one wants to
> Women who tease, without wanting to engage in sexual activity
> Women's refusal to take responsibility for their own sexuality
> Women who use their sexual attractiveness in a manipulatory fashion
> The excessive modesty of women (they want the lights off)
> Passive women
> Aggressive women
> Necessity to say you love the woman even if it isn't true
> Being expected to know all about sex
> Inability to communicate feelings or needs during the sex act

These responses imply that many couples in bed together might as well be on separate planets, for all the similarity of their perceptions and purposes. (This generalization applies mainly to unmarried people in their late teens or early twenties. Older single men and women are probably much more alike in outlook than younger ones.) The sex-and-love tangle may be the factor that is most responsible for such misunderstandings. Women, more often than men, use sex to get love; men use love to get sex. In a recent survey on sex roles, more than half of the men but only 15 percent of the women said they had told a sex partner they cared more for her or him than they really did in order to have sex (Tavris 1973). In contrast, a fourth of the women but very few of the men admitted they had used sex to bind a partner into a relationship.

It's clear that among young people, stated attitudes and actual behavior have changed almost as rapidly as the cost of living, but sexual motives and concerns have changed far less. Some old, familiar themes can still be heard, especially when the issue is whether sex can be separated from love, or ought to be. Men, more often than women, regard sex and love as unconnected experiences. In the *Playboy* survey, 60 percent of the males and 37 percent of the females thought premarital coitus was all right for men even without strong affection, but only 44 percent of the men and 20 percent of the women gave the same privilege to women. The double standard has been weakened, but it is not gone.

extramarital sex

after marriage, boys will be boys
and girls will be faithful

Kinsey found that men were more likely than women to have sex not only before marriage but outside of it. Though he did not present exact statistics, he estimated that about half of the husbands he interviewed had intercourse with a woman other than their wives at some time during their married lives. In contrast, only about one-fourth of the wives had sex with someone other than their husbands. Even this percentage of women is inflated because Kinsey included a disproportionate number of divorced women in his calculations, and they were more likely than never-divorced wives to have had extramarital sex. When Hunt recomputed Kinsey's statistics, taking this overrepresentation into account, he estimated that the incidence of extramarital sex in Kinsey's time was closer to one woman in five.

People have always been fascinated with adultery even as they condemn it. In recent years Americans have become more tolerant about extramarital sex. While only a few believe it should be encouraged, an equally small number think it is always wrong under all circumstances. Studies find that the majority of people regard extramarital sex the way they regard eating garlic. It's fine for them, but they don't want anyone near them to do it—especially their spouses.

The most dramatic change in attitudes toward extramarital sex, and in behavior, has come from young women. In Kinsey's time, only some 8 percent of the married women under age twenty-five had had extramarital sex, but today the estimated figure has jumped to 24 percent (Hunt 1974).

A generation ago, only a third as many young wives as husbands reported an extramarital experience, but today three-fourths as many young wives as husbands do. "The change," says Hunt, "is not a radical break with the ideal of sexual fidelity but a radical break with the double standard."

Although as many women as men may soon be having extramarital sex, differences between men and women in number of partners and in motives remain. In the *Psychology Today* survey, twice as many males as females reported six or more extramarital partners (14 percent to 7 percent), a finding supported in other surveys as well. It could be that men have more partners because they have more opportunities; the *Redbook* report found that employed wives are more likely to have sexual affairs than unemployed wives (though some smaller studies have found the opposite). But it is also possible that women enter extramarital liaisons, like premarital ones, less for lust than for love. For women, having sex outside marriage is still strongly correlated with marital dissatisfaction (Levin and Levin 1975). Men are more likely to try to distinguish emotionally the casual encounter for sex's sake from the marriage. Thus husbands are initially more enthusiastic than wives about unconventional forms of extramarital sex. Hunt found that among couples under age twenty-five, 5 percent of the husbands but only 2 percent of the wives had tried mate-swapping—which is often called wife-swapping, with good reason: all the available studies show that when the wife first participates it is often at the husband's instigation or insistence. In the *Psychology Today* survey, 41 percent of the husbands but 22 percent of the wives expressed an interest in swapping.

homosexuality

In the United States, laws against homosexuality—or more precisely, against behavior associated with homosexuals (anal intercourse, oral sex, mutual masturbation)—are the same for both sexes. But they are not enforced even-handedly. With his usual thoroughness, Kinsey looked up all convictions of homosexuals in this country from 1696 to 1952. He found not a single case involving lesbians. He also discovered that although thousands of males were arrested and convicted for homosexual acts over a decade in New York City, only three females were arrested, and all three cases were dismissed. Kinsey suggested several possible reasons for the greater prosecution of males, ranging from more public cruising by men to traditional religious sanctions against wasting semen.

Until the Kinsey study, people assumed that homosexual behavior must be very rare and that it would attract only the "sick" or "perverted." Kinsey redefined the whole question. Homosexuality, he said, is not an either-or-matter: "The world is not to be divided into sheep and goats." Sexual behavior falls along a continuum, with the exclusively homosexual and exclusively heterosexual at the two ends, and all mixtures in between. Some people enjoy coitus with a partner of the opposite sex but prefer same-sex relationships; some go through a lengthy period of exclusively homosexual activity and then become exclusively heterosexual; some have homosexual fantasies but no corresponding experience; and so on. Kinsey decided to avoid the label *homosexual* and instead to describe frequencies of homosexual behavior and ratios of homosexual to heterosexual experiences.

In Kinsey's sample, only 4 percent of the males were exclusively homosexual throughout their lives. However, by age forty-five about 37 percent of all men had experienced at least one homosexual encounter leading to orgasm. When Kinsey considered all erotic response, whether or not it involved orgasm or even sexual contact, fully half of the men said they had experienced homosexual arousal. Kinsey, to say nothing of the American public, was astonished by these findings.

In this area of sexuality as every other, the figures for women were lower. By age forty-five, 20 percent had had a homosexual experience, and the percentage fell to 13 percent when only encounters leading to orgasm were counted. Only 1 to 3 percent of the women said they were exclusively homosexual.

Many researchers are unhappy with Kinsey's statistics on homosexuality. A few believe his figures are too low, because some people were probably afraid to admit this behavior. But others, like Hunt, argue that the figures are too high. Kinsey sought out homosexuals to interview, so they were overrepresented in his sample. Further, his startling 37-percent figure for men included many who had a single exploratory experience, usually during adolescence. Hunt calculates that only about one in ten males in Kinsey's sample was "more or less exclusively homosexual" for three years or more after the age of fifteen. The female percentages were also inflated, because single women, who are more likely than wives to have homosexual experiences, were overrepresented. All in all, says Hunt, homosexual behavior is not as common as Kinsey's data indicate, nor has it increased much during the past two decades, though it has definitely come out of the closet.

Whatever the precise figures, surveys continue to find that males are more apt to try a homosexual experience and to be exclusively homosexual than females are. In the *Psychology Today* survey, 4 percent of the males but only 1 percent of the females said they were exclusively homosexual; 66 percent of the females but only 48 percent of the males said they had never had a homosexual experience and never would. Males also report more partners. Kinsey found that 22 percent of the male homosexuals but only 4 percent of the females had had eleven or more partners; Hunt's figures were 8 percent and 1 percent, respectively. Males tend to have short-term (though often intense) relationships, and about two-thirds say that they never have had an exclusive relationship lasting longer than a year (Weinberg and Williams 1974). Lesbians are more likely to have long-term relationships. In the *Psychology Today* sample, 60 percent of the female homosexuals but only 33 percent of the males said they were currently living with a lover. Most researchers report that lesbians, like heterosexual women, place at least as much importance on the romantic aspects of their relationships as they do on the sexual. One's experience and feelings during a sexual interlude seem to have less to do with whether one is gay or straight than with whether one is a man or a woman.

sexual fantasies

In Kinsey's sample, more men than women reported having fantasies about sex, though women were as far from being asexual in mind as they were in deed. A majority of both sexes (84 percent of the males and 69 percent of the females) reported having had erotic fantasies about the opposite sex. The figure for women may be higher today, because sexual fantasy is becoming recognized as normal and appropriate for both sexes. Recent books on female sexuality even encourage women to use fantasy to enhance their sexual experiences. E. Barbara Hariton (1973), a psychologist, recently interviewed a group of upper-middle-class housewives and discovered that 65 percent had sexual fantasies during coitus, and 28 percent reported occasional thoughts that could be considered fantasy. Many people, including some psychotherapists, have assumed that women who fantasize during sex are neurotic, bored, unhappy, or frustrated, but Hariton found no evidence of emotional instability, unhappiness, or neuroticism among the women who fantasized. Instead they tended to be creative, nonconformist, and sexually active and satisfied.

Kinsey reported that men and women differed considerably in their responses to erotic stimuli. Far more men than women reported being turned on by pornography and erotic materials. For example, 54 percent of the men said they had been aroused by photographs, drawings, or paintings of nude figures, compared to only 12 percent of the women. Although almost half of the men who heard erotic stories reported being aroused by them, the same was true for only 14 percent of the women—and more women than men said they were offended. Even Kinsey, who soon stopped being startled by the sexual preferences of his interviewees, was surprised at how few females reported being turned on by erotic stories. The only kind of psychological stimulation to which women seemed more susceptible than men came from ordinary movies, not hard-core pornography. Kinsey attributed this result to the romantic or emotional atmosphere that is part-and-parcel of erotic scenes in most movies.

But recent findings call Kinsey's into question. In a series of studies at the University of Hamburg, Gunter Schmidt and Volkmar Sigusch (1973) observed how college students reacted to sexually explicit stories, slides, and films. On the average, men reported slightly more sexual arousal to the materials than women, but in both sexes there was a lot of variation from individual to individual: 42 percent of the women who saw the films and slides were more aroused than the average man. Women were also more likely than men to describe themselves as shocked or disgusted by the erotica. In general, though, the sexual and emotional reactions of the men and women were more alike than different.

Most important, the majority of both women and men in the German studies reported physiological signs of sexual arousal to the erotica. When Schmidt and Sigusch grouped all kinds of reactions together—in men, pre-ejaculatory emissions, erections, and ejaculation; in women, vaginal lubrication, genital or breast sensations, and orgasm—they found that 80 to 91 percent of the men and 70 to 83 percent of the women had been aroused.

There are problems in generalizing from these results. College students are more permissive toward sexuality than many other groups, and in northwestern Europe they seem to be more permissive than their American counterparts. Studies such as Schmidt and Sigusch's do show, though, that there is nothing inevitable about a sex difference in reactions to erotic materials.

It may have occurred to you that women may be more likely to lie or at least to be evasive about their responses to pornography. Or they may be less sensitive to physiological signs of arousal. Julia Heiman (1975), a psychologist, recently got around these problems by recording the actual physiological responses of college men and women while they listened to taped erotic stories. Males wore a flexible circlet (rather like a rubber band) around the base of the penis. The device, called a strain gauge, is filled with mercury and measures blood volume and pressure pulse, recording the slightest sign of an erection. Women got a newly designed device called a photoplethysmograph, a small acrylic cylinder containing a photocell and light source. When inserted just inside the vagina, the photoplethysmograph registers changes in blood volume and pressure pulse, early indications of sexual arousal.

The students listened to four kinds of tapes: erotic stories about explicit sex; romantic versions of the same stories; stories that were both romantic and erotic; and control stories that were neither erotic nor romantic. In general, the women were as likely as the men to be turned on physiologically while listening to the erotic stories, and for both sexes straight sex was more arousing than romance alone. Further, there was no evidence that these women preferred romantic-erotic stories to those that were simply erotic. In fact, when the students evaluated the stories subjectively, the women rated the erotic ones as more arousing than did the men.

Although previous findings of a sex difference in response to pornography may have been due to women's difficulties in recognizing or admitting arousal, it's also possible that a real change has taken place since Kinsey's day. Women today are exposed to more erotica than they were then, and the content of the material is becoming more female-oriented. It is more permissible than it once was for a woman to enjoy magazines like Viva and Playgirl, to go to pornographic movies, and even to hang pictures of nude males on her bulletin board. Familiarity does not always breed contempt.

masturbation

To our grandparents masturbation was not only evil and disgusting but downright dangerous. Victorian physicians warned that stimulating yourself sexually could lead to acne, blindness, impotence, insanity, coughing spells, muscular convulsions, fever, and warts. Some worried that masturbation would drain men of semen, which they regarded as a scarce substance to be hoarded carefully and dispensed stingily on special occasions. Like a car without gasoline, it was thought, a man low on semen would soon stop running. For this reason, many experts also condemned nocturnal emissions (wet dreams) and too frequent coitus. Special horrors were reserved for the autoerotic woman. In addition to the usual illnesses, she would suffer loss of flesh, gastric and uterine disorders, emaciation, and bad breath. She risked turning into a pale, ugly, filthy nymphomaniac who would die a lingering death.

Victorian doctors frequently advised parents on ways to protect their children from themselves. Vigorous exercise and manly vows were recommended for males, but the treatment for girls could be much more extreme. Some doctors applied a hot iron to the offending clitoris or sewed the vaginal lips together (Hastings 1966). As late as the 1930s some standard American medical texts continued to advocate clitoridectomy and cauterization to treat female masturbation (Spitz 1952). To our knowledge, no one has ever cauterized or surgically removed a boy's penis because he masturbated, though plenty of parents have threatened to do so.

In the post-Victorian period, masturbation, like other forms of sexual expression, became somewhat more acceptable—for males. In females stimulation of the labia and clitoris, the commonest type of masturbation, was deemed immature and "masculine." Freud, whose writings greatly influenced sexual standards, considered the clitoris a stunted penis and felt that the sooner a woman accepted this fact and turned to bigger and better things, the happier she would be.

Because of the strong taboos against masturbation, most people in the pre-Kinsey era believed it to be quite rare. Kinsey set off shock waves when he announced that the practice was more popular than baseball. Virtually all of the men in his sample (92 percent) had masturbated, and quite frequently at that. But what really stunned people was Kinsey's report that 62 percent of the females he interviewed had masturbated, almost all to the point of orgasm. In the recent *Playboy* sample, about the same overall proportions of men and women had masturbated as in the Kinsey sample, but women were beginning to do so earlier and with greater frequency.

Thus, masturbation is widespread, but still many women never do it. This fact is important, because masturbation appears to play a crucial role in the sexual development of women. It is the most common source of the first orgasm, according to Kinsey, and the most important source of orgasm for single women.[3] The factor that best predicts whether a woman will have orgasms during marital coitus is whether she has had any orgasms, by whatever means, before marriage. Since the largest number of women achieve premarital orgasm through masturbation, masturbation is strongly related to the ability to have coital orgasms after marriage. Kinsey found that a third of all females who never masturbated to orgasm before

[3] For 40 percent of Kinsey's sample of women, the first orgasm occurred during masturbation. For 27 percent it was during coitus (either premarital or marital), for 24 percent during petting, for 5 percent during an erotic dream, for 3 percent during homosexual activity, and for 1 percent during "psychological stimulation."

marriage failed to reach orgasm in coitus during the first year of marriage, and in most instances during the first five years. Only 13 to 15 percent of those who did masturbate before marriage were totally unresponsive during the early years of marriage. Kinsey was aware that these statistics did not *prove* that masturbation makes coital orgasm easier, because those who masturbated before marriage might have been more erotically inclined in the first place. But he believed that there was a causal connection. In his section on female masturbation he wrote, "In many a specific history it appeared that the quality of the marital response was furthered by the female's previous knowledge of the nature of a sexual orgasm." He also observed the opposite, namely, that a girl who avoids sexual arousal throughout childhood and adolescence—"withdrawing from physical contacts and tensing her muscles in order to avoid response"—becomes conditioned, and does not shed these inhibitions easily after marriage.

If masturbation increases the probability that a woman will become orgasmic, it is undoubtedly because masturbatory orgasms are the easiest kind for women to have. Kinsey found that among women masturbation led to orgasm 95 percent of the time, in contrast to coitus, which was far less successful. He also discovered that masturbation brings rapid orgasm: 45 percent of the women who masturbated reached orgasm in one to three minutes; only 12 percent took longer than ten minutes. Kinsey concluded, "There is widespread opinion that the female is slower than the male in her sexual responses, but the masturbatory data do not support that opinion. It is true that the average female responds more slowly than the average male in coitus but this seems to be due to the ineffectiveness of usual coital techniques." [4]

Recent physiological research shows that Kinsey was right—women climax rapidly during masturbation because they provide continuous effective stimulation of the clitoris. During coitus, clitoral stimulation is usually less consistent, so it takes longer for a woman to reach orgasm. If the man has a climax too quickly, sex will be over for her before it's begun. Kinsey estimated that three-fourths of the men interviewed reached orgasm within two minutes after penetration, and many in less than a minute. Paul Gebhard, of Indiana's Institute for Sex Research, reports that interviews with over a thousand married women showed that penile intromission of less than a minute was insufficient to produce regular orgasm in most

---

[4] Masturbation therapy is widely accepted today as one of the most useful techniques for treating women who have never experienced orgasm. Women learn how to masturbate and find out what arouses them, then transfer the lesson to intercourse.

women. When intromission lasted one to eleven minutes, half of the wives had orgasms almost all the time. And when intromission lasted sixteen minutes or longer, two-thirds of the women reached orgasm almost all the time (Gebhard 1966). As Casey Stengel once said in a different context, "Nice guys finish last." Happily, there is recent evidence that Americans are now making love in a much more leisurely fashion than they used to (Hunt 1974).

Kinsey's findings made the topic of female sexuality popular, and the 1950s and 1960s brought a flurry of books, articles, and advisors to straighten out people's sex lives. The main item under discussion quickly became the female orgasm.

the great orgasm controversy

who has them and how?

Not so long ago, no one talked publicly about orgasms. It was understood that every man had them, but that for women they were unnecessary. In the absence of information about the physiology of sexual response, even doctors felt free to pontificate about what they didn't know. When Diana Scully and Pauline Bart (1973) analyzed gynecology textbooks published between 1943 and 1972, they found that some authors believed women couldn't experience orgasm during intercourse, or at least not very often. Many gynecologists assumed, and some still do, that men have an inherently greater need for sex. One textbook writer observed in 1943 that in women "sexual pleasure is entirely secondary or even absent" and that a common problem the gynecologist faces is "the vast and fundamental difference between the sexes in regard to sexual appetite." The writer added, "Women, with their almost universal relative frigidity, are apt to react to the marital relationship in one of three ways. (A) They submit philosophically to their husbands . . . (B) They submit rebelliously as a matter of duty . . . (C) They rebel completely and through refusal try to force the husband to adapt himself to their own scale of sexual appetite" (quoted in Bart 1974). According to this author, attempts to slow a husband down are doomed, because men cannot help being sexual virtuosos: "Biologically for the preservation of the race, the male is created to fertilize as many females as possible and hence has an infinite appetite and capacity for intercourse." Infinite!

The aim of many doctors who treated inorgasmic women was to

make life more comfortable for their husbands rather than to increase the women's sexual pleasure. If a woman could not respond with honest enthusiasm, her doctor often counseled her to fake it. In a 1952 text, two male physicians wrote:

> Unfortunate marital situations frequently arise because of the husband's resentment at the wife's sexual unresponsiveness . . . It is good advice to recommend to the women the advantage of innocent simulation of sex responsiveness, and as a matter of fact many women in their desire to please their husbands learned the advantage of such innocent deceptions (quoted in Bart 1974).

Notice that the good doctors did not worry about the wife's resentment, nor did they instruct the husband in ways to help the wife be more responsive, nor did they think men should try "innocent stimulations."

The popular assumption that most women were sexually uninterested or unresponsive was badly shaken by Kinsey's announcement that almost nine women in ten eventually respond with orgasm to sexual stimulation.[5] True, among women in their first year of marriage, 25 percent had no orgasms at all during intercourse, and only 39 percent almost always had orgasms. But by the fifteenth year of marriage, 45 percent of the women in Kinsey's sample almost always had orgasms and only 12 percent were completely nonorgasmic.

Even more shocking was Kinsey's report that some 14 percent of women said that they regularly experienced more than one orgasm during coitus. This finding was too much for some people. Two psychiatrists, Edmund Bergler and William Kroger, rushed into print with *Kinsey's Myth of Female Sexuality* (1954). Bergler and Kroger maintained that Kinsey had been taken in by "vaginally frigid" women, "nymphomaniacs" who were counting near hits as bullseyes. Despite the fact that multiple orgasms had been reported in several studies before Kinsey's, Bergler and Kroger insisted that they were a physical impossibility.

It took William Masters and Virginia Johnson to establish that they are not. In the midfifties Masters and Johnson launched the first major studies of the physiology of sex by recruiting volunteers to masturbate and to have intercourse in the laboratory. In all, 694 men and women participated. They ranged in age from eighteen to eighty-nine, and their only common characteristic was the ability to reach orgasm. These people were carefully

---

[5] Incredibly, the myth lives on in some gynecology texts. Scully and Bart report that of the nine books they examined that were published between 1963 and 1972, two claimed that most women are "frigid."

screened for signs of psychopathology, and volunteers who seemed motivated by a desire for sexual kicks were thanked and told to go home. Most volunteers acclimated rather rapidly to the laboratory, and women, supposedly the inhibited sex, did so more easily than men, possibly because the men felt more pressure to perform.

Masters and Johnson charted the sequence of changes that occur during sexual arousal. One of their most useful techniques was to have female volunteers masturbate while inserting a clear plastic artificial penis, containing a light and camera, into the vagina. This device allowed the experimenters to observe the interior of the vagina during sexual excitement and orgasm and to film the responses. During the twelve years of the laboratory research program, Masters and Johnson observed some 10,000 sexual cycles.[6] In 1966 they reported their findings in *Human Sexual Response*. A later volume, *Human Sexual Inadequacy* (1970), dealt with psychological barriers to sexual satisfaction.

Masters and Johnson's recordings established beyond doubt that orgasm is physiologically very similar for men and women. In both sexes, the main consequence of sexual arousal is vasocongestion of the genital area—blood flows into the organs and tissues and greatly distends them. Muscles tense and tighten; often the whole body becomes taut. Irregular muscle twitches gradually give way to more rhythmic movements. The skin flushes, the heart pounds, breathing becomes heavy. Though individuals of both sexes vary enormously in their orgasmic responses, Masters and Johnson report that orgasms vary more for women than for men, despite the fact that the physiology involved is the same. "The male orgasm is more a rose-is-a-rose-is-a-rose sort of thing," says Masters. "The female goes all the way from poppies to orchids." In an orchid orgasm, the whole body may convulse, and the person becomes insensitive to pain, ringing telephones, and the outside world. He or she appears to be more in torment than in ecstasy; the old Hollywood version of orgasm—dreamy, gentle, lovely—just isn't so.

Masters and Johnson divide the sexual response cycle into four phases, for ease of description. These phases occur in both sexes, and their sequence is the same whether the person is masturbating or making love. However, different types of stimulation may affect the onset or duration of a particular phase. In brief:

[6] Many critics of Masters and Johnson argued that the sexual responses they observed in a scientific environment would have to be unusual and deviant. They found it hard to believe that people could respond freely and emotionally while wired for sight and sound. However, Masters and Johnson's participants reported that they felt their orgasms in the lab were as good as those they experienced at home.

1. _Excitement._ In men, vasocongestion causes the penis to become erect within the first few seconds of arousal. In women, the first signs of arousal are lubrication of the vagina; droplets of moisture form on the vaginal walls. The vagina has no sweat glands, so it appears that the moisture comes from the congested vessels in tissues behind the semipermeable vaginal wall. The clitoris swells, and the cervix and uterus move up and back, which creates a "tenting" or ballooning of the inner part of the vagina.

2. _Plateau._ In men, the corona of the glans of the penis increases somewhat in diameter and may deepen in color. The testes increase in size and are pulled up into the scrotum. In women, the outer third of the vagina becomes so congested with blood that the passageway into the vagina is narrowed by as much as 50 percent. In contrast, the inner two-thirds of the vagina continue to balloon out and the uterus enlarges. The clitoris, now fully erect, retracts and seems to disappear, though it remains extremely sensitive to indirect stimulation.

3. _Orgasm._ The male orgasm is marked by contractions of several sets of muscles, occurring rhythmically about every .8 seconds. Three or four vigorous contractions of muscles at the root of the penis cause ejaculation of semen; several less regular and less intense contractions follow. In women, the muscles around the vagina push the lower part of the vaginal wall in and out. The first five or six of these muscular contractions are the most intense, occurring, as in men, every .8 seconds. The uterus also contracts, but the inner part of the vagina continues to expand.

4. _Resolution._ Muscular tensions subside and all bodily functions return to Start. If an aroused woman fails to reach orgasm, the resolution phase may take longer than usual. The pelvis may stay congested for up to an hour, and the woman may feel tense and uncomfortable. Men have joked for years about the "blue balls" problem—the pain of becoming highly aroused without orgasmic relief—but no one has given a name to the female equivalent.

Masters and Johnson confirmed and explained Kinsey's observation that some women can have many orgasms. After ejaculation, males have a _refractory period_ during which they cannot have another erection no matter how much they are stimulated. Sometimes the period is brief (one young fellow in the laboratory had three orgasms in ten minutes), but more often it lasts many minutes or even hours, and as a man ages it tends to become longer. Women, according to Masters and Johnson, do not have a refractory period. If a woman is regularly orgasmic, and if she is stimulated further after her first orgasm, she can continue to climax: the clitoris retracts again; the veins in the genital area refill with blood; the muscles contract. Many women in the laboratory oscillated between the plateau (preorgasmic) phase of sexual arousal and orgasm for a considerable length of time. Masters and Johnson reported that these multiple orgasms were physiologically identical to, and subjectively often more intense than, the first one. During masturbation, especially with an electric vibrator, some women can have as many as fifty consecutive orgasms.

In recording the physiology of multiple orgasm, Masters and Johnson were describing potential, not prescribing a standard. They did not suggest or imply that there is some ideal number of orgasms that women should strive for, or that a single orgasm is somehow inferior to a hundred consecutive ones. They intended only to report that multiorgasmic women are neither rare nor unusual. But because individual variations are so great, people keep wondering whether their own experiences are "typical" or "normal," and they are inclined to translate researchers' observations into unrealistic expectations. It's important to realize that no two women are exactly alike. Some women may indeed go from orgasm to plateau to orgasm as long as stimulation lasts. Others say they eventually have a "knockout" orgasm that brings them down to prearousal levels and leaves them insensitive to further stimulation. Still others are totally satisfied by a single, comparatively mild orgasm. The earth does not have to move, nor do orgasms have to occur in a chain, for a person to enjoy a sexual experience. Lots of things, from individual differences to the emotional context of the sexual encounter, contribute to any one woman's response and how she feels about it.

Variations in the male orgasm have received little attention from the public or from sex researchers. But now some observers are writing that men, too, can have multiple orgasms—that is, repeated climaxes, with or without ejaculation, during a single act of intercourse. According to Wardell Pomeroy, who worked with Kinsey and is still at Indiana's Sex Institute:

> A man's experience of multiple orgasm is somewhat different from a woman's. In the male, each orgasm is distinct; after ejaculation the penis again grows turgid, excitement builds, and another climax is achieved. With women, however, multiple orgasm is often experienced as waves of more and more intense climaxes, each blending into the other. . . . The man's experience might be compared to the up-and-down levels of a graph, the woman's to widening concentric circles (Pomeroy 1976, p. 204).

Pomeroy says that only about 20 percent of adolescent boys have this ability, which declines with age.

Researchers Mina Robbins and Gordon Jensen (personal communication) have brought the male multiple under scientific scrutiny. They found a young man who said he often had repeated orgasms without ejaculation, prior to his final, most intense orgasm with ejaculation. They brought him into their laboratory with his female companion, hooked him up to a polygraph, and found all the signs and symptoms of sequential orgasms: increased respiration and heart rate, muscular tension, urethral and anal contractions. After each climax, the man's erection lessened slightly for 15 or 20 seconds, and then the next build-up to another orgasm began. Robbins and Jensen have since observed more than 13 men, aged twenty-five to fifty-five, who have the same capacity for multiples; they now believe that the male multiple is much more common than we had assumed. But we know very little about why some men have sequential orgasms and others don't, or about why some men have multiples throughout their lives and others lose the ability.

the vaginal-clitoral debate

When people weren't worrying about whether women should have orgasms at all or whether they should have one or many, they were worrying about what kinds of orgasms were normal, natural, and right. According to Freud and his followers, young girls concentrate on the clitoris for sexual satisfaction, but as they mature the vagina is supposed to become more important. Clitoral orgasms, it was thought, are active, vigorous, immature, and typical of women who deny their true femininity. For Freudian Helene Deutsch a clitoral orgasm was rather like a good sneeze: "In some cases the vigorous antimotherly orgasm—as it may be termed—successfully realizes the woman's unconscious intention; by expelling the inflowing semen the woman can keep both the man and the undesired child away from her body." The mature vaginal orgasm, in contrast, was mellower, more lady-like:

> The typical function of the vagina during intercourse is passive-receptive. Its movements have the character of sucking in and relaxing, with a rhythm adjusted to that of the male partner. In the vast majority of women, if they are not disturbed, the sexual act does not culminate in a sphincterlike activity of the vagina but is brought to a happy end in a mild, slow relaxation with simultaneous lubrication and complete gratification (Deutsch, quoted in Moore 1961).

As Masters and Johnson later showed, Deutsch's physiological description was far off the mark. But Deutsch, like Freud, had no qualms about speaking of the "vast majority" of women.

Kinsey was one of the first critics of Freud's theory that mature women get sexual satisfaction from vaginal, not clitoral, stimulation. He noted that the theory assumed the vagina is sensitive to pressure and stimulation. To test this assumption Kinsey asked five gynecologists to touch 879 women on the clitoris, vaginal wall, cervix, and other parts of the genital anatomy. Few women were even conscious of a touch on the vaginal lining or the cervix, but almost all were very sensitive to a touch on the clitoris. This is just what one would expect, said Kinsey, given that the vaginal tissues contain few nerves. In fact, the interior of the vagina is so insensitive that operations can sometimes be performed on it without anesthesia.

One problem with Kinsey's study was that the examined women were not sexually aroused; perhaps the vagina becomes more sensitive than the clitoris during intercourse. Masters and Johnson got around this problem by having volunteers use the artificial penis to simulate intercourse. This allowed them to observe the vagina and clitoris during orgasm. They found that no matter what the site and source of stimulation—vagina, clitoris or breasts; penis, hand or vibrator—the clitoris is "the primary focus for sensual response in the human female's pelvis." [7] During coitus, the thrusting motions of the penis produce traction on the inner vaginal lips, which are attached to the clitoral hood. In turn, the hood swells and rubs the glans. As long as thrusting continues, therefore, the clitoris is indirectly but powerfully stimulated. Masters and Johnson concluded that it is useless (at best) to perpetuate the distinction between vaginal and clitoral orgasms.

But the controversy was not over. Before long some perceptive writers were pointing out that the physiological measurements that Masters and Johnson took were one thing but subjective experience was another. Women continued to report orgasms that felt different. For example, in a survey of 103 educated, articulate, and sexually active women, Barbara Seaman (1972) learned that some women always required direct clitoral stimulation to reach orgasm, while others swore that for a good orgasm they needed something—preferably a penis—in the vagina. Some women were certain that they experienced their orgasms in the clitoris, others were just as sure the site was the vagina. For a third group the site was sometimes the vagina and sometimes the clitoris. Some of these women felt that the vaginal variety was more restful or complete; others preferred the clitoral kind.

It is possible that Seaman's respondents actually shared the same experience but applied different labels to it. On the other hand, it is a bit pre-

[7] The penis and the clitoris both develop in the fetus from the same unisex "tubercle." Thus for all its tiny size, the clitoris contains as many nerve endings as the sensitive penis. It is the only organ in the animal kingdom that has sexual pleasure as its *only* purpose. Sex education books rarely say this, however. Many teach, incorrectly, that the vagina is analogous to the penis and the main source of pleasure for women.

sumptuous to decide that women don't experience what they say they do. Seaman reasonably remarks that we ought to avoid confusing the physiologically observable aspects of an experience with the total experience:

> Today we know that all female orgasms are similar physiologically, which is an interesting medical fact but should not be a revolutionary one. Did the public go into paroxysms when some nineteenth-century doctor discovered that all dinners are digested the same way? No, because the public *knew* that all dinners do not taste the same and that a feast of Boeuf Bourguignonne or Homard en Coquille is an entirely different *experience* from a hasty meal of brown bread and water (Seaman 1972, p. 62).

This brings us to the nub of the problem: which sort of orgasm reaches the standards of French cuisine, and which is merely plain and ordinary fare? Seaman refuses to answer that one, concluding wisely that "the liberated orgasm is any orgasm a woman likes."

You'd think the matter would stop there, but the labeling game goes on. The categorizing of orgasms wouldn't be so bad if people did not persist in arguing that one kind is better or healthier than another. Psychiatrist Natalie Shainess (1974), for instance, now distinguishes the clitoral orgasm from the "authentic orgasm." The former, she insists, is "alienated" and "mechanical"—a paltry, partial response "in which persistent, and therefore irritant and pathological, overstimulation of a particular and easily accessible site finally triggers an orgasm." The authentic type, by contrast, involves more generalized stimulation and supposedly is more satisfying. Only 10 percent of all women, declares Shainess, are psychologically healthy enough to have authentic orgasms. (The other 90 percent, we assume, need her therapy.) [8]

The vaginal-clitoral controversy is not simply a matter of scholarly disagreement or amusing misconceptions. The fact that the physiological facts have not stopped the discussion shows that personal interests and emotions are at stake. Some women have argued recently that the vaginal-clitoral distinction, which is still supported by many therapists and physicians, is an indirect way of maintaining the sexual double standard. Because the vagina

---

[8] Josephine Singer and Irving Singer (1972) take the novel position that there are not two but three varieties of female orgasm. The *vulval orgasm* is the one Masters and Johnson reported. The *uterine orgasm* occurs only during intercourse, and it does not produce the contractions of the vulval variety. Masters and Johnson missed this type of orgasm, the Singers believe, because it is emotionally very intense, and the atmosphere in the laboratory does not lend itself to such intensity of experience. Finally, the *blended orgasm,* as its name implies, combines elements of the other two types. Singer and Singer refrain from using moralistic terms such as authentic, but they do believe that uterine orgasms tend to be the most satisfying.

provides sexual pleasure to men, men would like to assume that the vagina is the main site of sexual pleasure for women as well. To acknowledge the importance of the clitoris is to admit that sex for women can be physically pleasurable even without a partner.[9] It is also to admit that what's good for the goose isn't always so great for the gander.

Beneath the polemics is a basic concern: can women be sexually satisfied without male partners? Are men dispensable? If women can produce orgasms all by themselves, some men worry that their sexual performance will be judged more severely—and that women may prefer masturbation or lesbianism to intercourse. At a logical level, such fears may seem foolish. Sex is more than a meeting of genitals; most people prefer sex with a warm, loving partner to sex with a mechanical, if reliable, vibrator; and most women prefer sex with a man. We know of no evidence showing that women who enjoy clitorally induced orgasms are tempted to throw out their men along with their copies of Freud, any more than men who masturbate lose interest in women. Although Kinsey found that most married men continue to masturbate at least occasionally throughout their lives, this fact has generated absolutely no debate about the relative merits of "manually induced" versus "partner induced" orgasms in men.

new problems in changing times

Ignorance about sex has caused pain to millions of people. Unfortunately, the preoccupation with sex that exists today may also cause pain. In just a few decades, women went from worrying about whether to have an orgasm at all, to worrying about what kind of orgasm it should be, to worrying about how many orgasms to have. Hardly had they gotten used to the notion that one climax was all right before popular books and articles were telling them that once was not enough. The demands on men increased accordingly. It wasn't enough to give a woman one orgasm; now she was going to want lots of them. Bernie Zilbergeld, a physician who heads a male sexuality program in San Francisco, reports:

> Of the men we see, most simply cannot follow their own inclinations in a sexual situation. They are so focused on pleasing their partners and being "real men" [that they sometimes can't say no when they want to or yes to what would

[9] Vaginally induced orgasms can be produced without a partner, of course, by using a finger, dildo, or some other object, and clitoral orgasms can be produced with the aid of a partner. But in the long debate over vaginal versus clitoral orgasms, vaginal orgasms have almost always been equated with the insertion of the penis into the vagina.

please them]. Thus, we find men making love when they don't want to, when they are too tense or uncomfortable to respond fully, ... in ways they don't like, and sometimes even with partners they find unattractive (Zilbergeld 1975).

The straight facts about human sexual response, which were supposed to liberate people, can also terrify them. Where people used to fear that they were the only ones doing it, now they fear that they are the only ones *not* doing it. A young girl recently wrote to Neil Solomon of the New York *Post* (July 6, 1976) for reassurance:

> Dear Doctor: I am a teenage virgin. My boyfriend tells me that the majority of teenage girls have had sexual intercourse and I am becoming an extinct species. Am I?

The doctor, who may be an M.D. but hadn't done his homework, told her:

> You represent a distinct majority (not extinct). A 1970 study by Michigan sociologists [unreferenced] stated that, among teenage girls, 72 percent had not had sexual intercourse. You do what you think is right for you.

The last sentence makes the most sense, but many people seem to find it hard to chart their own course. They want the weight of the majority on their side.

In a *Psychology Today* survey answered by 52,000 young adults, Phillip Shaver and Jonathan Freedman (1976) found that happiness may depend less on what you actually have than on what you expected to get. A great many of their respondents thought that the average person of their age and sex had had more sexual partners and was more sexually satisfied than they, but their comparisons were inflated. Among unmarried respondents, for example, 22 percent of the men and 21 percent of the women had never had coitus, but only 1 percent and 2 percent respectively thought their peers were virgins. Over half of the men (55 percent) and 34 percent of the women were dissatisfied with their sex lives, but only 29 percent and 19 percent respectively thought their peers were dissatisfied. Apparently many people think they are missing something sexually even when they are blessed with bounty. Sex therapists are beginning to report that their patients come for help not because they have serious orgasmic difficulties, but because they want their sex lives to be "better." Couples enter treatment because she is having "only" one orgasm during coitus or because he wants sex "only" three times a week. The sexual revolution, it appears, is a revolution of rising expectations.

biology and learning

Both women and men are biologically equipped to enjoy sexual arousal and orgasm regularly throughout their lives. But for all the talk about women's multiple orgasms, men have more orgasms than women—per episode, per month, per whatever. Kinsey found that by the time the average man married, he had had 1,523 orgasms, compared to 223 for the average women. The gap may be narrower today, but still it is a rare man who never has orgasms (in addition to the spontaneous emissions that result from sperm accumulation), while many women are years into a relationship before they reach orgasm during intercourse and a surprisingly large number—ranging to 20 percent—never do. In this society, sex seems to be more important to men than to women. On survey after survey they say they like it more, do it more, think about it more.

Many explanations have been offered for the sex difference in sexual activity, generally emphasizing one of two perspectives. Biological and evolutionary views argue for programed differences in sex drive between the sexes. Some people, such as Mary Jane Sherfey, think that women have the stronger sex drive but that it had to be suppressed long ago so that the family unit could survive. Others think that men developed the stronger sex drive because promiscuity was a necessary and efficient way to keep women pregnant and the tribe expanding. Learning explanations, on the other hand, maintain that the inborn sexual impulses of men and women are probably equal and that differences in behavior and attitudes result from the ways these impulses are shaped and directed.

Today, most social scientists think that both perspectives have something to offer and avoid taking an either-or stance. For example, John Gagnon and William Simon (1969, 1973) have set forth in some detail an explanation of sexual behavior that emphasizes learning but also illustrates the complex interplay between biology and culture. Like many other sex researchers, Simon and Gagnon believe that adult sexuality is conditioned to a large extent by adolescent experiences with masturbation and that sex differences in sexuality are linked to the fact that boys masturbate more often than girls. The increase of male hormones at puberty causes a boy to have frequent erections even when he is not preoccupied with erotic activities or thoughts, so his attention is directed to his genitals. At the same time, the social demands of the American masculine role, which emphasize aggressiveness, achievement, conquest, and potency, encourage the boy to experiment. For most boys, experimentation begins with masturbation, a purely physical experience detached from images or feelings of romantic love. Boys commonly masturbate in front of other boys—the one who ejaculates first may even win a prize—and many learn about masturbation from friends before they try it. The encouragement of his peers motivates a boy to experiment some more. Sex becomes a device for confirming one's status among other males, especially for working-class boys.

For girls, Simon and Gagnon say, anatomy and cultural rules produce another pattern entirely. It is much easier for a girl to ignore her genitals and to remain ignorant about them. The sign of male arousal, an erect penis, cannot be misinterpreted, but women often need time to learn to recognize signs of their own arousal. Girls are less likely to discover and practice masturbation; if they do, they usually make the discovery on their own and talk about it to no one. For many girls, the vagina and clitoris are untouchable, even unmentionable. (Many women refer only to a vague area "down there"; men have many words to call their genitals, and none of them are vague.)

For both anatomical and social reasons, then, Simon and Gagnon think that girls are less likely to learn about physical sexuality and orgasm. What they do learn about is romance, attractiveness, and the importance of catching a mate: "While boys are learning physical sex, girls are being trained in the language of love and the cosmetic values of sexual presentation through training in dress, dancing and other display behavior.... At no point is sexual expression valued in itself, independent of the formation of families" (Simon and Gagnon 1969). Boys, we might add, are more likely than girls to take communal showers and nude swimming lessons, to try group masturbation, and to have conversations about sex, experiences that give them different associations with sex from the ones girls learn. In short, most boys learn to think of sex as an achievement while many girls learn to think of it as a service to the male.

Biological and societal explanations also overlap to explain the well-known observation that boys reach their sexual peak in their late teens, women not until their mid-thirties. One line of reasoning is that hormones are responsible for the number of orgasms adolescent males have, which declines with age; impotence, we hear, is a "natural" occurrence in middle and old age. The explanation for the delayed peak in women is that they mature sexually only with pregnancy and childbirth, which increase the capacity of the pelvic area for engorgement and sexual tension. Kinsey, too, often attributed the sex differences he observed to biological causes. He thought men, like bumblebees, were designed to pollinate as many female flowers as they can.

But major social differences between men and women also could account for the discrepancy in sexual peaks. Young males are encouraged to sow their oats, women to hoard them. Women are taught to inhibit their sexuality all through adolescence, waiting for love as well as orgasm. It may therefore take a long-term relationship with a husband or lover before they feel self-confident enough, and trusting enough, to express their sexuality fully.[10] In addition, because women do not masturbate as much as men, it takes them longer to learn (and tell their partners) what pleases them. But the belief that sexuality is governed by biological rules sets up expectations about "normalcy" that may create self-fulfilling prophecies. If men expect their performance to decline with age, they are not surprised if it does—and their expectation may contribute to the decline. If women think they are going to be sexiest in their thirties, they may finally let themselves go, which contributes to their sexual pleasure.

the mangaian example

Perhaps the best way to appreciate the impact that social conventions can have on sexual behavior is to break out of our cultural cage for a moment. Donald S. Marshall, an anthropologist, spent a year in Mangaia, a tiny Polynesian island in the South Pacific. Mangaians of both sexes love sex, Marshall reports (1971), and their example suggests a high human capacity for sexual pleasure. Just as the Eskimos have many words for snow in all its various forms, the Mangaians have lots of words for intercourse and for the sexual organs. They have several descriptive words for clitoris alone, which suggests that they devote somewhat more attention to female anatomy than Americans do.

Mangaians start their sex lives early. Girls begin to have intercourse with orgasm at twelve or thirteen, and they have several lovers before marriage with no negative sanction from the community. From the start girls expect their lovers to satisfy them sexually. Boys entering puberty learn

[10] Sex therapists Georgia Kline-Graber and Benjamin Graber (1975) describe how such insecurity prevented one woman from enjoying sex even after she had been married for several years:

> J.B. was a 32-year-old married woman who at the time she came to the clinic had never had an enjoyable sex experience in ten years of marriage. She reported, "Each time we would go to bed, I would undress in the bathroom and make sure the lights were out before I climbed into bed. Roger always told me he found me attractive, but after three kids and with stretch marks and flabby hips I just felt ugly. . . . With the right clothes and makeup I look pretty good, but without the props I don't have much to brag about."

Young women seem to worry as much as older ones. A student who answered Carol Roberts' sex-problem question reported that one of her sexual worries was the way she looked to her partner during sex. "My butt jiggles," she complained. No doubt this characteristic was vastly erotic to her partner, but she was heeding the Madison Avenue ideal, not his.

about sex from older women, who teach them coital techniques, cunnilingus, foreplay, and how to bring a girl to several orgasms before they have their own. Mangaians all say that a girl must learn to have orgasms and that a good man teaches her how. Both sexes agree that a good man will be able to continue penetration for fifteen to thirty minutes or more, while a good woman moves her hips like "a washing machine." "A 'dead' partner who doesn't move," notes Marshall, "is universally despised."

Although Marshall did not collect detailed sexual histories from everyone on Mangaia, he found consistent, striking differences between Americans and Mangaians in sexual attitudes and frequencies. The Mangaian experience suggests that the two sexes are much more alike in terms of sexual potential than American performance statistics indicate, and that there is little biological inevitability to "premature ejaculation" or "frigidity." Young Mangaian couples typically reach climax three to five times a night —both sexes—but they are not overly concerned about orgasm, presumably because everyone achieves it. American girls link love and sex more readily than American boys do, but Mangaian girls happily take lovers for sexual pleasure. In Mangaia, the sexes do not have radically different "sexual peaks," and sexual frequency remains high for both sexes throughout life. No one is too old or too ugly to have a partner.

For years, physicians and poets chatted knowingly about sex without benefit of the physiological facts. Since Masters and Johnson, people chat more knowledgeably about the physiological facts but rarely put them into a psychological context. Sex is more than a matter of hydraulics. Masters and Johnson, so often accused of making sex mechanical, have said that when you treat sex as an exercise to be performed according to a set of directions, "you are dissecting and removing and depersonalizing the whole sexual experience." Sexual liberation is not just a question of dispelling physical hang-ups and freeing the body to respond. It is also a question of freeing the mind, so that one can enjoy—or reject—sex on the basis of choice, not coercion.

II

The sexes:
Explaining the
inequalities

4

Genes, hormones, and instincts: The biological perspective

People who believe that differences between the sexes are natural and necessary are apt to feel that the basic features of femininity and masculinity are somehow wired in at birth and that experience plays only an auxiliary role. For centuries people have justified the sexual status quo with arguments that women's inferior position was God-given or instinct-driven. Those who believe that the status quo is discriminatory and socially determined, on the other hand, often reject all hypotheses based on biology. They may readily admit that external chemicals (drugs) can alter consciousness and behavior but refuse to entertain the notion that internal chemicals (hormones) can do the same. People who believe the basic differences between the sexes are biologically determined tend to be politically conservative and to oppose sex-role equality, while feminists tend to deny sex differences altogether or say they are the result solely of social learning (e.g., Tavris 1973). Political preferences affect not only the kind of research scientists choose to do but also the way people react when they hear about the results.

Some biological determinists are given to sweeping statements. "It's the genes!" or "It's the hormones!" they proclaim, much as a beer-maker might boast, "It's the water!" Some environmentalists are just as extreme, dismissing biological explanations as sexist without even bothering to examine the evidence. Many laymen on both sides of the controversy have only the haziest notion of what "biological" means. If you press them, you find that they are not quite sure what a gene is, or just which hormones are supposed to influence which behaviors. Actually, it is not necessary to be an endocrinologist to understand and evaluate the basic issues raised by biological research.

Some scientists believe we can learn about biological predispositions in human beings by studying the behavior of our evolutionary cousins, the monkeys and apes. They argue by analogy: because these primates are so like ourselves but do not undergo the intricate and intensive learning process that we do, their behavior can tell us about our own biological inheritance. This approach avoids the complexities of human biochemistry as well as the ethical problems that make certain experiments impossible to conduct with people. We will consider this argument-by-analogy before turning to more direct evidence on our own species.

# of baboons and biology

Much of the behavior of nonhuman primates is *sexually dimorphic,* that is, more typical of one sex than the other, and certain primate species behave in ways that fit human stereotypes remarkably well. For instance, in some baboon species of Kenya, the males are clearly the more aggressive sex. They not only hold the top positions in the dominance hierarchy of the troop but they interfere in the fights of others, keep the peace, protect the troop, and form alliances with other males (DeVore 1965). Some writers have claimed that the adult males deserve credit for keeping the group socially stable. Male rhesus monkeys are also machos. Within a few months of birth the males are noticeably more active and aggressive than the females. They threaten each other by stiffening their bodies, staring each other down, retracting their lips, and baring their teeth ferociously—not unlike drunken cowboys in a saloon. When male rhesus monkeys play, there is lots of rough-and-tumble body contact. In comparison, females are calm and passive. They play more gently and are more likely than males to retreat or go rigid when approached by another animal. These sex differences emerge at an early age, when males and females do not differ much in size (Harlow 1965).

One way to find out whether such sex differences are learned or innate is to raise some monkeys in isolation, so that they have no adults to imitate. The pioneer in this sort of research was Harry Harlow, who wanted to know what would happen to infant monkeys that grew up without their mothers' protection, comfort, and affection. He raised generations of rhesus monkeys either in complete isolation or with inanimate surrogate mothers—some made of bare wire, some covered with cuddly terrycloth.[1]

When Harlow put the monkeys who grew up with the surrogate mothers into a specially constructed playroom, they behaved appropriately for their sex: by the second month of life, as shown in Figure 3, the males were more aggressive and the females more passive (Harlow 1962, 1965). Harlow concluded that sexual dimorphism must be innate in the rhesus monkey:

> It is illogical to interpret these sex differences as learned, culturally ordered patterns of behavior because there is no opportunity for acquiring a cultural heritage, let alone a sexually differentiated one, from an inanimate cloth surro-

[1] The original aim of Harlow's work was to determine the importance of breast-feeding in the infant's attachment to its mother. Harlow found that the mother's ability to provide contact comfort was more important to the psychological health of infants than her ability to provide milk. The cloth mothers got more love from the baby monkeys than the wire mothers, even when the latter provided food.

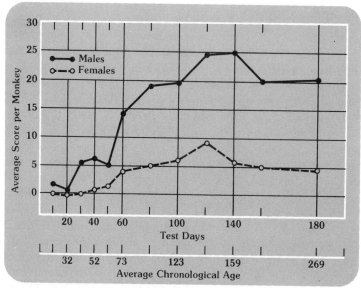

Threat Responses

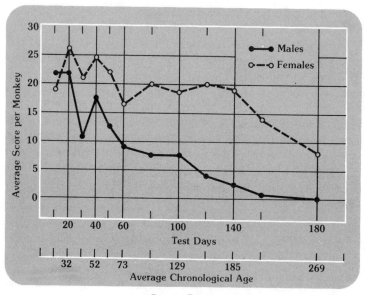

Passive Responses

Figure 3. When rhesus monkeys are raised with surrogate mothers and then put in a playroom together, they soon show a sex difference that is typical of normally raised members of their species: males behave more aggressively, females more passively. AFTER Harlow 1965.

gate. When I first saw these data, I was very excited, and told my wife that I believed that we had demonstrated biologically determined sex differences in infants' behavior. She was not impressed and said, "Child psychologists have known that for at least thirty years, and mothers have known it for centuries" (Harlow 1965, p. 242).

Harlow believes that his results apply to human beings. "If you are not interested in human applicability," he says, "then there is no sense in studying monkeys." Harlow and others see an obvious similarity between little simians and young children. Harlow tells of a school picnic for second-graders, at which the girls simply stood around or skipped about hand in hand but the boys, like little male monkeys, tackled and wrestled with each other. Although none of the girls chased the boys, some of the boys did go after some of the girls (Harlow 1962).

Other writers too have generalized from animal studies to human beings. Lionel Tiger, in *Men in Groups,* and Tiger and Robin Fox, in *The Imperial Animal,* maintain that there is a fundamental difference between males and females in all primate species including *Homo sapiens.* Robert Ardrey, Konrad Lorenz, and Desmond Morris have all written popular books that attempt to explain many human phenomena—war and territoriality as well as sex differences—by comparing us to our evolutionary neighbors. Psychologist D. O. Hebb says that anyone who works with chimpanzees is bound to see how clearly their sex differences are reflected in ours. "It might do some good if all psychologists worked with chimps before they were turned loose on people," Hebb says.

> You see, the female chimpanzee is the smarter of the two. If the male gets mad at you, he blusters and openly charges. But if the female gets mad, it's all milk and honey until you get within reach. . . . If the female is caged with a larger animal she can't dominate, she manipulates the situation. . . . I think we can see the same sex difference in people. Women are better than men at manipulating social situations. They don't run away from the bigger male, but stick close and see if there is a way that they can turn the situation to their benefit. (Hebb 1969, p. 22).

Analogies between human and animal behavior are tantalizing, but they are also risky. In the preceding chapters we pointed out that human sex differences confirmed by research are neither as numerous nor as universal as popular stereotypes would predict. Behavior that characterizes the average rhesus monkey may be engaged in by people, but much less commonly. One could argue that more (even all) human beings *would* behave like monkeys were it not for upbringing and experience, but that is a bit like saying that most of us would swing from trees if we had not been taught otherwise. In the course of evolution our species has outgrown many old ways.

Futher, two species may behave in a similar fashion, but that does not necessarily mean that the determinants of the behavior are the same. Here's a fascinating example from Maurice Temerlin, a psychologist who with his wife, Jane, reared a chimpanzee named Lucy. Temerlin (1975) reports that until Lucy reached sexual maturity she treated her human "father" with spontaneous, playful affection punctuated by many wet, exuberant kisses. But when Lucy began to menstruate the relationship suddenly changed. During her periods of estrus, which mark sexual receptivity, Lucy rejected Temerlin entirely. "She would not hug me," he complains. "She would not kiss me. She would not allow me to cuddle, hug, or kiss her. During the same period she made the most blatant and obvious sexual invitations to other men." Because Lucy's behavior was so clearly related to her cycle of reproductive readiness, which is controlled by hormones, Temerlin concludes that chimps probably have a built-in, biologically based incest taboo. Such a taboo has survival benefits for the species because it assures outbreeding and healthier offspring.

Every human society, too, has an incest taboo, but Lucy's example does not tell us whether our taboo is biologically based or not. Temerlin points out that people, unlike chimpanzees, have the ability to create rules governing their own behavior and to communicate those rules in language. It is possible—in Temerlin's opinion, very likely—that "the pressures designed to suppress sex within the [human] family are social rather than biological."

One of the most perplexing problems for those who wish to generalize from animal behavior to human is to decide which species to use as a standard. Primate behavior varies considerably. It is true, for example, that male rhesus monkeys in the wild are, by human standards, very poor fathers. They show no interest in newborn infants and may behave viciously if an infant gets too near. Male owl monkeys, on the other hand, often carry the infants, giving them to the mothers only for nursing. Male baboons outrank females in the dominance hierarchy. but gibbons do not seem to have such a sex difference. Are we more like rhesus monkeys or owl monkeys, more baboonish or more gibbonish? People who conclude that we are biologically programed like our primate cousins must pick and choose among their relatives, depending on what they would like to demonstrate.

Jane Beckman Lancaster, an anthropologist, thinks that researchers' personal opinions about human sex differences often influence what they notice about primate societies. For example, most ethologists have emphasized the role and importance of male animals, which are large and conspicuous, in dominance hierarchies. But among several macaque species, mother-infant pairs determine the dominance hierarchy. Lancaster (1973) writes, "These studies have come up with the startling conclusion that one can place almost any monkey in the group dominance hierarchy on the basis of its mother's identity and its birth order among its siblings. Among these macaques, the young monkeys take their ranks directly from their mothers."

Among the vervet monkeys that Lancaster studied, females band together and gang up on males who are monopolizing a food source or frightening an infant. Even the highest-ranking male will turn and run during such an encounter. And Shirley Strum's research with baboons in Kenya indicates that social stability, long thought to be the males' responsibility, is actually in the fuzzy hands of the females. The female baboons form lasting bonds with other members of their sex and tend to stay with their troop for life, while males frequently shift alliances (Strum 1975). Lancaster notes that among terrestrial monkeys, which travel across large territories to find food during all seasons, "it is the old females who are likely to hold the troop's valuable knowledge about range resources—especially the sources of food and water during bad years—for they are the only group members who have spent their entire lives in that area."

For all these reasons we think that observations of other primates, though thought-provoking, cannot provide conclusive evidence one way or the other on the question of whether human behavior is biologically based. That does not mean there is no such basis. At this point, we need to ask just how biological factors might operate in human beings to produce sex differences. One possibility is that genes and hormones program those differences even before birth. Another is that hormones make men and women different in adulthood.

prenatal factors

genes and gender

In human beings, the female ovum and the male sperm each possess twenty-three chromosomes, threadlike bodies that contain genetic material. When ovum and sperm get together to form a fertilized egg cell, the result is forty-six chromosomes, aligned in twenty-three pairs. One of these pairs determines the sex of the embryo: it consists of an X chromosome from the mother and either an X or a Y chromosome from the father. The sex chromosome from the father determines the sex of the child. If he contributes an X, the child has two Xs and is a girl; if he contributes a Y, the child has an X and a Y and is a boy. The X chromosome is much larger than the Y and carries more genetic material.

On rare occasions, for reasons not yet well understood, one of the sex chromosomes is lost either before or just after fertilization. The cell can survive this trauma only if the remaining chromosome is an X (Money and Ehrhardt 1972). In that case, the child will be a female with Turner's syndrome (XO), a condition involving birth defects that include the absence of normal gonads.[2] Because an X alone is sufficient to make a human being but a Y alone is not, a few writers have gleefully concluded that human embryos are basically female. Eve, they say, preceded Adam. This line of argument is a bit precarious, however. In other types of chromosomal abnormality, the egg cell has a single Y and more than one X—such as XXY, or even XXXY. In these cases, the Y always wins out and a male results, although one with certain abnormalities. Now it is the traditionalists who trumpet; clearly maleness drives out femaleness. When the war between the sexes descends to this level, it's probably time for all combatants to smile, shake hands, and try a different tack.

Some human traits are said to be *sex-linked,* which means that the genes for the trait are partially or totally carried on one of the sex chromosomes. The sex-linkage is almost always through the X chromosome, because the smaller Y chromosome carries less genetic material. In fact, only one trait not directly related to gender is thought to be carried on the Y chromosome: hairy ears. Because sex-linked traits are nearly always carried by the X chromosome, and because a boy always gets his lone X from his mother, sex-linked characteristics are transmitted from mother to son, not from father to son.

Often a trait is recessive, which means that the effects of the gene that carries the trait will be canceled by an analogous, dominant gene on the other chromosome. The implications of this fact are quite different for females than for males. If a female has one X chromosome carrying a recessive gene for a trait and another X carrying a dominant gene (no trait), then she becomes a carrier for the trait but does not show it herself. A female must have a recessive gene on each of her two X chromosomes in order to show the trait, and the probability of this happening is low. But a male is never just a carrier for an X-linked recessive trait. When his single X carries the recessive gene, there is nothing analogous on his Y chromosome to

[2] Strangely enough, a girl who has Turner's syndrome may have started out as a genetic male (XY). We know this because the syndrome has been documented in a case of identical twins. The unaffected twin was a normal boy with penis. Therefore, although the affected twin was born with female genitals, she must originally have been male (Money, unpublished manuscript).

cancel its effects. Therefore he will have the trait. That is why sex-linked recessive disorders, such as hemophilia and color blindness, are much more common in men than in women.

Hemophilia and color blindness are one thing; sex differences in personality and behavior are quite another. To date, no one has been able to demonstrate a direct connection between a specific gene and any of the sex differences discussed in previous chapters. Nonetheless, a strong argument can be made that one particular sex difference is the result of a genetic, sex-linked trait. This is the ability to identify embedded figures, to imagine objects in three dimensions, and to see faces in clouds—the visual-spatial ability discussed on pages 38−41.

genes and spatial visualization

Assume for the moment that good spatial ability is a recessive trait carried on the X chromosome. It is thus a trait that can be canceled by a dominant gene for poor spatial ability. So a female who has the trait must have two recessive genes, one on each X chromosome, but a boy who has the trait needs only one recessive gene, because there is no dominant gene on his Y chromosome to suppress it. Already it is clear that boys ought to show the trait more often than girls and that therefore they should perform better (on the average) on tests of spatial skill. But we can be more specific than that. Let's call the recessive gene for spatial ability s and the dominant gene, which leads to poorer ability, S. Females, who have two X chromosomes, can have four possible combinations of the two spatial genes; the combinations and their implications for performance on spatial tests are shown in Table 4. If these four combinations have an equal probability of occurring, only one-fourth of all women will have good spatial ability.

Table 4. Possible combinations of visual-spatial genes for females

Chromosomes X^1 X^2		Consequence
s	s	Good spatial ability
s	S	Carrier for good spatial ability but performs poorly
S	s	Carrier for good spatial ability but performs poorly
S	S	Poor spatial ability

(Gene combinations)

Now consider males. Males have only one X chromosome; their Y chromosome carries neither an s nor an S gene. Therefore, for males, there are only two possible gene combinations and two possible consequences, as shown in Table 5. If the two alternatives are equally probable, half of all males should have good spatial ability.

Table 5. Possible combinations of visual-spatial genes for males

		Chromosomes		Consequence
		X	Y	
Gene combinations		s	- - -	Good spatial ability
		S	- - -	Poor spatial ability

In other words, this genetic explanation predicts that about twice as many men as women will have good visual-spatial ability. Indeed, that is exactly what tests of spatial perception show (O'Connor 1943).

That is not all. Additional evidence comes from correlations between the spatial abilities of children and their parents. If the ability is inherited, boys can get it only from their mothers, because their X chromosome, which carries the trait, comes from her and not from the father. Girls, on the other hand, need a recessive gene from each parent. If a girl does get two recessive genes, she may or may not resemble her mother in spatial ability, since the mother may be only a carrier. But the girl will definitely resemble her father, because males are never just carriers: a man who transmits the gene for a recessive sex-linked trait always has the trait himself. Therefore, girls should be more like their fathers than their mothers in spatial ability. In fact, four separate studies have found this cross-sex pattern (Stafford 1961; Hartlage 1970; Yen 1973; Bock and Kolakowski 1973). Boys' scores of spatial ability tend to be correlated with those of their mothers and not with those of their fathers. Girls' scores are correlated with the scores of both parents, but especially with their fathers'. These findings are not easy to explain in terms of cultural factors or experience, but they are perfectly in accord with a genetic explanation.

The evidence for a sex-linked genetic contribution to spatial ability, though persuasive, is inferential. Further, it does not mean that women are invariably bad at spatial tasks. The 25 percent of them who have good ability do as well as the 50 percent of men who have good ability (and better than the 50 percent of men who do not). And almost everyone has enough spatial ability to manage ordinary tasks like cutting a dress pattern, packing a suitcase, and reading a map. Finally, few traits are determined by only one gene. There are undoubtedly other genes, carried on different chromosomes, that also contribute to spatial ability.

This genetic explanation, like any other, refers only to the potential of each sex. Training and experience are crucial to whether people develop the ability as far as their potential allows. American males and females do not show differences in spatial ability until adolescence, by which time much learning (as well as puberty) has occurred. Studies of Eskimos find that the sexes do equally well on spatial-ability tests (Berry 1966; MacArthur 1967). This could be because the Eskimos encourage both sexes to develop the skill, though it is also possible that natural selection in the arctic environment has produced different gene frequencies from our own.

Here as in all discussions of genetic components in sex differences, it is well to keep the "so what" question in mind. Research may unearth other sex-linked traits, but such data should not be used to limit an *individual's* opportunities. Too many people believe that to say a trait is sex-linked means that *all* men and *no* women have it, or vice versa. This is obvious nonsense; baldness is genetically linked, too, but not all men go bald. Whether or not a trait or talent is distributed equally among men and women should not dictate whether an individual who has the ability may act on it.

prenatal sex hormones

Another way that genes might promote sex differences in behavior is by programing the activities of the sex hormones, which, like other hormones, are secreted by endocrine glands. Their effects are particularly noticeable during fetal development and at puberty.

Until an embryo is about six weeks old, there is no way to tell whether it will become male or female without examining the chromosomes in its cells. Every embryo contains tissue that eventually will develop into either testes (the male gonads) or ovaries (the female gonads); a genital tubercle that will become either a penis and scrotum or a clitoris and labia; and two sets of ducts, one of which will become the internal reproductive structures appropriate to the embryo's sex. In males, the Wolffian ducts develop into the vas deferens epididymis, seminal vesicles, and prostate. In females, the Müllerian ducts develop into the Fallopian tubes, uterus, and vagina. (In each sex, the ducts that do not develop eventually degenerate except for vestigial traces.)

The sexual differentiation of the embryo proceeds like a relay race, to use John Money and Anke Ehrhardt's simile. The first lap, at six weeks, is run by the genes. If the embryo is genetically male (XY), the testes begin to form; if it is genetically female (XX), the ovaries will appear a few weeks later. Once the testes or ovaries have developed, they take over for the second lap: the sex hormones that the gonads manufacture determine which set of internal reproductive structures and external genitals the embryo will have. In males, the dominant sex hormones are called *androgens*. The most potent androgen is *testosterone*. In females, the major sex hormones are *estrogen* and *progesterone*. Researchers used to think that these hormones belonged exclusively to one sex or the other, but now they know that everyone has some of each. Males produce some estrogen in the testes, and females produce androgens in the ovaries and the adrenocortical glands.

Nature's plan, in a nutshell, is that the embryo will become a female unless two "extras" make it male. The first is the Y chromosome, which turns the embryo's unisex gonads into testes; if the Y is lost, the fetus will become a female with Turner's syndrome. The second requirement is the male sex hormone testosterone. If the testes cannot produce this hormone, the result is not a neuter organism but one with female genitals. As far as endocrinologists can tell, the anatomical development of the female fetus does not require the female hormone. All that is necessary is the absence of male hormones.

Animal studies suggest that there is a second critical period, after gender has been determined at six weeks, when the presence of testosterone influences the development of the brain. Experiments with rats and guinea pigs show that testosterone during this period affects the hypothalamus, which is responsible, among other things, for controlling the pituitary gland. In adults, the pituitary gland in turn stimulates the ovaries to release eggs and secrete estrogen and the testes to produce androgens. It turns out that no matter what the original genetic sex of a rat happens to be, if it gets a dose of testosterone at the critical period (which for rats is during the first few days after birth) its brain will always be sensitive to male hormones and insensitive to female ones. If it does not get testosterone at this period, its brain later will be sensitive to female hormones. There are striking effects on the animal's sexual behavior.[3]

[3] For example, female rats treated with testosterone after birth will not behave like sexually normal females when they grow up, by arching the back and elevating the pelvis, even if you give them injections of female hormones. If you give them more male hormones at maturity, they will go through the whole male sexual ritual of mounting another rat and, undeterred by the fact that they don't have male genitals, they will make thrusting motions (Levine 1966). Similarly, male rats that have been castrated at birth (the testes are removed so that no testosterone is produced) later respond to injections of female hormones by trying to behave sexually like females (Young, Goy, and Phoenix 1964; Levine 1966).

In nonhuman primates, as in human beings, the critical period for sexual differentiation occurs before birth, so experiments have to be done with fetuses. William Young and his colleagues (1964) injected testosterone into pregnant rhesus monkeys and thereby produced "masculine" female offspring. These females, the researchers observed, threatened other monkeys more than normal females do; they initiated more rough-and-tumble play; they were less likely to withdraw when another monkey approached them; and their sexual behavior was much like that of males. Apparently rhesus monkeys are born with a hormonally determined predisposition toward certain sex-typed behaviors.

Of course, as we argued earlier, findings from animal studies may or may not hold true for people. Fortunately for science, it has been possible to make use of some of nature's errors to understand better the relative contributions of hormones and experience to human behavior.

hermaphrodites On rare occasions during fetal development, the hormone system goes wrong and produces a *hermaphrodite,* an organism that has both male and female tissue. True hermaphrodites have one ovary and one testicle, or a single organ containing both types of tissue. The external genitals are usually ambiguous in appearance—the individual has what could be a very large clitoris or a very small penis. (Remember that the genitals develop from the same original tissue in the embryo.) A *pseudo-hermaphrodite* has only one set of gonads—testes or ovaries—but its external genitals are either ambiguous-looking or in actual conflict with its internal system. Thus it may have ovaries and a penis. True hermaphroditism is extremely rare in human beings; in this century only sixty cases have been reported world-wide (Katchadourian and Lunde 1975). Most of the cases in medical literature, including the ones to be described here, are pseudo-hermaphrodites. Following the practice of most writers on this subject, we will use the term "hermaphrodites" to refer to both kinds.

In genetically female human fetuses, hermaphroditism usually occurs in one of two ways. First, the female fetus may produce too much androgen, because of a malfunction of the adrenocortical glands. This error occurs too late to affect the internal organs but in time to change the appearance of the genitals, and the baby is born with the *adrenogenital syndrome*. Doctors can suppress the further production of androgens after birth by administering cortisone. If this is not done, the child develops a masculine appearance and body build. Second, the fetus may be exposed to a synthetic hormone that has a masculinizing effect. A few decades ago, some pregnant women took such a hormone, progestin, to avert miscarriage, and a few of their babies were born with *progestin-induced hermaphroditism*. Needless to say, the hormone is no longer prescribed for pregnant women.

Fetuses that are genetically male can also develop into hermaphrodites, having genitals that are ambiguous or that look more like a clitoris than a penis. There are two primary causes of this problem. A rare, genetically caused metabolic error may prevent the fetus from manufacturing androgen, which is crucial for male development. Or a genetic defect may cause the cells of the fetal organs to be insensitive to androgen. The testes produce testosterone normally, but the body cannot use it, so neither the internal reproductive organs nor the genitals develop normally. From the outside the baby usually appears to be female. This condition, known as the *androgen-insensitivity syndrome*, cannot be treated by administering androgen after birth, because the cells remain incapable of responding to the hormone.

If one could show that the hormonal imbalance that affects the physical appearance of hermaphrodites also alters their psychological make-up, that would be a feather in the cap of the biological determinists. Let's see what the evidence shows.

Money and Ehrhardt (1972) investigated a group of twenty-five hermaphrodites who were genetically female and who had undergone corrective surgery on their enlarged genitals and had been raised normally as girls. Those with the adrenogenital syndrome had received cortisone therapy as well. Money and Ehrhardt matched these androgenized girls, who ranged in age from four to sixteen at the time of the study, with a control group of normal girls who were similar in age, IQ, socioeconomic background, and race. They interviewed all the girls and their mothers and gave them many psychological tests.

Although the androgenized girls definitely considered themselves female, Money and Ehrhardt judged them more likely than the controls to regard themselves as tomboys, to play outdoor sports and games, to wear pants and shorts instead of dresses, and to prefer "boys' toys" to dolls. Most of the androgenized girls were unenthusiastic about babysitting and taking care of small children, and unlike the control girls they were more concerned about their future careers than with marriage. However, they were no more aggressive than the girls in the control group, and they showed no signs of lesbianism.

The researchers concluded that the tomboyism of the androgenized girls was probably due to a masculinizing effect of the male sex hormone on the fetal brain. They also speculated that the abnormal amount of androgen before birth might have blocked pathways in the brain that would normally promote maternal behavior, though no one has ever identified any such pathways. Finally, Money and Ehrhardt hinted that personality traits in women might be tied to variations in their hormonal levels: "No one knows how many genetic females born with normal female genitalia might, in fact, have been subject to prenatal androgen excess insufficient to influence the external anatomy, though perhaps sufficient to influence the brain." It is only one more step to the conclusion that prenatal androgen is behind the masculine behavior of little boys, and its absence behind the feminine behavior of little girls.[4]

Before we take that step, though, some problems with this study must be settled. For example, Money and Ehrhardt relied heavily on interview data, which are notoriously subject to distortion and bias. True, the androgenized girls in the study described themselves as tomboys and their mothers reported them to be very energetic and active. But we do not know whether an impartial observer would have noticed differences between the androgenized girls and the control girls. Even if the girls did behave differently, one would have to rule out the possibility that this was due to differences in upbringing. That is, the mothers of the androgenized girls may have reacted to their energy with the attitude, "Well, yes, she's very active, but that's probably natural, considering the extra dose of androgen she got before birth," while the mothers of the controls may have discouraged the same behavior as too masculine.[5]

transsexuals Judith Bardwick (1971) has made an interesting suggestion: that prenatal hormones might help explain one of the most fascinating puzzles of human sexuality, transsexualism. Transsexuals are people (usually males) who say they feel trapped in the body of the wrong sex. They are not homosexuals in the usual sense, because homosexuals are as satisfied with

[4] There is not much direct evidence on boys. Ehrhardt and Baker (1974) report that when boys receive too much androgen before birth, they differ in only one way from their normal brothers in the family: according to their mothers, they are more energetic. Money and Ehrhardt found that when genetic males with the androgen-insensitivity syndrome are raised as girls they become stereotypically female, but in such cases it is impossible to separate the effects of learning from the possible effects of the androgen deficit.

[5] No one really knows how common tomboyism is (or even *what* it is). According to one study, most little girls report themselves to have been tomboys at some time, and most women, looking back on their childhoods, recall having been tomboys (Hyde, Rosenberg, and Behrman 1974). Behaviorial studies are needed to find out whether these self-reports reflect reality.

their anatomy as anyone else, whereas transsexuals feel that somehow they got stuck with the wrong set of genitals. Thus a male transsexual typically thinks of himself as a woman who desires heterosexual contact with a man (Green 1974). Transsexuals are often so disgusted with their appearance that they request sex-change operations, and some male transsexuals, in desperation, have even tried to remove the offending genitals themselves. Christine Jorgensen became famous for her successful sex-change operation during the 1950s, and more recently Jan Morris, an English writer who had a wife and children, published a book (*Conundrum*), about her transformation. In 1976 Renee Richards, formerly a male physician, caused consternation and curiosity when she tried to enter the women's tennis circuit. Some female transsexuals also have sex-change operations, but less often. A penis can be constructed out of sensitive tissue, but it does not have erections.

Transsexualism is a puzzle because there does not seem to be a simple environmental explanation for it. Many transsexuals grow up in families where there is a protective "smother-mother" or a domineering mother and a weak father, but others do not (Stoller 1967; Benjamin 1966; Pauly 1965). The brothers and sisters of transsexuals are usually normal. Further, transsexualism appears very early in life; transsexuals commonly report that they knew they were in the wrong body as far back as they can remember, and that even as preschoolers they preferred the clothes, toys, and activities usually associated with the opposite sex (Green 1974).

The prenatal hormone theory, if correct, would add some pieces to this puzzle. Transsexuals may be people who suffered some prenatal error in androgen production after the external genitals had been formed but before the brain was sexually "set." The result: a person whose sense of himself is out of phase with the physical evidence and with the social role assigned him on the basis of his anatomy. This theory might also explain why more transsexuals are men wishing to be women than the reverse: because male development depends on the addition of androgen at critical times, it is more complicated and allows more room for error. All this, however, is conjecture.

labels and identity

Normally, genes, hormones, internal organs, and genitals are all congruent with the label the child gets at birth: "It's a boy!" or "It's a girl!" Hermaphrodites give us the chance to ask what happens when the label— boy or girl—disagrees with a physical attribute. In most cases the sex of assignment seems to override the discordant feature. For example, a study of androgenized girls who grew up as females but did not have cortisone treatments showed that although they developed deep voices, facial hair, and other male secondary sex characteristics, they still considered themselves to be female and had no desire to change sex (Hampson and Hampson 1961; Hampson 1965).

The clearest evidence on this question comes from comparisons of hermaphrodites who are born with the same physical condition but assigned different sexual identities. In one case the doctors and parents may decide the child is to be reared as a boy; in the other they decide the child should become a girl. One child goes home in a blue blanket and the other in a pink one. If prenatal hormones are the strongest influence on gender identity, one of these decisions is right and the other is tragically wrong. But if environment is more critical, the success of either decision rests on the consistency with which the parents raise the child.

Money and Ehrhardt describe several such pairs. For example, two genetically female hermaphrodites, both born with the adrenogenital syndrome, had surgery early in life to correct their enlarged clitorises. But whereas one was feminized and raised as a girl, the other underwent "penis repair" and was raised as a boy. According to Money and Ehrhardt, both children grew up secure in their respective gender roles. The girl was somewhat tomboyish, but she appeared attractively feminine to those who met her. The boy was accepted as male by other boys and expressed a romantic interest in girls.

Such studies seem to show that fetal hormones do not determine one's gender identity in any automatic way. Money and Ehrhardt, whose other work tends to demonstrate the power of prenatal hormones over environmental influences, say, "Matched pairs of hermaphrodites demonstrate conclusively how heavily weighted is the contribution of the postnatal phase of gender-identity differentiation. To use the Pygmalion allegory, one may begin with the same clay and fashion a god or a goddess."

Indeed, the label a child is given and the way he or she is raised can even override genetic gender and prenatal hormones working together. Money and Ehrhardt describe a fascinating case of a normal male child who, at the age of seven months, had his penis burned off during what was supposed to be a routine circumcision by electrocautery. For some months the parents agonized over what to do. When the child was seventeen months old, they authorized the transformation of their little boy into a little girl. A few months later the surgical reconstruction of the genitals began.

If some demented scientist had planned all this in order to do a controlled experiment, he could not have done better, for it happened that this little boy had an identical twin brother. Thus it was possible to compare the development of the newly created girl with that of a genetically identical individual who had the same prenatal hormone history. If the twins grew to differ in gender-related behavior, the results could safely be attributed to differences in rearing. Money and Ehrhardt have reported data on the child's early years. (She is now in late childhood.) One of the first changes that the parents made was in the child's clothing. The mother started to dress her daughter in little pink slacks and fancy blouses, granny gowns, bracelets and hair ribbons, and she let her hair grow. Not too surprisingly, the child came to prefer dresses and long hair, and she would sit under the hair dryer for hours to have her hair set. The mother also encouraged her daughter, as she grew older, to help with the housework. The little girl would copy her mother and try to help clean up the kitchen, while her brother totally ignored such chores. When the son urinated in the flower garden, his mother laughed at his antics and could not bring herself to scold him; when the girl once pulled her panties down, the mother swatted her on the rear and told her that nice little girls didn't do such things. By the age of four and a half, the girl was much the neater of the two children. At Christmas the girl requested, and received, a doll house and a doll carriage; the boy requested, and received, a toy garage complete with gas pumps and tools. Except for a certain degree of tomboyishness (the girl was very energetic and active), the little girl who had been a boy was a perfect picture of traditional femininity.

sex hormones in adults

During childhood, girls and boys do not differ much in their levels of androgen and estrogen, which are fairly low in both sexes. But at puberty the testes begin to increase their production of testosterone, and the ovaries increase production of estrogen. The result is reproductive fertility and the development of secondary sex characteristics. Boys grow pubic and underarm hair; their voices deepen; their genitals get larger; their testes begin to produce mature sperm. In girls the first sign of puberty is usually breast development, followed by *menarche* (the onset of menstruation). Girls' bodies also begin to produce male sex hormone, though not nearly as much as boys'. Adrenal androgens seem to be responsible for the growth of pubic and underarm hair in girls (Money and Ehrhardt 1972).

Many endocrinologists—and nonprofessionals—believe that the sex hormones have psychological as well as physiological effects on human beings. Fluctuating hormones, they argue, are responsible for emotional ups and downs, especially in women, and may even help explain some of the status differences between the sexes. Most of the empirical research in this area has concerned the effects of menstruation, which is a regular, visible, cyclic reminder of the role of hormones in reproduction.

menstruation and mood

Throughout history, men have reacted to menstruation with a mixture of awe, pity, disgust, and fear, as described in Chapter 1. Superstitions about menstruation die hard, and even in the sophisticated United States many people still feel uneasy about this basic biological process. As Karen Paige points out, the term "sanitary napkin" implies that menstruation is unsanitary, and menstrual blood is considered unclean and disgusting. Paige found that half of the women and men in a representative sample in the San Francisco Bay area had never had intercourse during a woman's period, although there is no medical reason for abstaining (Paige, in press). One of our students informed us that she and her female classmates at parochial school were asked to stay home at the beginning of the menstrual period. The nun who made the request was afraid that menstrual odor would distract and disturb the boys. For that matter, "menstruation" is not a word customarily used in polite conversation. Instead, women resort to euphemisms: it's "that time of the month," or "Aunt Flo is here," or one is "on the rag," or "riding a white horse." Southern women speak of "falling off the roof"; French women say "the English have arrived."

Even those who do not fear menstruation may regard it as a physical or mental handicap. The menstruating female is said to be unusually vulnerable and fragile, in need of protection. It used to be conventional wisdom that one must not wash one's hair or go swimming during the period, and a girl could feel entirely justified in asking to be excused from physical education classes (even though exercise is a good remedy for cramps). Some girls still accept these restrictions. Even more common is the assumption that menstruating women are emotionally unstable and hard to live with. Here is what psychologist Kenneth Moyer says, summing up the prevailing view of many husbands and social scientists:

> Although in humans violent and aggressive behavior is overwhelmingly committed by the male, any husband can testify that women are not immune to hostile feelings and aggressive tendencies. Feminine hostility has, of course, many causes, but there is now good evidence that there is a periodicity to the irascibility of women and that it is related to the hormonal changes occurring over the course of the menstrual cycle. . . . Emotional instability is characteristic of a number of women during the premenstrual period (Moyer 1974, pp. 358–59).

Despite the mystery that surrounds it, the biology of menstruation is quite straightforward. Each month the pituitary gland, under the control of the hypothalamus, sends out a chemical message (a hormone) that signals a woman's ovaries to increase their production of estrogen.[6] The estrogen causes rapid growth of cells in the lining of the uterus and signals the pituitary to release a second substance, which causes one of the follicles in the ovary to rupture and release an egg (ovulation). After ovulation, which usually occurs midway between periods, the follicle that released the egg changes form and becomes a temporary gland that secretes progesterone, another female hormone. Progesterone, the "pregnancy hormone," helps prepare the lining of the uterus to receive the egg, should it be fertilized. If conception does not take place, a decrease in estrogen and progesterone occurs, along with degeneration of the now unnecessary uterine lining. The result is the menstrual flow. After menstruation, the entire process begins anew.

Estrogen reaches its peak at midcycle, dips, rises again, remains fairly high until right before menstruation, and then falls off rapidly. Progesterone remains low until midcycle and then rises after ovulation, reaching a peak a few days before menstruation; then it too drops dramatically. These curves are shown in Figure 4.

The periodic fluctuation in female hormone levels has led many researchers to look for relationships between shifting hormones and shifting moods. In 1939 two psychoanalysts, Thérèse Benedek and B. B. Rubenstein, published the first study of the relation between hormone levels and emotional states. Based on reports from fifteen women in therapy, they concluded that at midcycle, when estrogen is high, the women were happiest and most self-confident; just before and during menstruation, when the hormones ebb, the women became passive, narcissistic, anxious, and tense (Benedek and Rubenstein 1939 a and b).

Thus was folklore enshrined in science. Psychologists hurried to document further the symptoms that collectively became known as the *premenstrual syndrome*. Unfortunately, they could not agree on how to define the syndrome. Some of them included dysmenorrhea (unusually painful menstruation, generally from physical causes) as well as other physical complaints such as headache and backache. Others restricted the definition to emotional symptoms such as irritability, depression, hostility, and anxiety. In addition, researchers have used vastly different methods to study the syn-

---

[6] *Estrogen* is actually the term for a class of female hormones, analogous to male androgens. Just as testosterone is the most potent of the androgens, estradiol is the most active of the estrogens. In nontechnical discussions, however, *estrogen* is the commonly used term.

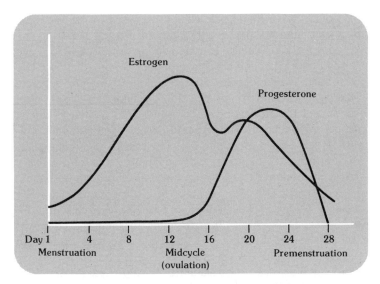

Figure 4. During the menstrual cycle, hormone levels rise and fall. Estrogen peaks at midcycle, dips, rises again, and then falls off just before menstruation. Progesterone rises after midcycle, peaks a few days before menstruation, and then declines abruptly. Several studies find a relation between phases of the menstrual cycle and changes in mood.
ADAPTED FROM William D. Odell and Dean L. Moyer. 1971. *Physiology of reproduction.* St. Louis: The C. V. Mosby Company. Used by permission of the publisher and the authors.

drome. Some simply asked women whether they experienced various problems at menstruation, ignoring the possibility of fallible memories and self-fulfilling prophecies. Others asked women to keep a daily diary. Still others examined what women spontaneously said about themselves or their lives at various points in the cycle. Some of the best-known studies, like Benedek and Rubenstein's, generalized from women in therapy to all women.

Although work on the premenstrual syndrome has been flawed by faulty methodology and unfounded interpretations, the consensus among most researchers today is that changes in mood are correlated with phases of the menstrual cycle for many women (see Parlee 1973 for a critique). But for how many? There's the rub. Estimates of the incidence of the premenstrual syndrome among American women range all the way from 15 percent to 95 percent, depending on how the syndrome is defined and who does the defining (Paige 1973). Not every study finds anxiety or depression to be higher before menstruation. For instance, Harold Persky, using a battery of psychological tests, found little change in mood across the menstrual cycles of twenty-nine normal, healthy women (Persky 1974).

In one well-known study, Melville Ivey and Judith Bardwick (1968) had twenty-six college women relate memorable experiences from their lives into a tape recorder. Each woman spoke for five minutes on four separate occasions—at midcycle (ovulation) and at premenstruation, for two months. The researchers scored the stories for emotional themes related to death, mutilation, guilt, separation, shame, and diffuse anxiety—and for some positive themes, such as self-esteem and optimism. They discovered that anxiety and hostility were significantly higher at premenstruation than at ovulation, while the stories at midcycle reflected a high level of self-esteem and confidence.

For example, at ovulation one young woman chose to talk about a vacation she had recently enjoyed: "We just went to Jamaica and it was fantastic, the island is so lush and green . . . and the place is so fertile and the natives are just so friendly." A psychoanalyst would be quick to point out that the word "fertile" was no coincidence; in any case, the theme is certainly a happy one. The same woman, at premenstruation, said this: "I'll tell you about the death of my poor dog . . . oh, another memorable event, my grandparents died in a plane crash. That was my first contact with death and it was very traumatic."

The alert reader may have noticed a methodological problem. Ivey and Bardwick's women were aware that the research in which they were participating had something to do with the menstrual cycle, and this might have biased them to respond in a particular way. Bardwick counters this objection by citing the case of one woman, interviewed on the fourteenth day of her cycle, when ovulation and optimism would be expected. She told a story with dismal themes of death, mutilation, and separation. The next day she began to menstruate, two weeks early. This single example, however, does not rule out the possibility that a general bias was operating in the study.

If mood changes are associated with the menstrual cycle, what are the causes? Many researchers automatically assume that hormones must be causing the emotional swings, and work is now going on to pin down the exact physiological mechanisms involved. Possibilities range from altered levels of the enzyme monoamine oxidase (MAO), which could affect the nervous system, to hypoglycemia (low blood sugar). Some scientists believe that aldosterone, an adrenocortical hormone, is involved, perhaps through its ability to cause water and salt retention.

But, as statisticians like to say, correlation is not causation. When two variables, A and B, tend to occur together, it does not mean that A is causing B, or vice versa. It is also possible that another factor, C, is causing both A and B. Or that C causes A but D causes B, and both C and D are caused by E—well, you get the point. The premenstrual syndrome (B) may be caused by physiological factors alone (A), but psychological (C) and cultural explanations (D) are also possible. When you consider the thousands of years of mystery, ritual, and taboo surrounding menstruation in all societies, it would be astounding if the negative feelings that the phenomenon evokes were purely physiological in origin.

The anxiety that emerges with each menstrual period, in other words, may be no more than anxiety about menstruation itself. Paige (1971, 1973) has explored this hypothesis in a clever series of experiments. She conducted a study similar in method to Ivey and Bardwick's, but she divided 102 married women into three groups: 38 women who were not taking an oral contraceptive; 52 who were taking the combination birth-control pill, which provides a constant level of both estrogen and progesterone for twenty days; and 12 who were on the sequential pill, which more closely mimics normal hormonal fluctuations. Paige found that women on the combination pill did not show menstrual anxiety but those on the sequential pill did, a finding that seems to support the hormones-as-cause theory. But Paige did not stop there. "If premenstrual blues are linked to menstrual bleeding and not to hormone levels," she reasoned, "then pill users whose flow has decreased should report fewer complaints than pill users whose flow has remained the same."

And that is exactly what happened. Menstrual anxiety was directly related to the amount of flow a woman reported during her period. Among women on the combination pill, those who had a reduced flow were less anxious at menstruation than women whose flow remained unchanged by the pill; but those who still had a normally heavy flow were just as anxious at menstruation as nonpill women. Paige explained her results by suggesting that women who have less of the "mess, worry, and fuss" of menstruation are less apprehensive about it and therefore feel less menstrual anxiety. (However, some people think it is also possible that the women with reduced flow had different hormone levels to begin with, which were responsible *both* for reduced flow and lower anxiety. The pill does not necessarily produce identical hormone levels in all women.)

Paige also thinks women learn to use menstruation as a way of explaining physical discomfort or psychological stress actually caused by other events. "When a woman feels irritable and has backaches during her period," she writes, "she may attribute these feelings to the fact that she is menstruating, while if she has the same feelings after a hard day's work, she will attribute them to the tensions of the job. . . . *None* of the symptoms that women report during menstruation are unique to menstruation; most are common reactions that both men and women have to psychological stress" (Paige 1973). In a second study of 352 unmarried college women, Paige found that women who reported menstrual problems were more likely than others also to report psychological stress, aches and pains, and illness not associated with menstruating. Apparently women who regard menstruation as an illness are most anxious and nervous in general and are most likely to respond to any stress with physical symptoms. Some psychoanalysts have argued that menstrual distress is a sign that a woman is denying her true femininity. According to this view, the ambitious, career-minded woman (whom many analysts consider unfeminine) should report the worst symptoms. Paige's research finds this assumption incorrect. "On the contrary," she says, "the traditionally feminine woman is the one who tends to get the cramps and the blues."

This line of research makes it clear that we must go beyond raging hormones to understand why some women get the menstrual blues and others don't. Paige and Paige (in press) have studied an international sample of tribal societies, and they find that while all of them have some menstrual taboos and myths, in some cultures women do not report any menstrual symptoms. They don't even know what the ethnographer is talking about when he or she inquires about such symptoms. Women in one tribe began reporting symptoms to health officials only after the arrival of Western female missionaries.

In short, all sorts of factors may account for reactions to menstruation, which differ among individuals within a society, and across societies: variations in hormone levels, diet, exercise, attitudes, and pain tolerance. The most important is probably cultural context, which determines the reactions that are socially acceptable. But not all menstrual distress is "psychological." Doctors do not yet know much about the causes of menstrual cramps, for example, or about why many women stop having such cramps after childbirth. The lack of information, unfortunately, does not stop some gynecologists from dismissing women who have pain during their periods as whining hypochondriacs. Researchers are trying to find out how the mind and body work together in producing a range of symptoms; the object is not to make women feel guilty, neurotic, or unliberated for having them.

Now the big question: so what if women get the menstrual blues? Studies have shown that people who are highly anxious do poorly on difficult intellectual tasks, though a moderate amount of anxiety seems to energize people. Certainly, depressed people are not motivated to do their best. Therefore, we must consider the possibility that premenstrual distress, whatever its causes, leads to poor intellectual performance in women. Lots of people think it does. Lionel Tiger worries that "an American girl writing her Graduate Record Examinations over a two-day period or a week-long set of finals during the premenstruum begins with a disadvantage which almost certainly condemns her to no higher than a second-class grade. A whole career in the educational system can be unfairly jeopardized because of this phenomenon" (Tiger 1970). Mercy! Does this mean that menstruating women will have to be excused both from physical education classes *and* from final exams?

Let us relieve the female reader's anxiety at once by answering: no. Study after study has failed to find a relationship between menstruation and intellectual performance. The one piece of research that seemed to support Tiger's worry was inconclusive. In 1960 Katherina Dalton reported that in a group of English schoolgirls, 27 percent got poorer test grades just before menstruation than at ovulation. But Dalton did not say how *much* worse they did, nor did she report any statistical tests that would have determined whether the results were reliable or due to chance. Besides, 56 percent of the girls in the study showed no change in test grades, and 17 percent did better at premenstruation—a fact that several writers have overlooked when citing this study.

Recently Sharon Golub did a much more extensive study in which she gave a number of psychological and mental tests to fifty women, once during the four-day period before menstruation and once two weeks later. Golub found, along with everyone from Benedek to Bardwick, that the women's anxiety and depression increased significantly at premenstruation. But she did not find any corresponding decreases in test performance. On eleven of the thirteen tests of intellectual ability there were no menstrual-cycle effects. On one of the remaining tests, women who were first tested at midcycle did better at midcycle; on the other, most women did better premenstrually (Golub 1975). It seems that monthly mood changes are not great enough to affect a woman's ability to think and work. As Julia Sherman (1971) dryly puts it, "Women apparently are motivated [during menstruation] to carry on as usual."

Well then, if menstruation doesn't make women dumber, perhaps it makes them dangerous. A great deal has been made of the dramatic correlations between premenstruation/menstruation and the incidence of antisocial behavior among women. Half of the women who commit suicide, half of those who commit crimes, and almost half of those admitted to hospitals for psychiatric reasons are either menstruating or about to (Dalton 1964). At first glance, these are impressive statistics. Given a random distribution, one would expect only 29 percent of all female suicides, crimes, and psychiatric admissions to occur during the eight days before and during menstruation. Some people have concluded that females go a bit berserk during menstruation. In some countries, menstruation is deemed an extenuating circumstance in criminal cases, and in France, severe premenstrual tension can qualify as temporary insanity.

But remember, correlations can be interpreted several ways. The crime statistic, for example, really tells us only that women who commit crimes (and get caught) are more likely than chance to be in the premenstrual/menstrual phase. It does *not* tell us that all women in this phase are more likely than usual to commit a crime. It is possible that those women who are already predisposed to commit a crime are pushed over the edge at this time; for others, premenstrual tension may set off a burst of creativity or sustained work. Another fascinating but often overlooked interpretation of the correlation is this: Being arrested, having an accident, or entering a hospital are all highly stressful events, and great stress itself can bring on an early menstrual period. Physician William Nolen (1975) notes that it is not uncommon for stress to provoke a period two weeks early. So it may well be that the popular notion that menstruation "causes" women to commit crimes, have accidents, and have psychiatric difficulties actually works the other way around: committing a crime, having an accident, or entering a hospital may "cause" earlier menstruation.

Finally, it would be a mistake to assume that menstruating women are more anxious, tense, or antisocial than the average man. Few studies of the premenstrual syndrome have used men as comparisons. However, Persky (1974) reports that menstruating women score about the same on various psychological tests as their male classmates. And because crime, accident, and suicide rates (though not suicide attempts) are much higher for males than for females, researchers might do better to study men at all weeks of the month than to worry about women during their one critical week.

menopause and melancholy

Psychologists do not yet know very much about the psychological consequences of menopause. But ignorance about the topic has not prevented writers from pontificating about it. Edgar F. Berman, a Baltimore physician, fretted thus about female hormones:

> If you had an investment in the bank, you wouldn't want the president of your bank making a loan under those raging hormonal influences at that particular period. Suppose we had a President in the White House, a menopausal woman President, who had to make the decision of the Bay of Pigs, which was of course a bad one, or the Russian contretemps with Cuba at that time?

Woman is in a double bind. For thirty years she is unreliable because she menstruates; then she's unreliable because she stops menstruating.

Menopause occurs most frequently when women are in the late forties, though it can begin earlier or later. The ovaries gradually atrophy and stop producing estrogen and progesterone (this is called the *climacterium*). Menstrual bleeding stops and the woman becomes infertile, although sometimes ovulation continues for a year or two after the end of menstruation. The adrenal glands continue to produce some estrogen, but the level falls to about one-sixth of what it was before menopause.

The menopausal symptom most often reported is the hot flash or flush. The woman suddenly feels warm from the waist up and perspires profusely; then, when the flash is over, she may feel chilled. Hot flashes seem to be due to a hormone imbalance. As estrogen declines, the pituitary gland releases an excessive amount of the hormones that stimulate the ovaries. This affects the vasomotor system, which regulates the diameter of the blood vessels.

Estrogen seems to be important for many functions in a woman's body, and when it falls off a number of physical effects may occur. The mucous lining of the vagina becomes thinner and less elastic, and it is more easily eroded. Sometimes there is pain during intercourse, but the probability of painful intercourse is greatly reduced if a woman has had regular sexual relations. The bones lose some calcium, and some women develop "dowager's hump" as the vertebrae compress. Some doctors believe that lowered estrogen is related to the increase in susceptibility to heart disease and cancer in postmenopausal women; before menopause women are much less vulnerable to these diseases than men. Other complaints common during menopause include headache, nausea, fatigue, heart palpitations, and backache, all of which may or may not be linked to a reduction in estrogen.[7] As if those woes were not enough, a few researchers argue that lowered estrogen levels affect the hypothalamus, and through it, the rest of the central nervous system, which causes the menopausal woman, like the premenstrual woman, to feel depressed and anxious.

The symptoms of menopause can be rather upsetting to a woman who has grown up in a society that makes a fetish of youth. But menopause is made even worse by the gloomy writings of some medical men. For example, David Reuben, who will tell you everything you wanted to know even

[7] Several doctors have reported dramatic success in treating menopausal symptoms with estrogen replacement therapy (See *Feminine Forever* by Robert Wilson). However, this treatment is increasingly controversial, as suspicions grow of a link between synthetic estrogen and cancer.

if he doesn't know it himself, writes, "Without estrogen the quality of being female gradually disappears. The vagina begins to shrivel, the uterus gets smaller, the breasts atrophy, sexual desire often disappears, and the woman becomes completely desexualized." Reuben (1969) serenely announces that during menopause a woman "comes as close as she can to being a man." She grows facial hair, her voice deepens, and her features become coarse. "Not really a man, but no longer a functional woman, these individuals live in the world of intersex."

As Barbara Seaman points out in *Free and Female* (1972), Reuben's description is both insulting and inaccurate. Most women continue to enjoy sex during and after menopause, sometimes more than they did when they had to worry about pregnancy. The other signs and symptoms Reuben describes are considerably exaggerated. "If a woman were to believe one-quarter of the repulsive things Dr. Reuben has told her about herself," says Seaman, "she would not feel very lovable and would hesitate to expose her coarse and hairy face and hairless head in public, much less reveal her atrophied breasts and shriveled vagina to a man." Fortunately, many women haven't read Reuben and have a sexually active old age.

Though the physical symptoms associated with menopause are fairly well defined, no one is quite sure how many women suffer from them. This is because menopause is often studied (if at all) using special groups of women, such as those in therapy. So we don't know much about the majority. Recent estimates are that about three-fourths of all women experience some discomfort during menopause, but that very few are incapacitated by it. Bernice Neugarten (1967) asked 100 normal women what changes during middle age worried them the most; only four mentioned menopause. Widowhood, getting old, fear of cancer, and having children leave home caused greater concern. Neugarten thinks that "the change" has received a worse press than it deserves. Most of the women in her study rated the experience as more unpleasant for other women than for themselves. This might mean that they are denying their own distress, but it could also indicate that the real menopause is not as bad as the expected one.

It is hard to assess theories about the psychological problems that may come from menopause because they cannot easily be separated from problems of aging in general. Certain symptoms have been blamed on menopause when they almost certainly should not have been. Aging can be agonizing for both sexes, not because of hormones but because of attitudes and society's limited roles for older people. Testosterone levels in most men decline gradually, not abruptly, yet men, too, often go through a turbulent emotional period during their forties and fifties—the "male menopause." They do not have a visible physical change to which to attribute their emotional state, as women do with menopause, so few researchers have looked for hormonal explanations of their midlife crisis.

As Paige pointed out in her explanation of menstrual ailments, there are many sources of irritability and depression that have nothing to do with hormones. If a woman experiences vaginal discomfort during intercourse, and if her spouse is less than understanding, that alone could make her cross. So could reading Dr. Reuben. Pauline Bart (1971) and other sociologists remind us that menopause occurs at a stage in life that is difficult and depressing for women whose sole identity has come from being a wife and mother; children leave the nest when most women are in their midforties. A woman's self-esteem and the way she regards aging will certainly affect her response to pain or discomfort during the "change of life."

For some women, menopause is a difficult time, whether for physiological reasons or mental ones. But others barely notice it. Seaman tells about her mother-in-law, a busy novelist, mother, and grandmother, who at the age of fifty-two was asked by her doctor when she had had her last period. She suddenly realized that it had been months, went home and checked the medicine cabinet, and discovered that the box of Kotex she had bought the summer before was almost full. That was her menopause. Though physicians often blame menstrual distress on psychological hangups, many assume that all menopausal women suffer hormonally caused symptoms. And they don't listen. One woman's doctor asked her, "Do you find that you are nervous and depressed?" "No," she replied. "Here," he said soothingly, "have this prescription filled; it will help."

testosterone and temperament

If fluctuating estrogen levels affect the female psyche, perhaps fluctuating testosterone levels affect the male. Do men have raging hormones? A simple, straightforward, obvious question, but one that hardly has been studied. One reason for the lack of attention, until recently, was that methods of measuring testosterone in the blood were very unreliable. Another reason, we think, is that it rarely occurred to researchers that *male* mood swings could be hormonally caused. Without a visible sign, such as menstruation, few scientists thought to ask whether testosterone fluctuates regularly, and whether it is related to changes in mood or behavior.

Male sex hormones do affect behavior in some species. If you inject testosterone into immature male mice, which normally are not very aggressive, they become as aggressive as adult male mice. In several rodent species, aggressiveness drops when the male is castrated and rises again when male hormones are injected. Biological determinists often use such animal data to argue that the male's testosterone is responsible for his dominance over weaker males and females. Not all animals are alike, though. In dogs, castration does not lessen aggressiveness, nor does it affect a dog's position in a dominance hierarchy (Moyer 1974).

Robert Rose and his colleagues (1971) carefully observed the social interactions of thirty-four rhesus monkeys who were living together in a compound, and they collected blood samples from which they could analyze testosterone levels. They found that high testosterone levels were correlated with aggressiveness (which consisted mostly of threats and chasing rather than real fighting) and with dominance rank in the group. However, monkeys that submitted to their "superiors" did not necessarily have low testosterone. This result is not as contradictory as it seems, because an animal can be both aggressive to its subordinates and submissive to higher-ups in the hierarchy. Rose and his colleagues also discovered that aggressiveness did not lead automatically to dominance; the most dominant animal, for example, ranked only twelfth in aggressiveness.

This study recalls the old refrain, correlation is not causation. Testosterone may cause aggressiveness, or being aggressive may cause testosterone to shoot up. When Rose, Gordon, and Bernstein (1972) paired two male monkeys who were low in dominance with females they could dominate and have sex with, the males' testosterone levels went up. Then the researchers put each male in with an established group of males, who lost no time in attacking the newcomer and putting him in his place. The poor monkeys' testosterone levels fell drastically and stayed low for weeks after they were taken out of that competitive cage.

The evidence on the relation between hormones and behavior in human males is no simpler than that from animal studies, and is more meager. In one study, Harold Persky and his colleagues (1971) gave eighteen healthy young men (age seventeen to twenty-eight) and fifteen healthy older men (age thirty-one to sixty-six) a battery of psychological tests and measured their testosterone levels and rate of testosterone production. For the younger men, but not for the older, both hormone measures were related significantly to hostility and aggression. Before we start worrying about letting a man with high testosterone run for public office, we must note that at least one study did not replicate Persky's (Meyer-Bahlburg et al, 1974). Another study, with prison inmates, had mixed results: the men's plasma testosterone levels were unrelated to aggressiveness as measured by psychological tests and to their history of aggressive acts in prison. But men who had high testosterone levels were more likely to have committed violent crimes as adolescents than men with low testosterone levels (Kreuz and Rose 1972).

Testosterone levels do fluctuate in human males, but over time the peaks and troughs are not as stable and regular as the estrogen shifts in women. Charles Doering and his colleagues (1974) at Stanford University measured testosterone in a group of twenty young men, taking blood samples every other morning for two months. In addition to giving psychological tests, they had the men keep a daily diary of moods and events. They found that each man's testosterone level fluctuated considerably from day to day and week to week. Of the twenty men, twelve had regular cycles, ranging in length from eight to thirty days. It is not clear why some of the men showed these cycles and others did not. For the group as a whole, self-reported depression and testosterone were positively related, while self-reported hostility and testosterone were weakly correlated. (A later report [Doering et al. 1975] indicates that the relation between depression and testosterone was weaker than originally reported, and that the correlation with hostility was not statistically significant.) But for individual men, every kind of relationship showed up. That is, for one man high testosterone might go along with increased hostility, while for another high testosterone might predictably be related to *low* hostility. Further, some men whose plasma testosterone changed a lot did not show great mood swings. It's hard to know what to say about these findings beyond what the researchers themselves say: "These findings . . . provide sufficient encouragement for further work."

the maternal instinct

In most animal and human societies, females do most of the childcare. Some explain this fact by postulating a maternal instinct or a biologically programed "readiness" to mother. Fathers learn to love their children, to be sure, but mothers are merely doing what comes naturally.

There is some controversy about what an instinct is. According to traditional definitions, an instinct is a genetically fixed behavior pattern that is performed automatically by every member of a species, even if an individual has been raised in isolation and has never seen the behavior in question. Styles of nest-building are instinctive in some birds. A young wolf instinctively howls in a certain way, whether or not it has heard the howl of another wolf. Spiders will spin an elegant web without a blueprint or demonstration. Chicks produce the usual chick sounds even if they are deafened right after hatching.

By this definition, human mothering is too complex to be considered an instinct. There are hundreds of different behaviors that go into infant and childcare—feeding, supervising, cleaning, teaching, dressing, and providing piano lessons, to name a few—and none of these activities can be called instinctive in the narrow sense. Even the desire to become a mother does not appear in all human females, and not all females who want and love babies are instant experts at caring for them. One of the first American psychologists to reject the notion of a maternal instinct, John Watson, took a cold, hard look at young mothers and said this:

> We have observed the nursing, handling, bathing, etc. of the first baby of a good many mothers. Certainly there are no new ready-made activities appearing except nursing. The mother is usually as awkward about that as she can well be. The instinctive factors are practically nil (quoted in Shields 1975, p. 751).

Many contemporary ethologists prefer to explore biological factors that may *predispose* an animal or person to have offspring and care for them. Their idea is that although females are not born knowing how to mother, they acquire maternal behaviors more easily and rapidly than males, under natural conditions. Much of the research on this issue has been done with lower animals, and the clearest results come, as usual, from rats and mice. After female rats give birth, they immediately set about doing rat-motherly things. They nurse, build a nest for the young, retrieve pups that wander off, and so forth. Virgin rats also will react maternally, but it takes them longer to get started. If you inject them with blood plasma taken from rats that have recently given birth, however, their maternal behavior begins more readily (Rosenblatt 1967, 1969). Perhaps it is the balance between progesterone and estrogen that is crucial to a rodent's responsiveness to newborn animals. Prolactin, which causes milk production, may also be involved.

But hormones aren't the only influence. Male rats usually stay out of the baby-care business and sometimes even attack newborns, but if helpless newborn rats are inflicted on them for five or six days, they relent and begin to lick and retrieve them, though not to feed them or to build nests (Rosenblatt 1967). Strangely enough, it seems that testosterone, the male hormone, stimulates maternal behavior in male rats when it is injected directly into the preoptic area of the brain. Rats treated in this way build nests and retrieve and groom the young (Fisher 1956).

Parenthood for primates depends more on learning. The female monkey's tendency to mother an infant will not survive if she has missed out on having a good parent herself. The female monkeys that Harlow reared in isolation refused to care for their own young when they became mothers.

Wild female chimps who have never assisted at a birth are sometimes frightened by the sight of their own infants. H. Hediger (1965) reports that a female chimp at the Zurich zoo took one look at her baby, uttered a piercing cry, tore up the umbilical cord, and ran away. Other zoo animals, totally inadequate at infant care, carry their babies upside down, which prevents them from finding the nipple. The infant may have to be taken away from these clumsy mothers and raised by a human being, but sometimes an observant mother watches the zookeeper or another animal and learns what to do. An animal usually improves as a mother with her second infant, and while some of this improvement may be due to physical maturation, Hediger believes that learning is more important. Sometimes the chimps learn the wrong lesson, though. One female, whose first baby's umbilical cord had been cut by the zookeeper, patiently waited for his assistance after delivering her second.

Because the female of the species bears the young and nurses them, research has concentrated more on mothers than on fathers. But in many species males take an active part in infant care. Male mice regularly help care for their young. Some male birds, such as penguins, take their turn sitting on the egg and feeding the young after they hatch. The male kiwi has complete charge of incubating the egg, which takes ninety days. In wolf packs, males may aid in feeding by regurgitating food, and in one zoo group, the dominant male helped carry and clean the pups, suffering no loss of wolfhood in the process (Ginsburg 1965). Young adult male hamadryas baboons often hug young infants and take them away from their mothers.

Primate males can learn to become good fathers even if they are not fatherly in the wild. Gary Mitchell and his colleagues (1974) have shown that the male rhesus monkey, ferocious father though he normally is, can become intimately attached to an infant in a laboratory. Mitchell et al. paired adult males with orphan infants of both sexes and waited apprehensively to see what would happen. The males did not immediately embrace their new charges, but eventually they warmed up and became exemplary parents. They played with their adopted children, groomed them, and protected them from the incursions of meddlesome researchers.

Some ethologists today object that studies of animals in abnormal environments (such as labs and zoos) are not a fair test of the animal's readiness to mother. This readiness, they say, emerges only in the species' natural environment. They acknowledge that all primates are tremendously flexible in their ability to learn but say that this does not mean there are no biological differences between the sexes. The true measure of biological predispositions, they believe, is not what an animal *can* learn but what it most easily *does* learn in the wild. Thus while male monkeys can learn to care for infants, as Mitchell showed, they are relatively slow and reluctant learners compared to females, and they are not affectionate parents under natural conditions.

This approach has the advantage of getting us away from older, fixed notions about an automatic maternal instinct. But the argument is difficult to validate with human beings: what are the "natural conditions" for our species? Another problem is that arguing that instinct is equivalent to readiness means there is no way to demonstrate the instinct does *not* exist. If the maternal behavior occurs, then the conditions must have been right: ergo, a maternal instinct. If the behavior does not occur, then the conditions must have been wrong: ergo, there's still an instinct, but it wasn't activated. It's like saying we all have an instinct to eat lasagna, but conditions allow Italians to express that instinct more readily than Chinese.

It is interesting that so many people are so reluctant to give up the notion of instincts, especially the maternal variety. When most scientists finally agreed that human beings have no "instincts" in the traditional sense of the word—behaviors inevitable for all members of a species—the next step was not to drop the idea but to redefine it.

Ultimately, biological theories must deal with the many examples of unmotherly behavior that dot human history. Infanticide has been a popular method of population control, and often it is the mothers who do the killing. Lloyd DeMause, who spent five years studying the history of childcare, reports that infanticide was common in ancient Greece and Rome, and that "every river, dung heap, and cesspool used to be littered with dead infants." A priest in 1527 admitted that "the latrines resound with the cries of children who have been plunged into them" (DeMause 1975). The practice of killing unwanted children continues in many tribes today, to say nothing of the current epidemic of child abuse in this country.[8]

In sum, the evidence that biological factors contribute to the readiness to mother is persuasive for many animal species, but for human beings

[8] See Una Stannard's article, "Adam's Rib, or The Woman Within" (1970), for a witty argument—that although women have the babies, it's the men who have the maternal instinct:

> Men, not women, have historically shown the most compassion for children. It was women chiefly who killed children, and not just illegitimate children. . . . Although women had always had the opportunity to observe infants and were presumably supplied with a maternal instinct to guide them, they had not learned how to take care of them. . . . [Children] had always died in such great numbers and disease was not the chief killer; it was maternal ignorance and neglect.

> When the supposed maternal instinct met the social ostracism that came with having an illegitimate child, instinct yielded. Great numbers of Victorian women, in the heyday of the female ideal, killed their own illegitimate children.

direct evidence does not exist. Until more evidence is gathered, we think the folk notion of a maternal instinct should be abandoned. The idea that all normal women want and need to be mothers has led to much guilt and suffering among women who cannot or choose not to have children. Too many women (and men) who would have been happier without children have been pressured into having them, with sorry results. Belief in the existence of a maternal instinct surely is not crucial to the preservation of the species; many people will continue to want children and to produce them. And perhaps fewer new mothers will be shocked at how much they have to learn and more new fathers will be eager to participate in caretaking if there is less talk about woman's "natural superiority" in this field.

evaluating the biological perspective

The evidence for some biological influence on some sex-typed behavior is substantial enough to warrant serious attention, even though the findings from animal studies are more conclusive than those from studies of people. Biological determinists make us confront the fact that biologically speaking, men and women are not exactly alike, and they probe the logically possible relations that may exist between biological and psychological differences. Their work reminds us that we are not disembodied brains: it appears, for example, that mood changes in some women and hostility and aggression in some men are related to hormone levels.

But it is also clear that neither genes nor cycling hormones lead to specific actions in any simple, direct way; our bodies are not straitjackets for personality. For one thing, research shows that experience and learning can override biological factors to a remarkable degree: a normal infant boy can be transformed into a normal infant girl. For another, high testosterone does not make all men violent and sex-mad, and low estrogen and progesterone does not make all menstruating or menopausal women anxious and depressed. Bodily changes interact with social cues. Stanley Schachter and Jerome Singer (1962) demonstrated, in a classic experiment, how this interaction works. They injected volunteers with a shot of adrenalin, which is what energizes a person to fight or flee. It causes unmistakable bodily changes, such as heart palpitations and tremors. People who thought the adrenalin was a shot of vitamins and did not know what physical reactions to expect reacted emotionally according to what others around them were doing: they got into emotional states as different as euphoric playfulness and sulky anger. Similarly, people may interpret and label—or ignore—the feelings caused by changing hormone levels according to cues provided by the social context.

We think that one reason for the controversy about this perspective is that researchers tend to become immersed in the viewpoint of their own field, rather like the blind men who tried to describe an elephant. Biologists always say they recognize the importance of learning, and most learning theorists say that of course biological dispositions matter. But a scientist whose research is designed to show that hormones can make a female rat behave like a male or a male rat behave like a mother is naturally going to think that a biological approach to behavior is the most interesting and useful one. A scientist whose research is designed to show that people are amazingly malleable depending on their experience or environment naturally tends to pooh-pooh biological arguments. Elephants are very large, and they convey different impressions from different angles.

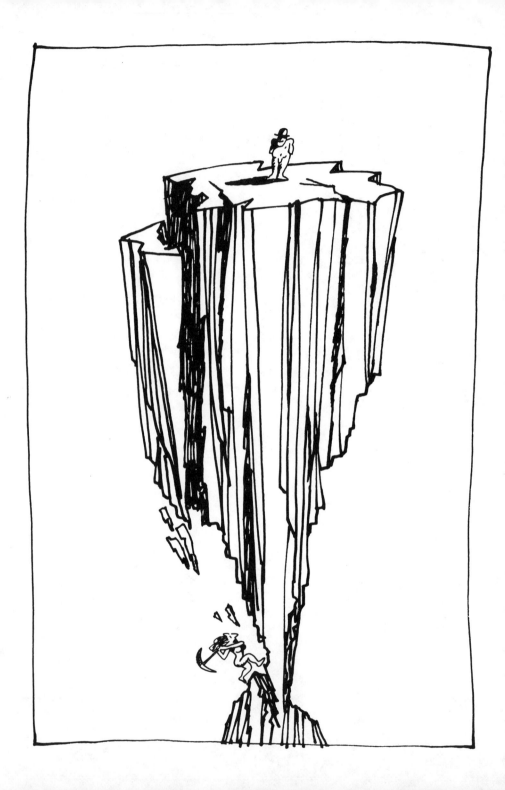

5

Freud, fantasy, and the fear of woman: The psychoanalytic perspective

When we asked a class of students exactly what they knew about Sigmund Freud, we got a momentary silence. Then came a tentative answer, "A male chauvinist." And a somewhat more tolerant reply, "A prisoner of his Victorian cage."

It's a bit more complicated than that. In the last few years criticisms of Freud have become more vociferous, both from psychologists who question his methods and assumptions and from feminists who challenge what they consider his patriarchal attitudes and biased conclusions. Because Freud left such a strong legacy, one that has influenced psychological theory and therapy for most of this century, his critics seem to feel that he must be utterly demolished. His defenders—mostly practicing psychoanalysts—are equally extreme, usually maintaining either that Freud was completely right or that their particular interpretation of him is.

The debate has polarized the psychoanalytic camp and its opponents. Feminist Eva Figes, for example, believes Freudian theory has had dire results:

> Of all the factors that have served to perpetuate a male-oriented society, that have hindered the free development of women as human beings in the Western world today, the emergence of Freudian psychoanalysis has been the most serious. . . . Psychoanalysis, whatever individual therapists may say, does tend to encourage conformity which may amount to something like brainwashing (Figes 1970, p. 148).

But Juliet Mitchell, also an active feminist, has written a valiant and energetic defense of Freud, arguing that an understanding of his work—as opposed to popularized Freudianism—is essential "for challenging the oppression of women. . . . However it may have been used, psychoanalysis is not a recommendation *for* a patriarchal society, but an analysis *of* one" (Mitchell 1974).

Those who believe that Freud was arguing *for* patriarchy cite, among other evidence, the protective and condescending letter he wrote to his fiancée, Martha Bernays:

> It is really a stillborn thought to send women into the struggle for existence exactly as men. If, for instance, I imagined my sweet gentle girl as a competitor it would only end in my telling her, as I did seventeen months ago, that I am

fond of her and that I implore her to withdraw from the strife into the calm uncompetitive activity of my home. It is possible that changes in upbringing may suppress all a woman's tender attributes, needful of protection and yet so victorious, and that she can then earn a livelihood like men. It is also possible that in such an event one would not be justified in mourning the passing away of the most delightful thing the world can offer us—our ideal of womanhood. I believe that all reforming action in law and education would break down in front of the fact that, long before the age at which a man can earn a position in society, Nature has determined a woman's destiny through beauty, charm and sweetness. Law and custom may have much to give women that has been withheld from them, but the position of women will surely be what it is: in youth an adored darling and in mature years a loved wife. (Freud 1961).

Echoes, indeed, of centuries of male talk about woman's tender attributes and her destiny to be sweet, charming, and sexy.

But Freud did not deny that changes in upbringing, law, and custom could change female destiny, and allow women to earn their livings too. He even suggested that might not be so bad. Moreover, he never tried to stifle the career ambitions of his illustrious daughter Anna, a bit of inconsistent behavior for a true patriarch. In fact, Freud warmly welcomed a significant number of women into the psychoanalytic sanctum, including Karen Horney, Clara Thompson, Ruth Brunswick, Lou Andreas-Salome, Helene Deutsch, and Jeanne Lampl-de Groot, and often referred patients to female therapists when he felt they would be better served by a woman. Nor did Freud invariably brainwash his female patients into adopting traditional roles. One of his most famous patients, Anna O., became a social worker and active feminist after her hysterical symptoms were resolved. Neither Freud nor the psychoanalytic movement discriminated against women as harshly as other medical and psychological establishments have before and since Freud's time.

The difficulty in finding the "real" Freud is that we must get through a series of onion-like layers: what Freud himself said originally, what he said later, what his followers did with what he said, what his detractors thought he said, and what his current defenders wish he had said. Few psychoanalysts today are pure Freudians, faithful to every tenet of the master's theories, but all share a language—a set of terms and concepts—and a way of seeing the world. People today often use that language to explain everyday behavior: "What a castrating woman!" "I guess I did that unconsciously." "He repressed his guilt." "Oops, a Freudian slip." "I must be regressing to my childhood." "I don't need to have sex with you; I can sublimate." In this chapter we will begin with the core of the onion, Freud's theories of the unconscious and of psychosexual development, with special attention to the controversial Freudian concept of penis envy. Next we will consider some criticisms of that concept and discuss a complementary idea, men's fear and envy of women, which has been developed by later psychoanalytic writers. Finally, we will evaluate the onion as a whole—that is, the larger framework and perspective of psychoanalysis and its approach to sex differences.

the unconscious

To follow Freud is to journey through the mind and explore the realm beneath our daily thoughts and conscious actions. The map he used to chart his course took its signs and signals from unlikely sources—fantasies, dreams, free associations, slips of the tongue, myths, and folklore—which most of his predecessors considered trivial or irrelevant. The recurring themes in these diverse sources, which one might expect to be idiosyncratic, persuaded Freud that there are universals in human experience and that the mental transformation of those universals lives in the deep recesses of the mind. Conscious thought is merely the tip of the iceberg. To skeptical colleagues and laymen who were accustomed to equating *mental* and *conscious,* Freud argued that the unconscious was the wellspring of the mind, the font of motivation and energy. Moreover, he said it was possible to identify the laws that govern this subterranean territory.

The mental apparatus, according to Freud, consists of three parts: the *id,* which serves as the reservoir of the instincts or libido (the psychic energy that fuels sexual and aggressive drives); the *ego,* which is the rational control mechanism; and the *superego,* which is the internalized voice of authority in both its rewarding (the ego ideal) and punishing (the conscience) aspects. These three structures develop sequentially and represent different desires. The id says, "I want, now"; the superego says, "You can't have it; it's bad for you"; and the ego, mediating, says, "Well, maybe you can have some of it—later." As a result, there is an inevitable war within every individual as he or she grows up. Defeat for the ego creates a disturbed person, perhaps one who is governed primarily by the impulsive, hedonistic id and seems to have no conscience; or one who is so inhibited by the authoritarian force of the superego that he or she cannot express any of the life energies.

Freud came to his conclusions about the unconscious and the origins of neurosis after years of studying patients who had bodily or mental disturbances (such as paralyzed limbs, tics, obsessive habits) but who showed no evidence of organic illness. As the patients talked, he realized that their fantasies and childhood memories had more power over them than their real experiences. He theorized that their symptoms represented mental conflicts, not physical ailments, and that his task as therapist was to help dredge up those conflicts from their unconscious depths.

Not that the conflicts are ever fully resolved. Tension between self-expression and self-denial always exists within a person, as it always exists between an individual and society. Every child must learn to control and redirect the libidinal impulses, to replace the *pleasure principle* that governs infancy with the *reality principle* of maturity. Analogously, societies must control and redirect the sexual drives of their members for the greater good of the group. The greatest cultural and artistic achievements of the human mind, Freud said, are expressions of sexual energy sublimated in this way.

> We believe that civilization has been built up, under the pressure of the struggle for existence, by sacrifices in gratification of the primitive impulses, and that it is to a great extent forever being recreated, as each individual, successively joining the community, repeats the sacrifice of his instinctive pleasures for the common good. The sexual are among the most important of the instinctive forces thus utilized: they are in this way sublimated, that is to say, their energy is turned aside from its sexual goal and diverted towards other ends, no longer sexual and socially more valuable (Freud 1960, p. 27).[1]

The sexual sublimation that civilization requires takes a heavy toll on everyone, Freud wrote, but the worst victims are women. The double standard at least allows men some sexual freedom before marriage (and after), but women are supposed to repress every sexual urge and inclination until their wedding night, at which time sexual bliss is to arrive full-blown. This impossible demand on women, said Freud, along with widespread sexual ignorance, lack of safe contraception, and unrealistic pressures for marital fidelity, were responsible for many sad cases of female frigidity and unhappiness. Unfortunately for women caught between their desires and their sense of duty, the only way out is neurosis. The civilization trap makes infidelity unthinkable, even when that would be, according to Freud, "the cure for nervous illness arising from marriage" (1908, p. 195). After all, nothing protects a woman's virtue as securely as illness. Freud's analysis of the wife's dilemma and how it becomes transformed still stands as a poignant indictment of some marriages.

[1] Freud was trying to describe, without moralizing, what he considered to be an inevitable conflict between individual desires and social needs. "I must confess that I am unable to balance gain against loss correctly on this point," he said (1908, p. 196). When pressed, Freud generally sided with the reality principle over the potential anarchy of the pleasure principle, but he also acknowledged the need to reform sexual morality. Many people who were attracted to psychoanalysis in the 1920s and 30s, however, read Freud as saying that sexual repression and sexual sublimation were unequivocally bad and caused all manner of ailments. They set about remedying that matter at once.

Consider the very common case of a woman who does not love her husband, because, owing to the conditions under which she entered marriage, she has no reason to love him, but who very much wants to love him, because this alone corresponds to the ideal of marriage to which she has been brought up. She will in that case suppress every impulse which would express the truth and contradict her endeavours to fulfil her ideal, and she will make special efforts to play the part of the loving, affectionate and attentive wife. The outcome of this self-suppression will be a neurotic illness; and this neurosis will in a short time have taken revenge on the unloved husband. . . . A neurotic wife who is unsatisfied by her husband is, as a mother, over-tender and over-anxious towards her child, on whom she transfers her need for love (Freud 1908, pp. 203, 202).

Our point is that for a man who basically shared the patriarchal biases of his society, Freud expressed considerable sympathy for the plight of modern woman, and he was fully aware of the ways in which culture, custom, and law shape human destinies and desires.

At the same time, Freud maintained that cultures and economic systems come and go while the unconscious goes on forever. To Freud, the unconscious is primary. The cultural system derives from it, not vice versa. This point is very important for understanding the psychoanalytic explanation of sex and status differences. The unconscious is the battleground for the forces of order and anarchy, and from the resolution of that war comes patriarchal law and civilization. "Where id is," wrote Freud, "there must ego come to be" (1933, p. 80). To Freud, the anatomical distinction between the sexes *as the unconscious interprets it, not as the rational mind regards it,* was responsible for the historical fact of male supremacy.

the psychosexual stages of development

Freud hypothesized that the sex differences he observed in personality and power were a result of an invariant sequence of stages in a child's development. While the specific form and length of each stage might vary in different societies, the psychological significance of the sequence was fixed and universal. The question he confronted was how civilization, personified by the parents, could transform the savage infant filled with surging libidinal desires into a properly socialized man or woman.

Freud maintained that sexual energy expresses itself from the moment of birth and takes different forms as a human being matures. This idea of infantile sexuality shocked his colleagues and laymen, who believed that sexual fantasies, drives, and behaviors were adult matters, and it is by no means fully accepted even today. In the first three years of life, Freud said, babies discover different erotogenic zones, or areas of sexual gratification: first, the *oral*, in which pleasure is centered in the mouth and sucking; second, the *anal*, in which pleasure comes from defecation; and third, the *phallic*, in which boys get their primary erotic pleasure from the penis and girls from the clitoris. During the phallic stage (from about age three to age six), children develop the *Oedipus complex*, the resolution of which establishes proper sex-role identification and other personality traits. This complex gets its name from the Greek legend in which Oedipus unwittingly kills his father and marries his mother. During the Oedipal phase of development, Freud says, there is a sort of love triangle within the family. The child wishes to possess the opposite-sexed parent and perceives the same-sexed parent as a rival. Freud was certain about how the Oedipus complex occurred and was resolved in boys, but its female equivalent perplexed him. His early and late views on the subject are not wholly consistent and are still the object of fevered debate.

the Oedipus complex

In boys, the Oedipus complex follows this course. The boy feels an intense attachment to his mother, who, after all, has been the more nurturant parent, and he harbors an incestuous wish to possess her sexually and to displace his father in her affections. His father becomes a competitor, a hated rival. The child's sexual gratification at this age comes from masturbation and his pride at possessing a penis, which he assumes everybody has. When he sees a naked girl or woman for the first time he is shocked. Since she does not have the precious organ that is giving him so much pleasure, she must have been castrated. If it happened to her, it could happen to him —and his father could be the one to do it. (If his parents have warned him that masturbation will make his penis drop off, this conclusion will be strengthened.) The panic of *castration anxiety* forces the boy to repress his desire for the mother. He yields to the superiority of his powerful father and transforms his feelings of rivalry into positive identification with him. In this way, the boy regains confidence that he'll keep the prized penis; giving up a few impertinent impulses is a small price to pay. He incorporates the father's authority and standards into his newly formed superego, so that conscience and the incest taboo are assured of victory over the narcissistic drives of infantile sexuality. At this point the boy enters the latency phase of late childhood, a time when sexual instincts are relatively quiescent. During the next few years he has some sexual rest and relaxation before puberty, which leads to the stage of mature genital sexuality.

Girls too go through an Oedipal stage, but with far different results. Whereas the boy worries that he *might be* castrated, the girl, after seeing a penis for the first time, worries that she already *has been* castrated. As Freud describes it, "When she makes a comparison with a playfellow of the other sex, she perceives that she has 'come off badly' and she feels this is a wrong done to her and a ground for inferiority" (1924a, p. 178). She is, to say the least, angry that she lacks the marvelous male organ and has an inferior clitoris. She blames her mother for this deprivation, rejects her, and seeks to displace her in her father's eyes. She becomes daddy's darling.

The problem for girls, said Freud, is that they do not have the powerful motivating fear of castration to break up their incestuous feelings and instill a strong superego. As far as girls are concerned, the worst has already happened; they have lost the penis. Thus "penis envy," not "castration anxiety," motivates the resolution of the female Oedipus complex. The girl hopes her father will give her a penis. When this wish remains unfulfilled, she finds a compensation: "Her Oedipus complex culminates in a desire, which is long retained, to receive a baby from her father as a gift—to bear him a child. . . . The two wishes—to possess a penis and a child—remain strongly cathected in the unconscious and help to prepare the female creature for her later sex role" (Freud 1924a, p. 179).

consequences of penis envy

The Oedipus complex in females doesn't die a quick and merciful death; it just fades away. Freud speculated on the consequences for women's personalities and behavior as follows:

1. Women have weaker superegos than men, because they have less motivation to incorporate the conscience of paternal authority. As Freud mused,

> I cannot evade the notion (though I hesitate to give it expression) that for women the level of what is ethically normal is different from what it is in men. Their super-ego is never so inexorable, so impersonal, so independent of its emotional origins as we require it to be in men (Freud 1924b, p. 257).

2. Women feel inferior to men and contemptuous of other women.

> After a woman has become aware of the wound to her narcissism [realizing that she lacks a penis], she develops, like a scar, a sense of inferiority. When she has passed beyond her first attempt at explaining her lack of a penis as being a punishment personal to herself and has realized that that sexual character is a universal one, she begins to share the contempt felt by men for a sex which is the lesser in so important a respect (Freud 1924b, p. 253).

The origin of male contempt for women is the same: men disparage the sex that lacks the essential organ. As Freud put it, a boy's reaction to female anatomy is either "horror of the mutilated creature or triumphant contempt for her" (1924b, p. 252).

3. Women develop a personality constellation that is characterized by masochism, passivity, vanity, and jealousy. Masochism—feeling pleasure in pain—is a female trait because the girl's frustrated attachment to her father teaches her to accept the female predicament. That is, she must accept the painful realities of first intercourse, passive sexuality, and childbirth, and even learn to get erotic pleasure from them. (Masochistic fantasies and behavior can also occur in men, of course, but in that case they represent a desire to play a "feminine" role.) To avoid the grief of rejection by the father, the little girl must develop her threatened ego and self-esteem by making herself loved and adored—by becoming a passive love-object rather than an active love-seeker.[2] If she cannot have a penis, she will turn her whole body into an erotic substitute; her feminine identity comes to depend on being sexy, attractive, and adored. Female jealousy is a displaced version of penis envy.

4. Women learn to give up their infantile gratification from masturbation of the clitoris and to prepare for adult gratification through vaginal intercourse. Freud assumed that little girls are unaware of vaginal sensations. However, he theorized that in the course of the Oedipus complex they begin to get less pleasure from "masculine masturbation"—stimulation of the clitoris—probably because the girl realizes that "this is a point on which she cannot compete with boys and that it would therefore be best for her to give up the idea of doing so" (1924b, p. 256). This realization is essential for her acceptance of femininity and vaginal receptivity. As we said in Chapter 3, Masters and Johnson have discredited the vaginal-clitoral distinction on physiological grounds, but we should note that Freud was talking about a psychological transference from clitoris to vagina as much as a physiological one.

For Freud, the resolution of the girl's Oedipus complex answered some questions about femininity that many contemporary observers still raise: why women so readily submit themselves to male authority (father, hus-

[2] This was the only sense in which Freud considered women "passive." He was otherwise adamant against what he considered the facile equation of masculine-active and feminine-passive. "Even in the sphere of human sexual life you soon see how inadequate it is to make masculine behaviour coincide with activity and feminine with passivity. A mother is active in every sense towards her child. . . . Women can display great activity in various directions, men are not able to live in company with their own kind unless they develop a large amount of passive adaptability. . . . We must beware in this of under-estimating the influence of social customs, which similarly force women into passive situations" (Freud 1933, p. 115).

band, boss); why their primary source of self-esteem and identity is sexual attractiveness rather than intellectual accomplishment; why they seem so willing to endure pain and humiliation for the sake of love and to sacrifice self-interest for the sake of lover, husband, or children. These characteristics were necessary, Freud thought, if women were to take their place in partriarchal culture and willingly accept the pains of childbirth and the self-sacrifice entailed in caring for children.

"anatomy is destiny"

At this point it is important to clarify what Freud meant by his famous cry "Anatomy is destiny." He borrowed the phrase from Napoleon, who was a maximum misogynist, but he did *not* use it to mean that biology dictates the kind of person we will become or that we are hopeless prisoners of our sex. Freud's theory of psychosexual development did not rely on biological imperatives such as the maternal instinct or female hormones to explain why women and men assume different roles. In fact, he dissociated himself from many of his woman-hating colleagues. When Paul Moebius sought physiological causes for women's intellectual inferiority, Freud argued instead that the lack of female achievement had a *social* reason: "the inhibition of thought necessitated by sexual suppression" (1908, p. 199). Also, as noted earlier, Freud was well aware that child development takes place in a societal context. He even observed that the resolution of the Oedipus complex in girls had more to do with "the result of upbringing and of intimidation from outside which threatens her with a loss of love" (1924a, p. 178) than was the case for boys.

What Freud *did* mean by "Anatomy is destiny" is that sex-role development begins with the child's unconscious reactions to anatomical differences, precipitated by the shocking discovery that one sex has a penis and the other does not. Remember that Freud was not talking about a literal, rational response to sex differences. When he says that women envy men or that men fear women he does not mean they do so consciously. He was trying to describe how a real anatomical fact is dealt with by the mind in profound, unconscious ways. He continually disparaged the efforts of feminists—male and female—to persuade people that the sexes were equal, because of the psychological effects he believed must follow from the fact that women would never have the beloved penis.

Although men and women could never be identical, neither were the sexes as opposite as had been assumed. One of the most important themes in Freud's work is that human traits and behaviors are not dichotomous categories—normal/abnormal, homosexual/heterosexual, masculine/feminine—but continua. We all carry both sides of each of these pairs, though in different degrees. To a world used to thinking in terms of mutually exclusive opposites this notion was (and still is) startling.

Freud maintained, for example, that no one passes clearly and cleanly through the stages of development and comes out normal at the end; we remain a mixture of influences from each stage. Rather than being determined by one event, however traumatic, a person's adult character is over-determined, the result of many experiences and innate motivations. All of us are to some extent normal and to some extent neurotic; unless our behavior reaches a self-defeating extreme, we need not be concerned about it. Freud reminded his colleagues that every lover could be said to have an idiosyncratic preference, fetish, or "perversion" of some sort—and, indeed, "the less repellent of the so-called sexual perversions are very widely diffused among the whole population, as every one knows except medical writers on the subject" (1905a, p. 51). Imagine that! People who deviated from Victorian sexual norms were neither uncommon, inhuman, nor organically warped; and Freud went further still. Forty years before the American Psychiatric Association decided that homosexuality was not an illness, Freud wrote to a woman who was devastated by her son's sexual preference:

> Homosexuality is assuredly no advantage, but it is nothing to be ashamed of, no vice, no degradation; it cannot be classified as an illness; we consider it to be a variation of the sexual function. . . . Many highly respectable individuals of ancient and modern times have been homosexuals, several of the greatest men among them. . . . It is a great injustice to persecute homosexuality as a crime— and a cruelty too. . . .
>
> What analysis can do for your son runs in a different line. If he is unhappy, neurotic, torn by conflicts, inhibited in his social life, analysis may bring him harmony, peace of mind, full efficiency, whether he remains homosexual or gets changed (Freud 1961, pp. 419—20).

To a world firmly convinced that masculinity and femininity were polar opposites, Freud argued that these concepts, like homosexuality and heterosexuality, overlapped. "In human beings pure masculinity or femininity is not to be found in a psychological or a biological sense. Every individual on the contrary displays a mixture of the character traits belonging to his own and to the opposite sex" (1905b, pp. 219–20n). If you consider that researchers are only now getting around to agreeing with this statement and giving an official name (androgyny) to the psychological blend of masculine and feminine, Freud seems remarkably prescient. To the extent that we all begin with a bisexual potential and behave in both stereotypical "male" and "female" ways throughout life, and to the extent that biology does not confine us to a rigid set of traits and talents, anatomy is not destiny. To the extent that the unconscious interprets the significance of our sex organs, it is.

attacks on penis envy

No sooner did Freud commit his provocative theory to paper than criticism began. Most of it came from two groups: from people within the psychoanalytic establishment who accepted Freud's overall framework and assumptions but challenged specific points of interpretation; and, later, from psychologists who took issue with psychoanalysis itself, both as theory and as method.

As you might expect, female psychoanalysts were not too happy with Freud's emphasis on penis envy as a motivation for women. The argument began in 1922, when Karen Horney wrote "On the Genesis of the Castration Complex in Women," and it continues to this day. Some critics have denied that penis envy exists at all. Some have maintained that the concept is to be taken symbolically rather than literally, as denoting women's envy of male power and status. What women envy, according to this line of thought, is not the penis itself but the prerogatives that go with having one. As psychoanalyst Clara Thompson put it, "It is the male who experiences the penis as a valuable organ and he assumes that women also must feel that way about it. But a woman cannot really imagine the sexual pleasure of a penis—she can only appreciate the social advantages its possessor has" (Thompson, in Miller 1973). And some have argued that while women do envy the penis, Freud overlooked the fact that men envy the womb; each sex, in other words, envies the unique organs of the other.

a social metaphor?

Horney's rebuttal of Freud stressed social realities. To assert that one half of the human race is discontented with the sex assigned to it, she began, "is decidedly unsatisfying, not only to feminine narcissism but also to biological science." Horney accepted Freud's notion that anatomical differences have psychological consequences, but she emphasized that the latter are strongly influenced by the real-world disadvantages that women endure, "the actual social subordination of women." It is impossible, she said, to judge the weight of unconscious motives like penis envy in the psychology of women as long as women are kept in second-class roles.

Horney also asked some tough sociological questions about the psychoanalytic assumption that femininity requires masochism. Instead of assuming that girls automatically turn masochistic at the realization that they lack a penis, she maintained, one ought to look at the *circumstances* that make women emotionally dependent on men. First, is it in fact true that women in all cultures, and only women, seek pleasure in the pain of self-sacrifice and exploitation? (No.) Second, are there alternate, social explanations of masochism to be considered? (Yes.) Women in most cultures, Horney pointed out, have few opportunities for sexual and professional expression. They are restricted to roles that emphasize or are built on emotional bonds —the family, religion, charity. Further, they are usually economically dependent on men and psychologically dependent on the family for self-esteem and fulfillment. A complete psychology of women, Horney said, must include these social facts as well as the anatomical ones. Otherwise psychoanalysis will do no more than add another ideology to buttress the existing patriarchal establishment.

> There may appear certain fixed ideologies concerning the "nature" of woman; such as doctrines that woman is innately weak, emotional, enjoys dependence, is limited in capacities for independent work and autonomous thinking. One is tempted to include in this category the psychoanalytic belief that woman is masochistic by nature. It is fairly obvious that these ideologies function not only to reconcile women to their subordinate role by presenting it as an unalterable one, but also to plant the belief that it represents a fulfillment they crave, or an ideal for which it is commendable and desirable to strive (Horney, 1967 p. 231).

Then Horney turned the whole problem of penis envy around and argued that if we are really to understand why men have kept women under control and why the sexes distrust each other, we must look at men's envy and fear of women. Many of her male patients, she said, revealed an intense envy of pregnancy, childbirth, nursing, and motherhood, and simultaneously feared these mysterious, bloody abilities of woman. Men cope with this envy and fear with the psychological mechanisms of denial and defense. By glorifying the male genitals they compensate for their inability to give birth; by fighting to maintain superior status they control their fear of woman's sexual power; by treating women with superficial love and adoration they conquer their dread.

"Dread of what?" one may ask, and Horney's answer takes us back to anatomy.

> The clearest aspect of this dread is revealed by the Arunta tribe. They believe that the woman has the power to magically influence the male genital. This is what we mean by castration anxiety in analysis. It is an anxiety of psychogenic origin that goes back to feelings of guilt and old childhood fears. Its anatomical-psychological nucleus lies in the fact that during intercourse the male has to

entrust his genitals to the female body, that he presents her with his semen and interprets this as a surrender of vital strength to the woman, similar to his experiencing the subsiding of erection after intercourse as evidence of having been weakened by the woman (Horney 1967, p. 116).

Freud had observed, though not emphasized, the same "fear of women" in an essay on the widespread taboo of virginity.

> Wherever primitive man has set up a taboo he fears some danger and it cannot be disputed that a generalized dread of women is expressed in all these rules of avoidance [the sexual and reproductive taboos on women]. Perhaps this dread is based on the fact that woman is different from man, for ever incomprehensible and mysterious, strange and therefore apparently hostile. The man is afraid of being weakened by the woman, infected with her femininity and of then showing himself incapable. . . . In all this there is nothing obsolete, nothing which is not still alive among ourselves (Freud 1918, pp. 198—99).

Shades of Samson and Delilah, Enkidu and the courtesan. Women sap your strength!

Both Horney and Freud are saying that during intercourse, adult males may suffer a resurgence of the castration anxiety that originated during the Oedipal period. This time, however, the one who wields the guillotine is not the father but the man's sexual partner. After all, the man unconsciously believes that females have already suffered castration, no doubt for some terrible wrong-doing; they are not to be trusted. Further, the man has committed his erect penis, the symbol of his very masculinity, to the dark interior of the female body, from whence it will emerge a mere shadow of its former self. Sex may be overwhelmingly pleasurable, but it is also a risky operation.

Men may fear women, then, because of what women might do to them, but they also dread what women can do that they cannot—the mysterious processes of menstruation, conception, childbirth, nursing. To psychoanalysis, the "otherness" of these female activities from the male viewpoint, combined with the obvious importance of childbirth to the perpetuation of the species, provokes large amounts of resentment, envy, and fear.

We now have two hypotheses about the reason for status differences between the sexes, which seem to be about 180 degrees apart: (1) women, lacking the prized penis, the symbol of power and pleasure, stand in awe and fear of men and therefore come to accept their inferior status; (2) men, lacking the mysterious womb, symbol of the power of procreation, and frightened by the figurative loss of the penis during intercourse, stand in awe and fear of women and must therefore force them into inferior status. Note that while the feelings of sex toward the other are the same (awe and fear), the female's response is to knuckle under while the male's is to assert himself.

How would you evaluate the truth of these ideas? Which, if either, has more merit? We will consider two efforts on the part of contemporary psychoanalysts to investigate the effects of woman-envy and woman-fear. Each stepped outside his clinical practice to reach for rich mines of data: Bruno Bettelheim, in *Symbolic Wounds* (1962), took evidence from schizophrenic boys and primitive tribes; Wolfgang Lederer, in *The Fear of Women* (1968), went to myths, fables, art, and folklore.

men's envy of women

Bettelheim began to develop his ideas about womb-envy by observing the rituals that four schizophrenic boys developed upon reaching puberty. Their monthly ceremonies had four aspects that intrigued him: secrecy from adults; the fact that the boys cut themselves in a secret part of their bodies; the loss of blood; and the boys' belief that the ritual was necessary for adult sexual satisfaction. Bettelheim was struck by the similarity between the boys' rites and the initiation rites of many primitive societies, which use the rituals to mark the adolescent's passage into the adult community. In both cases, Bettelheim says, the rites "originate in the adolescent's attempts to master his envy of the other sex, or to adjust the social role prescribed for his sex and give up pregenital, childish pleasures." The ceremonies serve the dual purpose of incorporating the female's magical power and of symbolizing for the boys what menarche (the onset of menstruation) does for girls: today you are an adult. Bettelheim supports his theory of womb-envy with examples of several kinds of male rites that mimic or compensate for menstruation and childbirth.

1. *Circumcision and subincision.* In many primitive tribes circumcision takes place at puberty, with many magical rituals welcoming the boy to manhood. Bettelheim notes that many circumcision rites involve not only painful self-mutilation but symbolic sacrifices of the foreskin, blood, or teeth to women.

> Among the Western Arunta, the foreskin is presented to a sister of the novice, who dries it, smears it with red ochre, and wears it suspended from her neck. In some tribes, after a boy has been circumcised, the blood from the wound is collected in a shield and taken to the mother, who drinks some of it, and gives food to the man who brought it to her (p. 93).

Sacrifice, whether to goddesses who are not of this world or to women who are, always assumes that the donor will get something in return: a good harvest, a victorious battle, an A in algebra, a share in supernatural power. In the case of male puberty rites, the rewards include a sense of manhood and a feeling of participation in female mysteries.

Subincision is a rare and radical surgery that makes men anatomically more like women. During some initiation ceremonies the underside of the penis is slit, sometimes an inch and sometimes the whole length; and in many cases the healed wound, which may even be called "vulva," is reopened periodically and bleeds. This is perhaps the most extreme effort on the part of men, says Bettelheim, to reproduce the female sex organs and symbolize the cyclic nature of menstruation.

> Statements made by the people themselves confirm such an interpretation. The Murngin say: "The blood that runs from an incision and with which the dancers paint themselves and their emblems is something more than a man's blood—it is the menses of the old Wawilak women" (p. 105).[3]

2. *Couvade.* According to Bettelheim and other psychoanalysts, men in tribal societies could cope with the ultimate miracle, childbirth, in two ways. The first was to deny the woman's contribution to conception and view her simply as a passive receptacle, a fertile field for the man's seed. The homunculus theory of sperm (that the sperm carries a complete miniature person who grows in the womb) reflects this "so much for you, ladies" opinion of women. It has appeared in countless cultures, from the Pilagá of South America to the ancient Greeks, and was not completely discredited in Europe until the mid-nineteenth century. The second was for men to take on the actual or symbolic role of life-giver and try to upstage the women.

Couvade is a childbirth ritual that gives men the starring role. In a typical couvade, the woman has the baby and shortly returns to work. Meanwhile the father takes to bed with moans and groans, follows various taboos about what he may and may not eat, and receives guests. Sometimes the man appears actually to experience all the signs and symptoms of pregnancy and labor that his wife does, and he may take longer than she to recover. Among the Arapesh, a tribe studied by Margaret Mead, "the verb 'to bear a child' is used indiscriminately of either a man or a woman, and child-bearing is believed to be as heavy a drain upon the man as upon the woman" (Mead 1963). An Arapesh father grants life to his child as literally as its mother does, though with more freedom of choice. When the baby is born, he directs the women who are attending the birth either to wash it (and let it live) or not to wash it (and assure its death.)[4]

---

[3] In Chapter 8 we will discuss the problems of trying to explain social customs by what people *say* about their behavior, and also consider the economic—rather than symbolic—functions of such rituals.

[4] Arapesh men as well as women, reports Mead, spend much time in childcare and raising infants; the male role doesn't stop with couvade. If you comment on a middle-aged man that he's good-looking, the Arapesh are likely to reply: "Good looking? Ye-e-s, but you should have seen him before he bore all those children."

Some anthropologists explain couvade rituals as a male effort to establish social paternity: "That's *my* kid; I bore him." Bettelheim thinks couvade is the closest a man can come to the experience of childbirth, even though he can mimic only its superficial aspects. "Women, emotionally satisfied by having given birth and secure in their ability to produce life, can agree to the couvade; men need it to fill the emotional vacuum created by their inability to bear children."[5]

3. *Ritual transvestism.* When the wearing of women's clothes by men is made into a ritual, it gives boys an officially sanctioned chance to play female—in particular, the role of mother. In one New Guinea tribe, the male sponsor of the boy to be initiated dresses up in widow's weeds, binds his stomach to imitate pregnant women, and wanders around the village calling for his "child" in a squeaky falsetto. According to Bettelheim, such rituals allow men to institutionalize and regulate their envy of women. Some tribes also allow girls to dress as males on symbolic occasions, but this is less common than ritualistic male transvestism. (When transvestism is not part of a ritual, of course, it is socially disapproved for both sexes, though in men it is likely to be regarded as a sign of sexual "perversion" while in women it may be greeted with a relatively benign understanding that they are merely trying to acquire some of the male's superior status.)

4. *Rebirth.* According to Bettelheim, it is now widely accepted "that initiation is a symbolic rebirth, usually with the male sponsors acting the part of those who give birth to the initiates . . . Again and again, in tribe after tribe, anthropologists report puberty rituals in which rebirth plays a prominent part. Among more sophisticated peoples, it is sometimes an abstract, symbolic drama. Among others it is a frank acting out of childbirth." Some initiation rites go to great extremes to duplicate birth: the boys must spend time in womb-like huts, curl up in the fetal position, submerge themselves in water. The adult men behave like mothers, caring for the infants, and at the end of the ceremonies the boys are reborn as men. Bettelheim concludes that ritual rebirth, like the couvade, gives men a sense of full participation in the creation of new life.

5. *Separation.* Many initiation rites, in primitive tribes and American fraternities, require absolute secrecy. Women and children must never know the dark and brooding deeds that go on in the men's world, and the boys are threatened with various tribal equivalents of hellfire and damnation if they tell. The common psychoanalytic interpretation of the severity of initiation rites in general, and of the male-bonding nature of them in particular, is that

[5] Lest you think that couvade is a quaint custom of primitive tribes, consider the popularity of natural childbirth in this country, and the renewed participation of the father in the whole process. Is Lamaze a modern couvade?

the rites serve to break Oedipal ties; the mother's power over the boy must be severed so that he can follow in his father's footsteps. Another explanation, which follows the same lines but is somewhat more social, is that the boy, who has typically spent his childhood being cared for by women, now must learn to be a man and to value male activities. By going through a difficult and painful initiation procedure, boys come to identify with the male role and feel closer to other men. They can finally assert themselves against those mysterious females (Burton and Whiting 1961; for a criticism of this view, see Parker, Smith, and Ginat 1975).

Secrecy is the final piece in Bettelheim's jigsaw puzzle of initiation rites. Secrecy, after all, should convince outsiders that the insiders are really onto something; it suggests that they have magical powers and are superior creatures. The male creation of secrets that are kept from women parallels the ultimate secret that women keep from men: how to have babies. The fact that male initiation rites exclude women persuades Bettelheim that they are not simple celebrations of *rite de passage* and that their main function is symbolic rather than educational.

Bettelheim does not look for the reasons behind initiation rites in a culture's economic system, kinship structure, or sex-role patterns. Nor does he deal with the fact that not every society has all the above initiation rites for its boys, and some do not have any. His explanation for these rituals begins with unconscious needs, and he shares with Freud the premise that men and women are psychologically bisexual. Therefore, he concludes, they will seek to express their sexually opposite traits in whatever ways society allows. Some cultures regulate the expression of femininity in boys with limited ceremonies like those described above. Others try to inhibit such expressions totally. Bettelheim believes that it is human nature for each sex to envy the other, and that the closer we come to allowing men and women to express both masculinity and femininity, the better off everyone will be.

men's fear of women

According to Bettelheim, envy between the sexes implies mystery and perpetual difference. According to Lederer, fear is the force that keeps the sexes apart. To support his case, Lederer takes his readers on a roller-coaster ride through the major themes of human mythology. They reveal, he says, not what women are really like but what men have imagined women to be.

In the beginning was the earth goddess, symbol of fertility. The first deities that mankind worshipped were female, the source of life and food. Figurines and statues created in the woman-worshipping cultures have many breasts and are fat and voluptuous. There are few thin-hipped, thin-lipped fertility dolls. Mother Earth—she creates life, nurtures it, feeds her children. What's so scary about her? Well, for starters:

1. *Menstruation.* This is the greatest mystery, Lederer believes, and accounts for the widespread fears of the menstruating woman, who supposedly can blight crops, contaminate men, infect food, and cause all manner of mishaps and mayhem. Lederer thinks this mystery explains why in some places women are relegated to special menstrual huts for the duration of their periods and must be ritually cleansed before they can rejoin the community:

> The fear we encounter here, attested to by so many defensive taboos, is undoubtedly real enough, and pertains to the other-ness of woman, the particular mystery by which she manages to bleed, and to transform blood into babies, and food into milk, and to be so self-sufficient and unapproachable in all of it (p. 34).

2. *Sexual treachery and insatiability,* female characteristics we reviewed in Chapter 1.

3. *Power.* Women destroy as well as create. Earth mothers who give life can also take it away, and they can get very bloodthirsty if they do not receive the proper sacrifices.

> The fertility of the Mother demands the blood of men, the Earth needs to be fertilized with corpses if she is to revitalize the dead from her full breasts; and if she is to bring forth new life, new crops, new infants, then she demands the sacrifice of infants. Thus we universally find, *wherever on this earth the Great Mother ruled, that child sacrifice was brought in her honor* (p. 132).

Ambivalence toward the powers of the Earth Mother is perhaps best represented by Kali, the Black One, the "Great and Terrible World-Mother" of India. "She is black with death," writes Lederer, "and her tongue is out to lick up the world; her teeth are hideous fangs. Her body is lithe and beautiful, and her breasts are big with milk." The Snake Woman of the Aztecs, too, granted fertility only with terrible blood sacrifices "in which the victim's hearts were torn out of their living chests, and their flayed skins worn by the priesthood." Note the symbolic connection between the blood required for the sacrifice, the blood that is the symbol of life, and the mysterious menstrual blood of women. Since it is obvious that Kali, the Snake Woman, and their myriad counterparts did not actually speak to their believers, we must be dealing here, says Lederer, with powers that men attributed to women.

Mother, good dear mom, a horrifying creature? Yes, the theme is common. There are far more female ogres and monsters than male in myth and fairy tale. Lederer did an informal survey of two hundred of Grimms' fairy tales and came up with the following tally: sixteen wicked mothers or stepmothers to three wicked fathers or stepfathers; thirteen treacherous maidens who kill or endanger their suitors to one evil suitor who harms his bride; twenty-three wicked female witches to two wicked male witches. (The three emphatically good women or mothers in the tales were slightly outnumbered by five emphatically good fathers.) Dad is a nice guy; mom, more often than not, is a witch.

In the course of time, Lederer theorizes, came the Patriarchal Revolt. Men replaced their fearful worship of the all-demanding earth mother with allegiance to male gods. New myths of creation specified that men, not women, were responsible for the creation of the world and of life. The male gods created man first and woman as an afterthought, from man's rib, thumb, foreskin, urine, or—as recounted by a sixteenth-century German poet—from a dog's tail. Thus began the era of misogynistic religions.

The idea that woman-as-mother is not only nurturant and fertile but ruthless and bloodthirsty is as common, and as paradoxical, as the idea that woman-as-lover belongs either on a pedestal or in the gutter. The ultimate fear of woman, Lederer thinks, came from her link not just with the mysteries of life but with the inevitability of death. Lederer views woman-worship and woman-loathing as reflections of the same fundamental male dilemma and insecurity.

We've come a long way from penis envy. If Freud thought it was an essential concept in his theory, Bettelheim balances it with womb envy—and Lederer dismisses it altogether. There is no evidence from myth, anthropology, or clinical psychology, he argues, that women want a penis of their own; they just like to borrow one once in a while for intercourse, and *that* they have always been able to do. The desire for a penis does not appear in girls' play or women's dreams, in female fantasy or delusion, except in rare and unusual cases. The evidence indicates, Lederer concludes, that "the literal, physical possession of a penis is a matter of no consequence to women. They are, in fact, rather amazed at the fuss we men are making about the little appendage." Whatever would Freud say!

Whereas Bettelheim believes that each sex should experience and express both its masculine and feminine aspects, Lederer concludes that opposites attract. Despite his denial of penis envy, he would agree with Freud that equality between the sexes is neither possible nor desirable, because the sexes are unique and hence eternally different. Equality would deprive us of that tingle of mystery and difference; worse, women would lose their magic appeal.

> Today our defensive strategem is the cry for equality. And in promoting loudly women's equal status, we fondly hope that she will thereby feel promoted, and not just kicked upstairs. For under the cloak of "equal rights" we attempt to deny the specifically feminine. To make woman equal means: to deprive her of her magic, of her primordial position; and means further: to deprive Shiva [the masculine component of the Hindu god Shiva-Shakti] of Shakti [the feminine component], and Man of his inspiration (Lederer 1968, p. 285).

The main business of woman is to inspire man—an odd conclusion for someone who has written an entire book detailing the dire consequences of man's fear of woman. Lederer refrains from arguing that men *should* fear women, but unfortunately he fails to explain how, if men continue to view women as magic vessels, their fear and hostility can subside. Indeed his own fantasies, both wishful and hostile, appear to have remained intact.

> Woman, anyway, has no use for freedom: she seeks not freedom, but fulfillment. She does not mean to be a slave, nor unequal before the law; nor will she tolerate any limitations in her intellectual or professional potential: but she does need the presence, in her life, of a man strong enough to protect her against the world and against her own destructiveness, strong enough to let her know that she is the magic vessel whence all his deepest satisfactions and most basic energies must flow (Ibid.).

It would be interesting to know what Freud would have thought of this effort to throw out the concept of penis envy and still maintain that it is woman's lot to fulfill her biological destiny under the care and protection of a strong male.

evaluating psychoanalysis

How shall we evaluate the relative worth of psychoanalytic theories of sex and status differences? Do the modifications of Freud's work represent advances, side-steps, or irrelevant elaborations?

Some of Freud's earliest critics, who were sympathetic to some of his insights but could not accept them as literal truths, suggested gently that the best way to regard psychoanalysis was as an elegant metaphor—a set of literary perceptions rather than scientific ones. Havelock Ellis was one of these; Freud, he said, was a great artist, not a scientist. Freud, feeling insulted, replied that of course he was a scientist, committed to recording his meticulous observations and deducing general principles in a calm, unbiased way. It wasn't *his* fault if the people who disagreed with him showed neurotic defenses and resistance to the unpleasant truths he revealed. However, he did admit, sometimes with coy humility, that he was dealing in theory, not in the empirical evidence that people today require of science. "If you reject this idea as fantastic and regard my belief in the influence of lack of a penis on the configuration of femininity as an *idée fixe,* I am of course defenceless" (Freud 1933, p. 132).

science or art?

Many contemporary psychologists have little patience for the fanciful word castles of Freudian theory and for the intramural bickering and debates among his followers. Quite apart from the matter of testing specific ideas within psychoanalytic theory, there are these problems with the approach as a whole:

1. *Drawing universal principles from the experiences of patients living in a specific class and culture.* Many critics of Freud have commented on this point. How, they asked, could he possibly conclude that the Oedipus complex was universal when he knew little about family structure in other societies? Some post-Freudian psychoanalysts have tried to strengthen their interpretations by seeking data from anthropology. But most simply assume, as Freud did, that the stuff they find in their own patients' dreams and free associations is the stuff of human nature.

2. *Using the retrospective memories of patients to construct developmental sequences.* Freud and his followers did not observe random samples of children at different ages in order to postulate a theory of development. Instead they worked backwards, recreating the significant childhood stages and themes from the patients' adult recollections. The room for distortion is vast: no one's memory is infallible, and the memories of adult patients, who by definition have psychological problems, are particularly suspect. To the argument that memory is a poor guide to reality, Freud replied that memory was the very reality he sought. This approach might be fine for treating the patient, but it is dubious as a basis for theoretical principles that supposedly apply to everyone's unconscious reality. In other words, another problem with Freud's approach is that he was:

3. *Generalizing from neurotic patients to all human beings.* Freud formed his theory about human development from reconstructions of his patients' early lives and fantasies. He assumed that normal people go through the same stages and crises that neurotics do, and that neurotics just get bogged down along the way. Thus, if a woman patient adored her father and was jealous of the male role, she simply had an especially bad case of the penis envy that all women feel. Freud based much of his speculation about castration anxiety and the Oedipus complex on the case of Little Hans, a five-year-old boy whose father had been a patient of Freud's. Hans was somewhat confused about sexual anatomy because his mother had told him that women have penises too. Yet Freud thought nothing of concluding that all children expect both sexes to have the male organ.

Such reasoning is characteristic of many clinicians, who assume that their patients represent the larger population. For example, despite Freud's generous remarks, clinicians and psychiatrists defined homosexuality as an illness for many years, because the homosexual patients they saw tended to be unhappy and to experience conflicts and guilt in connection with their homosexuality. Not until psychologists studied homosexuals who were not in therapy did the homosexuals-are-sick idea begin to fall apart.

Another problem with generalizing from one's experiences with patients is that the nature of the relationships between particular therapists and particular patients helps determine how problems are defined and what patients reveal. Karen Horney's male patients showed signs of womb envy; Sigmund Freud's male patients did not. Lederer's patients never indicated penis envy; Freud's patients did. Thus the difficulty of drawing conclusions about normal development from an analysis of one's patients' development is compounded by:

4. *The subjective, personal nature of the analyst's interpretations.* Freud recognized that this criticism would be made immediately—that people would feel that dreams, fantasies, and myths are open to many readings. He tried to argue that the symbols expressed in these unconscious forms were, like hieroglyphics, a language that followed clear rules. While some translators would obviously be more skilled than others, their interpretations ultimately would have to agree, so long as they followed the grammar of the unconscious.[6]

Since Freud was the one laying down the rules, he tended to stamp "Correct" mainly on interpretations that matched his own. If some analyst found no evidence of castration anxiety in his patients, Freud blamed the analyst's faulty powers of observation, not the theory. He remarked: "One

---

[6] Even Freud realized eventually that folks were getting a bit carried away when they interpreted every long, narrow object as a phallic symbol and every round or watery object as a womb symbol. Sometimes a cigar has phallic connotations, he said, "and sometimes a cigar is only a cigar."

hears of analysts who boast that, though they have worked for dozens of years, they have never found a sign of the existence of a castration complex. We must bow our heads in recognition of the greatness of this achievement, even though it is only a negative one, a piece of virtuosity in the art of overlooking and mistaking" (Freud 1924b, p. 254n). There is nothing wrong with trying to distinguish the merits of one interpretation over another on the basis of intellectual zip, theoretical neatness, or personal preference, which is the way one might decide, say, whether Laurence Olivier's rendition of Hamlet or Richard Burton's is "better." But those are not *scientific* ways to judge conflicting ideas, much less to select the one that is nearest the truth.

For example, consider Karen Horney's theory of the origins of the castration complex in women. She agreed with Freud that girls do have castration fantasies, but she disagreed that they are the result of penis envy. She said that penis envy, while unconscious, is not that deeply hidden in the mind. The motivating fantasy that really gets the guilts churning is the girl's desire to have intercourse with her father. Horney has now posed a cause-and-effect question that speculation alone cannot settle. Does envy of the penis cause the little girl to desire her father and identify with him, as Freud thought, or does the fantasy of sleeping with him lead to penis envy, as Horney thought?[7]

experimental evidence

Psychoanalysts argue that verification and modifications of their theories can come only from clinical settings and from the raw materials of the unconscious: dreams, play, folklore. They maintain that attempts to subject their concepts to the cold methods of experimental psychology are doomed to fail, because experiments can measure only conscious, overt behaviors and attitudes. The truth that psychoanalysis reveals, they say, is deeper than anything you'll find in a lab. Like the existence of God, the validity of psychoanalysis can't be proved. It is a matter of faith.

Still, efforts have been made to translate some central psychoanalytic concepts into terms that can be studied experimentally. Psychologists have devised projective tests that try to measure unconscious processes, such as the Thematic Apperception Test (TAT) and the Rorschach Ink Blot Test;

[7] None of the methodological problems discussed above is unique to psychoanalysis. Very often, contemporary experimental psychologists generalize from one group of people to everyone (perhaps from male college students to all American men—and women) and rely on the uncertain memories of informants. All scientific interpretations involve a degree of subjective judgment.

they have developed various projective tests for children too. Others have made behavioral predictions based on psychoanalytic theory and tested them, despite the possibility of error in moving from an abstract and complicated theory to specific behavior and back again. Neither line of research has had clear-cut results (for a review, see Sherman 1971). One reason is that the researchers often have as much difficulty agreeing on the interpretation of the tests as analysts do agreeing on the meaning of their patients' dreams.

For example, although studies that have tried to find support for the *literal* interpretation of penis envy have produced equivocal and ambiguous findings, considerable data suggest that both women and men value the male role more highly than the female role. In survey after survey, more women than men report having wanted to trade places with the opposite sex, and both sexes tend to agree that men have an easier time of it in society and have more advantages.

As for the *symbolic* interpretation of penis envy, believers and nonbelievers alike resort to children's spontaneous expressions to bolster their opinion. The classic demonstration of castration anxiety, for example, is the little boy's shocked reaction to seeing a naked girl for the first time: "Mommy, she doesn't have a penis!" We are pleased to report two modern examples that counter Freud's theory. One writer reports that her young daughter, on seeing a naked boy for the first time, rushed to tell her, "Mommy, John Frederick doesn't have a vagina!" But the most damning blow to the penis-envy theory comes from the little girl who took a bath with her young male cousin, observed the differences in silence, and said nothing until her mother tucked her in bed that night. "Mommy," she said softly, "isn't it a blessing he doesn't have it on his face?"

Researchers have also tried to demonstrate the universality of the Oedipus complex. Again, when the concept is interpreted literally rather than as a metaphor for the struggle between infantile pleasures and societal demands, the evidence falters. Between the ages of three and five, supposedly the years of marked conflict, both sexes prefer the mother. Some little girls go on to identify with (that is, to take on the traits and goals of) their fathers rather than their mothers, but no data show that these girls are the neurotic victims of unresolved Oedipus complexes (Mahl 1971). As Freud himself admitted, "In general our insight into these developmental processes in girls is unsatisfactory, incomplete and vague" (1924a).

It seems clear that some parents do treat their opposite-sex children seductively; that sexual tensions do thrive in many families; and that young children do have sexual impulses. But social scientists have not demonstrated that family love triangles and their effects are inevitable, or that families deal with them in the same ways, or that children's motivations are exclusively sexual. The Oedipus complex remains an illuminating metaphor or an unfounded hypothesis, depending on your point of view.

existential identity and vulnerability

Even though few mainstays of Freud's theory have been verified empirically, the theory has the virtue of raising some difficult questions about the relationship between men and women. For example, few other branches of social science even acknowledge the important themes of existential identity and vulnerability.

Many writers, from Margaret Mead and Sigmund Freud to Simone de Beauvoir and Norman Mailer, have said that one *is* a woman; one *learns to be* a man. Femininity is a function of the female body. Women are secure in their roles by virtue of their reproductive function and the monthly reminder that they are female. But masculinity must be learned, earned, and constantly re-won. It is thus much more fragile than femininity. Further, if women are born female but men must define themselves as male, then femininity is the given and masculinity is deduced from it. That is, in order to have a secure sexual identity, men must define themselves and their proper spheres of behavior as the opposite of what women do. As Mead puts it:

> A girl *is* a virgin [or] a mother. . . . Stage after stage in women's life histories thus stand, irrevocable, indisputable, accomplished. This gives a natural basis for the little girl's emphasis on *being* rather than *doing*. The little boy learns that he must act like a boy, do things, *prove that he is a boy, and prove it over and over again*, while the little girl learns that she *is* a girl, and all she has to do is refrain from acting like a boy (Mead 1968, pp. 182—83).

This line of reasoning, tenuous though it may seem, does suggest why equality—a world in which men and women do the same things and share the same desirable traits—would be deeply threatening to men. If they must base their sexuality and selfhood on being different from women, their historically consistent and virulent reaction to feminism and movements for women's rights is somewhat understandable. Conversely, it may be that men feel insecure *because* their identity rests on vague standards of masculinity defined in terms of what they can't do (womanly things) rather than what they should do.

Think of the argument this way: women make babies; men make civilizations. If men make civilizations because they can't make babies, then naturally they will resent female efforts to usurp their role. Since they can't take over the female role, sharing can only mean that they get less. But if the premise itself is faulty (as it would seem to be, since conception requires sperm), then both sexes could define their roles and choose their activities on some basis other than sex. Logically, there is no reason to assume that reproductive and nonreproductive activities are analogous just because both are "creative."

Psychoanalysts believe that the anatomical difference between the sexes will always entail mystery, no matter how much physiology we study or how many naked bodies we observe. Further, mystery invariably evokes interest and attraction, as well as fear and hostility. If you could wipe out the mystery, they imply, you might get rid of all that is fearful in sexual attraction but lose all that is fun, too.

The psychoanalytic perspective also holds that men and women have different kinds of sexual vulnerabilities that are anatomically determined (though both are equally susceptible to emotional hurt). For women, sexual anxieties are bound up with fears of being overwhelmed, violated, impregnated, raped. For men, sexual anxieties are linked to performance and fear of impotence. Each sex's fears have objective bases—rape and impotence do occur—but psychoanalysis argues that these fears also act on an unconscious level, influencing in subtle ways the quality of male-female relationships.[8]

The twin themes of identity and vulnerability contribute in some measure to the tension and outright hostility that is often evident between the sexes. Freud and the other early psychoanalysts deserve much credit for deromanticizing the Victorian vision of men and women dallying in idyllic and nonsexual love relationships, and for probing the earthy origins of the sexes' animosity, passion, and lust. The psychoanalytic perspective puts more emphasis than any other approach on the emotional qualities of male-female relationships.

In the opinion of many, however, psychoanalysis overemphasizes the dark side of life. No matter where Freud looked he saw conflict: between love and hate, creativity and destructiveness, sex and death. After a lifetime of thought he concluded that such conflicts are inevitable, both within and between individuals, and that the chances for permanent peace were vir-

---

[8] It is interesting that there are more jokes reflecting the male's fear than the female's. "All the woman has to do is lie there and fake it," men grumble. "There's no way to fake an erection." They tell many impotence and "castrating women" jokes:

A man, frustrated at his girlfriend's reluctance to sleep with him, finally in exasperation unzips his pants, takes out his organ, and shouts at her: "Look at me! Do you know what this is?" "It looks like a penis," she replies coolly, "only smaller."

tually nil. His emphasis on subterranean unconscious processes accounts for the mood of sexual envy, fear, and distrust that immersion in psychoanalytic theory tends to generate. Not all psychoanalysts are as pessimistic as Freud, though. Karen Horney offered one reason that the sexes might ultimately get it together after all:

> Love succeeds in building bridges from the loneliness of this shore to the loneliness on the other one. These bridges can be of great beauty, but they are rarely built for eternity and frequently they cannot tolerate too heavy a burden without collapsing. Here is the answer to the question posed initially of why we see love between the sexes more distinctly than we see hate—because the union of the sexes offers us the greatest possibilities for happiness (Horney 1967, p. 117).

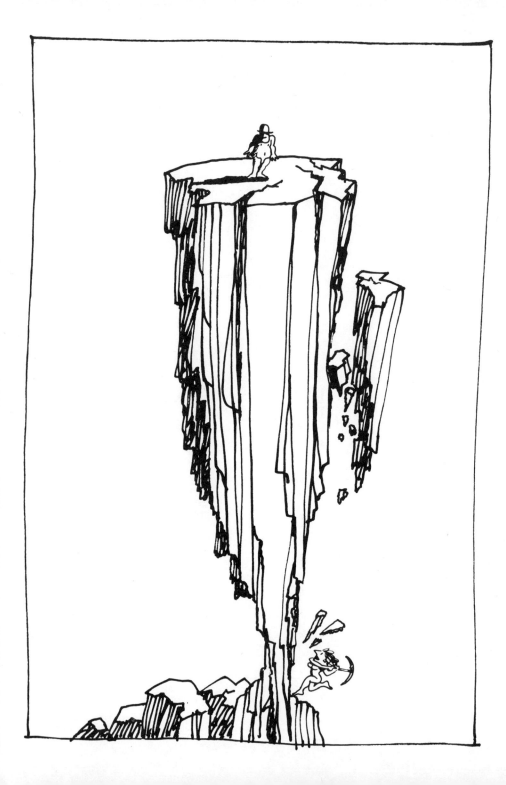

6

Getting the message: The learning perspective

Jessica Offir came home from school one day stirred up by an incident that had occurred in her sixth-grade class. It seems that one classmate, Susie, had been tormenting another, Scott, by trying to kick him in the groin. In frustration, the boy turned on her and gave her a whack. At that moment the teacher interrupted the fight to admonish the boy loudly: "Scott, don't you know we *never* hit girls?" Scott's crime, the teacher was saying, was not hitting itself but striking a female—who by definition was defenseless and fragile—even though in this case the female was half a head taller than her male opponent.

The learning perspective says that experiences like this one, multiplied thousands of times during childhood, eventually fit us for a social system in which males go one way, females another. Most laymen and many psychologists think that the basic ingredients of personality are set in childhood (some even say within the first few years of life) and that virtually from the moment of birth boys and girls take different roads to different personalities. This view implicitly accepts the idea that stereotypes about the sexes have a strong basis in reality: that men are more independent and aggressive, for example, and women are more nurturant and emotional. But it also says that there is nothing inevitable about these differences. They are learned from books, films, parents, and other people. As a result, this perspective says, no sooner have children learned to speak than they can tell you who wears dresses and who does not, who plays with baby dolls and who wouldn't touch them with a ten-foot pole, who will grow up to become a nurse and who a doctor. Children also learn many subtleties of personality and behavior, even how to sit, stand, and talk, that mark them as feminine or masculine as surely as bows and britches.

The learning perspective has intuitive appeal because it fits personal experience better than other approaches. People can't recognize the effect of a prenatal hormone on their behavior. Few can remember having an Oedipal conflict when they were four. But almost all of us can recall events from childhood that seem to explain, post hoc, why we are what we are, or why we never became what we wanted to. For example:

1. Did your parents encourage you to have a paper route when you were younger, or to babysit?

2. Could boys take home economics in your school and girls take shop? Which did you take?

3. Did you go out for Little League? Other sports? What did your parents think about your athletic abilities? Did you ever try out for football? Cheerleader?

4. Did anyone ever give you a toy nurse's kit? Doctor's kit? Chemistry set? Tea set?

5. Did anyone ever tell you that if you worked hard you could be an astronaut? Policeman? President of the United States? What was your earliest ambition?

6. Did your mother often talk to you about how wonderful it would be to marry and have children when you grew up?

In its broadest outlines, the learning perspective has to be right. As we saw in Chapter 4, experience can override biology: studies of hermaphrodites show that the gender assigned to a child at birth is more important for his or her eventual sense of identity as a male or female than genes and gonads. And as we noted in Chapter 1, activities and occupations labeled feminine in one society are labeled masculine in another. A Chinese woman can operate a crane or fly a plane without defending herself with, "I'm not one of those weird women's libbers." A Danish man who happened to be a dentist would be a minority in a "woman's" occupation. Since cultural norms for men and women vary so drastically, the process of socialization, which transforms infant savage into civilized adult, must explain a lot about sex differences. No gene determines that boys shall play football and girls shall wave pompoms.

The big question today is whether "sex typing"—teaching girls and boys separate rules for feminine and masculine behavior—is good or bad. In the 1950s and 1960s, scores of psychologists spent thousands of person-years trying to discover how parents turn out "properly" sex-typed children. Most implicitly assumed that good parents communicate the rules effectively and that sex-typed children are well adjusted and happy; woe to the girl who wants to play baseball and to the boy who wants to be a nurse. Now some social scientists think that sex-typing is socially discriminatory and psychologically unhealthy. And they are also beginning to argue with the assumption that a child's personality ballot is marked in indelible ink during those "formative years."

This chapter reviews some of the uncommon problems of this common-sense perspective. It is one thing to say that sex differences are learned, and something else again to say precisely how this learning takes place. "I treat all my children alike!" parents like to assert (though they will probably think that *their* parents played favorites), and finding out whether people do what they say can be as hard as catching a mouse with a butterfly net. In the first part of this chapter we consider the major theories of socialization, efforts to explain the *process* by which girls turn out girlish and boys boyish. In the second part we look at the content of that process, at the messages, explicit or subtle, that children learn about masculinity and femininity. The research, it turns out, confirms some common assumptions but not others.

socialization theories: two sexes and how they grow

social-learning theory

The basis of much contemporary research on sex typing is social-learning theory, a product of the behaviorist school of psychology. Behaviorists emphasize observable events and their consequences rather than internal feelings or drives. Years ago they formulated a set of principles to describe simple learning in animals; later they applied these principles to the complex learning skills and social behavior of people (thus the term *social*-learning theory). Behaviorists believe that all learning, including how we learn to be masculine or feminine, can be explained with the same basic rules.

The most important learning principle is that *behavior is controlled by its consequences.* An act that is regularly followed by a reward, or reinforcer, tends to occur again; an act that produces punishment—or is ignored— drops off in frequency. In the animal lab, for example, a hungry rat that gets a tasty morsel when it presses a bar will probably press the bar again. A rat that gets an electric shock when it presses the bar will soon stop pressing. The same principle works with people. If parents reward little girls for playing with dolls ("What a sweet little Mommy you are!"), girls will tend to play with dolls. If adults punish them for playing with baseball bats ("You don't want *that* for Christmas, silly"), girls will not develop much interest in Little League. Whether the rewards and punishments are handed out deliberately or not, the effect is the same.

With human beings, direct on-the-spot reinforcement is often unnecessary because language offers some convenient shortcuts. For instance, parents can tell their daughter that they disapprove of her hitting other children and that they like it when she helps in the kitchen. Anticipated rewards and punishments affect behavior just as real ones do. As psychologist Walter Mischel (1966) says, "A man does not have to be arrested for wearing dresses in public to learn about the consequences of such behavior." In addition, children can learn about the consequences of what they do by observing what happens to other people. Being the intelligent little persons that they are, they participate vicariously in the experiences of others and draw their own conclusions.

Most learning theorists feel that reinforcement alone cannot explain how children learn everything that their sex is expected to do and not to do. Parents would be kept busy twenty-four hours a day rewarding and punishing, rewarding and punishing, for each detail of behavior. Besides, most adults are not aware of the many mannerisms, gestures, and speech habits that are part of their sex roles. Such nuances, say the theorists, must be learned through imitation. Children do a lot of apparently spontaneous imitating; possibly they copy other people because adults have rewarded them for copying in the past, or perhaps they are simply natural mimics.

Most studies of imitation (or *modeling*) have been done in the laboratory rather than in real-life settings, and in the laboratory psychologists can often predict what sorts of models children will choose to imitate. For example, they tend to imitate adults who are friendly, warm, and attentive (Bandura and Huston 1961). They also imitate powerful people, that is, adults who control resources that are important to the child, whether intangibles like the privilege of playing outside or tangibles like cookies and toys (Bandura, Ross, and Ross 1963a; Mischel and Grusec 1966). Because parents are the most nurturant and powerful people in a child's world, they are assumed to be very effective models.

In order to explain how girls become feminine and boys masculine, social-learning theory assumes that children copy people similar to themselves—in particular, the same-sex parent and friends. As Mischel (1970) observes, "Boys do not learn baseball by watching girls and girls do not learn about fashions from observing boys." But research has not confirmed this key assumption. When children in an experiment have a chance to copy adults, they show no consistent tendency to mimic one sex more than the other. Researchers who have tried to correlate more global personality traits of parent and child (rather than concentrating on a particular action) do not find that children resemble the same-sex parent more than the opposite-sex parent (Maccoby and Jacklin 1974).

One plausible explanation for the discrepancy between theory and data is that children observe both sexes, but as they grow older they are most likely to do what they have learned by imitating same-sex models, because that path leads to reward and the other to punishment (Bandura and Walters 1963; Mischel 1970). "Both men and women know how to curse or to fight or use cosmetics or primp in front of mirrors," Mischel comments, but they don't do these things equally often. A three-year-old boy may innocently dress up in his mother's clothes and make-up, but if he does so at age fifteen he'll be in trouble.

Parents may be potent models, but children grow up with many influential people, not all of whom agree on what behavior is appropriate. (One of us recalls a favorite uncle who could be counted on to give her a really good "boy's toy" amidst all the dolls and clothes on her birthday.) For that matter, parents often do not agree on how to treat their children. Children have an entire smorgasbord of models to copy—parents, teachers, friends, siblings—with the result that each of us is a unique composite of many influences. Children must sift through conflicting demands and expectations, often finding, for example, that they cannot please both parents and friends at the same time. They have to figure out why something they did pleased their mother but angered their father, and why they were punished for fighting at one time but not another. And they have to deal with the fact that the behavior a parent displays may not be the one the parent rewards.[1]

Several writers have pointed out that fathers can teach their daughters to be feminine and mothers can teach their sons to be masculine, either by encouraging sex-typed behavior directly or by playing a complementary role (Mussen and Rutherford 1963). A parent may even communicate what's expected of the child by being mildly seductive (Chodorow 1974). Despite his liberated attitudes, a friend reports, "I tend to see little girls as cute, cuddly, and flirtatious—actually sexy—and I have quasi-sexual responses to them. Little boys evoke a completely different reaction in me." This friend is no dirty old man; he is simply perceptive about reactions that appear to be common though not always conscious.

cognitive-developmental theory

Social-learning theory views the child from the outside. It describes how the child is shaped by external events but has much less to say about what goes on in the child's head. Lawrence Kohlberg (1966, 1969) proposes another approach that emphasizes how children think. As learning theorists see it, children (and adults) of all ages learn things in the same ways— through reinforcement and modeling. But cognitive theory, like psychoana-

[1] Parents often punish aggressive children by spanking them. In doing so, they are modeling the very behavior they would like to get rid of: "Hitting is bad" (whack!). To their chagrin, the parents may discover later that their children have learned to express anger by hitting; aggressive children tend to have parents who harshly punish aggressiveness in the home (Bandura 1960; Sears, Maccoby, and Levin 1957). Social-learning research suggests that the best method is to praise the behavior you do want and ignore—rather than punish—the behavior you don't.

lytic theory, says that all children pass through certain *stages of develop-ment,* and that the way they learn depends on the stage they have reached. The Swiss psychologist Jean Piaget has shown that children's ability to reason and their understanding of the physical and social world change in predictable ways as they mature. Kohlberg argues that these changes affect the way they assimilate information about the sexes.

Thus, although two-year-olds can apply the labels "boy" and "girl" correctly to themselves and others, their concept of gender is very concrete. Preschool children rely on physical features such as dress and hairstyle to decide who falls in which category. Girls are people with long hair; boys are people who never wear dresses. Many children at this stage believe they can change their own gender at will simply by getting a haircut or a new outfit. They do not yet have the mental machinery to think of gender as adults do. All the reinforcement in the world, Kohlberg believes, won't alter that fact.

At this age, children can be quite rigid in their insistence that the rules they see as appropriate for a certain category of people or objects be obeyed. For example, a preschool girl may become confused or upset if her mother wears a man's suit to a Halloween party or if her father carries the mother's purse at the supermarket. The child seeks a tangible sign to distin-guish between male and female and between herself and the opposite sex. A girl may reason, for instance, that since boys wear pants but girls often wear skirts, she'd better stick to skirts. One colleague recalls that she was the despair of her liberated relatives when, at four, she insisted on wearing dresses instead of practical jeans.

By the age of six or seven, children understand that gender is permanent. This is a consequence not of rewards and punishments, in Kohlberg's view, but of a growing ability to grasp that certain basic characteristics of people and objects do not change even though less basic ones may. Just as the amount of water remains the same when it is poured from a short, fat glass into a tall, thin one, a woman remains a woman when she wears pants. Children at this age know that they are and always will be female or male. Now their task is to find out what to do to bring their actions into line with the label. Social-learning theory says that girls learn feminine behavior and boys learn masculine behavior because they are rewarded for doing so. Cognitive-developmental theory takes a different position: it assumes that children and adults try to maintain a coherent and balanced picture of themselves and the world, in which beliefs, actions, and values are con-gruent. The knowledge that gender is permanent motivates the child to discover how to be a competent or "proper" girl or boy. As a consequence, she or he finds female or male activities rewarding. Reinforcements and models help show children how well they are doing, but essentially children socialize themselves.

Despite the differences between social-learning and cognitive-developmental theory, it is often hard to choose between them when explaining an observation. For example, one study found that bright children preferred dolls of the same sex as themselves—regarded as a sign of sex-typing—at younger ages than children of average intelligence (Kohlberg and Zigler 1967). The cognitive interpretation is that the bright child matures earlier in mental capacity and therefore understands and assimilates sex-role demands faster than the average child. That is, the bright child goes through the same developmental stages in the same order as other children, but more quickly. The social-learning interpretation is that intelligent children need fewer lessons (fewer reinforcements) before they know what is expected of them (Mischel 1970).

identification

Many psychologists believe that a third process accounts for sex-role learning: the tendency of children to identify with the same-sex parent. The child wants to be like the parent and copies his or her values, mannerisms, personality, and ambitions, not just specific acts. Because of identification, children develop a stronger emotional commitment to their sex role than to behavior that is not tied to their masculinity or femininity. Freud's theory of psychosexual development (Chapter 5) is an identification theory *par excellence,* and it was Freud who first introduced the term. Freud believed that children incorporate ("introject") large chunks of the same-sex parent's personality into their own, mainly as a way of reducing the anxiety and conflict caused by Oedipal desires. Today most theories of identification do not give such a central place to sexual motivation. Instead they emphasize the child's desire to be similar to someone of the same sex; to be like someone who is powerful; to enjoy vicariously the position of someone who has status; or to reproduce the feelings experienced when the model gave the child love and attention. In some theories, attachment and dependency cause identification; in others identification leads to attachment and dependency.

One appeal of this approach is that it is more encompassing than, say, the behaviorists' attention to specific acts. Instead of counting reinforcements and situational forces that cause a boy to strike back at the neighborhood bully, identification theories can leapfrog over particular events and concentrate on a global personality trait, the boy's aggressiveness. Most behaviorists do not much like the concept of personality; they prefer to concentrate on events they can see and quantify. Personality theorists think that people acquire certain motivations and traits—ambitiousness, warmth, aggressiveness, dependence, and so on—that lead them to behave consistently across situations. The problem, as we saw in Chapter 2, is that personality is hard to measure. Suppose you want to know, as many researchers do, what sorts of parents produce demure little girls and tough little boys. There are more studies on this than summer sunflowers, but they yield a tangle of conclusions. Most studies try to account for some personality trait in the child by looking at the parent's personality, perhaps by relating the child's aggressiveness, dependence, or "femininity" to the parent's warmth, hostility, or child-rearing philosophy (for example, permissive vs. restrictive). These efforts are like trying to photograph bacteria with a Brownie. The method is usually too clumsy for its object.

The general concept of identification is plausible, but in practice it is hard to say when identification has occurred. Often people use the term loosely, as in, "I respected my father, but I identified with my mother." Psychologists define the term differently, depending on who is theorizing. For one it means that a child wants to be like a parent; for another that a child actually behaves like the parent; for a third that a child feels closest to the parent. You can see how hard it is to interpret this concept. If you walk, talk, and bake like your mother, if you have her endearing mannerisms and infuriating habits, but you have the literary tastes of your father and want to be an accountant like him, with which parent have you identified? In addition, in some studies people say they are "most like" one parent but "feel closest to" the other. Clearly the idea that girls learn to be feminine by identifying with their mothers and boys learn to be masculine by identifying with their fathers is too simple.

Identification has been used to explain not only the traditional course of sex-role learning but less traditional outcomes. For example, numerous researchers have been interested in why some girls become career women. They generally find that girls whose mothers worked outside the home or had a career are more likely than girls with homemaking mothers to follow a career and to have unconventional attitudes toward the female role (Frieze, Parsons, and Ruble 1972; Tangri 1972; Almquist and Angrist 1971). But some nontraditional women apparently got that way by identifying with (feeling closer to) their fathers rather than their mothers (Tangri 1972). The conclusion at the moment is that a girl is most likely to grow up nontraditional if she identifies with either her father or her nontraditional mother. (Until very recently, little work was done with nontraditional men, possibly because they are an even rarer species.)

Even when a child does turn out like a parent, "identification" is not necessarily the process responsible. Indeed, the child's behavior may not be based on the parent's at all. Albert Bandura (1969) illustrates this point with a parable about a big-game hunter who came face to face with a hungry lion. "As he prepared to shoot the onrushing beast, the gun jammed. Helpless and terrified, the hunter promptly closed his eyes and began to pray rapidly. Moments passed and, much to his surprise, nothing happened. Puzzled by this unexpected turn of events, the hunter cocked his head and slowly opened his eyes to find the lion also bowed in prayer. The jubilant hunter loudly exclaimed, 'Thank God, you are responding to my prayers!' The lion promptly replied, 'Not at all. I'm saying grace.' "

Despite such problems, identification theories raise some interesting issues. For example, in many ways growing up may be easier for girls than for boys. Most theorists believe than infants of both sexes start out with a stronger attachment to the mother, because she does most of the childcare and provides most of the nurturance. For girls, identification is relatively simple; they just continue the attachment to the mother.[2] For boys, the matter is more complicated. In order to become masculine and enter the world of men, they must break away from their mothers and identify with their fathers, who are around the house less often and are less involved with the children. Girls have many examples around them of what women do, but boys have a much vaguer idea of what men do; they are surrounded by female relatives and teachers in their early years. David Lynn (1966) thinks that "the father as a model for the boy is analogous to a map showing the major outline but lacking most details." A boy knows he should *not* be a sissy but has a harder time figuring out what he *should* be. He may turn to fiction and symbolic models, following a fantasized stereotyped image of the male role instead of identifying with a real person, as girls do.

These three theories give us some good ideas of how sex-typing occurs in general, but it is hard to predict how any given child will turn out. A child does not copy the parents in a mechanical way. The child may follow in the parent's footsteps only if the parent is wearing comfortable shoes—and is satisfied with his or her role (Frieze, Parsons, and Ruble 1972). If a mother chronically complains about her fate, her daughter may vow, "I'll never be like her!" Or the mother may seem happy enough, but her daughter may imitate the father for reasons that have nothing to do with gender. Perhaps she just likes him more. Maccoby and Jacklin tell of a little girl who held tenaciously to the belief that only boys could become doctors, even though her own mother was a physician. Apparently she was influenced more by the attitudes and behavior of people outside her family than by the real-life model who was closest to her.

[2] Freudians would disagree; see Chapter 5.

It is easier to play quarterback on Monday morning, and all th[e] theories can trace an individual's adult behavior to childhood antecede[nts] after the fact. A social-learning theorist would look at the person's history ⌐. rewards and punishments—all that family attention for good grades and apathy for making the team (or vice versa). An identification theorist would try to see which parent the person resembles most, especially in values and ambitions. A cognitive theorist would point to the child's mental processes and ways of assimilating information.

Although learning, cognitive, and identification theories emphasize different aspects of sex-role learning, many psychologists help themselves to a little of each. For example, social-learning theorists are supposed to stick to observable behavior, but many of them feel comfortable with the idea that identification is more than just imitation and that children adopt not only behaviors but rules and values. Kohlberg's ideas have influenced many researchers who began their work in the social-learning tradition. Eventually the best elements of the three formulations may be combined into one unified approach.

We turn now from the sex-role learning process to sex-role messages. What do children learn is the content of the male and female roles in this society?

sources of socialization

parents: perceptions and lessons

Many parents feel that they know their babies quite well when the infants are only a day or two old. "She's such a contented little dumpling," they say, or "he's quite an assertive little man." With such remarks, sex-typing begins. Psychologists Jeffrey Rubin, Frank Provenzano, and Zella Luria (1974) interviewed thirty first-time parents, fifteen of girls and fifteen of boys, within twenty-four hours of the baby's birth. Each baby had been routinely examined after birth by hospital personnel for physical and neurological characteristics such as color, muscle tone, and reflex irritability, and there were no objective differences between males and females, even in size. Yet the parents of girls rated their babies as softer, more finely featured, smaller, and more inattentive than did the parents of boys. Fathers especially were influenced by the gender of the child. They described their sons as firmer, larger-featured, better-coordinated, more alert, stronger, and hardier than the mothers of sons did; men thought their daughters were more inattentive, weak, and delicate than the women did. There was only one exception. Mothers rated sons cuddlier than daughters, and fathers rated daughters cuddlier than sons—a finding that Rubin et al. call the Oedipal Effect.

In interviews, parents of older children are apt to say they think the sexes have distinct personalities. For example, Canadian parents in one study thought boys were rougher, noisier, more active, more competitive, more mechanically minded, and more likely to defend themselves than girls, while they said girls were neater and cleaner, quieter, more reserved, better mannered, more sensitive to the feelings of others, more likely to cry, and more helpful at home. The same parents felt that boys and girls alike *ought* to be neat and clean, helpful at home, and able to care for themselves. Both sexes, they said, should rarely cry, get angry, or do dangerous things and both sexes should be able to compete and to defend themselves (Lambert, Yackley, and Hein 1971).

The important question is whether parents actually act on their attitudes and the answer to it is, it depends. The pressures on boys and girls to act in certain ways are uneven and unequal—with more flexibility generally granted to girls. Until adolescence, it is more permissible for girls to behave like tomboys than for boys to behave like sissies, an observation that draws many explanations. One is that parents fear that boys who prefer traditionally feminine activities may become homosexual; another is that masculinity is a more precarious identity than femininity, so boys must stick carefully to the rules. Some sociologists explain the matter in terms of status and power: lower-status groups, whether women or minorities, are understood to aspire to the status above them and forgiven when they try to move up. When a higher-status person takes a step down, however, society's pressures are brought to bear on him. In one study, parents of preschoolers were asked to react to hypothetical situations in which a child chooses a particular activity. When a little girl chose a boyish activity the parents were not especially concerned, but when a boy stepped over the line the parents, especially the fathers, reacted negatively (Lansky 1967).

Almost all parents encourage some sex-typed behavior in their children, for example by buying more trucks than dolls for boys and more dolls than trucks for girls. Jerrie Will, Patricia Self, and Nancy Datan (1974) observed eleven mothers as they played, one at a time, with a six-month-old child. Taking advantage of the fact that male and female infants look much alike, the researchers told six of the women that the child was a boy named Adam, and the other five that it was a girl named Beth. Then they looked to see which of three toys—a doll, a train, and a fish—the women would offer the child. Those who thought they were playing with Beth handed her the doll more often than those who thought they were playing with Adam, and "Adam" got the train more often than "Beth" did. Afterwards, two mothers commented that Beth was a real girl, because she was sweeter and cried more softly than a boy would. In fact, Beth was a boy. The notable thing about this study was that all of the women claimed to believe that males and females are alike at this tender age, and none said that she would treat her own son and daughter differently. On the contrary, nine insisted that they encouraged rough play with their daughters, and ten said that they encouraged their sons to play with dolls.[3]

Many people believe that adults punish boys who behave like girls and encourage boys to separate from their mothers, which teaches them to be "manly" and independent (Lynn 1966, 1969; Chodorow 1974). Psychologists have taken this assumption and run with it, speculating on the good and bad consequences. Some think that early pressure on boys to earn their masculinity explains why more boys than girls have childhood problems with adjustment, school, and health. Others assume that an early break of the mother-bond gives boys a greater sense of separateness, independence, and self-confidence; it's hard to explore the world if you're tangled up in apron strings. Psychologist Lois Hoffman (1972) even suggests that perhaps "girls need a little maternal rejection if they are to become independently competent and self-confident."

But when we turn to tests of the assumption that parents grant more autonomy or freedom to young boys than to young girls, we find a surprise. Most studies, Maccoby and Jacklin say, do not support the assumption. In fact, some research shows that parents claim to restrict preschool boys *more* than girls. They set firmer rules for boys; they are more apt to lay down the law with boys and to make sure it is obeyed. Possibly parents think that boys are more rambunctious and therefore keep closer tabs on them.

The research on aggressiveness is also contradictory. In 1957 Robert Sears, Eleanor Maccoby, and Harry Levin did a large interview study and reported that mothers allow boys to be more aggressive than girls, both

[3] The overall package of research on parent-infant exchanges is contradictory. Some studies find that mothers touch boy babies more often than girls; some find that they touch girls more; some find no difference. The same is true for studies of how much the mother talks to the child and of how quickly she responds to the baby's cries and coos. The kind of attention a parent gives to a child varies with social class and the age of the child. Highly educated mothers respond more quickly to the sounds and cries of female infants, but the reverse is true for less well-educated mothers. Parents may hold or touch a child of either sex more at one age than another, although in general parents tend to regard daughters as more fragile than sons and treat them more gingerly (Maccoby and Jacklin 1974). The data don't give any strong indication of how, or even whether, such parental behavior is related to the child's behavior later in life.

toward parents and toward other children. More recent studies, however, find that parents punish boys who fight more often than girls, or at least they say that they do.[4] Social-learning theorists can explain both these findings: girls fight less than boys because they are punished more consistently for doing so; boys fight more than girls because parental attention can be reinforcing even when it takes the form of spankings and scoldings. They might have more trouble explaining why girls find parental disapproval punishing while boys find it rewarding, but as we observed in Chapter 2, Americans are somewhat ambivalent about aggressiveness and violence, especially in males. Parents may convey to their sons, but not to their daughters, a covert admiration for feistiness.

teachers: the hidden curriculum

Fortunately, some good observational studies are now being done in schools. One recent study of teachers and children in fifteen nursery-school classrooms supports the position that adults do treat boys and girls differently, but in subtle ways. Even people who talk equality sometimes remain unconsciously traditional. Lisa Serbin and K. Daniel O'Leary (1975) trained observers to record exactly how and when preschool teachers spoke to the children. They were especially curious to find out how the teachers responded to boys and girls who were aggressive or dependent. Here are three of their main findings:

1. Teachers did reward the boys for being aggressive, but not by saying, "Terrific, Tommy, clobber him again." They responded over three times as often to boys who misbehaved as to girls who misbehaved. When they rebuked the girls, it was briefly, softly, out of other children's hearing. When they scolded the boys, they called public attention to their naughtiness—which only inspired the boys to continue in their ways. Serbin and O'Leary describe a typical encounter:

> John was a five-year-old bully. When someone didn't follow his directions or give him the toy he wanted, John lost his temper. He pushed, shoved, shouted, and threw things. When we first watched John in his classroom, he was playing peacefully with another boy at building a Tinker-Toy tower.
> Then John asked the other child for a piece of material the boy was using. When he was refused, John began to tear the tower apart. The other boy

---

[4] Most research on aggression is based on interviews with parents. Sometimes parents and children are observed at home or in a laboratory, but Maccoby and Jacklin found no studies in which researchers watched how parents actually react when their child brawls with other children outside the home.

protested, and John raised his hand threateningly. The other children across the room instantly sang out in chorus: "Teacher, John's hitting!" Mrs. Jones looked over and ordered John to stop. She strode across the room, pulled John away, and spent the next two minutes telling him why he shouldn't hit people. Five minutes later, John was hitting another classmate (Serbin and O'Leary 1975, p. 57).

One can easily conjure up an image of John, thumbs in lapels, basking in the limelight. Serbin and O'Leary explain that the example shows how teachers can reinforce exactly the behavior that's causing a problem: "For John, as for many children, being disruptive is an effective means of getting a far larger dose of attention than good behavior can bring." The solution, incidentally, was to ignore the bullying. When the teacher learned to over-look John's aggressiveness it stopped abruptly.

2. Teachers did reward the girls for being dependent, but not by say-ing, "How nice, Sally, that you're tugging on my skirt." They responded more often to girls when they were nearby than when they were out of arm's reach, and rarely sent the girls off to work on their own. In contrast, the teachers paid the same amount of attention to boys whether they were close to them or not, and encouraged the boys to do independent work.

3. All fifteen of the teachers paid more attention to boys. Boys were twice as likely as girls to get individual instruction on a task: they got more tangible and verbal rewards for academic work; and they got more help than girls did when they asked for it. The sort of help the boys got was the kind that creates independence and capability. A child's ability to solve problems is related to the amount of detailed instruction an adult gives. The best instruction teaches how to solve the problem without actually provid-ing the answer (Hess and Shipman 1967). Now consider what happened in one classroom that Serbin and O'Leary observed, when the children were busy making party baskets. When it was time to attach the paper handles, the teacher showed the class how to use the stapler. Then she held the handle in place so each boy could staple it himself. But if a girl failed to staple the handle on her own initiative, the teacher simply took the basket and attached the handle for her.

Serbin and O'Leary believe that the teachers' unwitting encourage-ment of the boys' aggressiveness explains why more boys than girls have reading problems and learning disabilities: their rowdiness prevents them from paying attention when they should. On the other hand, the extra instruction they get helps their problem-solving skills. Girls, praised for stay-ing close to their mothers and teachers, learn more easily to talk and read, but not to solve problems on their own. Other researchers find that parents, too, pay more attention to boys, both punishing and praising them more.

Why this is so is not known. Maccoby and Jacklin write, "In some situations boys appear to be more attention-getting, either because they do more things calling for adult response [such as breaking lamps and catching frogs] or because parents and teachers see them as having more interesting qualities or potential."

Maccoby and Jacklin's comment points to the chicken-or-the-egg problem common to all scientific endeavors. Some teachers and parents react more harshly to boys' aggressiveness than to girls'. Does that explain why more boys than girls fight, or do adults react to boys more harshly because boys are more aggressive to begin with? Parents usually say the latter; most will tell you that it's easier to raise a daughter than a son. "She'll sit and play quietly for an hour while he tears the house apart, plank by plank," they complain, shaking their heads in amused resignation (or dismay). One teacher in Serbin and O'Leary's study said that it was harder for her to ignore boys because "boys hit harder." We can't know for sure whether she was influencing the child's acts or whether he was influencing hers—or both.

The fifteen teachers in Serbin and O'Leary's study were not aware that they were treating boys and girls differently. Neither was the staff of a nursery school that Carole Joffe (1971) observed, in which there was a deliberate attempt to avoid sex-typing. Despite the egalitarian philosophy, the teachers and the mothers who worked with them perpetuated the stereotypes. They complimented girls on their dresses but said nothing when the girls wore pants, and they seldom commented on the way boys were dressed. They praised the boys for defending themselves well in a fight, for being "brave little men," though the school had a rule against fighting.

In some homes and classrooms, the overt sex-role philosophy of the past has gone underground, and the messages parents and teachers communicate to children are as complicated as they are subtle. A parent, teacher, or a casual observer may miss them, but children do not.

media messages

Anyone who reads, watches television, or goes to the movies can verify that media stereotypes are far from subtle. Everywhere one goes, one runs smack into the same images of women and men; yet they are so ubiquitous, so "natural," that people don't always realize they are there. As Sandra and Daryl Bem (1976) observe, "We are like the fish who is unaware that his environment is wet." There is no mystery to the media's message about what each sex should do and be: like the purloined letter, it is right there in front of us all the time. This section discusses the images of males and females in books and television, but much of what the research shows also applies to magazines, songs, movies, newspapers, and professional journals.

children's books: fairy tales about the sexes Preschool picture books, grammar-school readers, textbooks in science and social studies—all are populated primarily by males. When Women on Words and Images (1972), a New Jersey group that studies sexual stereotypes, surveyed 134 children's readers from fourteen different publishers—a total of 2,750 stories—it discovered these ratios:

Boy-centered to girl-centered stories   5:2
Adult male to adult female main characters   3:1
Male biographies to female biographies   6:1
Male animal stories to female animal stories   2:1
Male folk or fantasy stories to female folk or fantasy stories 4:1[5]

The WWI study, like others, found that boys and men in children's readers monopolize the traits that Americans regard highly: ingenuity, bravery, perseverance, achievement, sportsmanship. Boys make things. They rely on their wits to solve problems. They are curious, clever, and adventurous. They achieve; they make money. Girls and women are incompetent and fearful. They ask other people to solve their problems for them. They typically react to a crisis by dissolving in a puddle of tears. They spend most of their time baking cookies and sewing, and they are constantly concerned about how they look, which boys never are. In story after story, girls are the onlookers, the cheerleaders, speaking such lines as "Oh, Raymond, boys are much braver than girls," and even accepting humiliation and ridicule. In sixty-seven stories, one sex demeans the other—and sixty-five of these involve hostility of males against females. Boys exclude girls from groups, show them up as scaredy-cats, and make fun of their domesticity. The girls often join in the derision of their sex: "I'm just a girl, but I know enough not to do that"; "Even I can do it and you know how stupid I am."

The anti-female jokes common in American culture (see Chapter 1) have their parallel in some children's books. In one story the shrill, nagging wife of a kindly inventor is dumped into the garbage by a robot the inventor created for the express purpose of collecting trash. In another, a man accidentally makes money when he unintentionally kills his wife; his good fortune inspires other men in the town to bump off their old wives, too (U'Ren 1971).

[5] In a recent update using books published after 1972, when the first survey was published, WWI found that the ratio for biographies had improved markedly (to 2:1), but the ratio of boy-centered to girl-centered stories had worsened (to 7:2). Some individual books had changed, but the overall picture was not much altered.

Grammar-school readers offer many models for boys to emulate, but few for girls. WWI tallied 147 occupations for boys (including astronaut and cowboy), but only twenty-six for girls (including circus fat lady and witch). The full lists are shown in Table 6. In the 134 books examined, only three working mothers appeared—and in one, a young bully's bad behavior is chalked up to the fact that his mother wasn't home during the day to take care of him. For that matter, mothers, whether working or not, usually come out as mindless, dull, and punitive. Lenore Weitzman et al. (1972) explored the roles of women in prize-winning preschool picture books and found that women are the wives of the kings, judges, adventurers, and explorers, but they themselves are not the rulers, judges, adventurers, and explorers. Even eminent women have a way of fading into the background. One study of grammar-school textbooks in California recorded an illustration of Eve Curie, the Nobel Prize–winning chemist, peering from behind her husband's shoulder as he and a male colleague conferred (U'Ren 1971).

Publishers give various explanations for the portrayals of women and men in their books. One is that the books simply describe reality, since girls do grow up to live more routine lives than boys.[6] Critics respond that half of all women with school-age children work outside the home, yet they are rarely portrayed; further, even the most dedicated housewife does more than wash dishes and bake brownies. Nor are the boys' adventures remotely related to what adult men do; their escapades would cause the parents of real boys to drop dead of heart attacks. They rescue people from fires, protect their mothers from grizzly bears, leave home to pan for gold. They don't prepare to become what most real boys will become—insurance salesmen, factory workers, plumbers, office workers, teachers, and the like. The exaggerated male figures in children's fiction are not meant to be realistic, of course; they are supposed to teach values, such as persistence and courage. The important point is that female characters do not portray these positive qualities.

television: truth down the tube Almost everyone in America watches television, children more than anyone else. In a national sample of viewers, George Gerbner and Larry Gross (1976) found that half of the twelve-year-olds in the country watch an average of six or more hours per day. The typical teenager today has spent more time in front of the tube than in school. Television programing has truly become a "universal curriculum."

[6] Another is that boys should predominate in books to offset the fact that real boys, who are constantly surrounded by women (mothers and teachers), lack good male role models. Further, because boys have a harder time learning to read, they need the extra motivation of seeing themselves in exciting fantasy images. These points are well taken, but they don't explain why exciting male models must exist at the expense of exciting female ones.

Table 6. Occupations of Adult Males and Females in Grammar-School Readers

Male Occupations

airplane builder
animal trainer
architect
artist
astronaut
astronomer
athlete
author

babysitter
baker
balloonist
band conductor
banker
barber
baseball player
blacksmith
botanist
building contractor
businessman
bus driver

carpenter
circus keeper
clerk
clockmaker
clown
coach
computer operator
construction worker
cook
cowboy
craftsman

decorator
detective
deliveryman
dentist
doctor
doorman

electrician
engineer
expert on art
explorer

fairgroundsman
farmer
figure skater
film maker
fireman
fisherman
foreman
forest ranger

gardener
gas station attendant
glassblower
guard

handyman
humorist
hunter

ice cream man
inn keeper
inventor

janitor
judge
juggler

king
knight

landlord
lifeguard
lighthouse keeper
lumberman

magician
mailman

mathematician
mayor
m. c. in nightclub
merchant
milkman
miller
miner
mineralogist
monk
mover
museum manager

naturalist
newspaper owner
news reporter

organ grinder
outlaw

painter
parent
peddlar
pet store owner
photographer
pilot
pirate
plumber
policeman
pony herder
popcorn vender
priest
principal
professor
prospector

radio reporter
railroad inspector
restaurant owner
roadmaster
rocket firer

Table 6. Occupations of Adult Males and Females in Grammar-School Readers (continued)

sailor	steamshovel operator	train conductor
salesman	stonecutter	train engineer
scientist	storeowner	trapper
scoutmaster	submarine operator	trashman
sea captain		trolley driver
shepherder	tailor	truck driver
sheriff	taxidermist	
ship builder	teacher	veterinarian
shoemaker	telephoneman	
silversmith	telephone lineman	watchman
ski teacher	TV actor	whaler
soldier	TV man	woodcutter
space station worker	TV newsman	World War II hero
stagecoach driver	TV writer	
statesman	ticket seller	zookeeper

Female Occupations

acrobatist	ice skater
author	librarian
babysitter	painter
baker	parent
cafeteria worker	queen
cashier	recreational director
cleaning woman	school crossing guard
cook	school nurse
doctor	secretary
dressmaker	shopkeeper
fat lady (in circus)	teacher
governess	telephone operator
housekeeper	witch

SOURCE: Women on Words and Images 1972, pp. 73–74.

Television stories are children's textbooks in motion. The same stereotypes and sex ratios prevail: three-fourths of all leading characters on prime-time network TV are male. On adventure shows, men are usually freewheeling cowboys, cops, and secret agents; the women on these shows are interested only in romance, their families, and the boss's welfare. Most TV women don't have jobs, and those who do are in half as many occupations as men (Women on Words and Images 1975). During the early 1970s, Mary Tyler Moore was one of the few women to hold a responsible job among men; she was also one of the few women not portrayed as dumb and bungling. Recently Wonder Woman, Police Woman, and the Bionic Woman have helped shift the statistics, but it is interesting that Wonder Woman, when she isn't saving the world, works as a secretary, and the Bionic Woman teaches elementary school. Heroines such as Charlie's Angels usually take their orders from an authoritative man instead of figuring out who dunnit. Even Angie Dickinson's competent policewoman is often bailed out of a jam by her male partner. Heroines typically unmask the villain by accident or by luck. When women succeed, these programs seem to be saying, it is not by virtue of their own talents. (Real women attribute success to luck more often than skill, too, as we will discuss shortly.) To land the job of TV heroine, a woman must be slender, beautiful, and young. A male adventurer may be fat (Cannon), bald (Kojak), old (Barnaby Jones), or paralyzed (Ironside).

Sarah Sternglanz and Lisa Serbin (1974) analyzed ten popular children's programs during the 1971–72 season. Once again, males came out as aggressive, constructive, and helpful, and they were more likely to be rewarded for their actions. Females were deferential and passive more often than males, and sometimes they were punished for being too active. Females did not have as much impact as males on the course of events, except when they used magic. Indeed, four of the five female title-role stars were witches of some sort, modern-day versions of the ancient image of women as mysterious, magical, and unpredictable.

Commercials are another breeding ground for stereotypes. We are all familiar with the harried housewife who agonizes over waxy yellow buildup and ring-around-the-collar. In ads about cleaning products, women speak more, but 96 percent of the authoritative voice-overs are male (Women on Words and Images 1975). Men tell women how to care for sick children, bake a cake, wash dishes, and read dogfood labels. True, more recent commercials have begun to break away from the old stereotypes, showing wives who work, husbands who cook, and daughters who play football and provide their mothers with dirty clothes to wash. Overall, neither sex is especially intelligent or likable in commercials. Adults may be able to shrug off the exaggerated portrayals that interrupt a program every ten minutes, but young children seem to regard commercials as mini-programs—and often as more lively and appealing than the "real" program in progress. A parent and child may pass each other in the hall as a commercial starts, the former heading for the refrigerator and the latter eager for a chance to sing along with a favorite jingle.

It would be a mistake to assume, as some feminist critics seem to, that *only* women come across badly on TV. In comedy series, in contrast to adventure shows, men and women appear in nearly equal numbers, and men are as likely as women to be dingbats. In fact, often it is the wives who are wise, witty, and patient, and who end up deflating their husbands' puffed-up egos. Possibly men get their comeuppance in situation comedies because sitcoms ridicule everybody, or because the family is the female's domain and the male role at home is ambiguous and changing, an easy target. The point is that, overall, there are many more competent and admirable men on TV than there are women. Analogously, there are anti-male jokes as well as antifemale jokes (see Chapter 1), but many more of the latter than the former.

Most people who have documented sex stereotypes in the media assume that they contribute to sex differences in real life—that if children are exposed to endless images of dependent females and assertive males, they will ape what they see. Yet the connection is not as clear as all that. People who saw Bonnie and Clyde rob banks and kill people on film did not dash out and do the same. Writers on media stereotypes sometimes seem to believe that TV has an impact on everyone but their friends and them—somehow they have the resources to withstand the onslaught of dumb blondes and strong men.

The problem of proving a connection between media stereotypes and real-life behavior is the same one that researchers have when they try to show that people imitate TV violence and crime. In laboratory experiments, children will usually imitate an aggressive adult they have observed in a filmed episode. For example, if children watch an adult punch an inflated Bobo doll and are then left alone with a similar doll, they will punch it too (Bandura, Ross, and Ross 1963b). But it is harder to prove that films affect what viewers do outside a laboratory. Stanley Milgram set up an elaborate study to try to demonstrate such a causal relationship (Milgram 1974; Milgram and Shotland 1973). He wrote an antisocial scene about a man who steals from a charity box, inserted the scene into a real TV program ("Medical Center"), and had the program aired in certain test cities. Some viewers saw the altered program and some saw the same show without the stealing. Finally, he gave a sample of viewers an opportunity to imitate what they had seen. Milgram thought the people who had seen the antisocial act would be more likely to imitate it, but he was wrong. He tried time after time to set up an experiment that would demonstrate that people imitate what they see on TV, but he was never successful. Television executives were delighted. Milgram was not.

Milgram's research doesn't prove that TV crime *never* leads to real crime, of course. But most people probably learn to regard the portrayals they see on TV as cartoon images, exaggerations, flights of fancy. Most adults, anyway. Children may not be as skilled at distinguishing reality from fantasy, and so they may be more susceptible to filmed violence, crime, and sex stereotypes. Each program a child sees may be like a drop of water falling on a rock; a single drop has little effect, but if enough drops fall, an impression is made. The ideal test would be to find a group of children alike in class, intelligence, and home environment, expose half of them to sex-typed TV programs for a few years, and keep the rest from ever seeing such a program. You would have to take care that all the children had the same exposure (preferably none) to other sources of stereotyping—books, magazines, radio, movies, songs, friends. At the end of the experiment you might know whether TV images affect viewers or merely reflect society's norms. Obviously, such an experiment is only a psychologist's dream and a parent's nightmare. But it raises a critical issue: how other factors in a person's life—background, parents, intelligence, books, personal heroes—intervene between what the person sees in the media and how he or she responds in real life.

subliminal communication

Children can pick up sex stereotypes not only from books and film but by observing how people around them act toward each other. For example, sex differences in status are apparent in the way we talk and write, though most laymen are not aware of it. And there you see the problem. Can women be laymen? Many feminists believe that the use of "men" or "mankind" to refer to humanity, and the use of "he" to refer to any person, sex unspecified, communicates the notion that "male" and "human" are synonymous while females are outsiders. It is no accident, they say, that feminine forms can never be used in the general way that masculine forms are, that we never say "All women are created equal," "No woman is an island," or "These are the times that try women's souls." As Simone de Beauvoir wrote some twenty-five years ago,

> A man never begins by presenting himself as an individual of a certain sex; it goes without saying that he is a man. The terms *masculine* and *feminine* are used symmetrically only as a matter of form, as on legal papers. In actuality the relation of the two sexes is not quite like that of two electrical poles, for man represents both the positive and the neutral, as is indicated by the common use of *man* to designate human beings in general; whereas woman represents only

the negative, defined by limiting criteria, without reciprocity. . . . Thus humanity is male and man defines woman not in herself but as relative to him; she is not regarded as an autonomous being (de Beauvoir 1953, pp. xv–xvi).

Some linguists think that feminists simply have a case of pronoun envy; but in practice, masculine forms are not nearly as neutral in the generic sense as these linguists claim. Wendy Martyna (in press) argues that even when people seem to be using "he" to include both sexes, they often are really thinking about men only, which may become apparent from context. Thus two psycholinguists, discussing, of all topics, how pronouns are used to indicate status and power, write: "The progressive young Indian exchanges the mutual T [a kind of pronoun] with his wife" (Brown and Gilman 1960). As if all progressive young Indians were male! School textbooks are notorious for this sort of thing, as when they talk about "the settler and his wife." One textbook defines Standard English as "that language spoken by the educated professional and his wife" (Burr, Dunn, and Farquhar 1972).

The sexes learn early about styles of speaking, too. Girls aren't supposed to curse or speak too assertively, and some words are off-limits for one sex or the other. Women may use certain adjectives (*adorable, lovely, divine*), adverbial phrases (*awfully nice*), and euphemisms (*powder room*) that men must avoid. Some linguists think that men give orders more directly, using true imperative forms (*Open the window; Shut the door*), whereas women soften their commands by disguising them as questions (*Would you mind opening the window? Could you please shut the door?*). How much men and women actually differ in their language is still unknown, however. Sex differences may meet the ear less often than we suppose.[7]

----

[7] Of course, the times are changing rapidly. As more women enter male bastions, the language will have to bend to reflect the change. Or maybe it won't. When Mrs. Elizabeth Lane became England's first female High Court Justice, British protocol went into a crisis. What should she be called? As *Time* magazine reported:

"My Lord" seemed confusing at best, while traditionalists cringed at the sound of "Mrs. Justice." After grave deliberation, the Lord Chancellor's office has duly issued its decision: henceforth, Mrs. Lane will be Mr. Justice Lane, and may indeed be called "My Lord." "There simply isn't any precedent for calling a woman anything different," argued a harassed official. "We've taken what seems the least absurd decision." His Lordship, Mr. Justice Lane, is also entitled by ancient judicial tradition to a bachelor knighthood . . . (quoted in Epstein 1970, pp. 88—89).

Some occupations have been more flexible. A New Jersey town recently made the switch from "councilmen" to "members of the council." And on the Santa Fe railroad, men who had the job of calling rail crews to work were referred to as "call boys." Obviously women with this job could not have the comparable title. The railroad, embarrassed, came up with a new title for both sexes: "crew caller."

The way we address other people depends both on how intimate we are with them and on how powerful we are in comparison with them (Brown and Ford 1961). Because gender is related to intimacy and power, we should expect forms of address to be different for men and women. In keeping with the pedestal-gutter syndrome, men are at once respectful toward women (they are not supposed to offend the ladies by swearing) and overly familiar. One of us recalls a telephone conversation during which a man, an attorney whom she had never met, kept calling her "doctor." "Please, let's be more informal," she suggested. "OK, dear, now where were we?" he shot back. It's a rare woman who would address a male colleague with a cavalier "honey" or "doll." Coming from a woman, such terms are likely to be construed as a bid for sexual intimacy, not power.

Communication does not need to be verbal to be effective. Nancy Henley and Jo Freeman (1976) argue that a clear message of which sex has more power is transmitted in touches: females, they maintain, are touched more than males are, and this marks them as subordinate. Of course, people touch each other for many reasons—to be friendly, to show affection, to initiate sex—but touch also functions to show who outranks whom. In our society, touch implies privileged access to another person. For example, who would be more likely to touch the other by throwing an arm around the shoulder or putting a hand on the back: teacher or student, master or servant, policeman or accused, doctor or patient, minister or parishioner, businessman or secretary? "As with first-naming," note Henley and Freeman, "it is considered presumptuous for a person of low status to initiate touch with a person of higher status." Thus, they continue, when male diners pat waitresses or a male professor touches a female student, the intent is not necessarily sexual. But if a woman touches a man, her gesture, like the familiar "honey" or "dear," usually will be interpreted as a sexual overture even when it is not, "since it would be inconceivable for [her] to be exercising power."

Henley (1970) supports this thesis with personal accounts of what happened to her when she broke the usual pattern of who initiates touching. (Readers may try a small experiment for themselves by deliberately touching a person of higher status.) She also asked a male student, unaware of her theory, to observe and record touches in an outdoor setting. Apart from lovers, he noted, men were more likely to touch women than women were to touch men. Perhaps children use such nonverbal signals along with more obvious ones, like who makes decisions, to figure out which sex is more powerful.

Because Henley and Freeman are concerned with the political implications of nonverbal communication, they concentrate on messages about power and status. However, children undoubtedly draw inferences about other things as well. They may decide that females are more nurturant, because their mothers usually comfort them when they're hurt, encourage lap-sitting, and rock them to sleep when they're sick. They may conclude that males are the more aggressive sex, because their fathers most often roughhouse with them, toss them into the air, and accept their invitations to play touch-football. Children probably generalize from personal experience to reach conclusions about the "natural" traits and duties of men and women.

some consequences of socialization

By the time they are three or four, children tend to choose sex-typed toys, activities, and games. Boys especially are likely to prefer "boy-toys" and avoid "girl-toys" like the plague (Maccoby and Jacklin 1974).[8] Their sense of masculinity at this tender age, and perhaps later, seems to hinge on not being like girls.

By the time they enter kindergarten, children have a pretty good idea of what is going to be expected of them as adults—they know for sure that boys can be firemen and policemen and girls can be teachers and nurses. An undergraduate student, Linda Ollison, asked twenty-nine kindergarten girls and twenty-nine boys a revealing question: "What do you think is the most important job in the world?" Boys and girls alike listed policeman, fireman, and doctor, while girls added teacher. Then Ollison asked, "Do you think you could do that when you grow up?" and found that the boys were much more optimistic. Twenty of the twenty-nine boys answered yes compared to twelve of the twenty-nine girls. Further, only six boys conceded that a girl could do the most important job in the world, but twenty-two girls said that a boy could do the work.

The messages of socialization, overt and subtle, teach children what toys are okay to play with and which jobs are all right to aim for. The lessons hit home within the first few years of a child's life. But that's the way it has been in virtually every society in history. Why now are so many

[8] But nothing about children's toy preferences is engraved in stone or biology. Sarah Sternglanz (personal communication) found that when teachers rewarded young girls and boys for playing with each other (with attention and praise), cross-sex play increased quickly and the toys became unisex. When such play was ignored and same-sex play got the teacher's attention, the boys went back to their trucks and the girls to their kitchens.

people arguing that separate-but-equal treatment of children, as of blacks, is discriminatory and unfair?

One answer is that the messages about the sexes are out of synch with reality, and that both girls and boys should learn about the variety of roles they will be expected to play in their lives—as spouses, parents, employees, students. Nine out of ten girls born today will work for a substantial period of their lives, but most grow up to believe (incorrectly) that marriage will be their permanent, full-time job. Another answer is that the current system of socialization has two negative consequences for women: females grow up thinking that they are not quite as good as males, or maybe that they are not worth very much at all; and they suppress or deflect the motivation to strive and succeed. To many writers, the resulting sex differences in self-esteem and achievement motivation account for the greater prevalence of males in politics, business, science, and art. To be creative you have to be confident; to advance in your field you need some drive and energy. If socialization squelches a girl's ambitions and self-regard as it encourages a boy's, the implications for sex differences in social status and personal happiness are serious.

self-esteem vs. self-dislike

"I never yet knew a tolerable woman to be fond of her own sex," wrote Jonathan Swift, who wasn't terribly fond of either men or women. Indeed, many women throughout history have been willing to proclaim the inferiority of their sex. "I'm glad I'm not a man," confessed Madame de Staël, "for if I were, I'd be obliged to marry a woman." One of the early goals of the women's movement was to banish the longstanding belief that women don't like themselves or each other very much, that a "real woman" prefers to spend her time with men and gets her self-esteem vicariously, through the man she loves. These efforts, like the "black is beautiful" movement, were aimed at least in part at creating a self-fulfilling prophecy—at encouraging women to like their own sex.

Psychologists have tried to find out whether females really have lower self-esteem than males, usually by asking people to rate their own self-regard. The results are not what you might expect. After surveying a slew of self-esteem studies with children and college students (and a few with older adults), Maccoby and Jacklin concluded that females feel no worse about themselves than men do. This conclusion may be premature. Self-esteem is another personality trait that is hard to measure. People do not like to admit dissatisfaction with themselves or their lives; they may insist that they are happy as larks even when they are suffering from psychosomatic disorders brought on by stress and anxiety (see Chapter 7). So we need to consider other evidence.

1. Females envy males more than males envy females. More females than males suspect that the grass is greener on the other side of the fence and say they have fantasized about being a member of the other sex. The belief that males have more fun arises early in life. When Ollison asked her kindergarteners, "If you could, would you rather be a girl [boy]?" twenty-eight of the twenty-nine boys said they would rather fight than switch, but six of the girls were ready to change. Of course, such results don't necessarily mean that females think males are inherently superior; children of both sexes may simply perceive that it's a man's world and want to join. It's possible, though, that envy leads to a belief that males really are more valuable human beings, that a man's destiny matters more than a woman's.

2. Many women hold other women in low esteem and devalue their intellectual competence. It takes time to learn this attitude. When Ollison asked her kindergartners whether boys or girls are smarter, two-thirds of each sex replied that their own sex was smarter. Not one girl conceded that a boy could have the edge on intelligence. But when Ollison asked whether mommies or daddies are smarter, she heard a portent of things to come: over half of the girls replied that daddies were smarter.

By the time they are grown, some females are prejudiced against their sex. Philip Goldberg (1968) asked college women to rate several short articles for persuasive impact, profundity, and overall value, and their authors for writing style, professional competence, and ability to sway the reader. Half of the women got articles purportedly written by men (for example, John T. McKay) and half got the same articles signed by women (for example, Joan T. McKay). The women consistently gave higher marks to articles allegedly written by men. Another study, which asked people to rate a male or female painter, had similar results (Pheterson, Kiesler, and Goldberg 1971). However, some recent variations on the Goldberg study got mixed results. One study (M. B. Morris 1970) found that women gave higher ratings to articles written by *women*. Another (H. Mischel 1974) found that high-school and college students of both sexes tended to rate male authors higher in male-dominated fields, but female authors higher in female-dominated fields. Yet another study found that raters were unaffected by the sex of the author or the topic of the article (Levenson et al. 1975). Apparently antifemale bias is on the wane, has gone underground, or both. Probably people are more sensitive than they once were about openly expressing a low opinion of women (or blacks or Chicanos), but their inner feelings do not always keep pace with public statements. These feelings show up when, for example, they avoid consulting a female (or black or Chicano) doctor or lawyer.

Many psychologists believe that when people disparage the group they belong to they reveal a hatred of themselves. Self-disparagement is not uncommon among minorities, who are exposed to the same cultural images of their groups as the majority is; there are anti-Semitic Jews and white-supremacist blacks. Helen Mayer Hacker (1951), in a classic essay on women as a minority group, observed twenty-five years ago, "Like those minority groups whose self-castigation outdoes dominant group derision of them, women frequently exceed men in the violence of their vituperations of their sex."

3. Females have less self-confidence than males. In several studies, college students have predicted how well they will do at some particular task. Men are consistently more confident than women about their perform-ance, and they are also more satisfied with themselves after completing the job. This is true even when the task is one at which women do just as well as men, such as anagrams (Feather 1968, 1969). Similarly, if you ask stu-dents to estimate their grades for the next term, men usually expect to do at least as well as they have in the past, and perhaps better, while women expect to do worse. In one typical study, female college students predicted lower course grades than males did, despite the fact that actually the women's grades turned out to be slightly higher than the men's (Crandall 1969; see also Deaux 1976).

Of course, it's possible that what we have here is merely a case of feminine modesty and male bravado. But an important line of research suggests a different explanation, based on differences in the way the sexes interpret success. When you do well at something, you can react in various ways. You may believe you did well because you're competent, because you worked very hard, because the task was easy, or because luck was on your side that day. Psychologists find that many people consistently favor one sort of explanation over another. Those who attribute success to their own ability or effort are said to have an *internal locus of control*. Those who attribute success to the ease of the task or the fickle finger of fate are said to have an *external locus of control*. During childhood the sexes do not differ in this regard, but by college age more women than men have an external locus of control (Rotter and Hochreich 1973, cited in Frieze 1975; also Simon and Feather 1973).

Kay Deaux, Leonard White, and Elizabeth Farris (1975) had the imaginative idea of observing what kind of games men and women sought out at a county fair. As they predicted, the women went for games of luck (Bingo), while the men liked games of skill (ring tosses). Intrigued, they set up their own fair in the laboratory and found again that 75 percent of the men chose to play a skill game while 65 percent of the women chose a luck game. Why? Expectancy seems to be the key, the researchers believe. Women thought they would do better in a game of luck and men thought they would succeed more often in a game of skill.[9]

Ability is something you can count on, but luck is not; it's here today, gone tomorrow. If women have learned to attribute their success to luck, that could explain why they feel more insecure than men do about their future performance (Frieze 1975). To make matters worse, some studies (though not all) find that women feel that their lives are externally controlled only when it comes to success. When they fail, they suddenly turn internal, blaming their poor showing on a lack of ability. These women are caught: if they do well, they sacrifice the credit, but if they bomb, they shoulder the blame. Sooner or later a woman in this situation is likely to decide that if at first she doesn't succeed, she might as well forget it.

the achievement motive

The differences between men and women in their evaluation of their abilities suggests another explanation for sex differences in status and power. It is that girls do not acquire the same drive to achieve, to meet a personal standard of excellence, that many boys do. Psychologists usually regard the need to achieve as a stable disposition that a child acquires early in life. Some years ago David McClelland and his colleagues developed the Thematic Apperception Test (TAT) to assess how strong an achievement motive a person has. The TAT is a series of ambiguous pictures, and the person taking the test is asked to make up a story about each one. The stories are scored for themes related to achievement, using a carefully defined scoring system. Suppose a picture showed a middle-aged man talking to a younger man. A person who said that the young man was trying to convince his boss to try a new system to increase the company's productivity would get a higher need-for-achievement score than one who said a father and son were discussing the fun they had on a fishing trip.

Achievement-motivation theory, as originally formulated, said that people with a strong need to achieve would want to do well in situations

[9] Women don't always choose luck explanations. Deaux studied men and women in top management positions and asked them how they got there. Obviously a successful manager can't attribute her or his position to luck. Yet even here women were reluctant to say "I'm really good, that's how." They tended to say hard work and effort were the reasons, while men invoked ability as well as effort (Deaux 1976).

requiring intelligence and leadership (McClelland et al. 1953). If you put them in such a situation and gave them the TAT, the number of achievement fantasies should shoot up. This prediction turned out to be true—for men, but not for women. Indeed, TAT scores were usually related to actual achievement—especially school grades—for men, but not for women. The research with women kept confounding the theory. The response of psychologists was like that of the proverbial man who dropped his wallet in a dark street but searched for it beneath a street light because he could see better there: they stopped studying women. In 1958 an 873-page compilation of the research on achievement and related motives appeared; research on females was confined to a single footnote (Atkinson 1958).

In the sixties, psychologist Matina Horner (1969) turned a searchlight on the dark street men had ignored. She argued that women, unlike men, have a motive to *avoid* success, a fear that achievement will have disastrous consequences. Because women learn that achievement (especially intellectual achievement) is aggressive, and therefore masculine, they worry that they will be less feminine if they compete. Anxiety about this conflict makes women feel defensive if they do achieve and may prevent them from achieving in the first place. Able men do not have this problem because achievement and the masculine role go hand in hand.

To test her theory, Horner asked ninety female undergraduates to tell a story based on the following sentence: "After first-term finals, Anne finds herself at the top of her medical school class." Eighty-eight men responded to the same sentence, but about John. When Horner scored the stories, she found that most of the men (90 percent) were comfortable about John's success and saw a rosy future for him. "John is a conscientious young man who worked hard," wrote one male. "John continues working hard and eventually graduates at the top of his class."

But a majority of the stories written by women (65 percent) contained images that reflected what Horner called a fear of success (FOS). The most common theme was that Anne's academic success would bring her social rejection. She would be unpopular, unmarried, and lonely. Another was that Anne would feel unfeminine. One young woman saw particularly dire consequences for Anne: "Anne starts proclaiming her surprise and joy. Her fellow classmates are so disgusted with her behavior that they jump on her in a body and beat her. She is maimed for life." Some stories solved Anne's "problem" by having her drop out of medical school to marry a successful doctor or to enter a more "feminine" field, such as social work.

Next Horner compared the way students performed on tests when they worked alone or in a competitive group. Men tended to do better when they were competing with others, as did women whose stories about Anne did not show fear of success. Most women who showed high fear of success (77 percent) did better when they worked alone. Horner concluded that a psychological barrier of anxiety blocks achievement for many bright women.

When Horner published her work, a chorus of "Aha's!" went up throughout the land. Researchers thought they now understood why women had been ruining their studies. College women had a reason for their uncertain career plans. Journalists announced that an explanation had been found for women's low status in the world of work: the fault lay not in the stars but in women themselves. They might want to achieve, but they also wanted to be feminine, and the two motives were as incompatible as oil and water.

In the years that followed, dozens of follow-up studies were done all over the country and the world—Yugoslavia, Italy, Norway, the West Indies. The more data that came in, the more it appeared that the matter of women's lack of achievement was not quite solved. Criticisms of Horner's work began to appear (Tresemer 1974; Condry and Dyer 1976; Shaver 1976).

One problem is that men often show as much "fear of success" as women, and sometimes more. David Tresemer reviewed dozens of studies and found a remarkable range of results. In forty-five experiments, the proportion of women who wrote fear-of-success themes varied from 11 percent to 88 percent, with a median of 47 percent. In the twenty-two experiments that included men, the proportion of men who wrote fear-of-success themes varied from 22 percent to 85 percent, with a median of 43 percent—not significantly different from the median for women. In fourteen studies, men showed *more* fear of success than women did. One of these is especially important because it was an exact duplication of Horner's work. The study, by Lois Hoffman (1974), was conducted at the same university, in the same room, at the same time of year, with a similar male experimenter and similar students. Slightly more males than females (77 percent to 65 percent) wrote fear-of-success themes.

So the "motive to avoid success" is not limited to women. But the sexes do seem to regard the perils of achievement differently. Women associate success with social rejection; men question the value of success in the first place. They wonder whether hard work really pays off. In their stories, John may drop out of medical school to write a novel or take a 9-to-5, blue-collar job. Or John may find that his victory is a Pyrrhic one: "He graduates with honors and hates being a doctor. He wonders what it was all for." "It's great for his parents, but he doesn't give a shit" (Hoffman 1974). Anne suffers by becoming unpopular and dateless, but John suffers by dropping dead prematurely (Robbins and Robbins 1973).

New interpretations argue that the stories about Anne and John reflect not deep-seated motives but realistic attitudes—an assessment of the consequences of conforming or not conforming to social convention. In this view, it is not success that women fear but deviation from traditional roles. Studies that ask both sexes to write stories about John and Anne find that men and women recognize that female achievement is unusual, and that it frequently brings down punishment on the head of the achiever. In fact, men are sometimes more disturbed by Anne's number-one status than women are—they write more negative themes about her than women write about either Anne or John. So perhaps women are right to worry about the consequences of doing better than men; if they step too far toward the front of the line, they may arouse the worst in some males.

To avoid the consequences of being number one, women may turn to achievement in "safe" areas such as homemaking, philanthropy, or civic work. Or they may choose to do their work well but not to aim for public recognition or positions of power—the "woman behind the throne" side-step. If this speculation is true, then women's fear-of-success scores should be lower when the cue is less threatening than Anne at the head of her class in medical school. And indeed, fear-of-success imagery does drop if women are given the story line, "After first-term finals, Anne finds herself at the top of her class" (Alper 1974), or if the story states that half of Anne's medical-school classmates are women (Katz 1973).

John Condry and Sharon Dyer (1976) offer a nice analogy to show that fear-of-success themes may reflect an understanding of social realities rather than fear of achievement. Suppose you gave people a description of an interracial couple who had just gotten married and were about to set up housekeeping in rural Georgia. You ask them to write a story about what will happen to this couple. If you took each story that mentioned negative consequences and labeled it "fear of interracial marriage," you would be making a serious mistake. The people who predicted bad things for the couple would not necessarily be afraid or bigoted; they might just know which way the racist wind blows.

The assumption that fear-of-success motives affect a person's actual performance has also been questioned. Some studies support Horner's finding that women with this motive do worse in competition with men than when they work by themselves. Other research finds the opposite pattern. When the motive affects performance, its impact is usually rather small. Tresemer points out that the women in Horner's group who were most likely to show fear of success were honors students. "If the people who show FOS imagery are the ones who get good grades," he says, "just how deeply debilitating is it?" On the other hand, perhaps even more women would be high achievers in school if it were not for fear of success. Also, school achievers do not always achieve after graduating.

Researchers still disagree about whether fear of success has actually kept anyone from succeeding in a career. But even if worry about being different does not actually block achievement, it may cause women to feel ambivalent and guilty about their accomplishments and create considerable personal anguish.[10] When women compete in male-dominated professions, they may rein in their ambitions and play down their achievements. Or they may suffer from psychosomatic ailments due to emotional strain (see Shaver 1976). Their conflict will be especially painful if they have been punished for competing in the past, as by losing a man they loved.

evaluating the learning perspective

Hardly anyone denies that children are raised differently depending on their sex. Socialization takes place in many ways: through inadvertent as well as deliberate rewards and punishments, and through language, media messages, and adult examples. Sometimes the only way to experience the ubiquity of sex-role images in this society is to immerse oneself in another culture. China, for example, shakes up one's expectations. You see a soldier, rifle on back, walking along; you pass him and discover he is a woman carrying not only a gun but a baby. You attend a surgical operation and see two men and two women working on a patient. The women are the doctors; the men, the nurses.

In studying how socialization creates sex differences, however, many researchers have tried to stuff real people into rigid stereotypes, which don't fit flesh-and-blood human beings very well. They lose sight of the fact, as Mischel observes, that "there are many different acceptable ways of being a boy or girl, and even more diverse ways of being a man or woman." The learning perspective itself allows for this range of behavior, but the demands of the laboratory often force researchers to narrow their horizons.

To explore the flexibility of actual sex roles, Sandra Bem developed a measure of *androgyny*—the extent to which a person believes he or she possesses desirable attributes of both sexes. Bem (1975) reports that about half of the students she tested at Stanford University are traditionally femi-

[10] Black college women seem less likely than their white sisters to feel conflict between achievement and femininity, and they get lower fear-of-success scores (Weston and Mednick 1970). There is a problem in this study, though, because only highly motivated members of minority groups tend to go to college.

nine or masculine. Fifteen percent are cross-sex-typed; they score higher on traits associated with the opposite sex than on those associated with their own sex. And 35 percent are androgynous in Bem's terms: they score about the same on masculine and feminine qualities. (To see how androgynous or sex-typed you are, take the test in Table 7.) In a series of experiments, Bem found that androgynous people behave in feminine or masculine ways depending on the situation. They can be nurturant and sympathetic on one occasion, and assertive and independent on another. This flexibility, Bem thinks, enhances their mental health. Sex-typed people are restricted to a narrower range of behavior. A "real man" wouldn't dream of diapering a baby, and a "real woman" wouldn't consider changing a fuse. Today researchers are not as likely as they once were to regard masculinity and femininity as opposite ends of a continuum, and they are exploring more situations in which men and women behave alike rather than differently.

Another issue raised by the learning perspective is the common assumption that basic attitudes, abilities, and traits are set rather firmly in childhood. Just as most psychologists have paid little attention to variation within sex roles, they have also tended to ignore changes in people's behavior and personalities during adulthood. The learning approach does not rule out the possibility of adult changes; social-learning theory, in particular, stresses that as rewards change, so will a person's behavior. But in practice, researchers and laymen often think that adults are not really able to choose freely what path they will follow—their course was established in those "formative years." [11] The conclusion, therefore, is that if you want to teach children to conform, or *not* to conform, you'd better get them young. Thus Sandra and Daryl Bem (1976) write:

> The free will argument [of role choice] proposes that a 21-year-old woman is perfectly free to choose some other role if she cares to do so; no one is standing in her way. But this argument conveniently overlooks the fact that the society which has spent twenty years carefully marking the woman's ballot for her has nothing to lose in that twenty-first year by pretending to let her cast it for the alternative of her choice. Society has controlled not her alternatives, but her motivation to choose any but one of those alternatives (p. 184).

Psychologists are starting to reconsider this belief. Adult experiences matter too, as any adult who has ever changed careers or marriages or returned to school can testify. Take the matter of self-esteem. Overall,

---

[11] An early goal of social-learning theorists was to translate some of Freud's ideas and explain some of his observations in learning-theory terms. Freud's emphasis on early childhood was rarely questioned.

Table 7. How Androgynous Are You?

Instructions: Indicate on a scale of $1-7$ how well each of the following characteristics describes you. A 1 means the item is never or almost never true, and a 7 means that it is always or almost always true.

1. self-reliant	22. analytical	41. warm
2. yielding	23. sympathetic	42. solemn
3. helpful	24. jealous	43. willing to take a stand
4. defends own beliefs	25. has leadership abilities	44. tender
5. cheerful	26. sensitive to the needs	45. friendly
6. moody	of others	46. aggressive
7. independent	27. truthful	47. gullible
8. shy	28. willing to take risks	48. inefficient
9. conscientious	29. understanding	49. acts as a leader
10. athletic	30. secretive	50. childlike
11. affectionate	31. makes decisions easily	51. adaptable
12. theatrical	32. compassionate	52. individualistic
13. assertive	33. sincere	53. does not use harsh
14. flatterable	34. self-sufficient	language
15. happy	35. eager to soothe hurt	54. unsystematic
16. strong personality	feelings	55. competitive
17. loyal	36. conceited	56. loves children
18. unpredictable	37. dominant	57. tactful
19. forceful	38. soft spoken	58. ambitious
20. feminine	39. likable	59. gentle
21. reliable	40. masculine	60. conventional

Scoring: a) Add up your ratings for items 2, 5, 8, 11, 14, 17, 20, 23, 26, 29, 32, 35, 38, 41, 44, 47, 50, 53, 56, and 59, and divide the sum by twenty. This is your Femininity Score.

b) Add up your ratings for items 1, 4, 7, 10, 13, 16, 19, 22, 25, 28, 31, 34, 37, 40, 43, 46, 49, 52, 55, and 58, and divide the sum by twenty. This is your Masculinity Score.

c) Subtract your Masculinity Score from your Feminity Score, and multiply the result by 2.322. (This approximates the score derived by more complicated statistical procedures.) If the result is greater than 2.025, you are sex-typed in the feminine direction. If it is smaller than -2.025, you are sex-typed in the masculine direction. Bem considers a score between 1 and 2.025 to be "near feminine" and a score between -2.025 and -1 to be "near masculine." A score between -1 and 1 means you are not sex-typed in either direction; you are androgynous.

AFTER Bem 1974.

women probably have lower self-esteem than men. But self-esteem, like any other personality trait, can change with time and place. Paul Mussen (1962) found this shift in a study of adolescent boys. Those who had highly masculine job interests liked themselves better, had more self-confidence, and were better "adjusted" according to psychological tests than boys who had less traditional, more feminine interests. Observers rated the masculine teenagers as more carefree, contented, and relaxed. This makes sense: boys who buck their peers in adolescence risk some bad times and heavy social pressure. But because Mussen's data came from a longitudinal study, he was able to take the rare step of seeing what happened to the boys when they reached their late thirties. He found that the boys who had been very masculine as teenagers now were *less* self-confident and self-accepting than the "feminine" boys.

Parents do shape their children's behavior and attitudes, of course, but adult role models can mitigate or even reverse the effects of childhood models. Elizabeth Tidball (1973) found that the number of faculty women at a college is an excellent predictor of how many career women the school will produce. Ironically, in this heyday of efforts to integrate schools, women's colleges produce more ambitious, less traditional graduates.

The learning perspective explains women's second-class status by pointing to the different personality traits that men and women acquire as they grow up. It acknowledges but does not emphasize the influence of social norms and institutions on people. To the question, "Why do most women hold low-ranking jobs?" this perspective answers, "Because women have acquired certain traits—fear of success, dependence, sociability, noncompetitiveness—that limit their aspirations and their abilities." Sociologist Jessie Bernard (1975) summarizes the views of feminist critics who observe that defenders of the status quo can say, "Sorry, girls, too bad you haven't got what it takes; you're afraid of success and all that. I know it isn't your fault; I know it's the way you were socialized as a child; you'd be just as superior as I am if you had played with trucks instead of dolls. But what can I do about it, after all?"

Today the cradle-to-grave approach to human development is becoming increasingly popular. There may be no point at which we can say of a person, "She lived happily (or miserably) ever after." And some critics of the learning approach point out that whatever their childhood experiences, people grow up to face a world that assigns different (and discriminatory) roles to women and men. According to them, personality differences do not wholly explain status differences. One must also understand the social roles that adults are expected to play and the value society places on those roles. Parents and the media do not get their ideas about how boys and girls should behave from thin air. Where do these ideas come from? Many writers, Jessie Bernard notes, feel that "emphasis on socialization merely offers an easy out; it does not open doors." A thousand more studies on the development of personality differences will not give us the whole answer to the lesser status of women. We need rather to attack "the institutional structure which embalms these differences in the form of discrimination against women. The name of the game is power."

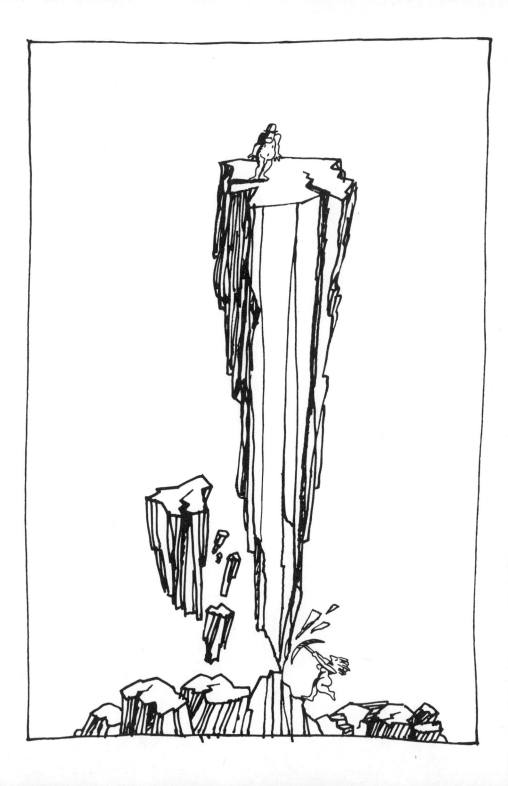

7

Earning the bread vs. baking it:
The sociological perspective

Michael and Marian have been going together for two years, and both of them agree that he is the dominant one. He generally decides where they will go and what they will do, and when they disagree on something Mike usually persuades Marian that he is right with an onslaught of reason and rhetoric. But Marian is not a doormat, she'll tell you. "If there's something I really want," she confides privately, "I can get it by pouting or sulking for a few days. And I can get the world from him if I cry. He can't stand it when I cry."

John and Martha are both department managers in a large corporation, but they are as different in style as Laurel and Hardy. The people who work for John say he is fair-minded and friendly, helps his subordinates, and sees to it that work gets done. The people who work for Martha can't say the same, though. They complain that she is petty, picky about trivial rules, and petulant if things aren't done just her way. "Bitchy—a typical woman boss," one of her employees remarks. "I'll never work for one again."

Most people would explain Marian and Martha's actions by saying that women learn to get their way through indirect manipulation, so if they have to take a leadership role they don't know how to exercise power effectively. It is easiest to explain sex differences in the use of power and influence in personality terms: a person behaves in a particular way because of some internal, stable set of traits that he or she possesses. This chapter, however, shows how external forces—the people around us, the roles we play, the work we do, the situations we are in, the rules we unconsciously follow—shape and direct behavior. The most extreme form of this view, held by some social scientists, says there is no such thing as personality, that we are all totally malleable in the face of social pressure and the organizations we belong to.

Behavioral psychologists, such as learning theorists, also study how the rewards and punishments a situation provides can create behavior, but their focus is still on the individual. Sociologists focus on the circumstances that surround the individual. The difference between the two views is a matter of emphasis. Just as most people realize that nature *and* nurture contribute to human behavior, but biologists emphasize one side and psychologists study the other, most realize that personality *and* social roles influence what people do and become. But psychologists study the person and sociologists study social roles. In this psychological age people are used to thinking in terms of intrapsychic drives and motives, and psychological explanations are more popular than social ones. But now we'll ask you to suspend the familiar ways of explaining sex differences, and to regard their origin from an entirely different perspective.

Social pressure is like a cobweb—strong but hard to see. Not long ago, psychologist Stanley Milgram asked the city-wise New York students in his graduate seminar to do a simple little experiment. "Pick out someone on a crowded subway," he said, "and ask him to give you his seat." "Are you crazy?" said the students. "A person could get killed doing that." One brave volunteer finally agreed to approach twenty people at random and see what happened. Rumors soon began circulating through the psychology department: "They're getting up! They're getting up!" The student reported back to the class that half of the people he asked for a seat automatically got up and gave it to him, with no excuses offered or demanded. But most surprising to the student, the simple little request had proved extraordinarily difficult, and he couldn't finish the assignment of twenty people. So Milgram decided to try it himself. He barely succeeded. "The words seemed lodged in my trachea and would simply not emerge," he reports. "I stood there frozen." When he finally got up the nerve to ask a man for his seat—and got it—he collapsed in a fit of nervous tension.

Milgram's experiment, though it may seem trivial, points out a powerful fact about human behavior. Our actions are governed by a network of rules that operate whether we are aware of them or not. Often the rules become apparent only when we try to break them. "We are all fragile creatures entwined in a cobweb of social constraints," says Milgram. "If you think it is easy to violate [them], get onto a bus and sing out loud. Full-throated song, now, no humming. Many people will say it is *easy* to carry out this act, but not one in a hundred will be able to do it" (Milgram 1974).

The sociological view relies less on how people explain their own attitudes and behavior than on outside influences on their attitudes and behavior. For example, suppose you think of yourself as an assertive person who stands up for your beliefs. Now suppose you are called upon to defend a conviction of yours in the following groups: six women who agree with you; six women who disagree with you; six men who agree with you but don't like you very much; three women and three men with mixed opinions; and six men who oppose you. Would you feel as comfortable in all situations? Would you argue the same way? Change your convictions to go along with the majority? Chances are that your opinion of yourself might not change as you performed this exercise, but your behavior would (Ruble and Higgins 1976).

In this chapter we will look at some ways that two major institutions—work and marriage—affect and create differences between women and men. The sociological perspective argues that the roles people play in this society as spouse and worker perpetuate sexual inequality. Since inequality is built into the system, it says, equality can come only when institutions, organizations, and roles change, not just personal attitudes.

work: opportunity, power, and tokenism

If you were to go out and interview a random sample of American workers, you would probably find that some stereotyped beliefs about female employees would be supported. More men than women would be achievement-oriented, wanting promotions and raises; more women than men would be family- and friend-oriented, putting social life before job responsibilities. Joan Crowley, Teresa Levitin, and Robert Quinn (1973) did such a study and found, for example, that 64 percent of the men but only 48 percent of the women said they wanted to be promoted. Women were more likely than men, though not by much, to say that having friendly coworkers was very important (68 percent to 61 percent), and to attach importance to good hours, pleasant surroundings, and convenient commuting arrangements.

Employers sometimes use such information to explain why they don't promote women: the women are happy where they are. But Rosabeth Kanter, a sociologist, has marshalled persuasive evidence that three aspects of organizational structure—not personal preferences—account for the apparent differences between men and women at work: opportunity, power, and tokenism.

opportunity

In one large corporation that Kanter studied, she asked 111 employees how they felt about promotion. She got the same replies that Crowley et al. did: the men were more eager to move up in the hierarchy than the women and much more certain of the ability to succeed. The women didn't want promotions, they said, if their new responsibilities might interfere with family matters.

But Kanter (and Crowley et al.) also observed that men and women have dramatically different *opportunities* for promotion. In the company Kanter studied, men made up only a small proportion of the white-collar workers. Most men were trained professionals in positions that led up the steps to management. Most women, in contrast, held dead-end jobs as secretaries or clerks; the best job they could aspire to was executive secretary. When Kanter looked to see what the few women in high-ranking jobs (such as sales) thought about promotion, their achievement ambitions were no different from the men's. "Ambition, self-esteem, and career commitment were all flourishing among women in sales jobs, which are well paid and on the way to top management," Kanter (1976a) reported. Similarly, Crowley and her colleagues found that the *desire* for promotion among American workers is largely a matter of their *expectation* of promotion. Women want promotions as much as men do, when they think they have a realistic chance of advancing.

Achievement ambitions, it seems, are directly related to one's chances of achieving, and for women, the chances are low. Crowley et al. found that two-thirds of all American working women never expected to be promoted. "We would guess that to avoid frustration," the researchers noted mildly, "women, like men in the same situation, scale down their ambitions." Kanter reviewed some early research on work motivation in men. She found that when men's opportunities for advancement are blocked they behave like the stereotypic female. They play down the importance of their jobs, fantasize about leaving, emphasize family life over careers, and claim little interest in higher-status work. Male auto workers, meat packers, and factory workers have the same attitudes toward achievement and work as female secretaries and typists do.

Kanter also observes that the kind of job a person has determines what he or she enjoys about working. People whose work is exciting, challenging, and flexible will concentrate on it, putting in as many hours as they need to with a minimum of grumbling. If they are in an advancement hierarchy— with goals of becoming head of the department, dean of the college, manager of the business—they will do what it takes to get there. On the other hand, people whose work is repetitive and boring will be less involved with the work itself. They get more pleasure from other aspects of the job, such as working conditions, companions, opportunities for socializing. When work is dull, friends can liven it up. The result says Kanter, is that women seem more "talk-oriented" than "task-oriented" on the job and seem to care more about external conditions than about the intrinsic demands of the assignment. People sometimes use the stereotype of the gossipy female coffee klatsch to "prove" that women are more interested in people than in work and to explain why they don't achieve what men do. But talk or task orientations probably reflect the characteristics of the job more clearly than the personality of the woman or man who holds it.

Highly mobile jobs require that a person subordinate friendships with coworkers to work demands. "The competitive corporate world requires its participants to be willing to relocate, to surpass rivals without hesitation, to use other people to advance in status," Kanter writes. "The aggressive, striving junior executive is as much a creation of his place in the organization hierarchy as is the talkative, unambitious secretary."

A laboratory study reported by Kanter showed directly how the opportunity for advancement affects people's behavior in a group. Arthur Cohen set up some work groups of young men: the participants in half of the groups had good chances for promotion, while those in the other half had no such chances. Although members of each group had the same job to do and the same supervisors, their reactions and attitudes differed. The high-opportunity groups became much more involved with their task. "They dropped irrelevant chatter, and reported later that they cared more about the high-power people who were supervising them than about each other," Kanter says. "The nonmobile group members, by contrast, concentrated on each other. They virtually ignored the powerful supervisors, because they had nothing to gain from them anyway. They were more openly critical and resentful of people with power."

People do not make conscious decisions to emphasize or de-emphasize their work or coworkers. They don't say, "Gee, I guess this job is a dead end, so I might as well chum up with Diane," or "No sense bothering to make friends with these branch-office hicks, since I won't need them when I'm moved to New York." People tend to feel that the decision to make friends with Diane or to avoid people in the office is a matter of personal choice that has nothing to do with the job. But such "personal choices" are part of a vicious circle. People in dead-end jobs, whether male or female, lower their aspirations to accord with reality. Employers note that the workers don't have the attitudes or the ambition to warrant promotion and dismiss them from consideration, thus confirming the employees' impression that their jobs lead nowhere.

But perhaps, you say, women in high-achievement jobs got there because of personality factors: perhaps attitudes create opportunities, not the other way around. Perhaps men in low-achievement jobs behave like women because they don't have what it takes to get ahead. Most researchers in psychology have implicitly endorsed this view, for example by looking for personality traits that suit a person for a particular job rather than at how a particular job affects personality. In personnel testing, psychologists commonly give a battery of personality tests to applicants so that they can identify the "best" person for a position. Many developmental psychologists have tried to find out what personality characteristics acquired in childhood cause people to choose the occupations they do—or, as in the case of fear-of-success research, cause them to avoid competitive jobs.

Melvin Kohn and Carmi Schooler (1973) are doing a long-term study of the reverse hypothesis to find out how jobs affect personality. They have studied a random sample of 3,101 American men to see how certain structural aspects of their jobs (complexity, pace, pressures, fringe benefits, routinization) affect such individual characteristics as job commitment and satisfaction, anxiety, self-esteem, intellectual flexibility, and moral standards. Using complex statistics to tease out cause from effect, they found in all cases that "job affects man more than man affects job." The complexity of the job was especially important: it affected all facets of the men's psychological functioning and was directly related to their self-esteem. The reason high job-complexity makes for high self-esteem, the researchers say, is that a man's job "confronts him with demands he must try to meet." The average woman has less chance to rise to the occasion than the average man, since her work is less complex than his.

Other sociologists have also found that roles change attitudes more often than attitudes create roles. Twenty-five years ago, Seymour Lieberman did a field study in a factory, assessing changes in workers' attitudes when some of them became foremen and others became union leaders. The workers filled out a questionnaire about their views on labor and management; fifteen months later, they took the questionnaire again. The workers who had become foremen were now much more favorably inclined toward management and more critical of the union than they had been, while the new union leaders were more critical of management. Still later, some of the foremen became workers again—and their attitudes changed back to pro-union (Lieberman 1965). Most people who become managers start to think and behave like managers, not like workers in managerial disguise, even if they try hard to remember their humble origins. When a wolf wears sheep's clothing, in other words, it becomes a sheep.

power

Power is a hard thing to define to everyone's satisfaction. Sometimes it is used to mean influence, or the ability to get people to do what you want. Sometimes it means authority, or the legitimate right to issue orders and see that they are obeyed. The two meanings are not the same, because one person might hold a high office but lack the ability to influence others, while another might have considerable influence without being in an official position of power.

Many commentators on the sexual scene observe, with varying degrees of seriousness, that women have plenty of influence but not much authority. Women, they say, are the power behind the throne, the stage managers who make it all happen and then retreat to the wings, leaving the men to take the curtain calls. According to this line of reasoning, female power is based on womanly wiles and seductive persuasion. Tears are as effective as threats, and sexuality as powerful as strength. Since the ladies get exactly what they want, why make things even more unfair by giving them legitimate authority too? Didn't Helen of Troy have power? Carmen? Lady Macbeth?

Many people of both sexes are uncomfortable with the idea of a woman boss. In 1965 a survey of 2,000 executives showed that two-thirds of the men and one-fifth of the women said they would not want to work for a woman. In 1976 attitudes had not changed much. A Gallup poll found that most Americans still held negative views of women bosses.[1] Kanter reviewed the research on sex differences in leadership and found little consistent evidence. Another sociologist, Barbara Bunker (1976), also reviewed numerous studies comparing male and female leaders and reports that the myth of the mean female boss doesn't hold up. Field studies of leaders in real-world organizations show few sex differences, and subordinates and peers evaluate leaders of both sexes equally. In experimental situations, too, people are equally satisfied with male and female leaders. Workers of both sexes want a boss who is competent, dominant, and directive. If he or she is also a "nice guy," so much the better.

If men and women don't differ as much as people assume, why the assumption? One reason may be that female bosses are still rare enough to stand out. When people have a female employer they don't like, it is easiest to explain the feeling by reference to sex. But no one can dismiss a bad male boss with "he's only a man—what d'you expect?"

Kanter adds another explanation. She concludes that a manager's style of leadership depends more on whether he or she has real power than on whether he or she has a specific personality trait. "Real power" means that the organization has given the person the authority to make decisions, institute them, and hand out important rewards and punishments (promotions,

[1] Oddly enough, people find it easier to accept the idea of a woman president, perhaps because that possibility is so remote. The proportion of people who say they could vote for a female president has steadily risen, from 31 percent in 1937 to 73 percent in 1976.

raises, transfers, dismissals). Power comes not just from job title or a fancy office but from membership in the informal inner circles of the company and from recognition by coworkers. Kanter believes that a boss's style reflects his or her power. "Powerless leaders, men and women alike," she says, "often become punitive, petty tyrants . . . Blocked from exercising power in the wider hierarchy, they substitute the satisfaction of lording it over subordinates. Unable to move ahead, they hold everyone back." Bosses who have real authority tend to be more flexible about rules, to share information with employees, and to try to help able ones move on to better jobs.

Women are usually excluded from the informal power networks, the "old boys" circle by which company leaders bring their protégés into positions of power. The protégé system has made it difficult for women to succeed in business without really trying—unless they have a sponsor or a father in the ruling family. In a report on the ten highest-ranking women in big business in 1973, *Fortune* magazine observed that eight of the ten made it to the top because of family connections, marriage, or the fact that they helped create the organizations they now preside over (Robertson 1973). They did not start out in jobs with limited futures, nor did they have to work their way through a corporate hierarchy that discriminated against them. Cynthia Fuchs Epstein (1970) also talks about the difficulties women have getting a high-ranking sponsor to help them make it to the top in the academic world.

Because women are so rarely in visible positions of power, many people assume that women behave as they do because of their sex rather than because of their status. In truth, women who truly have authority behave as well or as badly as men, and men whose authority is uncertain or absent behave as well or as badly as women in similar spots. Kanter cites a study of Air Force officers which showed that men who had low status and little chance for promotion were more inflexible and authoritarian than officers of the same formal rank who had more power.

Sociologists believe that women use indirect methods of influence because they are barred from using direct ones, not because they are "naturally" manipulative and seductive. Any social group that does not have access to legitimized power develops indirect ways to influence the dominant group. Many writers have compared blacks and women in this regard; historically, both have had to rely on wiles and guile to get around the whims of the master, the white man (Hacker 1951; Myrdal 1944).

To see whether the sexes truly differ in their strategies of influence, and with what personal consequences, Paula Johnson and Jacqueline Goodchilds (1976) did an ingeniously simple study. They asked over 250 males and females to write a paragraph with the title: "How I Get My Way." The women were more likely than the men, 45 percent to 27 percent, to answer that they deliberately display some emotion. "I get my way by getting angry. If that doesn't work, I cry," wrote one young woman. "I pout, frown, and say something to make the other person feel bad, such as 'you don't love me,'" said another. "I'm not the type to come right out with what I want," said a third. "I will usually hint around. It's all hope, and a lot of beating around the bush."

The men tended to be more direct and unemotional, or so they said. "First I think out completely what I want and formulate a detailed plan of action that will cover all angles. I find out all the necessary information . . . and then present a master plan of what I intend to do." Of the men who got their way through emotional outbursts, half expressed anger and the rest played martyr by sulking or acting sad. Of the women who mentioned emotional strategies, 20 percent used anger, 40 percent used sulking, and 40 percent used tears. Overall, men generally said they get their way by reasoned argument. Women were more likely to say they bargain, deceive the partner, or become emotional.

Next Johnson (1976) set up an experiment to see what kinds of power strategies the sexes actually used. She asked each of 144 students to work at a computer console with a TV screen. The person believed that he or she was supervising a group of unseen partners, all linked by the console, and that the task was to sort IBM cards into a visual pattern in supposed competition with another group. Each supervisor communicated with the rest of his or her "team" by choosing one of six cards with a message, and each message represented a different kind of power tactic. Three times as many men as women chose a message based on expertise or authority: "Please sort faster; I know it's possible to go faster because I've worked on this sort of thing before and you really can go fast." Or "As your supervisor, I'd like to ask you to sort faster, please." But four times as many women as men resorted to messages based on helplessness: "Help; please sort faster; I'm really counting on you."

"Female" strategies, it turned out, were less effective than "male" strategies, and worse for the self-esteem of those who used them. Students of both sexes who used helpless, li'l-ole-me messages had lower self-esteem at the end of the experiment than students whose messages were direct and based on competence. Capitalizing on weakness, Johnson concludes, may be effective in the short run, but it does not bring the long-term effectiveness and self-regard that come from being viewed as a powerful person or group.

Neither sex regards the traditional feminine strategies of weakness and ingratiation as particularly admirable, either. Toni Falbo observed groups of students working together, and found that they rated the stereotypically feminine members negatively—least likable, least honest, least able to express themselves. Further, using Bem's androgyny measure (see page 198), Falbo found that only the most traditionally feminine women—and the men who scored "feminine" on Bem's scale—said they got their way through subtlety ("I hint around") or ingratiation ("I try to look sympathetic"). The androgynous and "masculine" students of both sexes, in contrast, claimed to be more direct in their appeals ("I become blunt and outspoken") (reported in Johnson and Goodchilds 1976).

the trouble with tokens

What situations tend to foster stereotypic feminine strategies? Rosabeth Kanter (1975) would answer that the single organizational factor surest to provoke stereotyped behavior is tokenism. Women in management are often isolated from each other, working as the sole female in groups of men. All individuals who have token status, Kanter believes—whether a female scientist or a male nurse or a black executive—share certain experiences. A token is always in the limelight: everyone notices her or him, and everything the token does is scrutinized. Coworkers tend to concentrate on qualities that make the token unique rather than on those the token shares with the rest of the group.

Kanter (1976a) reports a study by Shelley Taylor and Susan Fiske that showed how the heightened visibility of a token black man affected a group's perceptions of him. Their students listened to a tape of a group discussion and saw pictures that presumably were of the participants; then they described their impressions of each member. The photos showed either one black man in an all-white group or a group that was evenly mixed, black and white. The observers' opinions of the black man changed, even though the taped discussion (hence the man's objective participation) did not. Basically, the students paid too much attention to the black man in the white group. They thought his contribution was disproportionately large, and they stereotyped his personality traits. When they evaluated the mixed groups, they were as likely to recall information about whites as about blacks, and they rated their personalities equally.

A group not only *sees* a token in a stereotyped way; it also pressures the token to *behave* in a stereotyped way. Kanter (1976b) has identified a few traditional roles that a token woman can adopt if she wants to win acceptance by the group. She can play the *mother*, who is sympathetic and comforts the men, who bakes cookies for the department or office, who sews on buttons; or the *sex object*, the seductress, who provokes men to compete for her and woo her; or the *pet* or kid sister, who plays cheerleader to male ideas and adds humor without threat. If a woman does not take on one of these three roles (all of which deflect issues of professional ability and competition) Kanter observes that she will be regarded with suspicion, even hostility. She may be viewed as an *iron maiden* who insists on her rights and her competence. The iron maiden may be asked, "You're not one of those women's libbers, are you?" Regardless of her answer, men are inclined to regard her as a hard-hearted militant.

Carol Wolman and Hal Frank (1975) have examined the token's predicament in more detail. They observed and recorded the behavior of six working groups, ranging in size from nine to thirteen members, each of which had only one female participant. Three of the groups consisted of graduate students taking a course in T-groups (group processes and dynamics) and met for thirty hours each; three groups consisted of first-year students in psychiatry and met for six months. All these people were psychologically oriented and might have been expected to be perceptive about behavior. But in four of the six groups the woman was treated as an outcast, a deviant, no matter how hard she tried to win acceptance from the group. One woman isolated herself by choice. One was eventually accepted, but with low status and only after she had presented herself to the men as naive, less competent than they, and frightened. (In time she proved to be extremely competent and her status rose.) Some of the strategies the women tried reflect Kanter's four types:

> [Betty] fought for regular membership by rationally pointing out that she didn't fit the "little sister" stereotype the group had imposed on her. This earned her a "women's lib" label. . . . She was treated as a deviant for the duration of the group, and felt frustrated and unhappy.

> [Cora] presented herself as assertive, rational, and self-assured. The men provoked her into becoming emotional, and then defined her as deviant for being naive, bitchy, and overemotional. She felt that at times they ignored her, and at times they competed to control her as a way of establishing and maintaining their "pecking order."

Wolman and Frank observed that whatever the woman did to gain acceptance, the men countered by reinterpreting her efforts.

> If she acted friendly she was thought to be flirting. If she acted weak, the men tried to infantilize her, treating her as a "little sister" rather than a peer. If she apologized for alienating the group, she was seen as a submissive young woman knowing her place. If she asked for help, she earned a "needy female" label. If she became angry, or tried to point out rationally what the group process was doing to her, she was seen as competitive, in a bitchy unfeminine way. "Feminine" coping mechanisms increased her perceived differences; "masculine" ones threatened the men so that they isolated her more.

In short, the token women faced a damned-if-you're-feminine, damned-if-you're-masculine dilemma.[2]

The token woman in such a situation reacts (understandably) with depression, frustration, or anger. She tends to feel there's something the matter with her that has brought on the group's wrath or disdain. The men see things the same way. Few recognize that it is the structure of the group itself that creates the supposed failure of personality. This point becomes clearer if the participants but not the group structure are changed. Kanter (1976a) reports a study of male nurses in which men were the tokens in a female working world. The men were treated much like Wolman and Frank's lone females: they felt isolated and not quite accepted, and they often sensed disguised hostility and distrust from the group.

All tokens face the same predicament: how to lose their exaggerated visibility and win the group's acceptance. Some play the stereotype expected of them; Everett Hughes (1958) found that token blacks among white workers often become the group comedian. Others try to hide themselves and their accomplishments: many female executives describe efforts to minimize their female attributes and fade unobtrusively into the background (Hennig and Jardim 1977). One way to reduce conflict with male peers is to let a man take credit for one's accomplishments. Kanter (1976b) reports interviews in which some women "even expressed pride that they could influence a group of men without the men recognizing the origin of the idea, or they rejoiced in the secret knowledge that they were responsible for their boss's success."

Another kind of accommodation a lone woman sometimes makes to win acceptance is available to the rare woman who makes it to the top of a male-dominated profession. Such a woman can become a Queen Bee who has no use for other women. "If I made it, why can't they?" is her attitude. The women's movement, wrote the writer Helen Lawrenson, is a phony movement based on a phony issue. "Demands for equal political and legal rights, for childcare centers and equal pay for equal work are reasonable enough. . . . But what they are [really] demanding is the absolute subjugation of men. These are not normal women. I think they are freaks" (in Staines, Tavris, and Jayaratne 1974).

Queen Bees have strongly individualistic attitudes and tend to be anti-

[2] The experiences of the solo women in Wolman and Frank's study lend some credence to the idea that the women studied by Matina Horner and others (see Chapter 6) don't so much fear success as fear social rejection. If Anne is the only woman in her medical school class and gets the highest grades, she may have all the problems these female students had, times ten.

woman; their counterpart in the black civil-rights movement is the Uncle Tom. Graham Staines and his colleagues suggest several structural forces that help create the Queen Bee's personality and opinions:

1. *Cooptation.* The token woman, like any other token, faces considerable pressure from the majority group to take sides, to show loyalty to the majority, and to oppose other minorities. If the token keeps arguing, for example, that more blacks or women or Jews should be admitted, members of the dominant group may find their tolerance stretched. They can admit a token or two without shaking the system, but that's all they aim to do.

2. *Rewards for being special.* The token gets ample praise and attention for not rocking the boat. Queen Bees feel special: they are highly praised for "being so feminine" yet "thinking like a man." Wolman and Frank's study illustrates the tremendously frustrating double-bind the token is in. If the men decide that she is a remarkable exception to her sex, worthy of their friendship and acceptance, what relief and pleasure she must feel! How can she risk all her gains by reminding them, "Er, fellas, a lot of other women would like to work here . . ."

3. *Excluding the competition.* The Queen Bee doesn't want competition any more than the men do. Most tokens have worked very hard to be admitted to their groups, and they don't see why it should be easier for others. It can be fun to be the one-in-a-million woman at the top. Why let in everyone else and become just one of the crowd?

The structural forces that support stereotypes—blocked opportunities, powerlessness, and tokenism—affect not only women but members of any minority group who try to break into the majority system. This is why affirmative action programs are designed to change organizational conditions rather than people's attitudes or motivations—the assumption is that attitudes follow opportunity. For example, Kanter interviewed a woman who had been a secretary in a large corporation for twenty-five years:

> Five years ago, she would have said that she never wanted to be anything but a secretary. She also would have told you that . . . she was thinking of quitting. She said secretarial work was not a good enough reason to leave the children.
>
> Then came an affirmative action program, and Linda was offered a promotion. She wavered. It would mean leaving her good female friends for a lonely life among male managers. Her friends thought she was abandoning them. She worried whether she could handle the job. But her boss talked her into it and promised to help, reassuring her that he would be her sponsor.
>
> So Linda was promoted, and now she handles a challenging management job most successfully. Seeing friends is the least of her many reasons to come to work every day, and her ambitions have soared. She wants to go right to the top.

"I have fifteen years left to work," she says. "And I want to move up six grades—to corporate vice president, at least!" (Kanter 1976a, p. 91)

the changing face of the work force

People who believe that "woman's place is in the home" had better keep their heads in the sand if they want to avoid confronting the truth. In 1953, only 26 percent of all married women held jobs, and a woman with small children was likely to feel guilty if she wanted to work. Two decades later, in 1973, 42 percent of all wives were working, and a third of all mothers with preschool children (see Table 8). There are at least three reasons for the steady increase in numbers of working women:

1. *Economic conditions.* The old stereotype held that women work for pin money—extra frills and luxuries, rather than the family's meat-and-potatoes needs—or to mark time until they marry. This stereotype justified paying women less than men for the same work. "Husbands, the breadwinners, need the money more," employers could say; or "Why should I promote her? She'll just get married and quit." In fact, most women work for the same reasons men do—they need the money and they want the satisfaction (Crowley, Levitin, and Quinn 1973). In 1973 almost two-thirds of all American working women were either heads of households (single, widowed, or divorced) or married to men whose incomes were below the poverty line.

2. *Education.* More women are getting college educations and post-graduate training than ever before. Between 1970 and 1974, the number of women in college increased by 30 percent, compared to a 12 percent increase among men. The proportion of women in graduate school, which had been declining steadily since its peak in the 1930s, began to rise again. Women accounted for only 4 percent of the students in law schools in 1960, but by 1972 they were 12 percent and they reached 19 percent in 1974. (At

Table 8. Percentages of Married Women Holding Jobs, 1960–73

Year	All wives	Wives without children	Wives with children under 6	Wives with children 6–17
1960	30.5%	34.7%	18.6%	39.0%
1963	33.7	37.4	22.5	41.5
1968	38.3	40.1	27.6	46.9
1973	42.2	42.8	32.7	50.1

SOURCE: U.S. Department of Labor 1974.

western University's law school that year, half of the entering class was
]). In medical schools, women went from 6 percent of the total in
to 13 percent in 1972 to 18 percent in 1974 (Van Dusen and Sheldon
U.S. Department of Labor 1974).

3. *Declining family size.* Women are having fewer children. The birth rate
fell during the 1920s and the Depression years of the 1930s, hitting a pre–
World War II low in 1933 of 18.4 births per thousand of population. After
the war, women left the factories and businesses and went home to have
babies—lots of them. The *average* wife in the 1950s had four children, and
the rate held level at about twenty-five births per thousand people through
the 1950s. After 1960, however, the birth rate went into a sharp and steady
decline.[3]

In 1974 the birth rate hit an all-time low for this century, 14.8 births per
thousand, which meant that the United States had reached Zero Population
Growth: an average of 1.9 children per family (Van Dusen and Sheldon 1976;
Glick 1975). The proportion of women under thirty who say they do not
intend to have children has been rising each year. According to one 1974
estimate, 27 percent of wives aged twenty-five to twenty-nine did not expect
to have any children.

It might seem that soon women will not have to worry about tokenism
and powerlessness; with all that education and fewer children, they ought to
be able to get better jobs and more opportunities. Unfortunately, seeming
isn't so. Job segregation, in which the large majority of each sex clusters into
"women's work" and "men's work," continues. Although more women are
going into the professions, most doctors and lawyers are still men and most
women still remain in female-dominated, low-paying occupations. One statis-
tician argues that the small apparent decrease in overall job segregation
comes not from more women in men's jobs but from the reverse: more men
are entering traditionally female jobs as a result of the recent recession.
Another analyst notes that overall segregation could seem to be diminishing
simply because a few occupations are growing at fast rates. Indeed, between
1960 and 1970 the fields that became less sex-segregated were those that
were growing most rapidly, such as college and secondary school teaching,
computer work, and health technology (Van Dusen and Sheldon 1976). It

[3] The development of the birth control pill and worries about world overpopulation may
have caused the decline in birth rate, and then again they may not. Birth control made family
planning easier, to be sure, but it is also possible that families made the decision to have fewer
children for other reasons—the troubled economy, notably. It is important not to jump to
conclusions about cause and effect here, because if the economy improves and people can
afford more children, or if it worsens and women lose their jobs, we may see a return of the
1950s ideology and family size.

is too soon to tell what impact affirmative action programs will have; so far the evidence is that there has been more affirmative talk than action. Although more women are becoming pilots, carpenters, and plumbers, they are still a drop in the bucket and most occupations remain heavily sex-segregated.

Valerie Oppenheimer (1970, 1975) argues that the labor market in the United States is actually two markets, male and female, so that the sexes rarely compete for the same jobs. Sex segregation of jobs is not just a matter of women "wanting" poorly paid service jobs (such as waitress or nurse's aide). They are the only jobs women can get. The job market opened to women in the midfifties because the country needed not just more workers but specifically *female* workers. Women, says Oppenheimer, rarely *displaced* men, for example as teachers and typists; they merely *replaced* men when men got opportunities to move ahead. Women offered special qualities: they were cheap to hire, they were available, they were educated. Industrial society needs a pool of cheap but educated labor, and this need has kept women in low-paying, well-schooled jobs such as elementary school teaching and clerical work. "To substitute men," notes Oppenheimer, "would require either a rise in the price for labor or a decline in the quality of labor."

In times of crisis, such as the Civil War and World War II, women have gone to work when they were needed. In times of recession they are, like blacks, last hired and first fired. In spite of the women's movement and awareness about discrimination in salary in recent years, the income gap between the sexes has not narrowed. A 1975 government report found that nearly two-thirds of all full-time female workers earned *less* than $7,000 in 1972, while over three-fourths of all full-time male workers earned *more* than $7,000. The gap remains even when male and female workers are matched for skill, education, tenure on the job, and so on (Suter and Miller 1973; Levitin, Quinn, and Staines 1973).

Working women lose even more money once they marry. Two sociologists, Donald Treiman and Kermit Terrell (1975), analyzed representative samples of American women, aged thirty to forty-four, their husbands, and other men the same age. They found that women who had never married earned far more than women who had (or did have) husbands. To be sure, single women were also better educated, had higher-status jobs, and worked longer hours than their married counterparts, but these factors accounted for only part of their greater income. The single women got a higher return for their education, for example. Given the same number of years of schooling, single women can expect to earn three times as much as married women ($365 per year of school for singles, compared to $123 per year for married and divorced women).[4]

A sex-segregated marketplace supports these salary differences by making use of the fact that most women's primary allegiance is to their families. "Women's" jobs do not require long-term commitment or extensive sacrifice of time, so a woman can take a job, quit, and return as family responsibilities change. Because service and clerical jobs exist all over the country, women whose husbands are transferred can travel with them and pick up work in the new city. Employers, for their part, do not have to provide much training for female employees or invest time and resources in them. Geographically, married women are a captive labor force. Where they work is determined by where they live, which in turn is determined by where their husbands work. Further, most wives have to consider other attributes of a job than income and interest: they want their hours to correspond to the children's school hours, for example, or they decide to work nights while their husbands are home with the kids. If the husband's career means that the family moves a lot, or if the wife stops work while the children are small, she may change occupations several times in the course of a lifetime.[5]

The needs and demands of the economic marketplace, then, set limits on the work most women can do, and as studies described earlier indicate, the intrepid few who cross the boundaries are subject to group pressures. But as Treiman and Terrell's work suggests, there is another major barrier to equality between the sexes, a barrier that permits men's work and women's work to stay segregated. That barrier is the family.

marriage: cage or castle?

Suppose that 90 percent of the young men in this country were required to work for an influential company with branches in every state. They love the company and go to the job with high hopes and cheerful enthusiasm. After

[4] When the researchers compared the jobs and earnings of wives and husbands, the income gap remained. Wives get paid less than husbands for doing work of comparable status, even when work experience and number of hours on the job are the same. Black wives, who are significantly better educated than their husbands, are paid much less than black men, again for comparable work.

[5] We know a mother of four, now sixty-five, who has had three careers of about eight years each: newspaper reporter and editor, elementary school teacher, and real estate broker. She has enjoyed all three, she says. And yet, her friends agree, she has the drive and business sense of a corporate executive—which she might have become, if such jobs did not require the commitment of more time (both daily and in years) than she felt she could spare from her family.

a few years managers notice that the workers are wilting. Most of them have hypertension, peptic ulcers, headaches, and insomnia. Many are lonely, anxious, and depressed. Production slows down. Some employees stop working altogether.

What's wrong? Most observers would say that something is amiss with a company that can so transform its bright young workers. If you reread the above paragraph, substituting "women" for "men," "wives" for "workers and employees," and "marriage" for "the company," you'll have the same situation in different dress. Yet while unions and social scientists have paid in blood, time, and effort to document and change the effects of bad working conditions on employees, less attention has gone to the effects of marital conditions on families.

When Betty Friedan wrote about "the problem that has no name" in *The Feminine Mystique* (1963), she hit a responsive nerve in women who were unhappy with the role of happy housewife. During the last decade, research on women and marriage has shown a subtle change: instead of asking, "What's wrong with women who can't adjust to marriage?" researchers have begun to ask, "What's wrong with marriage that so many women can't adjust to it?" In this section we will look at the effects of marriage to see why they are so different for women and men. Because virtually all Americans marry (94 percent), an understanding of sex differences in achievement, status, and power must include an analysis of the ways marriage enhances or inhibits achievement in men and women. The picture is not black and white; contemporary marriage is a complex, changing institution, and its effects come in all shades of gray.

his and hers marriages

"Every woman should marry," wrote Benjamin Disraeli, "and no man." Take any book of famous quotations and look up marriage, and you will find such a wailing from men, such a catalogue of complaints, that you will wonder why any of them went through with the awful deed.

Alice Rossi, a sociologist, offers an explanation for the jokes men, but not women, make about wedlock. ("Bigamy is having one wife too many. Monogamy is the same.") Most men do marry, but they don't *have* to marry in order to meet masculine requirements of identity or fulfillment. For women, in contrast, marriage is an essential role through which feminine identity is achieved. Rossi observes that people feel free to joke and express doubts about roles that are peripheral to their sense of identity, but not about roles that are central. When it comes to work, a role that is basic to men's identity but peripheral to women's, the tables are turned. It is more permissible for women to express doubts about the value of work than for men to do so; women can also fall back on the housewife role without social censure if they choose not to take a job or to leave one (Rossi n.d.). In Crowley et al.'s 1973 survey of American workers, men and women responded differently to the question, "If you were to get enough money to live as comfortably as you would like for the rest of your life, would you continue to work?" Three-fourths of the men and the single women said yes, compared to half of the married women. The researchers explained this result by saying that the married women were more likely than men or single women to be working in unchallenging jobs; and some may have thought they were giving the socially approved answer (a "good wife" wouldn't want to work). In either case, wives have alternatives to work that men do not. A man without a job and a woman without a husband each lack the key ingredient to their respective identities. They are, some might say, like a meal without wine or a day without sunshine.[6]

The irony is that marriage, which many men consider a trap, does them a world of good, while the relentless pressure on them to be breadwinners causes undue strain and conflict. Exactly the reverse is true for women. Marriage, which they yearn for from childhood, may prove hazardous to their health, while the optional opportunities of work help keep them sane and satisfied. Let's look at this paradox more closely.

Jessie Bernard in *The Future of Marriage* (1972) says that the sexes get into marriage as they get into bed: with different desires, rhythms, and expectations. And they have entirely different experiences. Critics of marriage are often asked, "What's *wrong* with raising boys to be workers and girls to be wives?" One answer rests on accumulating data showing that marriage is neither as healthy nor as satisfying for wives as it is for husbands.

Bernard has gathered considerable evidence on the mental and physical health of married and single Americans. Overall, she found, married men are healthier in all ways than single men. They are even likely to get better jobs and higher pay. Single men get into more trouble than husbands: they commit more crimes, murder more often, have more traffic accidents, and kill themselves at a higher rate. Bernard recognizes that perhaps marriage should not get all the credit for civilizing young men; perhaps unhealthy, neurotic, criminally inclined men are simply not selected as mates. She has tried to get around this problem by comparing married men with widowers, to see what happens when men are thrown back into the single state. "They are miserable," she reports. "They show more than

---

[6] But note Flo Kennedy's contrary opinion: "A woman without a man is like a fish without a bicycle."

Table 9. Percentages of Married and Single Women and Men Scoring High on Mental Illness Measures

	Married women	Single women	Married men	Single men
Depression	54%	35%	37%	50%
Severe neurosis	11	4	17	30
Irrational fears	55	44	30	40
Passivity	74	57	50	66

AFTER Knupfer, Clark, and Room 1966.

expected frequencies of psychological distress, and their death rate is high." Studies that have compared married clergy with celibate priests—all men of similar background and health—found that the husbands lived longer than the celibates. Once married, men virtually crave the condition. Divorced and widowed men tend to remarry, and quickly. "At every age," Bernard observes, "the marriage rate for both divorced and widowed men is higher than the rate for single men. Half of all divorced white men who remarry do so within three years after divorce. Indeed, it might not be far-fetched to conclude that the verbal assaults on marriage indulged in by men are a kind of compensatory reaction to their dependence on it."

Among women, the situation reverses: married women show more mental and physical problems than single women. In 1966, in a study that aimed to see whether the mental health of single people was as terrible as commonly assumed, Genevieve Knupfer and her colleagues found that wives (like single men) were worse off than single women and husbands, as shown in Table 9.

In 1973, Walter Gove and Jeannette Tudor reviewed dozens of studies that compared the mental health of married men and women. No matter how they defined mental illness—as including neurotic disorders such as chronic anxiety or only true psychoses in which a person cannot function, such as schizophrenia, manic-depressive reaction, and paranoia—women are less healthy than men. Further, no matter who defined the mental illness, women are less healthy than men. More women are admitted to mental hospitals on an involuntary basis. More women are treated by general physicians on a voluntary basis. And more women show up ill on community surveys, when selection bias is largely eliminated.

There's a long list of symptoms that psychologists use to tell whether people are suffering from stress and distress, including nervousness, inertia, insomnia, nightmares, fainting, headaches, dizziness, heart palpitations, and feelings of impending nervous breakdown. On many studies that have now been done, of selected groups as well as national samples, more women than men, and specifically more wives than husbands, report these problems (Gurin, Veroff, and Feld 1960; U.S. Department of Health, Education, and Welfare 1970; Campbell 1975). Gove and Tudor believe, as Bernard does, that women do not show these higher rates of illness because they are women—and therefore weak, or permitted to complain—but because of strains in the roles they are called upon to play.[7] When Gove (1972) reviewed studies of marital status and mental illness that were done after World War II, he found without exception that wives were more likely to have a mental disorder than husbands. But when he compared never-married men with never-married women, divorced men with divorced women, and widowed men with widowed women, the men usually had the higher rates of mental illness. It would seem that something about marriage helps men and hurts women. What is it?

why wives wilt and husbands thrive: the housewife syndrome

The sociological view seeks to understand what it is about the structure of marriage that causes the sexes to react so differently. Not unreasonably, people tend to think there is something the matter with them if they cannot adjust to a new role, whether as spouse, parent, recruit, employee, or manager. But sociologists have managed to pinpoint some forces in the roles called for by marriage, not in the personalities of individuals, that produce sex differences in achievement, nurturance, self-esteem, and mental health.

Bernard and others believe that marriage exerts its most negative effects on women whose sole identity is as wife and mother. These women are subject to the "housewife syndrome." Employed wives show lower symptom rates than housewives, both in large-scale studies and in more select samples. In a recent *Psychology Today* survey on happiness (Shaver and Freedman 1976), housewives reported feeling more anxious and worried than employed wives (46 percent to 28 percent); more lonely (44 percent to 26 percent); and more worthless (41 percent to 24 percent).

[7] Some people have said that the sexes don't really differ in mental illness, it's just that women admit problems and pains more. Gove and Kevin Clancy addressed this problem by studying the effect of response bias—for example, the tendency to give answers that will win social approval, to agree to most questions asked, and to claim symptoms that are considered desirable—on reports of psychosomatic illnesses. They found that when they controlled for response bias, the sex differences in mental illness *increased*. So women don't have more symptoms because they think they should have them or are simply more willing to talk about them (Clancy and Gove 1975).

This response from women who read *Psychology Today* is interesting precisely because these women are more affluent, educated, and aware, on the average, than most Americans. If housewives who have these benefits still show the psychosomatic syndrome, then the stress of marriage is not only a result of being poor and having to manage a household on a shoestring.

Yet housewives are as likely as working wives to say they feel happy. A survey of a representative sample of Americans (Campbell 1975) finds the paradox that wives say they are happier than single women do, but single women are healthier than wives.[8] The researchers' explanation is that in this society women learn to require marriage as a condition of happiness: no matter how good their lives are without it, they think they are missing something; no matter how bad their lives are without it, they suspect that marriage would solve their problems.

The "housewife syndrome," once identified, became the subject of considerable study—and some derision. Some physicians have written disparagingly about the bored, neurotic wives who clutter their offices hoping to find a medical reason for their malaise. Housewives do consult doctors more often than men and single women do, and they are more likely to use and misuse such drugs as tranquilizers, barbiturates, and amphetamines (Fidell and Prather 1976; Bart 1971). Some writers have criticized American housewives as demanding, lazy, and domineering (see Philip Wylie's portrait of "mom" in *Generation of Vipers*). Some have argued that there is nothing wrong with marriage that a fascinating woman, a total woman, a *real* woman can't fix.

It is important to remember that there *are* many happy housewives in this country. As the glorification of family "togetherness" in the fifties gave way to feminism, the political pundits swung from trying to prove that all wives are contented to trying to prove that all of them are miserable (or ought to be). The real question is, who is which and why? A recent study by Myra Marx Ferree (1976) narrows down the conditions that cause a housewife to blossom or wither.

Ferree's sample consisted of 135 working-class women from the Boston area. About half of them worked outside the home, but not in glamorous professions: they were supermarket and department-store clerks, waitresses, typists, beauticians, and so on. Yet the wives who held jobs were happier and more satisfied with their lives than the full-time housewives.

---

[8] In Campbell's survey, "single women" meant women who had never been married. Divorced and separated women reported the greatest unhappiness and stress of any group of either sex, undoubtedly because, the researchers found, most were bearing all the economic responsibility and all the burdens of family care by themselves, and because they felt socially isolated.

Ferree speculated that housewives lack the social contact with customers and coworkers, and the regular paycheck, that bolster self-esteem and create a sense of accomplishment. Housewives typically lack recognition for the work they do; for that matter, there are no clear criteria for a job well done. Among Ferree's housewives, only one in fourteen said she was extremely good at taking care of a home, while three out of four felt incompetent. Most of the working wives (67 percent) also claimed to be poor homemakers. But *not one* of the employed wives said she felt incompetent at her job, and over half said they were "extremely good."

Ferree went on to see what allowed some of her housewives to feel happy with their lives and competent in their roles. The answer was that the happy housewives see family and friends regularly, and that their husbands and relatives value their work and give them moral support. They feel neither loneliness nor boredom, moods that are highly correlated with watching television and doing housework—the primary activities of alienated housewives (Shaver and Freedman 1976).

Not so long ago, housewives lived near their mothers, sisters, and other family members for most of their lives, and formed close-knit groups that exchanged support and help as well as news and advice. In recent decades, however, high job mobility and the exodus to the suburbs have broken up the extended family and stable neighborhood patterns. When housework and childcare became a solo pastime, it became a lonely one. Ferree's working wives said they had felt they were "going crazy staying home, not seeing anyone but four walls all day." Full-time housewifery, said one woman, "is like being in jail."

For many housewives, a lack of rewards for a job well done and social isolation create feelings of helplessness and hopelessness, accompanied by depression and a profound loss of self-esteem. One reason for the housewife's sense of helplessness is that years of taking care of a family, in exchange for being provided for by a husband, take a toll on one's sense of autonomy. "Women who are quite able to take care of themselves before marriage may become helpless after fifteen or twenty years of marriage," writes Bernard, citing the example of a fifty-five-year-old widow who did not know how to get a passport for herself even though she had run a travel agency in her youth.[9] Wives who do not work or have their own source of income are totally dependent on their husbands for money. In the opinion

---

[9] It works the same way for men, of course. Years of having all meals prepared, socks darned, and laundry cleaned may turn a self-sufficient bachelor into an inept widower who can't boil eggs or wash a shirt. In terms of self-esteem, though, the crisis of competence is more severe for the housewife, for she does not have another source of esteem in work as her husband does.

of many sociologists, this dependency perpetuates the use of "feminine wiles" rather than direct communication and keeps many women in marriages out of need rather than love. Many studies have shown that the more income the wife brings in, the more power she has in the family and the more she participates in decisions. This is true for wives of all races and classes. And the higher the husband's status, occupational prestige, and income, the greater his power in family decisions. So full-time housewives lack power as well as autonomy. Because the husband's income-producing job has higher status than the wife's job as homemaker, his needs and wants come first. Dair Gillespie (1976) argues that despite the egalitarian philosophy of most American marriages, husbands and wives have vastly unequal legal rights and obligations, financial resources, and power. "Women are *structurally* deprived of equal opportunities to develop their capacities, resources, and competence in competition with males," she observes.

Power, though, is not determined solely by who brings home the bacon and decides which car to buy. Many years ago, sociologist Willard Waller (1938) observed that among couples in love, the partner who is less involved has more power—a finding he promptly dubbed "the principle of least interest." The partner who is less committed to a love affair can call the shots, because he or she can always threaten to leave. Many sociological studies of economic bases of power overlook the emotions that can reverse predictions. We all know housewives who seem to be totally dominant over their successful husbands, and women who can turn their mild-mannered boyfriends into jealous maniacs with a mere hint of sexual adventure.

But even this route is apparently closed to many women. In various studies of housewives, the women are more likely than the men to say they feel unloved and unvalued; in Shaver and Freedman's affluent sample, for instance, the wives felt they loved their husbands more than they were loved in return (see also Bernard 1972). Women's magazines frequently offer advice to their readers on how to get their men to love them again, a topic rarely mentioned in men's magazines. Emotions may seem to have little to do with economics, but sociologist Arlie Hochschild (1975) argues that it is precisely because for women love has an economic motive—marrying the best breadwinner—that women are more likely than men to talk themselves into, and out of, love, and to seem obsessed with finding it and keeping it.

the working-wife syndrome

Most wives today are caught in a double bind. If they do not work outside the home, they have a high chance of coming down with housewife syndrome—feelings of depression and incompetence, and psychosomatic ailments such as insomnia and stomach aches. If they do work, they have an advantage over housewives in having higher self-esteem, greater power and participation in family decision-making, and fewer psychological and physical symptoms. The catch-22 is that marriage and work are in greater conflict for women than for men; the accommodation of the job's demands to family needs rests on women. A married mother who works has two jobs; a married father who works has one. Some women, such as the housewives in Ferree's study, take jobs that pay less or are less challenging in order to reduce pressure. They get the benefits of combining work and family with less strain—but less income, too. Other women opt for the whole show—a more-than-full-time career and a family.

Traditional wives, a category that includes the vast majority of women whether they work or not, take care of cleaning, shopping, meals, laundry, sewing, childcare and babysitters, and what Bernard calls "stroking." Part of a wife's role is to listen to her husband's troubles and bolster his ego. These support functions of a wife free her husband for other concerns. Ernest Hemingway wrote novels, and Mary Hemingway ran his estate. Einstein could pursue a problem long into the night because Mrs. Einstein saw to dinner. The President reached his high office because the First Lady attended the babies.

Rose Coser and Gerald Rokoff (1971) observe, as Rossi does, that our primary role allegiances are strongly sex-typed: "A man owes to his profession what a woman owes to her family." The prestige professions of men, Coser and Rokoff believe, require "selflessness and a devotion to a calling"— like the scientist who sacrifices money for the love of his work. But in another sense real professional achievement requires great selfishness. If you are hot on the trail of a breakthrough in biochemistry, if you have a brilliant idea for Chapter 3 of your novel, if you have a legal brief that must be ready by 9:00 A.M. tomorrow, you must selfishly seize the time. If you are worried about feeding the family, dusting the bookshelves, or cheering up your spouse who had a lousy day, you may not finish the task.

Note that we are talking about "selfishness" not as a personality trait but as a role requirement. Most jobs require a fixed amount of participation, and people know they can be fired if they fool around with the rules. A bus driver or a businessman may not want to leave a sick wife or child in order to work, but he may feel he must. Other careers simply are so demanding that they cannot accommodate people who would prefer to be flexible about hours and time with family. Some men and women today are deciding that professional achievement is not worth the pressure to behave egocentrically, but at the moment we are not talking about what should be or could be, but about what is. Currently, the "is" means that fewer women than men have been structurally able to meet the demands of full-time careers, because women don't have wives to take care of them. Margaret Adams (1971) says that women are caught in a "compassion trap"—the pervasive belief that "women's primary social function is to provide tenderness and compassion." Many women now face a dilemma at the heart of their lives: how to strike a balance between the "selfless" pleasures of giving and loving and the "selfish" pleasures of finding their own way in the working world.

Those women who do try for careers that demand more time and attention than a 9-to-5 job may receive more financial and psychological rewards than the average female worker, but the conflict between their two roles is especially intense (Hunt and Hunt 1975; Douvan n.d.; Rapoport and Rapoport 1972).[10] Margaret Poloma (1972) studied fifty-three couples in which the wife was actively working in law, medicine, or college teaching, professions that are predominantly male and require extended training and personal investment. Poloma wanted to know how these women managed their roles as wives and professionals. Most of her interviewees juggled their jobs and families with four kinds of "tension-management techniques":

1. They looked at the benefits, rather than the costs, of combining career and family. As one woman explained, "I am a better mother *because* I work and can expend my energies on something other than the over-mothering of my children."

2. They decided in advance which role to emphasize, in case of conflicting demands, and in virtually every case family crises took precedence over career crises. When the babysitter didn't show up or a child got sick, the wife, not the husband, missed work that day.

3. They compartmentalized the two roles as much as possible, keeping work and family distinct. Few of the women brought work home with them, for example, though their husbands did often. One lawyer wouldn't talk about her practice at home, says Poloma, so that "the children would not think that her work was more important than their father's."

4. They compromised. The wives controlled the extent of their career commitment to fit the circumstances of their family lives—how the husband's work was going, his income, the ages and number of children, the

[10] To the great majority of working wives, whose jobs are not glamorous careers, the idea of "role strain" on the part of successful, affluent, middle-class working wives is absurd, if not infuriating. But researchers on this topic, most of whom are married professionals, have tended to concentrate on how middle-class women combine career and family. (Myra Ferree is a notable exception.) Naturally, the subject is of considerable interest to them, and probably to their students too.

husband's support (or lack of it), and so on. "When one or more of these factors is out of kilter, the wife makes the necessary adjustment to manage role strain," Poloma found. "She generally expects little and asks nothing of the family to better enable her to adjust to family and career demands."

Coser and Rokoff note that every time a professional woman compromises in favor of her family, or stays home to wait for the babysitter, she confirms the prejudice that women don't really want to achieve and are not really serious about their work. Thus is another self-fulfilling prophesy created: because women do the compromising when family and career demands conflict, fewer job opportunities are opened to them, and career commitments become, for some, too heavy a burden.

Well then, some people say, if the conflict between home and work causes women such stress, let 'em stay home. What happens when bright, college-educated women avoid careers and choose a traditional family path?

Alice Rossi theorizes that women in their twenties who marry and have children are fulfilling their lives' ambitions, and thus should be at a peak of self-esteem and satisfaction. In contrast, their counterparts who are in graduate school or struggling in new careers have all the self-doubts and anxieties of men in professional training: Do I really want to be a doctor? Do I want to spend my life running this complicated agency? These women look at their friends and think: Wouldn't it be easier to drop out and have babies? Why didn't I do what Jane did, get married early and be taken care of? (Note that men do not have this back-up option.) Career preparations are demanding and exhausting for either sex. But a decade later, Rossi suggests, the situation shifts. Now, when the career woman is hitting her stride, the wife is losing ground. Her children are in school, and her life seems to have less focus and to offer fewer rewards. Now she is the one who feels envious.

Rossi's data from studies in the early 1960s support her argument that the family-oriented woman has higher self-esteem in the early years of marriage than the career-oriented woman; as we saw, Campbell and others have found that young married women are the happiest group of either sex at any age. Judith Birnbaum (1975) wanted to see whether Rossi's prediction about women in their thirties was correct. She took as her sample women who had graduated with honors from the University of Michigan fifteen to twenty-five years earlier, selecting twenty-nine who had married, borne children, and sought no further education or employment. For comparison, she also interviewed twenty-five married women with children and twenty-seven single women, all of whom were Ph.D.s on the Michigan faculty or M.D.s.

Birnbaum found Rossi's hunch confirmed. Of the three groups, as shown in Table 10, the homemakers had the lowest self-esteem and felt the

Table 10. Some Findings on the Health and Happiness of Housewives, Married Professionals, and Single Professionals

	House-wives N=29	Married pro-fessionals N=25	Single pro-fessionals N=27
Self-esteem score (competence in five areas: domestic, social, child-care, cultural, intellectual)			
Poor to average	31%	4%	15%
Average to good	55	42	31
Good to very good	14	54	54
Mental-emotional health			
Poor to average	39	12	12
Good to very good	61	88	88
Feelings of uncertainty about who you are and what you want			
Hardly ever	34	64	58
Fairly often	66	36	42
Feeling lonely			
Hardly ever	28	72	27
Sometimes to often	72	28	73
Would like to have more friends	40	12	11
Misses challenge and creativity	42	4	0
Feels "not very" attractive to men	61	12	58
Very happily married	52	68	—

SOURCE: Birnbaum 1975.

worst about their competence—even at childcare and getting along with people. They felt the least attractive, worried most about personal identity, and most often felt lonely. The only thing the professional women said they missed was enough time to do all the things they wanted, but the homemakers said they missed challenge and creative involvement.

Most poignant of all, the married professionals were happier with their marriages than the housewives who were devoting all their time to their families. In answer to the question, "How does marriage change a woman's life?" the housewives were far more likely than the married professionals to respond negatively. More than half of them (52 percent) said that marriage is restricting, burdensome, and demanding, compared to 19 percent in the professional group. This finding is especially interesting in light of our observation that, objectively, working wives do face more burdens and demands. Birnbaum felt that the housewives justified themselves by speaking of marriage as requiring sacrifice and subordination—Margaret Adams' "compassion trap." "Marriage is not for the self-centered woman," said one housewife. "It is a life of loving and giving in exchange for being wanted and needed and loved by her husband and later her children." While 62 percent of the housewives mentioned self-sacrifice in discussing the impact of having children, only one professional woman did. The gift of love, says Birnbaum, takes its toll in unhappiness and lower self-esteem among these martyr-mothers.

of housework and husbands

So far we have talked more in this chapter about women than about men, and there's a reason. When people talk about "liberating" women and ending discrimination, they are generally thinking of how to get women out of the home and into the work force—and perhaps especially into the top echelons of power. They are generally not thinking of how to get men to do more at home. Even countries that are justifiably proud of the equality achieved by their women usually mean that women now clean the streets, not that men now clean the house (see Chapter 9).

You may have wondered, in the discussion of the conflicts of working women, why husbands don't take some of the pressure off their wives. A good question—but they don't. In spite of the increasing number of married women who are going back to work, there seems to be no corresponding increase in the number of married men who are doing more at home. The result, that many women have two jobs instead of one, is true all over the world. Yugoslavian husbands don't like household chores any more than Peruvian husbands do.

An international team of social scientists, under the direction of Alexander Szalai, a Hungarian sociologist, has done an enormous study of how people spend their time. Two thousand citizens in each of twelve countries[11] filled out minute-by-minute diaries covering a twenty-four hour period in their lives. This extraordinary survey showed, first of all, that housewives have not been liberated by technology or by jobs. In countries that have a rich supply of washers, dryers, and other modern conveniences, women spend as much time on home and family chores as do women in countries where housewives still chop their own wood. The average woman in Osna-

[11] Belgium, Bulgaria, Czechoslovakia, East Germany, France, Hungary, Peru, Poland, the Soviet Union, the United States, West Germany, and Yugoslavia.

bruck, West Germany, has all the appliances she wants, yet she spends as much time doing housework—within a minute—as a wife in Kragujevac, Yugoslavia, who still draws water from a well (Szalai 1972).

Another sociologist, Joann Vanek (1974), found that the hours devoted to housework are remarkably constant not only across technological and national boundaries but across time as well. Today's average American housewife puts in as many hours as her grandmother did forty years ago: about fifty-three hours a week. True, notes Vanek, some jobs have become less time-consuming, such as sewing, cooking, and meal clean-up. But women still spend exactly as much time—in some studies, even more time —cleaning clothes (they clean them more often) and they spend more time transporting children and husbands from place to place. "Contemporary women spend about one full working day per week on the road and in stores compared with less than two hours per week for women in the 1920s," Vanek says. Parkinson's Law, which states that activities swell to fill the available time, must be operating. Vanek adds that because the value of housework and the criteria for a completed job are unclear, women apparently feel pressure to spend long hours at it.

Working wives spend less time than housewives on daily chores, averaging twenty-six hours a week. They aren't spending less time because they're getting more help, though. Vanek found that working wives are no more likely than housewives to have paid help—and no more likely to be helped by their husbands. "Contrary to popular belief," she says, "American husbands do not share the responsibilities of household work. They spend only a few hours a week at it, and most of what they do is shopping." As a result, working wives have about ten fewer hours of free time each week than either housewives or employed men. Working wives use weekends to catch up on the cleaning and shopping. Working husbands use weekends to do odd chores, and then catch up on their rest, watch TV, or play sports.

As the family grows larger, the husband's participation *decreases*. He does less childcare, housework, and cooking. The wife's housework time, however, increases between 5 and 10 percent with each child, whether she works or not.

Why don't husbands do more? Possibly for the same reasons that little boys won't play with "girls' toys"—women's work is less valued and threatens masculinity. Possibly because housework isn't much fun. Or possibly because the wives don't want them to. Nancy and John Robinson (1975), using a national sample of American households, found that only 19 percent of the women they interviewed said they wanted more help from their husbands. The majority of American men and women are more willing to accept equality for women in the marketplace than in the home; housework, they say, is the woman's responsibility (Osmond and Martin 1975). Women learn early that housework is a central part of their feminine role; indeed, single women spend one to two hours more per day on housework than single men do, and only twenty minutes less per day than do young wives without children.

The roles of husband and wife currently assign the bulk of the housework and childcare to women. This frees men to pursue professional or leisure activities, but it also deprives them of something they might enjoy: time with the children. Philip Stone (1972) used Szalai's international time data to study the amount of time spent on childcare in the twelve countries. He found that women—working or not—spend far more time with children than their husbands do. In only one nation, the Soviet Union, do husbands and working wives spend the same amount of workday time with their children, and even there, on weekends the mothers try more than the fathers do to catch up. Overall, fathers from Eastern European countries spend more time with their children than fathers from Western countries do. Can you guess how much time per day the average American father spends with his children? A half hour? An hour? Two hours? The correct answer is twelve minutes.

evaluating the sociological perspective

The sociological perspective deals with patterns across groups, and with the impact of the roles people play on their self-esteem and satisfaction. It maintains that marriage and work roles in American society encourage men to be achievement-oriented, aggressive, and dominant and withholds from them the option to stop work or spend more time with their families. Men haven't the time to be nurturant, runs this view, because they carry the breadwinner's burden. And women haven't the time to make it to the top of a profession, unless they forego children, get outside help, or postpone career decisions until the children are grown. It was easier for Golda Meir to manage Israel as a grandmother than it would have been as a young mother.

The evidence accumulated in the last decade shatters the stereotypes of the happy housewife and the trapped husband. It is easy to infer from this that marriage is awful for all women and wonderful for all men, that everyone should have a career, and that the pressures of the male role are simple and slight compared to those of the female—easy, but incorrect. The system has benefits and costs for each of us.

Just as research shows that women with two sources of self-esteem—family and work—are healthier and happier than women with just one, the same is true for men. Now that women are discovering work, men are discovering that work isn't everything. Many contemporary writers are saying that modern life should not require total commitment to any one role, that people feel better when they have many roles to carry out. Those who put all their eggs in one basket may be in for depression and helplessness when the basket breaks. Women who get their whole sense of identity from motherhood, and men who get theirs from work, are more likely to suffer and turn sick when the children leave home or the job ends through retirement (or firing). Not much will have been achieved, some people argue, if women's liberation merely gets women out of the house and into jobs that turn them into achievement-mad competitors, or makes contented housewives feel dissatisfied, or creates a generation of depressed househusbands.

The sociological view says that if men and women are to be equal in opportunity, then organizations such as work and the family must become more flexible, more integrated, and less sex-typed. Change can come only when institutions and laws change—people's hearts and minds will follow. But this is not as simple as it sounds, and there are limitations to the perspective. The force of socialized beliefs—for example, among women, that the house must be spotless and that it is their job to make it so and among men, that income and success are the keys to masculine identity—cannot be legislated away overnight. The behaviors and beliefs that people learn to regard as central to their feelings of masculinity and femininity are reinforced in many ways every day and reach into every corner of their lives.

Nonetheless, the contributions of sociologists have helped people psychologically. In Chapter 6 we discussed the difference between internal and external control—between people who feel they are captains of the ship and those who feel like barnacles. Among middle-class whites, especially men, a sense of internal control is associated with high self-esteem. But among minorities who are discriminated against, a sense of *external* control is associated with high self-esteem. Blacks and women who blame what happens to them on the system have higher self-esteem than blacks and women who blame themselves. This seems logical: it is psychologically satisfying to hold oneself responsible if things are going well but to locate blame elsewhere if they are not. Both consciousness-raising groups and black-militancy organizations have the same function: to help their members break out of helplessness and depression and organize efforts for change. The trouble is that blaming the system, like blaming anything else, can cut two ways. The belief that the system is responsible for the inequities that blacks and women face can provide emotional catharsis and energize people to change institutions. Or it can provide a scapegoat that becomes an excuse for resignation and inactivity. Which of these occurs may depend on how deeply powerless people feel—or, more sociologically, on how powerless they in fact are.

Sometimes one hears that if women ran the world we would greet a humane new era. In this view, because women are more nurturant, empathic, and sensitive than men, because they are closer to birth and the mysteries of life, they wouldn't get this little planet into wars and tyrannies; if mothers ruled the world, no son of theirs would ever see battle. This idea is based on the same assumption as the one that claims women are emotionally unfit for political office—namely, that the sexes are fundamentally different. But the sociological view predicts that women who are cast into positions of authority will behave just as men do, neither better nor worse. Certainly Indira Gandhi has been just as authoritarian, and Golda Meir just as ready for war, as any male leader. To be sure, these women were sole females in otherwise male-dominated systems. Nowhere on earth is there a system in which men and women truly share political power or in which women dominate. If we ever get a chance to observe one, we can see whether women bring "feminine" traits to office or whether office drums "masculine" traits into them.

This chapter has argued that the way a society sets up its work and family organizations determines how men and women will behave, what their ambitions will be, what opportunities they can reach for. The next question to ask is, how did the system get to be the way it is? No one sat at a pinnacle of power and decided what work would be open to women and what to men. So now we will move to the next perspective and explore some theories about the function and evolution of sex differences across societies and throughout history.

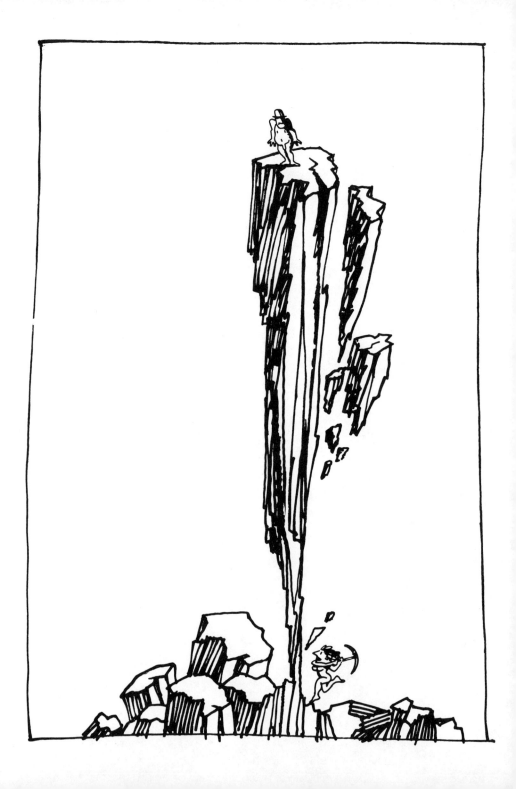

8

The origins of roles and rituals:
The evolutionary perspective

The Yanomamo Indians of South America are one of the most aggressive, warlike societies on this planet. Their principal ethnographer, Napoleon Chagnon, calls them the "fierce people," and even that is an understatement. Yanomamo men may be the ultimate male chauvinists; they are always brawling over real and imagined insults, and their victims are as likely to be women as men. "All Yanomamo men physically abuse their wives," writes anthropologist Marvin Harris (1974). "Kind husbands merely bruise and mutilate them; the fierce ones wound and kill." As a result, women are marked with brutal ugly scars, which they regard as a mark of their husbands' concern. Women are property, and little girls begin to serve their future husbands, sexually and domestically, when they are as young as eight or nine. Yanomamo men are continually fighting over women. If they capture females from another Yanomamo tribe, they gang-rape them, bring them back to their own village, rape them again, and distribute them to deserving warriors. The odd thing is that Yanomamos create the very scarcity of women that eventually sends the men to battle for wives: they kill infant daughters until they have a son.

Thousands of miles and a hundred years away from the Yanomamo, Iroquois women lived a very different life. They had high status and wielded significant political and economic influence. Although women could not join the highest ruling body, the Council of Elders, some of the older wives (matrons) had power to influence decisions of the Council, including those on war and peace treaties (Brown 1975). Iroquois matrons helped select, and could become, the tribe's religious leaders, and they reigned supreme in their households. The matrons guarded the tribe's treasury of stored food and valuables, and they had the right to dispense these goods, even those that had been acquired by men. An Iroquois male offended a matron at his peril.

How shall we account for the different status of women among the Yanomamo and the Iroquois? The perspective described in this chapter represents the broadest level of explanation. It takes as its unit of analysis not the individual, not the family, not even social roles, but entire societies. Each perspective in this book raises questions for its successor: there may be biological and anatomical differences between males and females, but how do those affect personality differences? Personality differences may be learned, but why are boys and girls socialized differently? Boys and girls may learn different lessons as they grow up because their society profits from a division of labor, but why does one society divide the sexes rigidly and brutally and another less so?

In trying to understand human behavior, most people cannot see the forest for the trees. The trees are the fascinating rituals (circumcision, couvade), the inconsistent attitudes (woman on a pedestal, woman in the gutter), and the apparently arbitrary sex-role assignments (women tend the chickens, men tend the cows). The evolutionary perspective makes us look at the forest—the whole package of economic and environmental factors that produced a given culture and its customs.

The data for this perspective come from anthropologists, who have collected thousands of case studies that demonstrate the remarkable plasticity of human nature. Anthropologists use tribes the way psychologists use laboratories: to isolate a unit for study. But not all anthropologists use them the same way. Those in the dominant tradition of anthropology take a basically descriptive approach. They want to identify the rules of each culture and explain them in that culture's own terms. The best way to find out what the rules are, these anthropologists believe, is to ask. You sit down with a wise village elder, for example, and ask him who marries whom, how women are treated, why men fight, who does what work. Margaret Mead's famous books on sex and temperament are an excellent illustration of this approach. Mead wants to know *what* the Arapesh and the Mundugumor do; she is less interested in *why* the Arapesh are gentle and cooperative while the Mundugumor are suspicious and nasty.

Another, more recent school of anthropology takes a materialist approach to the "whys." The materialists regard the rules, customs, and rituals of a given group as parts of an interlocking system. Basic to the system, they assume, are the material conditions in which the group lives—its economy, technology, and method of food production and distribution. Customs and rituals, in this view, result from identifiable circumstances and have predictable consequences for the functioning of the social system in which they occur. These researchers do not rely solely on informants to describe and explain group behavior, because people are often unaware of the most basic rules they follow (see the Milgram subway experiment in Chapter 7). The materialists are not content merely to know that the Machiguenga have this life-style and the Mundurucú have that. They want to know what forces caused different groups to evolve in different directions and whether there are any general principles that can explain the path taken by each. They try to identify such principles by looking for economic correlates of a society's customs and people's psychological attitudes. And they ask what purpose (or "function") those customs and attitudes serve for the group as a whole.

The materialist approach requires us to regard each culture as a product of its own unique history and environment. Customs that work in a particular social and economic system cannot be exported from one society to another like cheese. You may like the way Mbuti men treat women more than the habits of the Yanomamo, but even customs you don't like have a purpose. This is why people engage in rituals that seem, to outsiders, to be destructive or painful, such as superincision (making a slit in the penis) for males and infibulation (cutting and sewing up the vagina) for females (Hayes 1975). It doesn't advance our understanding to moan, "But why do women (or men) put up with that awful practice?" They put up with it because it is one element in an interconnected system of kinship, population pressures, and economic dependency.

This chapter illustrates a *strategy* that can be used in thinking about sex differences; it does not explain every riddle and ritual mentioned earlier. The units of study are small tribes rather than large, industrial nations (which are the topic of Chapter 9). Materialist anthropologists believe the principles behind social customs and cultural evolution can best be isolated and understood by studying small groups first. Some of the studies we have chosen offer new and controversial answers to old questions. They cover a lot of territory and may seem unrelated, but they share a framework, a way of approaching the relations between men and women, that we find creative and exciting. The first section describes researchers' efforts to explain particular phenomena: the Yanomamo treatment of women; the rituals of circumcision and couvade; and sexual customs that range from repressive to open. The second section reviews some theories that try to account for male dominance and variations in female status across cultures and throughout history. The third discusses the strengths and weaknesses of the evolutionary perspective as a whole, especially some problems shared by all functional theories, and the differences between biological and social evolution.

some customs in social context

the case of the Yanomamo

When Chagnon asked his Yanomamo informants why they were always fighting, he was told that the men fight to get women. They must constantly raid villages and steal females in order to have enough wives to go around. The Yanomamo are certainly short of women; the practice of female infanticide and wife-abuse results in an adult sex ratio of 141 males to 100 females. The puzzle is why the Yanomamo kill and maim the very object of all their lusts and struggles.

Chagnon accepts his informants' explanation, but Marvin Harris (1974, 1975) interprets the story of the Yanomamo differently. He looks at their practice of warfare, female infanticide, and male supremacy as connected parts of a system that has assured the survival of the tribe under particular conditions. "Any human activity will seem ridiculous or mysterious if we tear it into fragments and don't relate it to the historical picture," he says. "You must begin with a system's technological history and its local ecology."

A century ago the Yanomamo were nomadic hunters who traveled through the forests in search of animals. Today their staples are bananas and plantains, uncultivated foods that are high in calories but low in protein. As the Yanomamo settled into a fruit-based diet their population increased rapidly, and today they are one of the largest groups in the Amazon area. Yet, Harris says, they are starving. Though tropical forests seem to be full of fruits and good food, they are surprisingly deficient in game animals. In recent years the game supply has diminished rapidly, and meat is scarce. Hunters must range long distances to kill enough animals to feed the village. Sometimes they don't get enough to feed the expedition itself. Yanomamo villages are fairly close together in the forests, and hunters crisscross each other's territory as they search for food. Yanomamo villages are competing for scarce resources all right, Harris says, but they are protein, not women. The Yanomamo even have two words for hunger, one meaning an empty stomach and one meaning a full stomach that craves meat. Yanomamo songs and poems are full of themes of meat hunger (just imagine an American folk song called "Oh how I yearn for some beef in my stew"), and Yanomamo feasts celebrate meat.

The scarcity of meat creates a need to control population, and the Yanomamo, like many other tribal societies around the world, use infanticide to accomplish this goal. Females are killed more often than males because, when population pressures are great, a tribe needs fewer females to produce offspring and more males to hunt for rare protein. As Harris observes, male supremacist attitudes alone cannot account for the slaying of infant daughters, because women have too many opportunities to save them and to circumvent the demands of the men. For the women as well as the men a high male:female ratio means slower population growth. It also means more war, the price for raising sons.

You might reasonably ask why hunting and making war require male supremacy and the violent oppression of females. Why don't women learn to hunt and fight, too? Wouldn't a tribe be better off if everyone could search for game or snatch the sexually appealing members of a neighboring village? Harris thinks the answer is that brutal warriors must be highly motivated. How do you motivate them? You could deprive them of food and bodily comforts until they triumph in battle, but then you would have hungry, weak fighters. "But sex makes a terrific reward," Harris says. If sex is to be the reward for toughness in battle, he goes on, then women must be taught passivity.

> When the King told his knights, "If you slay the dragon, I'll give you one of my daughters," no one doubted that the daughters would go when given. The complement to male supremacy is female passivity. The training of fierce males requires the training of pliant females. You can't use the women for alliances and rewards if they are going to be equally aggressive (Harris 1975, p. 66).

This idea does not explain, though, why the men become the brutal fighters and the women the passive rewards. That division of labor, Harris thinks, is based on the male edge over females in physical strength. When war required hand-held weapons and face-to-face combat, warriors had to be aggressive and tough. ("If Napoleon had been a Yanomamo, he would never have become a general," Harris notes.) Further, a system of aggressive females and pliant males would probably have led to *male* infanticide, which is not an effective method of population control.

In Harris's interpretation, then, male supremacy is a result of ecological pressures on cultural groups that needed one group to be fighters and hunters. At no point does he resort to intrapsychic explanations based on biology or instinct. For example, he rejects the idea that males fight for the bloody pleasure of it because they are naturally aggressive and warlike. "The link between sex and aggression is as artificial as the link between infanticide and war," he believes. Men learn to fight when the conditions require them to. Indeed, the Yanomamo are quite rare among hunting and gathering societies: most hunting tribes are remarkably peaceful. They have no need to be otherwise, as long as their population is not too great for their food supply.

When population grows to an extent that threatens the food-producing capacities of the environment, Harris says, something must occur to restore balance. For the Yanomamo, that something is war and female infanticide; other tribal groups rely on gentler traditions to slow population growth. For instance, a small group may leave the larger one and establish itself in another territory (a process called fission). But food-rich new territories are becoming scarce. War is an adaptive mechanism of the last resort, a relatively new solution to the push of population against resources. It may be brutal, but it works: tribes that have learned to control their growth, whether through warfare or by splitting up, have survived more consistently than tribes that blundered along, continuing to eat until nothing was left.

Recently William Divale and Harris (1976) tested the idea that warfare and male supremacy are related by surveying 561 local village groups from 112 world societies. They found that when the need for warriors was great, female infanticide was a common practice. Thus, for the 160 bands and villages surveyed in the midst of war, the sex ratio among children was extremely lopsided as a result of female infanticide, while the adult ratio was balanced as a result of male deaths in battle (see Table 11). The groups surveyed within a generation after a war were in transition: there were more males than females at all ages, because boys who would otherwise have been killed in war survived. After a full generation, though, female infanticide had stopped and the sex ratio was almost even.

In the absence of effective birth control, Divale and Harris note, a tribe that averages three children per adult woman can remain stable in size only if *one third* of its female infants do not survive to adulthood. If most adult women have four children, then *half* of the female babies must not reach reproductive age—or the population will grow too rapidly. One alternative to infanticide is abortion, which is widely practiced around the world, but in tribal societies abortion has the unfortunate side effect of killing the mother almost as often as the fetus. Infanticide does not endanger the mother, and it allows the selective rearing of males under conditions when males are needed for war.

When war is adaptive for a society, as when it means more food and fewer people in an overpopulated group, it is self-perpetuating. With it

Table 11. The Relation Between Sex Ratios and War

	Male:female ratio below age 15	Male:female ratio above age 15
Warfare present at time of census (160 bands and villages)	128:100	101:100
Warfare stopped 5-25 years before census (236 bands and villages)	113:100	113:100
Warfare stopped more than 25 years before census (165 bands and villages)	106:100	92:100

SOURCE: Divale and Harris 1976.

comes male supremacy—a cluster of traditions and rituals that glorify males and subordinate females. Divale and Harris report various studies showing that frequent wars are highly correlated with patrilocal residence, patrilineal inheritance, polygyny, marriage by capture, bride price, restrictions on women's sexual behavior, and male secret societies. (War is *negatively* correlated with polyandry. In the few places where women may have several husbands, the chances of warfare are decreased.)

Harris's explanation of tribal warfare does not account for war in all times and places, however. In contemporary industrial societies, war serves other functions than population control—indeed, the awesome wars of this century, which killed millions upon millions of people, have slowed the growth of world population hardly at all. One analysis suggests that in modern nations war solves production deficiencies by permitting constant economic expansion (see Naroll and Divale 1976). But Harris would point out that regardless of its particular functions, warfare always serves economic and survival ends and does not reflect a biological "drive" to fight, which is why he is optimistic that human beings can eventually find less brutal solutions to their problems. Harris also notes that as long as warfare involves combat and thus requires physical strength and training, male dominance in this arena will connect with male dominance in others.[1]

One important problem with materialist interpretations such as Harris's, which argue that a custom exists because it has a survival "function" for the group, is that they are hard to prove or disprove. After something has occurred, it is easy to look back and say it had to be that way for survival reasons. Harris replies that these theories can be tested, not in the same way predictions can be tested in a laboratory, but against events that have already occurred. In the case of the Yanomamo, for example, Harris predicts that when the population is in balance with the environment and the people are no longer starving for protein, then both female infanticide and warfare between Yanomamo villages should stop. And they do. In some villages consisting of refugees from the more violent battles, the Yanomamo get protein from fishing and raise manioc, a potato-like root, as a staple. Here the sex ratio is back to normal; babies aren't left to die; and the men aren't so fierce.

You can begin to see the complexities of this perspective, because no single custom or attitude can be studied in isolation from the others. Further, a custom that serves one function in society Q may have an entirely differ-

---

[1] In the future era of push-button wars, heaven forfend, women will be able to "fight" like men, so we could predict the emergence of integrated armies—which is already happening in many industrial nations.

ent function in society R, and a ritual that is adaptive in one culture may be maladaptive in another.[2] We shall have more to say on these problems, but for the moment let's try out a different kind of materialist explanation for two common sex-related practices: circumcision and couvade.

social dilemmas and sexual rituals

circumcision When psychoanalysts try to explain the prevalence of sexual taboos and rituals, they look for answers in unconscious motives (see Chapter 5). For example, they usually account for circumcision practices in terms of castration anxiety and father-son rivalry. Some focus on the boy's motives. Circumcision, they say, represents the boy's willingness to sacrifice a part of his penis as a symbolic gesture of deference to his father's power: "If I give you this much, may I please keep the rest?" The trouble is that in no society do boys circumcise themselves, certainly not Oedipal-aged little ones. Another explanation is that circumcision represents the father's effort to head off the threat from his son, that it is a symbolic gesture meaning, "Buzz off, kid, your mother is mine." The trouble is that fathers rarely circumcise their own sons. The operation is usually done by a third party: the chief of the tribe, a doctor, the boy's uncle, and so on.

Karen Paige and Jeffery Paige (in press) have developed a theory to explain reproductive rituals and taboos that does not rely on unconscious mechanisms. They regard these rituals as "a form of psychological warfare used to influence and assess the opinions and intentions of other individuals when no more direct means of influence are available" (Paige, in press). Rituals are used to persuade and convince other group members of one's intentions.

[2] Food taboos are a good example. Harris argues that the Jewish and Muslim taboo on pork was ecologically adaptive for life in the Middle East. For nomadic pastoralists, like the Hebrews and Arabs, pigs were difficult and costly to raise. They can't be herded across long distances; they eat the same food as people do; they suffer in the heat because they cannot sweat. It would have been ecologically unsound to raise them in large numbers, but pigs taste delicious. The gods always initiate taboos where the greatest temptations lie, notes Harris, and so they forbade their followers to raise pigs (this taboo never exists in societies where climate and habitat favor pig-raising). Jahweh and Allah did not place taboos on cows and sheep, which can be herded and which can live in hot climates, even though these animals carry as many infectious and fatal diseases as pigs do. Indeed, anthrax (transmitted by cows) is far worse for human beings to catch than trichinosis. Having accounted for the opposite customs of pig-loathing and pig-loving in ecological terms, Harris (1975) then notes the exceptions. Obviously Jews in the United States who abstain from eating pork are not doing so for ecological reasons. For them, the taboo serves another function, such as giving them a sense of identity as a distinctive community.

If you live in a hunting and gathering society, your fortunes rise and fall with the prevalence of food in the forests, which may or may not be plentiful. The deer or the fish may not be abundant this year. People who depend on unpredictable runs of game or fish for their protein live under uncertain circumstances, and their resources are temporary, perishable, and of little value as objects to be inherited. Most hunters and gatherers do not acquire property that can be handed down from generation to generation. You can't bequeath twenty berries to your children or stash twenty fish under your bed for very long. Nor can you put a fence around forty acres of tropical jungle and try to live on the occasional wild pig or tapir that bounds through.

Now consider the advantages, and disadvantages, of settling down. Once you have some land to be plowed and animals to domesticate, you start worrying about how to protect them. One cost of wealth is the fear of losing it. If you are desert nomads, like the Bedouin, you had better keep a careful eye on your camels; in that blistering climate, they may mean the difference between life and death. If you cultivate land as your only source of food and income, you had better keep marauders and hungry neighbors away. Cows and camels can wander off; farms and fields can be raided. So property requires protectors.

Tribes that control stable economic resources face a critical social problem, the Paiges argue. Their need is for large numbers of sons to defend the group's property and boundaries against outside enemies. The danger is that some young men may break away and grab some property and camels for themselves. According to the Paiges, circumcision is a symbolic demonstration by fathers of their loyalty to the existing tribe.

The Paiges began their analysis by asking where circumcision occurs: most commonly in advanced horticultural or pastoral societies such as the Tiv of Nigeria and the Kazak of Russia.[3] Most of these societies share a common social organization, namely strong fraternal interest groups. That is, they consist of bands of related males united under common military or political leadership. These males have the power to defend property, control

[3] Some critics of studies based on samples of tribal societies point out that apparent correlations between their customs and rituals may be spurious. They argue that the process of cultural diffusion—when a society breaks up and spawns several offshoots—accounts for such correlations. That is, if several (or many) tribes in a sample once made up a single tribe, then of course a pork taboo in one will have many of the same economic correlates as a pork taboo in another. The Paiges, however, drew their tribes from the Standard Cross-Cultural Sample, which is a stratified sample of tribes taken from 186 distinct groups around the world. Each group consists of a cluster of societies that share similar culture, language, and location. Selecting one tribe from each group minimizes the effects of diffusion.

resources, and negotiate binding agreements over women and wealth. Since their power comes from their unity, male solidarity is essential. A son who moves away represents not just the loss of one man, but the loss of the son's sons and all their wealth and military strength. "In such societies, fission is not simply a cause for grumbling but a major political crisis," write the Paiges.

In hunting and gathering tribes that lack fraternal interest groups, fission is quite common. The son of a Mbuti hunter takes with him only what he can carry, and his departure means no loss of power or prestige for his father. It is only when military and political power depend on the continual expansion of males in the father's line that a son who leaves the tribe is a great threat.

The Paiges' next question was, for whom is the circumcision ritual performed? They believe it is done not to solve the psychodynamic conflicts of the individual father or his son, but to solve the political conflicts of the tribe. By allowing his son to be circumcised, the father demonstrates publicly to his brothers, chief, and other close kinsmen that he is loyal and will not leave. When a father hands over his son to the tribal establishment he is yielding to the group's authority and power. As we noted in Chapter 4, circumcision occasionally goes wrong even in a modern hospital; among primitive tribes, accidents are common and the child may even die. (Participants often make nervous jokes that illustrate their awareness of risk. Tiv fathers tell the circumciser: "Easy, easy, or many women will weep.") But that is the point. The ritual *must* involve risk, and risk of the man's reproductive ability at that, for it to counter the risk of fission. Circumcision is never done on the ear, or elbow, or ankle, but on the penis, organ of procreation and power.

Some anthropological explanations of circumcision regard the ritual as a rite of passage, a ceremony that initiates boys into manhood. John Whiting, Richard Kluckhohn, and Albert Anthony (1958) believe it serves to break a boy's emotional bond to his mother and assure proper masculine identity. One trouble with such interpretations, the Paiges say, is that the timing of circumcision rituals varies widely. Of the twenty-one tribes in their sample that practice the custom, boys are circumcised in infancy in four, in early or late childhood in ten, at puberty in six, and in late adolescence in one. This age distribution, and the fact that even members of the same culture may disagree over whether and when to circumcise their sons, persuades the Paiges that the purpose of the operation is not to impress masculine standards on the child. The child is a passive central character; the ceremony is not for him but for the adults. Among the Thonga the clan chief orders the ceremony for all boys between ten and sixteen, and if necessary he will use force to compel them to have the operation. This is the most common pattern—a village elder commands a reluctant father to have his sons circumcised.

The force of the ritual is made especially clear when a father disobeys. A man who does not allow the circumcision of his son is telling everyone that he can't be trusted, that he is an individualist who might leave the tribe at any time and had better be watched carefully. If he can't be counted on to sacrifice his son, at least symbolically, he certainly can't be counted on in the next war. (This is a function of many group rituals. A Mormon who drinks coffee and an Indian who eats the sacred cow are both announcing the limits of their loyalty to the group.) The Paiges describe in colorful detail the politics of circumcision in many tribes. Kinsmen are constantly fighting over who should do the operation and how old the child should be. Sometimes the timing of a circumcision settles a brewing feud, or escalates one. Victor Turner (1962), who studied the Ndembu tribe of western Zambia, observed one wily old chief who revived his flagging power over squabbling factions by deciding that a circumcision ritual must be done—and he presided.

Genesis 17 describes circumcision as a social bargain between God and Abraham: "This is my covenant, which ye shall keep, between me and you and thy seed after thee; Every man-child among you shall be circumcised. . . . And the uncircumcised man-child whose flesh of his foreskin is not circumcised, that soul shall be cut off from his people; he hath broken my covenant." The God of the Hebrews was explicit about the loyalty function of circumcision. When Moses broke the covenant by failing to circumcise his son, God threatened to slay the boy. Moses' wife Zipporah cut off her son's foreskin herself to save him (Exodus 4). The ancient Hebrews, as the Paiges point out, were advanced horticulturalists with precisely the kind of economic and political organization to which fission is the greatest threat. Indeed, the story of Genesis is a story of fissions and feuds, of a growing tribe that needed unity and struggled with dissensions. Circumcision, like any test of loyalty, reduces the threat only temporarily. "Ritual provides a means of gaining temporary political advantage, not final political victory," say the Paiges.

couvade "It's a wise child who knows his own father," the saying goes, and from the biological fact that paternity is rarely 100 percent certain comes a wide range of social customs attending childbirth. In some societies women are confined in special huts or moved to another community during childbirth, or their social contacts—especially with men—are severely curtailed, or they are regarded as unclean and dangerous, to be avoided at all costs. In other societies *men* follow the taboos and restrictions. In the most extreme form of husband involvement, couvade, fathers, not mothers, are expected to have labor pains and a long recovery period (see Chapter 5).

Many anthropologists have observed that the birth of a child is occasion for relatives to lay claim to the newborn's allegiance, inheritance, and eventual productive and reproductive capacity. Almost everywhere the rights of such control over the child belong to the father, but the biological father and the legal (sociological) father are not always the same person. The legal father may be the wife's brother, a clan head, a state agency, an ancestral ghost, or even a woman.[4]

Paige and Paige (1973) regard couvade and other birth rituals as symbolic efforts to assert claims to the offspring, made necessary by the absence of more potent means of assertion, such as binding contracts and legal machinery. "Ritual is a poor substitute for legal or political action," they write. "A potential claimant would be ill advised to spend two weeks in a hammock or avoid turtle meat if he could claim his child by hiring a lawyer or organizing a war party." Preindustrial tribes do not have these alternatives, and for them paternity rights depend on a complex set of bargains and rituals. The Paiges hypothesized that restrictions on the pregnant woman and participation of the husband in rituals like couvade would occur in different kinds of societies. Table 12 summarizes the birth practices found in their sample of 114 tribal societies. They found that, like circumcision, restrictions on women are most likely to occur in societies in which men are strongly organized and can enforce the restrictions, and in which wealth is exchanged at the marriage. A groom who pays a bride price expects a fertile wife. If she is barren or produces a defective child, the husband and his kinsmen may demand a refund from her father, in the form of an additional wife, some cows, even someone else's child. When males are not effectively organized, they cannot restrict women and control the birth process by careful monitoring of the female's activities and whereabouts. Without legal or military recourse, they must assert their claims another way: through ritual involvement. The Paiges found that couvade is most likely to occur in tribes that do not have strongly organized male groups, do not practice exchanges of wealth at marriage, and do not offer compensation to a husband for his wife's fertility problems. Both restrictions on women and the involvement of husbands are alternative male methods of asserting

[4] In twenty African tribes, such as the Ibos of Nigeria and the Simbiti of Tanzania, a woman can literally buy the status of "male" if she has accumulated enough cows or other wealth. She may then buy herself a wife and become a legal husband. She does not have sex with her bride but arranges partners for her, and the female husband will be the accepted father of any children that result (O'Brien, in Friedl 1975).

Table 12. Birth Practices in Tribal Societies

Maternal Restrictions

Social (high):

Structural seclusion	Confined to dwelling during pregnancy at least 2 weeks prior to delivery; secluded in special hut; moved to other community during birth process.
Social avoidance	Contact with people, especially men, restricted during pregnancy. Pregnant women avoided and believed to be unclean and dangerous, evil.

Personal (low):

Sex taboo	Sexual relations with husband restricted for at least 2 months before delivery.
Food taboo	Eating certain foods during either pregnancy or postpartum is restricted.
Minor	Restrictions on looking at ugly objects, wearing certain clothing, working too hard, etc.

Husband Involvement

Couvade (high):

Seclusion	Secluded in dwelling during pregnancy or postpartum with or without mother and child. May also be considered unclean. Avoids others.
Postpartum work taboo	Refrains from performing normal tasks during postpartum period. Must remain close to home; contact with others minimized.
Food taboo	Refrains from eating certain foods during pregnancy or postpartum.

Minor (low):

Minor observances	Minor ritual observances, such as seeking a vision, performs birth-related sacrifices. May help wife with daily chores.
Informal	Residual category: no changes in normal behavior. No ritual observances.

SOURCE: Paige and Paige 1973.

paternity and protecting their rights to the children, but which method is used depends on the economic and social structure of the community.

When the Paiges argue that rituals are a form of psychological warfare designed to persuade some individuals of other individuals' intentions, they are using psychological notions to link economic condition A with ritual behavior B. Many anthropologists would be content to find simply that A and B coexist. The Paiges want to show how the bargains that live in the heads of a tribe's members solve social problems: if I go through labor with my wife you will believe I am the child's real father; if I let my son be circumcised, you will believe I am loyal; if you share your meat from a successful hunt with me, I will share mine with you when I am lucky and you are not. The idea to think about is that these psychological bargains are effects, not causes. They result from conflicts that originate in a group's economic system, not from conflicts in people's minds.

sexuality vs. the system

To explain the sexual suppression of women, biological theories are frequently posed. Men have a stronger sex drive, which is why they have all those wives and mistresses and lovers. Polygyny (one man with several wives) is more popular than polyandry (one woman with several husbands)[5] because men want to have sex more often than women do; a man can satisfy many women but a woman can't quench the fires of many men. Social customs and marriage practices, this theory runs, result from this basic difference between the sexes.

Mary Jane Sherfey (1973), a psychiatrist who thinks that matriarchies were the earliest type of human social organization, believes that women, not men, have the stronger sex drive. In prehistoric times, she says, women were as sexually active as some nonhuman female primates are today. A female chimpanzee may have coitus twenty to fifty times a day during the peak week of estrus (her fertile period). She flirts and flaunts her charms in the most provocative way to attract a male, stimulating him to perform a series of copulations; when she is done she leaves him panting on the ground and seduces another male. A female may emerge from estrus with wounds inflicted by weary males who have had enough. Sherfey firmly

---

[5] Polygyny occurs 141 times more often than polyandry. In a random sample of 1,179 world societies, almost 15 percent practice monogamy; 85 percent practice limited or general polygyny; and only .6 percent—seven societies—practice limited polyandry (Divale and Harris 1976).

believes that "something akin to this behavior could be paralleled by the human female if her civilization allowed it."[6]

Female hypersexuality was adaptive at one time, Sherfey thinks, because it insured that women would continually be pregnant. But when in the course of evolution human females became even sexier than chimpanzees, and could have sex any day of the month instead of just around the time of ovulation, their sexual insatiability posed a social problem. It would never do to have women lurking in forests to lure unsuspecting males away from their work. Women who were thinking about sex all the time would not be content to stay at home, attending to maternal duties. In fact, they wouldn't want to stay home at all, which put the family in danger. As civilization developed to the point where it was based not on hunting and gathering but on settled agricultural economies, a stable family structure was essential. When the irresistible force of female sexuality met the immovable object of the family, something had to give. The suppression of female sexuality, Sherfey continues, was at times cruel and oppressive, but this was not because men were inherently sadistic or selfish or because women were inherently weak or masochistic. "The strength of the drive determines the force required to suppress it," she concludes.[7]

Sherfey's theory has many opponents and lots of loopholes. There is no evidence, as we noted in Chapter 1, that women originally ran the sexual show or that matriarchies were the prototypical form of human organization. There is no evidence, even from the hunting societies that today are closest to the original form of human social organization, that women behave or ever did behave like female chimpanzees in heat. Sherfey does not explain why *male* hypersexuality didn't "threaten the family." An even more telling problem with the theory, as with most biological arguments, is that it cannot account for societal differences. Women are not sexually suppressed in all

---

[6] See Chapter 4 for a review of some problems in comparing human beings to other primates. But Sherfey also bases much of her theory on Masters and Johnson's findings about the female multiple orgasm.

[7] Like Freud, Sherfey regards sexual energy as a powerful and rather dangerous force, and like him she seems ambivalent about the desirability of unleashing it. The logical implication of her theory is that if cultural restrictions on female sexuality are removed, women will be having sex day in and day out. The consequence of female and sexual liberation, Sherfey worries, may be a backlash: an "inevitable and mandatory" return to repressive rules, so that the family as a basic social unit can continue. We are including her theory partly because so many people today regard liberation movements as a threat to the family, and some husbands worry that if the Mrs. gets to "like it" too much, she will leave home for greener beds.

cultures; remember Mangaia? In societies that give women considerable sexual freedom, people still manage to get married and raise children. Sherfey's ideas are provocative, but it will not do to replace theories that overestimate the male sex drive with theories that overestimate the female sex drive.

For these reasons, we think it is necessary to look elsewhere to explain sexual customs. A good way to begin is by asking: what is the net effect of beliefs that couples can have sex only at certain times, or that women are dirty and to be avoided, or that women are inherently lustful (or lustless)? One answer from converging lines of research is that many of these attitudes and their corresponding rituals serve to increase the chances for conception when population is low and to decrease them when population is pressing against resources.

sexual customs and population control Ernestine Friedl (1975), an anthropologist, cites a recent study of the remarkable differences between two tribes that live in New Guinea. In the highlands, people believe that intercourse weakens men, that women are dangerously threatening and unclean, and that menstrual blood can do all sorts of terrifying things. Sex is considered powerful and mysterious; it must not be performed in a garden or the act will blight the crops. Antagonism between the sexes runs high. Men often delay marriage because bride prices are so high, and many remain bachelors. Not so far away, another tribe has an opposite view of women and sex. They think sexual intercourse is fun and even has a revitalizing effect on men. They think sex *should* take place in gardens, as it will foster the growth of plants. The only worry men have about sex is whether they can perform as well as custom decrees and as females like. The living quarters of men and women are not segregated, the way they are in the highlands. The sexes get along relatively well.

Why the two sets of attitudes? One explanation is that the highland people have been settled a long time and have little new land or resources; a population increase would seriously strain the food supply. Sexual antagonism, fear of coitus, and an acceptance of bachelorhood are all good ways to lower the birth rate, just as prosex attitudes are an excellent way to increase it. The sexy tribe lives in uncultivated areas, and it needs more group members to cultivate the land and help the group defend itself against hostile neighbors.[8]

---

[8] Friedl observes that the population-pressure explanation of sexual attitudes is not the only one possible. Several forces may reinforce each other. As Harris argues, the "warfare complex"—the entire constellation of battle, population control, kin structures, and political organization—all interact to produce a tribe's particular customs.

Many societies have sexual rules whose effect is to lower or raise the birth rate. In some tribes heterosexual intercourse is taboo for 205 to 260 days a year, and on New Britain Island (a territory of New Guinea) men are so afraid of sex that *they* are the ones who worry about being raped (Rubin 1975). In many societies sex is taboo after a woman has a baby, sometimes for several years. Conversely, the orthodox Jewish belief that a woman is unclean during her period and for seven days thereafter assures that intercourse will occur near ovulation. Certainly the Catholic taboo on birth control results in a higher Catholic birth rate.

Sexual freedom or repressiveness, in other words, has its origin in nonsexual events. In many Polynesian societies boys and girls are sexually free before marriage. At the other end of the sexual continuum, neither sex may have intercourse before marriage. In the middle are all sorts of variations: girls may have sex but woe if they get pregnant, or girls may have sex only with their fiancés, to whom they are betrothed as children. In reviewing the research on premarital sex rules, Friedl found that permissiveness occurs in tribes that do not require large-scale property exchanges at marriage. This makes good economic sense. In many tribes, elders control the economic resources of the group, and they determine which woman shall be exchanged for how much property. When marriages entail high bride prices that one kin group pays to another, you can bet that the buyer wants unused merchandise. Families limit the sexual activity of the young so as to increase the girl's value at marriage.[9] With this interpretation, one could have predicted that in the United States, as marriage evolved away from being a means of property exchange with women as the pawns, and as dowries vanished and the strength of kin groups diminished, the premium on female virginity would fade. As it has.

polygyny and polyandry Ester Boserup (1970), writing on the economics of polygyny, explains the usefulness of a man's having many wives in African tribal economies. In regions where land is widely available for cultivation, polygyny advances its development. A man with several wives gains workers for his fields and producers of his children, wealth on two counts. For their part, the wives are not unhappy with the system, or at least no more unhappy than monogamous wives are in the West. A Tiv

[9] One factor that does *not* seem to have much to do with premarital sex rules is the probability of illegitimate children. Even in the most permissive Polynesian societies, the rate of premarital pregnancies is low. For nutritional reasons, menarche occurs later than it does in industrial nations (age sixteen or so) and females tend to be infertile for the first year or two after menarche. When a premarital pregnancy does occur, no one is terribly concerned. The child is usually adopted by the girl's family.

woman expressed dismay when a visiting anthropologist, Laura Bohannan, told her that English men have only one wife at a time. "Only one? The poor wife! Who helps her hoe the fields, deliver her children, prepare the food, mend the clothes, and tend the infants?" (Who, indeed.) In most polygynous households, conflict among the wives is minimized by a set of rules that specifies how often the husband sleeps with each wife, and how often each wife must cook for the husband (Lamphere 1974; Leis 1974).

Polygyny, in other words, has survival benefits in certain kinds of societies. Horticultural tribes are much more likely than hunters and foragers to allow men to have several wives, and the reason seems to be, again, the greater accumulation of property and all forms of wealth among farming societies (Friedl 1975). Women become valuable possessions, not only for the sons they can bear for defense but for the land they bring with them at marriage, which unifies kin groups. The more wives a man has, then, the more wealth he has, and the more bodies are available to tend his property. It's a matter of economics, not sex drive.

Why polyandry never emerged as a safe means of population control is a mystery. If one woman hoarded several husbands the men would be reproductively redundant. But instead, as Divale and Harris (1976) note, "we find female infanticide limiting the number of females and polygyny exacerbating the shortage." The answer, they assume, is that the need to control population through the sacrifice of female infants overbalanced the desirability of having more adult females for sexual partners and workers. And more males than females were necessary because males were the fighters, defenders, and hunters.

Another factor that undoubtedly militated against polyandry was the little matter of paternity and lineage. Identifying a child's mother is both easy and, in a patrilineal system, rather unimportant. Identifying a child's father is crucial and, if a woman has more than one husband, very difficult. Early tribes could not solve this problem with rules for each man's access to the wife, because they did not understand the connection between intercourse, menstruation, and pregnancy. But the reasons for the absence of the custom are still not entirely known, possibly because until recently anthropologists were more interested in the causes and consequences of polygyny.

subsistence and status: why men matter more

the Marxist model

The original philosopher of materialism was Karl Marx, who thought that to understand behavior one had to start with the basic economic conditions of people's lives, not with the ideas in their heads. Economics, Marx thought, was the groundwork for the ideological superstructure of law, politics, custom, art, ideas. In preindustrial societies, as among hunters and gatherers, people produced or killed just what they needed. In capitalist societies, the aim is to create surplus goods that can be exchanged for labor. Preindustrial societies, Marx thought, were egalitarian; no group exploited another. But capitalism brought class structure, the emergence of an exploiting group that grew rich on the labor of workers. Marx believed that the inherent conflict between owners and workers would inevitably lead to revolution by the workers, and that a classless socialist system would be born from the ashes of the old. Although Marx was not overly concerned with sex and status differences, many writers have used his theory to account for the subjection of women around the world. As Gayle Rubin (1975) notes, "It has been argued that women are a reserve labor force for capitalism, that women's generally lower wages provide extra surplus to a capitalist employer, that women serve the ends of capitalist consumerism in their roles as administrators of family consumption, and so forth."

Marx's collaborator, Friedrich Engels, took the next step. In *The Origin of the Family, Private Property and the State*, Engels added sex to Marxist economics, noting that work is not the whole of human experience and that people do need to reproduce themselves. Although Engels' book shared some nineteenth-century misconceptions about the existence of matriarchies and the egalitarianism of primitive tribes, his work contributed a provocative idea: the monogamous family as an economic unit is what constrains women and assures their subjugation. Engels believed that "as wealth increased it made the man's position in the family more important than the woman's, and . . . created an impulse to exploit this strengthened position in order to overthrow, in favor of his children, the traditional [matriarchal] order of inheritance." The overthrow of "mother right," he went on, meant "*the world historical defeat of the female sex.* The man took command in the home also; the woman was degraded and reduced to servitude; she became the slave of his lust and a mere instrument for the production of children" (Engels didn't mince words). You may recall that Wolfgang Lederer, the psychoanalyst, also theorized about a patriarchal revolt against the myths of matriarchy, but his explanation concerned the minds of men, not the economic conditions of their households.

Just as Marx and Engels assumed a basic camaraderie between the sexes in classless societies, so they assumed that the sexes would reunite harmoniously once classless societies returned in the form of communism. Their view that ideas and relationships are shaped by the *tangible* conditions of people's lives—their property, their jobs, their involvement with work—had dramatic impact, both in politics and science. And, as Harris (1968) notes, Marxist theory fits well with a materialist approach to anthropology. But the theory is too narrow to explain such phenomena as Yanomamo hostility to women, sexual segregation among the Kwakiutl, and the practice of genital mutilation among the Sudanese. Nor can it explain why women's work was less valued than men's work long before capitalism dawned.

We turn now to some new efforts to account for the virtual universality of male dominance and for variations in women's status from culture to culture.

digression: a fable

Suppose you landed on an unexplored continent and discovered a species of animal called the uhurdu. They all look alike to you, but eventually you observe that some of them have a freckle behind their ears and others have a stripe on their bellies. Uhurdus live on fuzzy yellow plants that grow plentifully in their habitat, and all uhurdus gather them easily. After a few months, however, you learn that while the fuzzy yellow plants are necessary for the health of the uhurdu, they are not sufficient. Twice a year the species must eat a rare red berry that grows high above them on a steep cliff; if they don't get their dose of the berry, they will weaken and die. Now the freckled uhurdus leave for several weeks, maybe a month or even two, however long it takes to get enough berries for every uhurdu. The striped uhurdus stay behind, feeding fuzzy yellow plants to the newborn. When the freckles come back, they are greeted with celebration and carousing, and a big feast is held for all. The freckle who got the most berries is immediately surrounded by a bevy of flirting stripes.

Being a good anthropologist, you learn to speak hurdish and ask some of the creatures about their social organization. They all tell you that the freckled uhurdu are braver and more intelligent than the stripes, and more important, too. "But the stripes do important work," you object. "They produce small uhurdu, and feed them. They gather fuzzy yellow plants every day and carry loads of them to the nesting site. They make redberry pie and redberry beer and weave redberry skins for winter warmth." "True," the uhurdu tell you, "but any of us could do that. Only the freckles can reap the berries. Without the freckles' work, we would die."

It seems easy to understand why freckled uhurdu would be regarded as more valuable than striped. Their work, though less frequent than plant-gathering, is unpredictable, difficult, and essential. We would not expect the uhurdu to understand nutrition any more than we would expect squirrels to know why they hoard nuts for the winter. In the process of evolution, we would say, the species learned what it took to keep themselves alive.

Many anthropologists try to apply the same kind of analysis to human societies. They explain status differences between the sexes in terms of which sex produces the most food and which sex produces the essential food (protein); as in the case of the uhurdu, these are not always the same sex. Current theories suggest that status differences develop out of the division of labor and the way that food and wealth are distributed among a tribe's members. Such explanations begin with the survival needs a tribe faced. All groups had to reproduce themselves, feed themselves, and defend themselves; if they did not, they died out. For obvious reasons, the job of reproduction went to women. For convenience, their secondary job was gathering food near home base—plant foods, usually. Men, rather by default, devoted their primary energies to hunting animal food and, when necessary, to defense. This early and inevitable division of sexual labor, such theories argue, put men in a better position to acquire and control the valuable resources (Sanday 1973, 1974).

hunters and gatherers vs. horticulturalists

There are about 300,000 people on the earth today who still get food in the original way, through hunting and gathering. These tribes live on wild plants, animals, and fish, in whatever proportion and combination their environments permit. In such societies men are always responsible for hunting large game and deep-sea fishing, and these occupations always carry prestige. Women's work is gathering the staple foods and has less prestige. Sometimes women help with the hunting and fishing, but they are never in charge of these activities.

Although all hunting and gathering societies rely mainly on men to be the hunters, regional environments have created different patterns in the division of labor. Friedl (1975) cites four:

1. Both sexes spend most of their time gathering, usually on an individual basis; men forage for themselves, women forage for themselves and their children. Men spend only a little time hunting, and meat is rarely distributed. (Examples: the Hadza of Tanzania in Africa; the Paliyans of Southwest India.)

2. Both sexes work together to hunt, gather, and fish, though men actually kill the game. Usually, the participating households share in the proceeds; sometimes husbands and wives work as a team and keep their own food. In these societies women can join men on the hunt because game is plentiful or close; for instance, the sexes may join forces to net a large catch during heavy fish runs. (Examples: the Washo of the Great Basin of North America; the Mbuti pygmies of the African Congo).

3. The sexes are highly segregated, with men hunting alone or in small groups and women gathering vegetables and plants near the campsite. Women contribute more than half of the food supply, but men add 30 or 40 percent, which must be distributed to the whole group. This is the most common pattern,[10] and points to the importance of "women's work"—gathering—as the primary means of getting food, which we tend to forget in thinking of the glamour and status of hunting. (Examples: the Tiwi of North Australia; the Bushmen of Africa.)

4. Men provide virtually all the food. This pattern, of which the Eskimos are a familiar example, is the most rare; like the other patterns, it is determined by environmental conditions. Eskimo women have no vegetable gardens to give them a source of food or income: you can't grow corn in ice. Eskimo women, like their Yanomamo peers, have no rights, political or sexual. Men frequently take the women they desire by force, whether or not the women are married. Because women are totally dependent on men for protection and for every subsistence need—for their food and raw materials—their self-esteem comes from their role in the family and from their husbands' social status.

As you might expect, relations between men and women in these four different subsistence patterns range from quite egalitarian to supremely male-dominated. It is no coincidence that where women contribute to the needs of the society and work alongside men, sexual relationships are less hostile than in tribes where women contribute nothing. Notice that social customs and the degree of sexual segregation of tasks reflect the kind of food the environment offers and the ease or difficulty of getting it. Not all tribes adhere to our mythic image of Man the Mighty Warrior and Woman the Passive Gatherer. Yet this is the most common pattern, and from it

---

[10] In one sample of ninety hunting and gathering societies, the *primary* source of food was as follows (Martin and Voorhies 1975):

Gathering	52 societies
Hunting	22 societies
Fishing	7 societies
Gathering and hunting equally	3 societies
Gathering and fishing equally	3 societies
Hunting and fishing equally	3 societies

evolved some sex differences that many authors say are "intrinsic" to the species. How did that sexual division of labor come to pass?

why brawn gets the bacon The usual explanations of why men became the hunters and women the gatherers rest on physical sex differences. Men were better suited to fight and hunt because they were bigger, stronger, more muscular, could run faster, had greater lung capacity, and were more motivated by hormonally based aggressive drives. As we noted earlier, Marvin Harris thinks that physical strength was virtually the only reason that men became the warriors and hence the dominant sex. Some feminist anthropologists now take issue with the physical strength explanation. "The labor record of primitive women does not warrant the assertion that [women] were physically weak or helpless," says Evelyn Reed (1975). On the contrary, the heavy burdens that women carried, the hard work they did in the fields, the labor involved in everything from construction to domestic chores, all meant that women had to be extremely strong. Reed goes so far as to suggest that the many burdens of women's work "gave them a high degree of endurance and the strength to lift *heavier* loads than men."

Arguments about physical strength seem pointless because they cannot be resolved, but the issue itself is important. Newer approaches suggest that those who believe the egg came first should think about the chicken. For example, perhaps it was not that men became hunters because they were stronger than women; perhaps men became stronger than women once they had to be hunters. Analogously, Friedl (1975) observes that many people assume that the number of children a woman has determines how fully she participates in the work force: pregnancy and childbirth clearly limit her ability to work. But perhaps, Friedl says, a society's subsistence needs and its ecology set limits on how many children a woman can be "permitted" to have. In societies that require considerable female labor, an adaptive solution would be to generate taboos and sexual customs that would insure a greater spacing of children. Indeed, in hunting and gathering societies such as the Bushmen of Africa, where women contribute up to two thirds of the tribe's food, women nurse each child for four years. Women do not usually ovulate while they are breast feeding a child; thus female Bushmen (sic) can travel long distances to collect food without carrying more than one child at a time. In short, Friedl proposes that the spacing of children and styles of child-rearing are everywhere adjusted to the work that women have to do. Work is not adjusted to the frequency of childbirth. With one exception: child-bearing meant that women couldn't hunt.

Why not? Why didn't the sexes take turns searching for deer and tapirs and caring for the toddlers? In our modern, relatively flexible society, changing roles and alternating jobs seems a reasonable solution. One friend of ours thought it would be quite acceptable for tribal women to hunt now and then while the men cared for the young and very old. The only problems she foresaw were family squabbles: "You took *three weeks* and only brought back *one* deer, and now I'm supposed to catch twenty tapirs in three days?"

Friedl suggests that structural factors caused the assignment of men to hunting and women to gathering. First, women could not be hunters on a regular basis because they are the child-bearers, in two senses: they bear them during pregnancy and they often carry them around (for nursing and feeding) when they are small. A society in which females were raised, along with males, to be hunters would be wasting its efforts. Girls marry at just the time they could become skilled hunters, and they spend most of their child-bearing years pregnant or nursing.

When we say women couldn't hunt, though, remember that we are talking about a certain kind of subsistence hunting—the kind that requires roaming far from home for an unpredictable length of time. Child-bearing is perfectly compatible with hunting small game and fishing near home. It is not compatible, Friedl points out, with long-distance hunting. A hunter who hopes to bag a deer cannot also plan to carry home a sack of roots and berries, much less a tearful child. Because hunting is such an uncertain activity—meat may be found quickly or only after many days and miles of travel—a tribe that let "anyone" hunt would have found a maladaptive solution. Someone reliably has to feed the tribe each day while someone else chases the game. The most important consequence of the resulting male monopoly on hunting was that men controlled the valuable meat. All foraging cultures, Friedl says, have rules to assure the distribution of meat throughout the tribe, while the plant food that women collect tends to be for their immediate households only. This distribution system meant that men acquired a society-wide network of mutual exchanges and obligations, while women's influence was limited to the family. And thus was born a sex difference in power.

When human groups began to domesticate animals and cultivate crops, events that occurred only about 10,000 years ago, the fundamental nature of subsistence changed, and so did social customs and relationships. As we said earlier, settling down meant the need for a warrior class to defend property. Friedl explains the emergence of men as fighters in the same terms that account for their role as hunters: fighting, like hunting, occurs at irregular intervals and is incompatible with gathering and childcare.

Tribal societies based on horticulture[11] permit a much wider range of sex-role variations, because both sexes can work in the fields with children beside them. The only monopoly men seem to have in horticultural systems is that they clear the land, chopping down trees and cutting away the underbrush. After that, either sex or both may be responsible for cultivating and harvesting the crops. Friedl notes that clearing the land, unlike hunting, does not automatically give men the right to distribute food. Distribution rights vary across cultures, and women's fortunes vary accordingly.

protein and power The idea that women get higher status when they control a tribe's economic resources is supported by the case of the Iroquois (Brown 1970, 1975). The Iroquois depended on cultivated foods for their subsistence: men prepared the fields and women planted and harvested the crops. The tribe's basically vegetable diet was supplemented by fish, which both sexes caught, and game, which men hunted, occasionally joined by women. In many ways the sexes lived separate lives, even eating the daily meal apart from each other. The men were often away on war parties and hunting expeditions for years at a time. Iroquois women worked together in cohesive groups, and the distribution of food was left to the matrons, a select group of older wives. Their control over the political decisions of the Council of Elders, Brown believes, was related to their control of the provisions for the hunting and war parties. She quotes an observer who wrote, "The women could hinder or actually prevent a war party which lacked their approval by not giving the supplies of dried corn and the moccasins which the warriors required."

Some writers have attributed the power of Iroquois women to the matrilineal social structure of the tribe. But in other matrilineal societies, such as the Bemba, women did not have the status of the Iroquois women (Brown 1970). One major difference between the two tribes is that the Iroquois enjoyed rich plentiful harvests, while the Bemba endured recurrent scarcity of food. The abundant crops and stored wealth of the Iroquois women gave them a stable, predictable right to distribute resources. Among the Bemba, the shortage of food led to a centralized political system in which food was distributed by the chief. In adaptive terms, both tribes made good decisions. The object of food distribution, after all, is not to give all tribe members equal status but to see that all get fed.

[11] The difference between horticulture and agriculture is that horticulturalists prepare the soil and plant crops with a hoe and digging stick, whereas agriculturalists use plows or machines.

Peggy Sanday (1973, 1974) studied twelve societies, including the Iroquois, in which female status ranged from very high to nonexistent. She defined status as the degree to which women had the power to make decisions that affected the tribe as a whole, not just a woman's own family. She used four indicators of female status, as shown in Table 13: (1) material control—do women distribute food and wealth outside the family? (2) demand for female produce—is the work that women do valued outside the family, in the marketplace? (3) political participation—do women express opinions and influence policy in official ways? (4) group strength—do women belong to solidarity groups devoted to women's political and economic interests? In some of the societies that Sanday looked at, such as the Yoruba and the Iroquois, the answer to all four questions was yes. In others, such as the Toda and the Somali, the answer to all four was no.

When Sanday compared the status of women in each society with the percentage of food they contributed, she got the surprising results shown in Figure 5. When women's contribution was very low, their status was very low; Toda women contribute 10 percent of the food, for example, and their status was lowest. So far, not startling. But Sanday found that when

Table 13. Female Status in Twelve Societies

| | INDICATORS | | | | |
Society	Female material control	Demand for female produce	Female political partici- pation	Female solidarity groups	Status scale score
Yoruba	P	P	P	P	5
Iroquois	P	P	P	P	5
Samoans	?	P	P	P	5
Crow	P	P	P	A	4
Aymara	P	P	A	A	3
Tapirape	?	P	A	A	3
Rwala	P	?	A	A	3
Andamans	P	A	A	A	2
Tikopia	A	A	A	A	1
Azande	A	?	A	A	1
Somali	A	A	A	A	1
Toda	A	A	A	A	1

A = absent   P = present   ? = information unclear or unavailable
SOURCE: Sanday 1974.

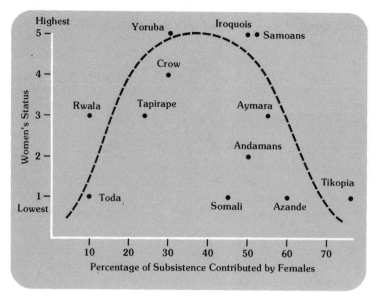

Figure 5. The relationship between female status in twelve cultures and women's contribution to group subsistence. Women have the highest status when they contribute about half of the food, not when they provide the least (10 percent)—or even the most (75 percent).
ADAPTED FROM Sanday 1974.

women's contribution was very *high*, their status was still very low. Tikopia women contribute 75 percent of the food, and they are no better off than the Toda. Female status was highest in tribes in which women contributed just about as much as men. Despite such exceptions as the Rwala and the Somali, a balanced division of labor apparently does the most to balance sexual status.

But even that is not enough to assure sexual harmony. Orna and Allen Johnson (1975), as well as many sociologists, have found another factor that affects how the sexes think of each other: how work is organized. When the sexes are mutually dependent and work cooperatively, as in husband-wife teams, sexual antagonism is much lower than when work is organized along sex-segregated lines. Among the Machiguenga Indians of Peru, where the sexes cooperate in growing manioc, fishing, and recreation, husbands and wives feel solidarity with each other, not with their same-sex friends. Among the Mundurucú, women and men work in same-sex groups, and friendships rarely cross sexual lines; women feel a sense of solidarity with other women, men with men. Among the Yanomamo (a tribe that apparently fascinates everyone), the women are alienated from men and isolated from each other. Sexual antagonism is highest in this case. Such research suggests that the question of which sex is more "affiliative"—whether in terms of male bonding or female sociability—has less to do with inborn traits than with social organization.

It is still puzzling that women have low status even when they control the production of most foods. Why don't the Tikopia women behave like the male Yanomamos or Eskimos? One answer comes from our uhurdu fable: the nutritional staples of a society do not necessarily provide its protein. Women may supply 75 percent of the tribe's total calories, but the remaining 25 percent may be nutritionally more valuable. High status requires the control not just of resources but of rare resources, the most valued ones. Imagine that you control "only" 10 percent of a Bedouin tribe's resources— but that the 10 percent is their water—and you will have an inkling of why male control of protein originally gave them such power.

Sanday, Friedl, and other anthropologists imply that certain psychological associations were established in people's minds as time rolled on. Hunting = essential activity; men = hunting; therefore men = essential activity.[12] This set of associations may have survived long past its literal validity for a tribe. Certainly it makes little sense for societies like our own, in which hunting is for recreation, not survival.

evaluating the evolutionary perspective

The connection between a tribe's economy and its sexual customs and attitudes is not a straight line between two points. Many intervening factors are important: availability of food, population pressures, need for warfare, the structure of work and family roles, technological inventions, and so on.

---

[12] Some readers will surely object: isn't reproduction an essential activity? Why does having babies bring less status than hunting game? One answer may be that hunting (like war) was more dangerous and therefore had to be glorified if anyone was to do it. Fighting and hunting are life-threatening activities that generate emotional energy for the participants and the tribe. Sherry Ortner (1974) thinks that societies put a higher value on all things, events, and activities that are under human control (culture) than on events they cannot control (nature). Women, by virtue of their reproductive functions, stand closer to nature than to culture, and thus women and women's work are devalued. But the question is far from answered.

The particular way a society weaves these factors together creates its particular set of rituals, customs, and beliefs about the sexes. As Michelle Rosaldo (1974) summarizes, inequalities between men and women are built into the unequal assignments of domestic and public work. The most egalitarian societies are those in which both roles are valued and both sexes participate in household activities and important public events. Women are oppressed and lack social worth, she says, to the extent that they are confined to the home, cut off from other women and the outside world.[13] They gain power and status when they leave the domestic sphere.

The advantage of the system perspective—that it tries to tie together many factors and show how they operate together—is also its disadvantage. The evolutionary view is tough to wrestle down to empirical bedrock. In the broadest sense, evolutionary arguments maintain that male supremacy has lasted for the same reason that there are two sexes instead of one or three: if alternatives were ever tried, they didn't work.[14] Although in the most general sense this explanation may be correct, it permits a "we're here because we're here" conclusion and allows for the belief that any system or practice that survives must be "good."

But social evolution is a constant process. At any one time it is hard to tell which systems and customs exist because they work and which are evolution's errors and will die. A critical issue for functionalists is to predict which is which. They cannot have it both ways. They cannot assume today that all existing customs are adaptive and tomorrow that any custom that has changed was maladaptive.

Obviously, it is easier to study a tribe of seventy-five members than a nation of seventy-five million. The larger and more complex a social system

---

[13] Boserup (1970) observes some unexpected implications of birth control in the rural African communities she studied. When women work long and hard in the fields, they are valued both as workers and wives. In tribes in which hired laborers do the field work (a "modern" convention), women are valued only as mothers, a lesser status, and especially as mothers of sons who will work the fields and earn money. Barren women are therefore considered useless. If birth control is adopted in such societies, Boserup warns, the result could be to lower the status of women even further.

[14] There are two sexes, actually, because two is the most efficient minimum number for the exchange of genetic information. An organism that reproduces itself gains no new material. Two sexes are sufficient for assuring the genetic recombinations necessary for variation and adaptation. A third sex would add no new genes but lots of social aggravation and sexual inefficiency.

becomes, the harder it is to relate one part of the system to the others—and the greater the time lag between a change in material conditions and a corresponding change in customs and beliefs. Functionalists use this observation to explain, and sometimes excuse, the failure of a prediction that an economic change will bring cultural change. But how many years shall we wait? Thirty? Three hundred? Three thousand? In almost every society, for example, men work with metals and women do not. There no longer seems to be a functional explanation for this division of labor. Friedl (1975) speculates that men acquired the ability because they originally used metals to make weapons for battle and hunting, but why have they kept it for so long? In modern industrial nations there is more room for a variety of traditions and customs, and it becomes even harder to know when the survival function of a practice is gone, leaving only a behavioral shell.

As sociologist Alvin Gouldner (1970) has pointed out, a functionalist approach makes survival the ultimate yardstick. It implies that any social practice that "works" not only will but should continue. Gouldner regards functionalism as basically conservative because it nods benignly at stability (and thus at the status quo) and views change with alarm, as a sign that something has "malfunctioned." People in positions of power can use functionalist theories to justify many of the questionable practices that have had long and healthy lives: not only male supremacy but war, slavery, infanticide, and wholesale imprisonment, oppression, and slaughter of outgroups of every description. For whom are these practices "functional"? Theories that concentrate on the consequences of a custom for the society as a whole may miss its consequences for particular groups within that society. American slavery, for example, was certainly dysfunctional for blacks, but it benefited plantation owners and it "worked" as a basis for the southern economic system. Similarly, it is not always obvious what the costs and benefits of women's lesser status are—for a society, for its women, or for its men.

Not all materialists believe in the conservative aspects of functionalism, by any means. Efforts to find economic causes of human behavior often feed the fires of change—as Marx's theory has. Harris believes that if we can identify the rational reasons for our apparently irrational practices—and understand that these customs are born from environmental pressures, not genetic ones—we can change the conditions that create dissatisfaction, exploitation, and war. His view raises again one of the most fascinating and important issues of our time: the control of our destiny. Do human societies evolve mindlessly, like anemones and aardvarks, or is there a place for human purpose?

cultural vs. biological evolution

The parallels between human evolution and the evolution of other species have tempted many writers since Darwin's day. To some, Darwin's principles of biological evolution—gene mutation followed by the retention of the traits that prove most adaptive for the species—seemed to apply to human societies as well. "Survival of the fittest" apparently explained why some cultures failed and others flourished. The social Darwinists assumed that evolution therefore meant progress, a steady move from the "primitive" toward the "civilized."

Today it is generally recognized that the evolution of human societies is not precisely analogous to the evolution of species. People, unlike cabbages and dinosaurs, have minds and language, which permit learning and communication. Today evolution means change, continuous adaptations over time, not necessarily "progress" (Wispé and Thompson 1976). Social groups can deliberately speed change up, slow it down, and alter its direction. Cultural and technological change can influence, even overcome, the impact of biological change. Poor eyesight would affect the survival chances of a New Guinea hunter, but a nearsighted editor in the jungles of New York can survive quite nicely with glasses.

Recently Donald Campbell (1975a, 1975b), an eminent social psychologist, has argued that one analogy between biological and cultural evolution is too important to lose. Campbell thinks that many of our social traditions have passed the test of evolution and thereby acquired a sort of historical wisdom. Some are institutions, such as marriage, which have existed in societies of every size and shape. Some are religious and moral injunctions, such as honoring one's father and mother and not murdering one's neighbor. Campbell calls these traditions "wise superstitions"—wise because they have helped people survive, and superstitions because people believe in them for reasons they do not fully understand. He explains:

> Evolution produces traditions that are beneficial and adaptive *without people knowing why*. That's why I think it's just as rational to follow religious rules that one doesn't understand as to continue breathing when one doesn't understand the role of oxygen in bodily metabolism. That's what I call a "wise" superstition (Campbell 1975a, p. 55).

As far as Campbell is concerned, people should proceed with caution when tempted to go against the wisdom of ages. We might not realize how necessary a tradition is to our survival as a group until it is too late.

This kind of argument is heard often these days, as in all times of social upheaval. Upstarts and revolutionaries are warned not to rock the boat as others try to etch the status quo in granite. But the same perspective that makes us aware of "wise superstitions" also shows that when conditions change, so do social systems. Human beings are not the pawns of evolutionary forces; they have at least some capacity to control the environment instead of merely responding to it. In the next chapter we will consider some twentieth-century efforts by modern nations to create the proper conditions for sexual equality.

9

Conclusion: The age of alliance?

There never was a good war or a bad peace.
—*Benjamin Franklin*

Only a peace between equals can last.
—*Woodrow Wilson*

"Male supremacy is on the way out in all industrialized nations," says Marvin Harris. "Male supremacy was just a phase in the evolution of culture." Harris, an anthropologist, makes his matter-of-fact assertion by taking the long view with an evolutionist's eye. In the twentieth century, for the *first time* in human history, conditions have permitted societies to experiment with equality. Birth control means that women can decide when and even whether to have babies. Overpopulation means that families must get smaller. Industrialization has brought affluence to millions and provided them with the leisure time to consider less traditional life styles. Warfare is largely mechanized, and males have no particular edge over females at pushing buttons to launch a deadly battle. The radically and rapidly altered conditions of life in this century suggest, says Harris, that male supremacy is just a long first act in a show that is not yet over.

Attempts at egalitarianism in this century have crossed national and ideological boundaries. In some countries, such as Sweden, a more equal division of labor between the sexes simply evolved, and political philosophy followed. Other efforts, such as the Israeli kibbutz, started from scratch as attempts to put theory and dreams into practice. Some nations, such as the Soviet Union and the People's Republic of China, went through complete revolutionary overhauls that brought millions of feudal peasants into the twentieth century in the flicker of an eyelid. By taking a look at how these experiments are turning out, and at how ideology and reality differ, we can get an idea of the barriers to equality and of the prospects for overcoming them.

We can also see what the idea of "equality" means in different countries, and how it relates to a country's particular needs, history, and economic and political system. Equality can mean getting women out of the home and into the work force, or assuring women of political power, or breaking down all personality and task differences based on sex, or getting rid of archaic laws designed to keep women barefoot and pregnant. Some cultures are so far from equality by any definition that it is remarkable if women are allowed to show their faces or choose their husbands. In others, the term implies equal opportunity at all levels. As New York's State Education Commissioner put it, "Equality is not when a female Einstein gets promoted to assistant professor; equality is when a female schlemiel moves ahead as fast as a male schlemiel." Your evaluation of a country's efforts at equality will depend on your definition and your values.

case 1: the Soviet Union

In every society, wrote Marx and Engels, "the degree of emancipation of women is a natural standard of the general emancipation." The Soviet Union was the first country to try to put this belief into practice; one of the first orders of business after the 1917 revolution was to change the laws affecting women. Women quickly got the right to work alongside men, to have abortions on demand for unwanted pregnancies, and to end unhappy, arranged marriages with easy divorces. During the first heady years after the revolution, reformers were optimistic that socialism, having destroyed the economic basis of inequality, would automatically bring the demise of the patriarchal bourgeois family and liberate women. Women would take their rightful place as "productive" members of society, doing work that benefited the nation as a whole and not just the individual or the family. The state would take over the service work, childcare, and household chores. As Engels wrote, "The modern individual family is based on the open or disguised domestic enslavement of the woman; private housekeeping should become a social industry." Communal dining rooms, government-run nursery schools, and professional laundries would solve the age-old problem of who does the dirty work.

In terms of the "productive work" part of this blueprint, the country's economic needs coincided with ideology. For most of this century the Soviet Union has suffered an acute shortage of men, because so many died during the revolution, a civil war, two world wars, periods of famine, and political upheavals. Before the revolution the ratio of women to men was about equal, but by 1938 it was 108.7 women for every 100 men. And the situation got worse. According to one estimate, nearly half of all the Russian men alive in 1939 died during World War II (Dodge 1966). That may be an exaggeration, but it is no exaggeration to say the country's losses were staggering. And they occurred during the decades when the Soviet Union was struggling to become a major industrial power. The government needed all the female workers it could get; its survival depended on them.

Female workers it got. Today nearly half of the work force is made up of women, and they work in virtually every sort of job. It is not unusual in the Soviet Union to see women as doctors, engineers, judges, professors, janitors, lawyers, sea captains, pilots, industrial laborers, bus drivers, builders. The staff of the Leningrad Institute of High-Molecular Compounds is fond of telling about the Western chemist who came to a conference on new technologies. "And tell me, please," he asked his hosts, "what are these beautiful ladies doing here?" The categories of beautiful lady and chemistry professor obviously did not overlap in his Westernized head (Mandel 1975).

The Soviet Union offers a good example of the glass-half-full, glass-half-empty phenomenon. William Mandel, an optimist, emphasizes how far Soviet women have come in a short sixty years. There is no unemployment, so women can freely enter the fields they want. No woman need be economically dependent on her husband (only one urban woman in ten, and one rural woman in six, depends on her husband for financial support). Women hold 47 percent of the public offices, and they make up almost one third of the two houses of the Supreme Soviet. Mandel interviewed female fighter pilots, astronomers, and sea captains who told him they were not unique, and who were in prestige positions they could never have held in this country. Every working woman is entitled to paid maternity leave. And the prosecution of rape is not the one-sided event it is in most countries, where the victim must defend her virtue.

> A man can get two weeks in jail for "gross behavior" toward his wife, simply on her say-so. Similarly, a man can get three to seven years for rape on the woman's say-so, with no witness needed. This does not mean that Russian courts ignore such realities as the woman who seeks to entrap a man into marriage. . . . But . . . the fact that one third of prosecutors, judges, and lawyers and one half of citizen juror-judges are women immediately makes a difference (Mandel 1975, p. 272).

The need for productive labor in the Soviet Union, and the high respect accorded to workers, means that women do not feel the need to defend themselves for doing "men's work," or "women's work," or any work at all.[1] Nor do they feel guilty about "abandoning" their children to daycare centers and nursery schools, because the cultural belief is that communal child-rearing is better for children and builds good citizens who put their country first.

Hilda Scott (1974), however, belongs to a group of observers who think the Soviet glass is half empty. She finds status differences alive and well in the U.S.S.R. and other communist countries of Eastern Europe. Women work, yes, but they are overrepresented in the lowest-paid, most menial jobs, such as janitors and construction workers. On the average, women still earn less than men do. The high-status jobs, she says, are all but monopolized by men, whether in science, industry, or government. Men still hold the executive jobs, and though many women work on local political committees, hold lesser offices, and belong to trade unions, few women hold positions of real power in the Communist Party or the government. Of the 360 members of the Central Committee of the Communist Party, fourteen are female. ("That figure," says Mandel bravely, "low as it is, is now the highest in the history of the U.S.S.R.") And as several people have noted, as women entered formerly male-dominated professions, the fields were redefined as "feminine"—notably pharmacy, dentistry, chemistry, and medicine (Safilios-Rothschild 1975).

Scott and others are skeptical of claims about female equality because they observe how often ideology has succumbed to circumstance. For example, abortion was readily available after the revolution because, it was said, women should be able to control their own bodies, avoid loveless marriages, and not be slaves to unwanted pregnancies. But none of the planners realized how popular abortion would become. By the 1930s, the government faced a declining birth rate, and in 1936 it did an about-face, outlawing abortion except for certain medical reasons and making divorce more difficult and expensive. Then it took positive measures to increase the birth rate: it offered premiums to women who had more than two children, payments that continued for the first four years of a child's life. Women who produced a number of children earned honors as well. A mother of five children won a Maternity Medal; seven or more children brought the Order of Maternal Glory; and ten or more won mom the title of Mother Heroine (Martin and Voorhies 1975; Field and Flynn 1970). Although Russia eventually liberalized its abortion and divorce laws again in 1966, another socialist

---

[1] The difference between the Soviet Union and the United States in this regard is nicely shown in the names of two magazines. For fifty years the Russians have published "The Woman Worker"—for workers who happen to be female. Finally the United States has gotten around to a magazine called "Working Woman"—for women who happen to work.

country, Rumania, outlawed most abortions and stopped importing contraceptives the same year (Scott 1974).[2]

The course of liberation, like love, never runs smooth. The clearest rumple in the socialist blueprint concerns ideology about the family. Somehow, no one in the Soviet Union ever got around to solving the logistical problems of providing millions of families with professional laundry service, food delivery, and childcare; doing so would have required shifting funds and energies away from more pressing problems. As a result, guess who does the housework and childcare?

The domestic side of life is still regarded by both sexes as the woman's responsibility. Although many children go to state-run nursery schools, the nurseries are not free and not yet available to every child. So most mothers rely on friends or relatives to help them with childcare, and in a crisis it is usually the mother, not the father, who compromises the job for the family (see Chapter 7). It is usually the mother, not the father, who interrupts a career for a few years in an effort to juggle the needs of children, household, and job. And it is usually the mother, not the father, who stands in long lines at the market, prepares meals without benefit of fancy appliances, and cleans the house. The men "help out"—evoking a few sarcastic reactions from women:

> No one who has followed the painful efforts to modernize socialist housework over the past three decades can fail to be struck by the way this is inevitably presented as "the debt we owe our women," as though women were responsible for all the wash that is dirtied and were the sole beneficiaries of clean windows and floors and ate all the potatoes that are lugged home (Scott 1974, p. 197).

> There's a bachelor I knew in three periods of his life. First when he was married and, by his own words, didn't know how to put a teapot on to boil, never mind eggs. . . . Then he got divorced. A miracle followed. He could have been a professor of homemaking. His room wasn't simply clean, it was downright sterile, and the dinners he made for friends were beyond praise. . . . Then he remarried. And immediately stopped cooking dinners, making pickles, and it took an argument for his wife to get him to go down for bread (Russian woman quoted in Mandel 1975, p. 211).

Lenin had berated men for shirking their domestic duties. "Very few

[2] Most of us are so concerned with the long-term consequences of overpopulation that it seems surprising that a government would want to *increase* its population. But a sudden drop in births can have serious short-term results—shortages of workers in critical occupations, reduced demand for consumer goods, a relative increase in the proportion of old people. Is the drop in the U.S. birth rate associated with efforts to strike down liberal abortion laws?

husbands, not even the proletarians, think of how much they could lighten the burdens and worries of their wives, or relieve them entirely, if they lent a hand in this 'woman's work.' But no, that would go against the 'privilege and dignity of the husband.' He demands that he have his rest and comfort." That he does. Soviet writers have considered many ways to lighten woman's burden: giving women less strenuous jobs, arranging part-time work for women or shorter working days, distributing better household appliances, building more childcare facilities, and so on (Field and Flynn 1970). But they seem to be overlooking Lenin's observation that the handiest labor-saving device is a husband.

case 2: the People's Republic of China

Before the revolution of 1949, the Chinese say, all people carried three mountains on their backs—feudalism, capitalism, and imperialism—but women had a fourth burden, male supremacy. A proverb sums up the treatment of women in prerevolutionary China: "A woman married is like a pony bought—to be ridden or whipped at the master's pleasure." Women had no rights—not over their property, their bodies, or their marriages. Fathers sometimes drowned their infant daughters and sold their surviving daughters as concubines and prostitutes. Husbands could beat or even kill their wives with impunity, and landlords could rape them. When a woman married she became subject to the wishes of her husband's family forever; divorce was almost impossible, and widows were forbidden to remarry.

The emancipation of Chinese women started in the nineteenth century, when capitalism began to break up the feudal system that had existed for thousands of years. Industrialization provided women with jobs in the port cities, and although both sexes labored from dawn to dusk for slave wages, women's small incomes did give them a measure of power in the family. Educational and professional opportunities for women increased slightly and feminist movements were organized, though these developments affected only a tiny minority of women. During the first half of this century the official policy of the government (the Kuomintang) was inconsistent. At times it reacted with cruel repression; in 1927, for instance, the Kuomintang executed several hundred women for wearing short haircuts, a symbol of liberation. At other times it became more liberal, at least on paper; in 1931 the Kuomintang gave women the rights to marry freely and to inherit property —though this change was never publicized, much less put into practice (Curtin 1975).

Long before it came to power, the Communist Party showed concern for the low status of women.[3] Party workers (cadres) discovered an effective way to rally women to their cause, to make women understand that their pains and burdens were shared and were not an inevitable part of being female. The cadres would go into a village and get the women to sit together and talk about their lives—nothing political at first, just their lives. Slowly, painfully, then bitterly, the stories came out: the beatings, the humiliations, the defeats. These sessions, which became known as Speak-Bitterness meetings, taught the Chinese women that they were not alone, that their experiences were the experiences of all women. And like consciousness-raising groups in the United States, the Chinese groups taught that in unity there is strength.

Then came 1949, Communist victory, and a series of sweeping reforms intended to clear away all the lingering feudal cobwebs. The new government quickly gave women property rights, a free choice in marriage, the right to vote, the right to divorce. It abolished polygamy, prostitution, wife-buying, and female infanticide. It declared that women were economically equal to men and would get the same pay for the same work. It wasn't easy to enforce all of these measures because of deep resistance from peasant males and even from loyal Communist males. Husbands did not want their wives going to Speak-Bitterness meetings before the revolution, and they were not happy about female equality after it. Some female activists who were sent to rural villages to explain the new rights of women were murdered by men who felt that their authority in the family and the community was under attack (as indeed it was). But gradually the measures gained acceptance, and attention turned to mobilizing women for productive work.

China today has had even less time than the Soviet Union to overturn centuries of feudalism and female subordination. Yet in twenty-eight years, scarcely a generation, extraordinary changes have taken place in the status of Chinese women. Ninety percent of them work outside the home, and there is a fairly extensive network of nurseries and daycare centers attached to the factories, hospitals, housing projects, and businesses where the parents work. As in Russia, women have entered jobs formerly reserved for

---

[3] One critic argues, however, that the Communists' concern fluctuated, depending on whether they were trying to fight the Kuomintang or form an alliance with it. During efforts at accommodation, the Communists held some reforms in check, including women's rights. When Kuomintang leader Chiang Kai-Shek turned them down, they returned to a more radical line (Curtin 1975).

men. They drive trucks, fly planes, and wield picks. (In 1957, China had a squadron of jet fighters run entirely by women.) They are doctors, teachers, engineers (Curtin 1975; Tavris 1974).

Of course, the entrance of women into the work force has not been steady and uncomplicated. Work for women has depended on the country's economic growth and on its shifting economic policies, as in Russia. Katie Curtin believes that an industrial slump in the mid-1950s was behind propaganda praising home life and the contributions of the housewife. (Similarly, a postwar slump in the United States evoked the "feminine mystique" that glorified large families and the joys of homemaking.) But when China developed an acute need for labor in 1958, and subsequently launched the "Great Leap Forward," the government proclaimed the liberating, patriotic effects of being a working woman. It set up daycare centers to make it possible for women to enter the work force in large numbers. The program was so successful that today a Chinese "housewife" is virtually an anachronism. In many places wives have gotten together to organize what they call "housewife factories," local enterprises that produce everything from embroidered pillows to insulation materials (Tavris 1974).

The Chinese Communists never were as concerned as the Russians about changing the basic nature of the family and sexual relations. The Chinese see no incompatibility between the family and female liberation; indeed, they believe the family is bedrock. Although a wave of divorces followed the revolution, ending thousands of brutal marriages, today divorce is more difficult to get, and a Chinese couple goes through considerable discussion and persuasion from colleagues and family before they make it to the divorce court. Further, the Chinese see no link between female liberation and sexual liberation. On the contrary. The Chinese are quite Victorian in their views: before marriage, the sexual rule is "all for none and none for all," and they will tell you seriously that their young people are too busy working for a socialist society to think of sex. Sex, the adolescents learn, saps your strength. Abortion and birth control are available to all women. The purpose, though, is not to make them sexually free but to keep the population down and the females working.

Although the Chinese have tried to strengthen, not eliminate, the family, they do believe it is unfair and uncommunist to expect women to handle all the domestic work as well as a job. How to right this common wrong, however, has not been figured out. When C. T. visited China in 1973, most of the people she talked to claimed to have egalitarian marriages, the political ideal. Whichever spouse came home first got the groceries (an easy task, since markets are attached to most housing clusters) and prepared the dinner.

Both did the cleaning and cared for the children, when they were not in school or daycare or with grandparents (everyone's favorite babysitters, even in modern China). Women explained to her, with smiles and lots of stories, that a husband can't get away with male-chauvinist attitudes any more. If he persists in his "feudal" ways, the local Women's Association may decide to reeducate him, and so will his comrades at work, his in-laws, his neighbors, and his union. On the other hand, members of the Committee of Concerned Asian Scholars (1972) got other answers to the same question. When they asked who does the cooking, cleaning, shopping, washing, and childcare, the usual reply was "The wife, of course."

The discrepancy is probably a result of the size of the country and the size of the gap between policy and practice. Policy says that women will be equal and men will do housework, that families should have only two children and that girls are as good as boys, that women get equal pay for equal work. But in practice the old ways haven't changed overnight or for everyone. In much of the countryside, families still prefer sons.[4] On communes, which are huge agricultural collectives of up to 50,000 people, a system of work points determines a person's share of the collective income. The more physically strenuous the job, the more points one gets. Women earn fewer work points than men because they don't do the hardest work, because they tend to work shorter days in order to do housework (which is not regarded as productive labor), and because they don't get points for maternity leave or for days off during the menstrual period if they take them (Diamond 1975). In the cities, men still seem to wind up doing different work from women, even in the same factory, and getting more money— although wage differences by sex are nowhere near as great as they are in this country.

Some occupations are still regarded as "women's work" in China: almost all teachers in primary school, nurses, daycare attendants, and flight attendants are women. All visitors observe that fathers and grandfathers have a warm and tender relationship with their young relatives and spend much time with them, but there have been no efforts to get men to work professionally with children. "Women have more patience, after all," C. T. was told. "They are more gentle." Conversely, women are still a tiny minority in top political circles, even though the number of women accepted into the Communist Party is increasing steadily (20 percent of the delegates to the Tenth Party Congress in 1973 were women). In the prestigious People's

[4] The Anshan Experiment, a new Chinese method of identifying the sex of a fetus, came up with this eerie, unintended finding. Of thirty fetuses that had been intentionally aborted after the mother knew its sex, twenty-nine were female (Campbell 1976).

Liberation Army (PLA), which produces the top political leaders, women work in separate battalions at service tasks such as running canteens, staffing offices, and giving medical aid. When C. T. asked why the PLA was segregated she was told, "Men are stronger, after all." This explanation was not convincing, because women get rigorous military training alongside men in the local militia units, where they have no apparent trouble learning to handle rifles, grenades, and machine guns.

To the Chinese, whatever remnants of male chauvinism still exist are mere trifles compared to what has been accomplished in the liberation of women. Because the majority of the population remembers the starvation, illness, and social problems that were so widespread before the revolution, the Chinese convey a spirit of optimism and strength. They believe they can solve whatever minor problems remain, and they are desperately determined to avoid the pitfalls that they believe entrapped the Soviet Union: a regression to capitalist competitiveness, renewed inequality between the sexes, and a premature complacency about the success of the revolution. Under Mao Tse-tung, who was unwavering in his fight against complacency, the Chinese believed that constant "revolutions" were necessary to keep a country from backsliding. Whether they will hold to that belief under the new leadership, and what priorities will be assigned to sexual equality in the future, is anybody's guess.

case 3: the Scandinavian countries, especially Sweden

Sweden and her sister countries are good examples of nations that are reaching sex-role equality through evolution rather than revolution. In Sweden, industrialization began much sooner than it did in the U.S.S.R., and it brought a decrease in the proportion of children and an increase in the proportion of city dwellers. Twenty years ago, Sweden faced certain issues and economic problems that are only now coming to the fore in the United States. In the mid-fifties two sociologists, Alva Myrdal and Viola Klein, wrote *Women's Two Roles: Home and Work,* a book that explored the difficulties of combining those roles and suggested some solutions. The ideology of sex-role equality that is still struggling for acceptance in the United States came to Sweden years ago.

But in Scandinavia, as in China and elsewhere, ideology is one thing and daily life is another. Today in the Scandinavian countries only about one third of all married women work (in Russia, Finland, Poland, and Hungary, the figure is 50 percent; in the United States it is 43 percent).

Scandinavian women are less likely to enter "masculine" professions than women in Eastern European nations, although they make up one fifth to one third of the physicians and lawyers and have taken over the fields of pharmacy and, especially in Denmark, dentistry. There are numerous government-sponsored nursery schools, though not enough for the children of all working women.

Because taxes and some legislation favor the two-income family, husbands and wives are redefining the division of labor in the household. Both partners are expected to share housework and childcare when both work, and—most radical innovation of all—husbands as well as wives have the option to stay home or work part-time. Sweden may be one of the few countries in the world in which a househusband is socially accepted. He may not be universally admired, but at least he need endure no snickers, and his masculinity is not questioned (Safilios-Rothschild 1975).

The role of Swedish women in the work force, like that of women elsewhere, has fluctuated with economic conditions. Between 1930 and 1946 droves of women left the labor force in what has been called a "mass flight" into marriage. "Aha," observers said. "See? Women are happier as housewives." However, their flight coincided with what a Swedish sociologist called an "enormously woman-hostile labor market during the Depression." After the Depression the economic standard was high enough for many women to afford to stay home, which has not been the case in the Soviet Union and Finland, for example (Haavio-Mannila 1975). In the 1960s, a shortage of labor meant that Sweden needed its women in the work force. Accordingly, official policy shifted, childcare facilities were improved, and a national educational campaign for sex-role equality began. The defeat of the social-democrat system in 1976, and the apparent return to capitalism after forty-four years of socialist programs, make it hard to predict whether Sweden's need for working women, or its efforts toward equality, will continue.

Elina Haavio-Mannila (1975) compared the efforts of three neighboring nations—Sweden, Finland, and the Soviet Union—to liberate women from housework. The three countries have different ideologies about sex roles and different industrial histories, to say nothing of political philosophies. Haavio-Mannila's study was based on interviews with 430 Soviet families in three cities (Leningrad, Moscow, and Pensa); 271 families in Helsinki, Finland; and 442 families in Uppsala, Sweden. She found *no differences* among these countries in the families' division of labor. It didn't matter whether the women had outside jobs or not, or how actively the government encouraged them to join the labor force or stay at home. In 70 percent of the households, only the wife bought food, made breakfast, fed

Table 14. Division of Household Tasks in Russian, Finnish, and Swedish Cities, 1966 [a]

Household task		Wife	Both spouses	Husband
Feeding the family				
Buying the food	Three Soviet cities	70%	18%	4%
	Helsinki	74	20	2
	Uppsala	71	17	5
Preparing breakfast	Three Soviet cities	72	10	3
	Helsinki	72	16	8
	Uppsala	76	9	8
Preparing dinner	Three Soviet cities	80	5	1
	Helsinki	85	9	2
	Uppsala	86	5	2
Washing the dishes	Three Soviet cities	64	20	1
	Helsinki	70	20	4
Cleaning and washing				
Daily cleaning	Three Soviet cities	67	14	4
	Helsinki	73	18	1
	Uppsala	80	12	2
Washing the windows	Helsinki	51	32	6
	Uppsala	76	9	5
Washing clothes	Three Soviet cities	90	2	0
(Helsinki: men's	Helsinki	80	4	11
shirts and stockings)				
Family finances				
Paying regular bills	Three Soviet cities	47	13	28
	Helsinki	32	19	48
	Uppsala	29	18	49
Repairing				
Fixing things around	Three Soviet cities	50	6	27
the house	Helsinki	6	7	82
	Uppsala	10	13	70
Childcare				
Feeding the children	Helsinki	74	20	0
(if small children in	Uppsala	70	17	0
the family)				

[a] Horizontal percentages do not add to 100 because in some cases a third person does the task.
AFTER Haavio-Mannila 1975.

case 3: the Scandinavian countries, especially Sweden   283

the children, and washed the dishes; in 80 percent she cooked dinner. As shown in Table 14, the men were more likely to fix things around the house —and that's all. Househusbandry may be an approved way of life in Sweden, but it is far from a popular practice.[5]

As these case studies illustrate, most modern nations have made great strides in their efforts to unravel the work and family knot. To get women into the labor force, they have used a variety of approaches to enable women to combine "their" responsibilities of home and job. In one summary review, Constantina Safilios-Rothschild (1975) studied the male-female division of labor in twenty-three countries at all levels of economic development and noted four patterns:

1. *The Soviet Union, Poland, Hungary, Finland:* Women work, many in formerly male occupations, but men do not do women's work. State-supported nursery schools and daycare and a national ideology that favors communal child-rearing help women work but require no changes on the part of husbands.

2. *Scandinavian countries:* Fewer women work, though the ideology favors complete equality. Men are encouraged to split housework and child-care equally, though there are many fewer househusbands than housewives.

3. *Argentina, Austria, Japan, Greece, Turkey:* About one third of the women work, and an even smaller proportion of wives. None of these countries provides daycare centers or nursery schools, except a few under-staffed ones for working-class women. Wealthy wives can combine work and family because maid service is cheap and available and the extended family still thrives. Grandmothers often do housework and babysit for their working daughters.

4. *The United States, Canada, and to some extent England, France, West Germany, and Australia:* In these countries the cultural values are at odds with the realities. While many women work (at least one third of all women, ranging to half), the reigning ideology is that childcare is a full-time occupation and that children need their mothers. These nations provide no system-wide professional help or daycare for working mothers, who are left to work out a solution on an individual basis. Partly because so many women in these countries must wait until their children are in school before

[5] For example, Sweden has a paid paternity-leave program: fathers can take up to seven months off after the birth of a child at 95 percent of full salary. (If the mother works too, the parents can share the leave period as they wish.) Though the number of participating fathers has more than quadrupled since 1974 and is still rising, only 7 percent of fathers took paternity leaves in 1976 (*New York Times*, December 19, 1976).

they can work full-time, women have not entered traditionally male occupations in significant numbers.

In most of these countries women are steadily (though in some, slowly) being absorbed into the work force, doing a great number of jobs. Some countries make it easier for women to work and raise families and some make it harder, but none has succeeded in getting men to share domestic work equally. And in no nation are women 50 percent of the key politicians and leaders.

Perhaps it seems that equality on a national level would be more difficult and complicated to achieve than equality in a small, manageable unit. For this reason the example of the Israeli kibbutz is an important story.

case 4: the Israeli kibbutz

Perhaps no experiment in equality has been scrutinized as minutely as the kibbutz (plural: kibbutzim). Scarcely had the idea been planted before researchers began pulling it out by the roots to see how it was doing. The kibbutz is especially fascinating today because it seems to provide clear evidence that equality is doomed, that left to their druthers men and women will lapse into the traditional division of roles, power, and labor.

Kibbutzim are rural communities in which members collectively own all property. The first kibbutzim were founded early in this century by young socialist emigrants from Russia and Europe, who wanted to escape what they considered the stifling atmosphere of traditional urban Jewish life. They had read Marx and Freud and were determined to set up an alternative community that would represent the best of both. The founders therefore rejected the nuclear family, which they regarded as patriarchal and antifemale, a breeding ground for the Oedipus complex and sexual hostilities. They rejected the values associated with capitalism, especially competitiveness and financial ambition, and sought instead a community based on physical labor, austerity, equality, and group loyalty. There would be no salaries and no status distinctions based on wealth. Each member of the group would get the goods and services she or he needed, regardless of the work assigned.

The decision to break up the nuclear family came about for several reasons. The founders feared that family loyalties would compete with allegiance to the larger community, and in the face of harsh external conditions for survival the kibbutz could not afford much internal dissension, family squabbling, or personal ambition. Ideologically, the founders also believed that if parents dealt with their children as friendly comrades instead of as stern disciplinarians, a more democratic bond between adults and children would result. The children would be more secure as well, because they would be children of the kibbutz, nourished and loved by everyone. Finally, the founders believed that when women were free for "productive" work like plowing fields and building roads, when they didn't have to worry about cooking meals and ironing shirts, they would become equal partners with men once and for all—politically, economically, and sexually.

The kibbutz made almost all housekeeping a collective enterprise. Kibbutz members eat together in a communal dining room; they get their clothes, toothbrushes, and soap at a communal commissary; and they send their dirty linen to a communal laundry. Though they live in private apartments, the rooms are small and do not require much care. Child-rearing too is a collective procedure. Within a few days or weeks after birth, babies are brought to a special children's house, where they are cared for by a specially trained professional called a *metapelet* (nurse). Children visit with their parents in the late afternoons and on weekends, but they eat and sleep in their own quarters. A child's friends, not parents, are the primary contacts, and as a result the kibbutz child develops a strong allegiance to the peer group.

Today there are about 250 kibbutzim, with some 100,000 residents, a small but influential proportion of the total Israeli population. They range in size from several dozen members to over 2,000; but most have a few hundred. The kibbutzniks have been remarkably successful at surviving in the face of extraordinary odds. Though life was hard and work seemed unending in the early days, today kibbutz members enjoy a standard of living that is higher than that of most Israelis. The collective principle still holds; residents together own all property and means of production.

In 1960–61 C. O. lived on a kibbutz for six months. Instead of working at a permanent job assignment she landed the job of pinch hitter, which gave her an opportunity to observe many kibbutzniks at work. Guess who was doing the cooking and childcare? Most of the kibbutz women, young or old, were cooking meals, cleaning toilets, scrubbing floors, ironing shirts, teaching children, and caring for infants. Not for their own families, to be sure, but for the several hundred souls on the commune. A few young women labored in the fields, but none drove tractors or worked in construction. C. O. never observed a man working in the children's houses or ironing. Though both sexes were required to do a month of kitchen duty every year (washing dishes, setting and waiting on tables), few men held permanent jobs in the kitchen. Some old men helped out regularly in preparing meals, doing chores like plucking chickens.

Recent studies confirm these informal observations about the sexual division of labor on the kibbutz. Lionel Tiger and Joseph Shepher (1975) studied some 16,000 women in two communes, and Martha Mednick (1975) interviewed a random sample of kibbutzniks from fifty-five settlements, 400 original settlers and 918 adults of the second generation. The women are in fact back at the service jobs in the kitchen, laundry, and schools, and those who do work in agriculture are concentrated in poultry-raising and plant nurseries. Fewer occupations are open to women than to men, and the dream of a fifty-fifty share in the work of production has vanished. As the kibbutzim prospered and the population grew, the need for support services and the desire for physical amenities increased, and the women left the fields for the household.

It might seem that a sexual division of labor could still be equitable. After all, feeding an entire community and raising loyal members of the kibbutz are as important as driving a tractor or picking apples. But that is not how it is on the kibbutz. The jobs that produce income for the community, the jobs that men do, are held in higher esteem than the jobs women do. And when members rate their own status in the community, women rate themselves lower than men.

> Work is the central value of the kibbutz. Moreover, *productive* work, that which results in economic gain, is valued most highly. On the other hand, services, which include the kitchen, the laundry, the clothing factory, and the dining room, are regarded as necessary, but *nonproductive* and therefore less valued (Mednick 1975, p. 88).

Men have the political power too, although there are no official barriers in the women's way. The kibbutz is a true participatory democracy. A general assembly of all members meets regularly to make major decisions, and each member has one vote. Yet women are not equal participants in this system. They rarely run for political office, although these positions rotate every few years; they show up in fewer numbers at the meetings; when they do attend they are less vocal than the men. Although almost half of all kibbutz members serve on community committees, women work on those connected with education, social welfare, and cultural activities, while men dominate on the economic committee—which determines economic goals and policies, controls the budget, and wields the real power (Mednick 1975). The second-generation women, says Mednick, seem quite content to leave political matters to men. So although there are no status differences based on class and wealth, the bane of Marxist theory, there *are* status differences based on work and political participation. And men have the prestige.

As the kibbutzim became more successful, the "intrinsic antagonism" between the family and the community shifted in favor of the family (Talmon 1972). Most (though not all) women are enthusiastic about the trend toward traditionalism and are actively promoting it. They want larger families, and they don't want to delay having children until they have finished vocational training (Gerson 1971). Cosmetics, dresses, and beauty shops— once regarded as signs of decadent bourgeois values—are gaining acceptance. On some kibbutzim, parents are trying to reverse one of the founders' basic principles and have their children live with them, though this is permitted on fewer than 10 percent of the kibbutzim so far.

The kibbutz, then, presents us with a puzzle. Kibbutz women are even more economically independent than women in socialist countries. They do not get status from their husbands' incomes or jobs. They have total job security no matter how many children they choose to have, and they are guaranteed high-quality care and education for their children. They do not have complicated housework to contend with and they do not have to feed their families or clean up after them. Yet kibbutz women lack political power, and they don't seem to want it. They do not work in the high-prestige occupations, and they don't seem to want to. The feminine mystique has returned with a vengeance.

the perspectives in perspective

Each of the perspectives in this book offers reasons for the continuing status differences between the sexes; for the difficulty of getting men to do women's work; for the "flight to the family" that women take even when they don't have to do household chores, as on the kibbutz.

A popular line of explanation today starts with biology. Tiger and Shepher (the latter a long-time kibbutznik) believe that the kibbutz is the perfect laboratory to test biological imperatives because there, if anywhere, every effort was made to create sexual equality in practice as well as in ideology. If the effort failed, they argue, it must be because equality goes against the grain that evolution has determined for us. They write, "There is at birth a basic diagram, a set of biologically determined dispositions which has been called a 'biogrammar.' . . . Culture (i.e., socialization) in its plasticity may go against those dispositions, but not for long and not for many people, without causing serious difficulties for both the individual and society" (Tiger and Shepher 1975). In other words, the kibbutz has reverted to the traditional ways because women have a universal need to be close to their children, care for their families, and leave the driving to men. Women by nature don't want to play politics or defend the group. All they want is a nest, a small, warm place to raise children. Women may tolerate the frustration of their basic needs in times of crisis, when their country needs pioneers, but as soon as conditions allow, Tiger and Shepher say, they inevitably "return to a pattern more typical of our species."

Similarly, the psychoanalytic view predicts that no society can eradicate the unique components of feminine personality that are based on unconscious motives and anatomical differences. Women will continue to feel inferior to men, whether they get equal pay for equal work or not, because no government can issue them a penis. They will continue to bear children as a substitute for the missing organ, and efforts to avoid the Oedipus complex by raising children in communal systems are doomed because of the deeply rooted needs and driving forces of the unconscious.

Most sociologists and learning theorists resist the reduction of complex social issues to biological or psychoanalytic imperatives. Jessie Bernard (1976) tears into the concept of the biogram, pointing out, for example, "that women of the nobility and upper classes have matter-of-factly and routinely turned their children over to the care of nurses and nannies for generations and that countless middle-class and working-class mothers would cheerfully do likewise if they could." Further, she observes, Tiger and Shepher occasionally bend their argument when it doesn't fit the data. People who believe in an instinctive mother-child bond often argue that when mothers go off to work, the children invariably suffer. But Tiger and Shepher are in somewhat of a bind because kibbutz children grow into happy, healthy adults, physically and emotionally. So, Bernard observes, they must concede that " 'the biogrammatical rules . . . need not be followed precisely; the kibbutz example suggests that one can drastically alter the ways of being a mother' and still turn out a great product." Finally, while Tiger and Shepher explain the very high level of dissatisfaction among kibbutz women in terms of the women's thwarted maternal instinct, Bernard thinks a more plausible explanation is the low level of prestige and professionalism of their work.[6]

---

[6] During her stay on the kibbutz, C. O. was struck by the tedium of most of the women's work. The women who ironed shirts and slacks for eight hours a day, for instance, liked the job about as much as you would. They took little professional pride in their work and made time pass quicker by gossiping and taking breaks. Of course, some of the jobs men did were just as boring, but C. O.'s impression was that on the whole men's work was more varied and challenging. Further, even men who had dull jobs had the satisfaction of meeting production quotas and earning income for the kibbutz. Ironed shirts don't generate income, and they invariably come back a week later dirty and wrinkled again.

Martha Mednick's explanation for the kibbutz's feminine "backlash" relies on events, not instincts. The return to family and home, she says, occurred because of these nonbiological factors:

1. The kibbutzim were founded in an atmosphere of economic and military crisis, in which "masculine" attributes and values were needed for survival and rewarded. The early emancipation of women came about as much out of need as ideology. (A similar argument can be made for Russia and China.)

2. Certain roles never changed. "Women had the *privilege* of working and fighting like men," she writes, "but men did not have the obvious reciprocal privileges." The care and education of children always remained tasks for women only.

3. As the early hardships lessened, the need for children to sustain the kibbutz increased, and pronatalist values returned. More children meant more support services; at the same time the economic successes of the kibbutzim spurred demands for more amenities, a more comfortable life. At this point it seemed natural, writes Mednick, for women to return to the traditional tasks and for men to continue in production; rationalizations about women's "true nature" followed this break from the original ideology of equality.

4. At present, the only female activity that is rewarded on the kibbutz and that brings self-esteem is having children. Women who have many children, though they may not get titles like "Mother Heroine," are highly regarded for producing more members of the kibbutz.

We do not need to postulate all sorts of biological urges and surges to understand why the sexual division of labor persists. The answers, we think, come from economics, sociology, and psychology. For sexual equality to occur, the economic conditions must be right; roles, laws, and organizations must be modified; and people's attitudes and values must change, too. All three developments overlap, naturally, but they evolve at different rates, which makes programs for change complex and seemingly interminable.

The learning perspective suggests that efforts at equality have failed so far because revolutionaries have not been able to overcome their own socialization histories. Male supremacy, after all, is older than any particular economic or political system. So it may be easier for people to accept physical labor in place of intellectual labor, or a communist system of distributing goods in place of a capitalist one, than to accept the concept of sexual equality. If the first generation of reformers cannot change their own deepest feelings about the place of women, they probably transmit those feelings to their children, professed egalitarian philosophies notwithstanding. Bernard cites a male kibbutznik's attitude toward women, unconsciously revealed while he was reminiscing with, of all people, Golda Meir. "He told Golda that though she herself was perhaps not sensitive to it, the men of her generation believed women to be weak and incompetent beings, and tried as best they could to keep them out of the way, at which point *he made the gesture one usually makes when brushing flies away.*"

The heat of a passionate ideology can blind people to the subtleties of socialization. Settlers on the kibbutz and revolutionaries in the Soviet Union seem to have assumed that by declaring the sexes equal and putting women to work, they had created equality. They did not worry about whether role changes would outlast crisis conditions. As Hilda Scott (1974) notes, if inequality is assumed to be merely a matter of the wrong economic system, then once you have changed the system there is no need to define equality, to see how men and women continue to treat each other, or to be concerned with whether women have overcome their low self-regard. "In other words, [there is] no need to unwrap people's minds and souls or air their misconceptions and prejudices. If patriarchal beliefs then continue to lie just below the surface in men and women, these are likely to determine the kind of equality that is set as the goal."

On the other hand, the sociological perspective suggests that no amount of consciousness-raising or bitterness-speaking can transform a society unless the organizations and distribution of power change also. As a result, efforts to change people's attitudes typically have mixed effects. For example, educational psychologist Marcia Guttentag and her colleagues set up an ambitious school program to nip sexism in the bud (Guttentag et al., in press). They developed a curriculum and got it accepted in three large school districts in the Boston area; over 1,000 children participated, from kindergarten, fifth grade, and ninth grade. The children read stories, saw films, acted out plays, and worked on special projects—a six-week crash course in equality. They learned that both sexes should share the good personality traits, such as competence and warmth, and that both sexes can work at any job and also have fun with their families, raising babies. The researchers kept in mind the unconscious messages that children pick up, so they taught the teachers to be careful not to treat the boys and girls differently. And they taught the children how the pressure of friends can influence acts and beliefs.

The researchers thought of everything, but their program did not work out quite as planned. They got the results they wanted among many of the girls, who at all ages were ready to accept the idea that women could combine both work and family and enter men's jobs. The ninth-grade girls in particular got a boost in self-esteem from the course. But the program backfired with the boys. In only one ninth-grade class, taught by a strong and enthusiastic teacher, did the boys become more egalitarian. In most of the others, the boys became *more* rigid and stereotyped in their views of women and women's place. This was true whether their mothers worked or not. Possibly peer-group pressures outweighed the lessons at school and the examples at home; in any case, a six-week program, no matter how thorough, could not overturn years of observation and experience.

Guttentag's study had a rather ominous outcome, since it increased the distance between the boys and the girls. The boys held tenaciously to traditionalism, which seemed to be in their own best interest, while the girls switched to feminism, which was in theirs. This is a common pattern throughout the world. Men, like other dominant groups, will accept equality when it doesn't require them to give up too much. They will vote for a woman president, they say, but they don't want to do housework, childcare, or cooking. That's woman's work.

The sociological perspective suggests that if this final distance is ever to be bridged, then woman's work must yield as many rewards from society as man's work: economic and psychological rewards, not empty words about the nobility of housework. Both sexes must feel that women are producers rather than consumers, and the work that both sexes do must generate income for the family. Then people will be able to make decisions about what they want to do on the basis of ability and temperament, not gender, and neither sex will be at the economic mercy of the other. All occupations, from raising children to raising soybeans, will be valuable. Some people object to this kind of argument, saying it reflects the crass materialism of American life. But we base our observation on the data from Chapter 8, which show that every culture in human history has valued income-producing work more than domestic work and child-rearing.

In recent years, social scientists have begun to talk about the importance of the housewife's work, which is the essential but invisible backbone of our economic system, and to try to assign it some monetary value. The calculations can get complicated. One way to come up with an estimate is to apply the going wage to all the jobs the housewife does, such as babysitter, cook, decorator, housekeeper, dishwasher, and chauffeur. The Social Security Administration, using this procedure in 1972, came up with a low average "salary": $4,705 for housewives of all ages, and a peak value of $6,417 for wives aged 25 to 29, when childcare is at its most time-consuming. Most observers of the housewife's role laugh at this estimate, and even the S.S.A. says the figures are conservative. Insurance companies, which estimate a wife's value to her family in the event of her death, put the cost of her yearly services at $15,000 (*New York Times,* January 13, 1976). But no social scientist has figured the value of housework the way a New York jury did in 1974. A man whose wife had been injured in a car crash had to do all the housework by himself for two whole months. The jury, sympathetic to his plight, awarded him $56,000. *Newsweek,* which reported the story, could not resist remarking that not even the woman's movement had suggested that a housewife's job is worth $336,000 a year. If it were, you can bet more men would be doing it.

The evolutionary perspective suggests that we must consider the functions that the economic roles of men and women have for a society. It predicts that as these roles change, so will relations between the sexes. John Kenneth Galbraith (1973), the noted economist, argues that the conversion of American women into an unpaid servant class was "an economic accomplishment of the first importance. Menial employed servants were available only to a minority of the pre-industrial population; the servant-wife is available, democratically, to almost the entire present male population. . . . The servant role of women is critical for the expansion of consumption in the modern economy." In other words, an economy that is based on spending and growth, as ours is, needs an "underclass" that does not cost employers anything and whose function is to spend what employees earn. The housewife role has been fundamental to the entire system, but its economic significance has been overlooked. As we move from an economy based on expansion to one based on containment (in a world that is slowly learning that resources are not infinite), the need for a class of consumers will diminish.

The evolutionary perspective says that a society's history, technology, and degree of affluence all help determine its particular beliefs and customs. Equality in China may not be equality to the Swedes, but the way both countries treat their women will be a result less of ideology than of material conditions. Americans may favor equality or staunchly defend traditional roles, but whatever accommodation we come to about women's roles will be a result of the fit—comfortable or uncomfortable—between the evolving needs of our society and its members. For that matter, our very definition of equality will reflect a fit between our economic system, its traditions, and the aspirations we have learned are within our reach.

For example, the Chinese are nation-oriented while Americans are self-oriented. "Fulfillment" to a Chinese woman means working where the country needs her; "fulfillment" to an American woman means working at the best, most ego-satisfying job she can get or having the best house and family on the block. The Chinese grow up with the slogan "Serve the people," and a child will not understand the question "What do you want to be when you grow up?" (In response the child looks puzzled and says, "I'll go where the country needs me.") Americans grow up with the slogan

"Do your own thing," and many children have adult ambitions by the time they enter school. The Chinese do not understand some of the issues raised by American feminists, such as what is wrong with the nuclear family, or how to get power in a male-dominated field, or why women should be "free" to "express their individuality." To the Chinese, liberation would not mean choosing to remain single, and it certainly would never mean leaving your spouse and children in order to pursue a personal ambition. It is no surprise that equality between the sexes is translated differently in each country. The Chinese cannot afford the luxury and unpredictability of an individualistic philosophy. They do not have the affluence and leisure that would permit millions of people to drop out to practice the mandolin or join a cult of meditation. American concepts of equality and freedom, in other words, are the product of an economic system that dispenses rewards for individual achievement and ambition rather than for communal effort, and that has attained a high material standard of living. People can afford to worry about their souls and psyches only when their stomachs are full and their bodies are clothed.

the hand that rocks the cradle . . .

To go wrong on the fundamental problem of "man and woman," to deny the most abysmal antagonism between them and the necessity of an eternally hostile tension, to dream perhaps of equal rights, equal education, equal claims and obligations—that is a *typical* sign of shallowness.

—Friedrich Nietzsche

I've been married to a fascist and married to a Marxist, and neither one of them took out the garbage.

—Attributed to a well-known actress

The evolutionary perspective persuades us that Nietzsche was wrong, that the sexes need not be antagonistic and that equality of women is on the way. Many countries are addressing themselves to the "woman question": appointing ministers to deal with the matter, passing laws to end the legal superiority of males, permitting women to enter occupations once for men only. The International Congress of Women held in 1975, for all the tumult and controversy it caused, would have been an historic impossibility as recently as fifteen years ago. Naturally, every country is proceeding at a different rate, some at the pace of molasses. But the worldwide trend is unmistakable. Women are awakening.

Some people overestimate what a society can accomplish in a short time, as disillusioned observers of Russia, China, and the United States tend to do. "We have been trying to educate and agitate around women's liberation for several years," wrote Marge Piercy. "How come things are getting worse?" But others underestimate the speed of change, once conditions are right, and no century has witnessed faster changes than ours. Each generation seems eons away from its parents. One of us has a cousin who is head of Rubin Grais and Sons Sportswear, a large company that grew from the skills of one good tailor, Rubin, fifty years ago. The company has always been led by the sons, and it never occurred to anyone in the family that a woman might one day run the factory, or, for that matter, that a woman might run anything but a house. One day the current president went to visit his daughter's oldest child, Jennifer, age eleven, and happened to ask her what she was planning to be when she grew up—a secretary? A nurse? "Oh, no," Jennifer said firmly. "When I grow up I want to be president of Rubin Grais and Sons AND GRANDDAUGHTER."

Maybe she will. But the trend is not inevitable. Future events, such as catastrophic war, economic recession, or decreasing population, could make it necessary for societies once again to glorify large families and send women back to hearth and home. In countries that lack a widespread system of daycare and a belief in the benefits of communal child-rearing, women may find that having two jobs, home and career, is one too many. And while we can predict with considerable confidence that increasing numbers of women will take their place alongside men in the working world, we have less confidence that increasing numbers of men will take their place alongside women in the nursery and the kitchen. No country has given the question top priority. Until it does, the hand that rocks the cradle will be too tired to rule the world.

Most uncertain of all is how women and men will get along during the decades of transition. Change is going to frighten some people and make others angry, and the line between liberation and loneliness will be blurred for a while. But we are optimistic that the alliance the sexes will forge on the far side of change will be stronger, and will make more people happier, than the uneasy compromises of the longest war.

References

Chapter 1
Introduction: The Longest War

Aronoff, Joel, and Crano, William D. 1975. A re-examination of the cross-cultural principles of task segregation and sex role differentiation in the family. *American sociological review* 40:12–20.

Bamberger, Joan. 1974. The myth of matriarchy. In *Woman, culture, and society,* eds. Michelle Zimbalist Rosaldo and Louise Lamphere, pp. 263–81. Stanford, California: Stanford University Press.

Barry, H.; Bacon, Margaret K.; and Child, I. I. 1957. A cross-cultural survey of some sex differences in socialization. *Journal of abnormal and social psychology* 55:327–32.

Beard, Mary. 1973. *Woman as force in history.* New York: Collier Books.

Broverman, Inge K.; Vogel, Susan R.; Broverman, Donald; Clarkson, Frank E.; and Rosenkrantz, Paul S. 1972. Sex-role stereotypes: a current appraisal. *Journal of social issues* 28:59–79.

Brown, Judith K. 1975. Iroquois women: an ethnohistoric note. In *Toward an anthropology of women,* ed. Rayna R. Reiter, pp. 141–57. New York and London: Monthly Review Press.

Brownmiller, Susan. 1975. *Against our will: men, women, and rape.* New York: Simon & Schuster.

Bullough, Vern L. 1973. *The subordinate sex.* Baltimore: Penguin Books.

D'Andrade, Roy G. 1966. Sex differences and cultural institutions. In *The development of sex differences,* ed. Eleanor Maccoby, pp. 173–204. Stanford, California: Stanford University Press.

Dinitz, Simon; Dynes, Russell R.; and Clarke, Alfred C. 1954. Preferences for male or female children: traditional or affectional? *Marriage and family living* 16:128–30.

Figes, Eva. 1970. *Patriarchal attitudes.* New York: Stein & Day.

Friedl, Ernestine. 1975. *Women and men: an anthropologist's view.* New York: Holt, Rinehart and Winston.

Gingold, Judith. 1976. One of these days—POW, right in the kisser. *Ms.* 5 (September):51–54.

Hunt, Morton. 1967. *The natural history of love.* The Minerva Press.

Lederer, Wolfgang. 1968. *The fear of women.* New York: Harcourt Brace Jovanovich.

Levitin, Teresa E.; Quinn, Robert P.; and Staines, Graham L. 1973. A woman is 58% of a man. *Psychology today* 6(March):89–92.

Myrdal, Gunnar. 1944. A parallel to the Negro problem (appendix 5), in *An American dilemma.* New York: Harper & Row.

Peterson, Candida C., and Peterson, James L. 1973. Preferences for sex of offspring as a measure of change in sex attitudes. *Psychology* 10:3–5.

Pomeroy, Sarah B. 1975. *Goddesses, whores, wives, and slaves—women in classical antiquity.* New York: Schocken Books.

Robertson, Wyndham. 1973. The ten highest-ranking women in big business. *Fortune* (April):81–89.

Rosaldo, Michelle Zimbalist. 1974. Woman, culture, and society: a theoretical overview. In *Woman, culture, and society,* eds. Michelle Zimbalist Rosaldo and Louise Lamphere, pp. 17–42. Stanford, California: Stanford University Press.

Roszak, Betty, and Roszak, Theodore, eds. 1969. *Masculine/feminine: readings in sexual mythology and the liberation of women.* New York: Harper & Row.

Shaw, George Bernard. 1891. The quintessence of Ibsenism. In *Selected non-dramatic writings of Bernard Shaw,* ed. Dan H. Laurence. Boston: Houghton Mifflin, n.d., pp. 224–30.

Shields, Stephanie. 1975. Functionalism, Darwinism, and the psychology of women. *American psychologist* 30:739–54.

Sommers, Dixie. 1974. Occupational rankings for men and women by earnings. *Monthly labor review,* United States Department of Labor, Bureau of Labor Statistics (August).

Treiman, Donald J., and Terrell, Kermit. 1975. Sex and the process of status attainment: a comparison of working women and men. *American sociological review* 40:174–200.

van Vuuren, Nancy. 1973. *The subversion of women.* Philadelphia: Westminster Press.

Webster, Paula. 1975. Matriarchy: a vision of power. In *Toward an anthropology of women,* ed. Rayna R. Reiter, pp. 141–57. New York and London: Monthly Review Press.

Zimbardo, Philip G., and Meadow, Wendy. 1974. Becoming a sexist—in one easy laugh: sexism in the *Reader's Digest.* Paper read at annual meeting of the Western Psychological Association, San Francisco.

Chapter 2
Sex Differences, Real and
Imagined

Argyle, M.; Lalljee, M.; and Cook, M. 1968. The effects of visibility on interaction in a dyad. *Human relations* 21:3–17.

Bardwick, Judith M. 1971. *Psychology of women: a study of bio-cultural conflicts.* New York: Harper & Row.

Bem, Sandra Lipsitz. 1975. Androgyny vs. the tight little lives of fluffy women and chesty men. *Psychology today* 9 (September):58–59ff.

Berman, Phyllis W. 1975. Attraction to infants: are sex differences innate and invariant? Paper read at 83rd annual convention of the American Psychological Association, Chicago.

Bernstein, R. C., and Jacklin, Carol N. 1973. The 3½-month-old infant: stability of behavior, sex differences, and longitudinal findings. Unpublished master's thesis, Stanford University, Stanford, California.

Block, Jeanne H. 1976. Debatable conclusions about sex differences. *Contemporary psychology* 21:517–22.

Broverman, Donald M.; Klaiber, Edward L.; Kobayashi, Yutaka; and Vogel, William. 1968. Roles of activation and inhibition in sex differences in cognitive abilities. *Psychological review* 75:23–50.

Droege, Robert C. 1967. Sex differences in aptitude maturation during high school. *Journal of counseling psychology* 14:407–11.

Feshbach, Seymour, and Feshbach, Norma. 1973. The young aggressors. *Psychology today* 6 (April):90–95.

Garai, Josef E., and Scheinfeld, Amram. 1968. Sex differences in mental and behavioral traits. *Genetic psychology monographs* 77:169–299.

Goldberg, Susan, and Lewis, Michael. 1969. Play behavior in the year-old infant: early sex differences. *Child development* 40:21–31.

Harlow, Harry F. 1971. *Learning to love*. San Francisco: Albion.

Hill, Charles T.; Rubin, Zick; and Peplau, Letitia Anne. 1976. Breakups before marriage: the end of 103 affairs. *Journal of social issues* 32(1):147–68.

Hollander, Edwin P., and Marcia, James E. 1970. Parental determinants of peer-orientation and self-orientation among preadolescents. *Developmental psychology* 2:292–302.

Horn, Jack. 1975. Bored to sickness. *Psychology today* 9 (November):92.

Jacklin, Carol Nagy; Maccoby, Eleanor E.; and Dick, Anne E. 1973. Barrier behavior and toy preference: sex differences (and their absence) in the year-old child. *Child development* 44:196–200.

Lewis, Michael. 1972. Culture and gender roles: there's no unisex in the nursery. *Psychology today* 5 (May):54–57.

Lewis, Michael; Kagan, Jerome; and Kalafat, John. 1966. Patterns of fixation in the young infant. *Child development* 37:331–41.

Lunneborg, Patricia W., and Rosenwood, Linda M. 1972. Need affiliation and achievement: declining sex differences. *Psychological reports* 31:795–98.

McCarthy, Dorothea. 1954. Language development in children. In *Manual of child psychology*, 2nd ed., ed. Leonard Carmichael, pp. 492–630. New York: Wiley.

Maccoby, Eleanor Emmons, and Jacklin, Carol Nagy. 1974a. *The psychology of sex differences*. Stanford, California: Stanford University Press.

Maccoby, Eleanor Emmons, and Jacklin, Carol Nagy. 1974b. Myth, reality and shades of gray: what we know and don't know about sex differences. *Psychology today* 8 (December):109–12.

Parke, Ross, and O'Leary, S. E. 1974. Mother-father-infant interaction in the newborn period: some findings, some observations, and some unresolved issues. [Cited in Maccoby and Jacklin 1974a.]

Parlee, Mary B. 1972. Comments on "Roles of activation and inhibition in sex differences in cognitive abilities" by Donald M. Broverman, Edward L. Klaiber, Yutaka Kobayashi, and William Vogel. *Psychological review* 79:180–84.

Rosenthal, Robert. 1966. *Experimenter effects in behavioral research*. New York: Appleton-Century-Crofts.

———. 1968. Self-fulfilling prophecy. *Psychology today* 2 (September):44–51.

Rosenthal, Robert; Archer, Dane; DiMatteo, M. Robin; Koivumaki, Judith Hall; and Rogers, Peter L. 1974. Body talk and tone of voice: the language without words. *Psychology today* 8 (September):64–68.

Shaver, Phillip, and Freedman, Jonathan. 1976. Your pursuit of happiness. *Psychology today* 10 (August):26–29ff.

Sherman, Julia. 1967. Problems of sex differences in space perception and aspects of intellectual functioning. *Psychological review* 74:290–99.

———. 1971. *On the psychology of women: a survey of empirical studies*. Springfield, Illinois: Charles C. Thomas.

Tiger, Lionel. 1969. *Men in groups*. New York: Random House.

Tobias, Sheila. 1976. Math anxiety: why is a smart girl like you counting on your fingers? *Ms.* 5 (September):56–59ff.

Wagman, Morton. 1967. Sex differences in types of daydreams. *Journal of personality and social psychology* 3:329–32.

Waller, Willard. 1938. *The family: a dynamic interpretation.* New York: Dryden.

Wechsler, David. 1958. *The measurement and appraisal of adult intelligence.* 4th ed. Baltimore: Williams and Wilkins.

Whiting, Beatrice, and Edwards, Carolyn Pope. 1973. A cross-cultural analysis of sex differences in the behavior of children aged three through 11. *Journal of social psychology* 91:171–88.

Witkin, Herman A.; Birnbaum, Judith; Lomonaco, Salvatore; Lehr, Suzanne; and Herman, Judith L. 1968. Cognitive patterning in congenitally totally blind children. *Child development* 39:768–86.

Wolfgang, Marvin E. 1969. Who kills whom. *Psychology today* 3 (October):54–56ff.

Chapter 3
Sexuality

Athanasiou, Robert; Shaver, Phillip; and Tavris, Carol. 1970. Sex. *Psychology today* 4 (July):37–52.

Bardwick, Judith M. 1971. *Psychology of women: a study of bio-cultural conflicts.* New York: Harper & Row.

Bart, Pauline B. 1974. Male views of female sexuality: from Freud's phallacies to Fisher's inexact test. Paper read at Second National Meeting, Special Section of Psychosomatic Obstetrics and Gynecology, Key Biscayne, Florida.

Bell, Robert R. 1966. *Premarital sex in a changing society.* Englewood Cliffs, New Jersey: Prentice-Hall.

Bell, Robert R., and Chaskes, Jay B. 1970. Premarital sexual experience among coeds, 1958 and 1968. *Journal of marriage and the family* 32:81–84.

Bergler, Edmund, and Kroger, William S. 1954. *Kinsey's myth of female sexuality.* New York: Grune & Stratton.

Brecher, Edward M. 1969. *The sex researchers.* Boston: Little, Brown.

Christensen, Harold T., and Gregg, Christina F. 1970. Changing sex norms in America and Scandinavia. *Journal of marriage and the family* 32:616–27.

Degler, Carl N. 1974. What ought to be and what was: women's sexuality in the nineteenth century. *American historical review* 79:1467–90.

Deutsch, Helene. 1945. *The psychology of women: a psychoanalytic interpretation,* vol. II. New York: Grune & Stratton.

Gagnon, John H., and Simon, William. 1969. They're going to learn in the streets anyway. *Psychology today* 3 (July):46–47ff.

Gagnon, John H., and Simon, William. 1973. *Sexual conduct: the social sources of human sexuality.* Chicago: Aldine.

Gebhard, Paul H. 1966. Factors in marital orgasm. *Journal of social issues* 22(2):88–95.

Hariton, E. Barbara. 1973. The sexual fantasies of women. *Psychology today* 6 (November):39–44.

Hastings, Donald W. 1966. Can specific training procedures overcome sexual inadequacy? In *An analysis of human sexual response,* eds. Ruth and Edward M. Brecher, pp. 221–35. New York: New American Library.

Heiman, Julia R. 1975. The physiology of erotica: women's sexual arousal. *Psychology today* 8 (April):90–94.

Hunt, Morton. 1974. *Sexual behavior in the 1970s.* Chicago: Playboy Press.

Kantner, John F., and Zelnik, Melvin. 1972. Sexual experience of young unmarried women in the United States. *Family planning perspectives* 4 (October):9–18.

Kinsey, Alfred C.; Pomeroy, Wardell B.; and Martin, Clyde E. 1948. *Sexual behavior in the human male.* Philadelphia: Saunders.

Kinsey, Alfred C.; Pomeroy, Wardell B.; Martin, Clyde E.; and Gebhard, Paul H. 1953. *Sexual behavior in the human female.* Philadelphia: Saunders.

Kline-Graber, Georgia, and Graber, Benjamin. 1975. *Woman's orgasm.* Indianapolis and New York: Bobbs-Merrill.

Levin, Robert J., and Levin, Amy. 1975. Sexual pleasure: the surprising preferences of 100,000 women. *Redbook* 145 (September):51–58. [See also Tavris, Carol, and Sadd, Susan, *The Redbook report: the sexual preferences of American women,* New York: Delacorte, in preparation.]

LoPiccolo, Joseph, and Heiman, Julia. In press. Cultural values and the therapeutic definition of sexual function and dysfunction. *Journal of social issues.*

Marshall, Donald S. 1971. Too much in Mangaia. *Psychology today* 4 (February):43–44ff.

Masters, William H., and Johnson, Virginia E. 1966. *Human sexual response.* Boston: Little, Brown.

———. 1970. *Human sexual inadequacy.* Boston: Little, Brown.

Moore, Burness E. 1961. Frigidity in women (panel report). *Journal of the American psychoanalytic association* 9:571–84.

Pomeroy, Wardell B. 1976. The male orgasm. *Cosmopolitan* 180 (April):203–05ff.

Reiss, Ira L. 1960. *Premarital sexual standards in America.* Glencoe, Illinois: The Free Press.

———. 1969. Premarital sexual standards. In *The individual, sex, and society,* eds. Carlfred B. Broderick and Jessie Bernard, pp. 109–18. Baltimore: The Johns Hopkins Press.

Schmidt, Gunter, and Sigusch, Volkmar. 1973. Women's sexual arousal. In *Contemporary sexual behavior: critical issues in the 1970s,* eds. Joseph Zubin and John Money, pp. 117–43. Baltimore: The Johns Hopkins Press.

Scully, Diana, and Bart, Pauline. 1973. A funny thing happened on the way to the orifice: women in gynecology textbooks. In *Changing women in a changing society,* ed. Joan Huber, pp. 283–88. Chicago and London: University of Chicago Press.

Seaman, Barbara. 1972. *Free and female.* Greenwich, Connecticut: Fawcett Publications.

Shainess, Natalie. 1974. Sexual problems of women. *Journal of sex and marital therapy* 1:110–23.

Shaver, Phillip, and Freedman, Jonathan. 1976. Your pursuit of happiness. *Psychology today* 10 (August):26–29ff.

Shorter, Edward. 1975. *The making of the modern family.* New York: Basic Books.

Simon, William, and Gagnon, John H. 1969. Psychosexual development. *Trans-action* 6 (March):9–18.

Singer, Josephine, and Singer, Irving. 1972. Types of female orgasm. *Journal of sex research* 8:255–67.

Sorensen, Robert C. 1973. *Adolescent sexuality in contemporary America (the Sorensen report).* New York: World Publishing.

Spitz, René A. 1952. Authority and masturbation. *The psychoanalytic quarterly* 21:490–527.

Tavris, Carol. 1973. Who likes women's liberation and why: the case of the unliberated liberals. *Journal of social issues* 29(4):175–94.

Weinberg, Martin S., and Williams, Colin J. 1974. *Male homosexuals: their problems and adaptations.* New York: Oxford University Press.

Zilbergeld, Bernie. 1975. Group treatment of sexual dysfunction in men without partners. *Journal of sex and marital therapy* 1:204–14.

Chapter 4
Genes, Hormones, and Instincts:
The Biological Perspective

Bardwick, Judith M. 1971. *Psychology of women: a study of bio-cultural conflicts*. New York: Harper & Row.

———. 1972. Her body, the battleground. *Psychology today* 5 (February):50–54ff.

Bart, Pauline B. 1971. Depression in middle-aged women. In *Woman in sexist society: studies in power and powerlessness*, eds. Vivian Gornick and Barbara K. Moran, pp. 163–86. New York: New American Library.

Benedek, Thérèse F., and Rubenstein, B. B. 1939a. The correlations between ovarian activity and psychodynamic processes. I. The ovulative phase. *Psychosomatic medicine* 1:245–70.

Benedek, Thérèse F., and Rubenstein, B. B. 1939b. The correlations between ovarian activity and psychodynamic processes. II. The menstrual phase. *Psychosomatic medicine* 1:461–85.

Benjamin, Harry, ed. 1966. *The transsexual phenomenon*. New York: Julian Press.

Berry, John W. 1966. Temne and Eskimo perceptual skills. *International journal of psychology* 1:207–29.

Bock, R. D., and Kolakowski, D. 1973. Further evidence of sex-linked major-gene influence on human spatial visualizing ability. *American journal of human genetics* 25:1–14.

Dalton, Katherina. 1960. Effect of menstruation on school girls' weekly work. *British medical journal* 1:326–28.

———. 1964. *The premenstrual syndrome*. Springfield, Illinois: Charles C. Thomas.

Delaney, Janice; Lupton, Mary Jane; and Toth, Emily. 1976. *The curse: a cultural history of menstruation*. New York: Dutton.

DeMause, Lloyd. 1975. Our forebears made childhood a nightmare. *Psychology today* 8 (April):85–88.

DeVore, I. 1965. Male dominance and mating behavior in baboons. In *Sex and behavior*, ed. Frank A. Beach, pp. 266–89. New York: Wiley.

Doering, Charles H.; Brodie, H. K. H.; Kraemer, H. C.; Becker, H. B.; and Hamburg, D. A. 1974. Plasma testosterone levels and psychologic measures in men over a 2-month period. In *Sex differences in behavior*, eds. Richard C. Friedman, Ralph M. Richart, and Raymond L. Vande Wiele, pp. 413–31. New York: Wiley.

Doering, Charles H.; Brodie, H. Keith H.; Kraemer, Helena C.; Moos, Rudolf H.; Becker, Heather B.; and Hamburg, David A. 1975. Negative affect and plasma testosterone: a longitudinal human study. *Psychosomatic medicine* 37:484–91.

Ehrhardt, Anke A., and Baker, Susan W. 1974. Fetal androgens, human central nervous system differentiation, and behavior sex differences. In *Sex differences in behavior*, eds. Richard C. Friedman, Ralph M. Richart, and Raymond L. Vande Wiele, pp. 33–51. New York: Wiley.

Fisher, Alan E. 1956. Maternal and sexual behavior induced by intracranial chemical stimulation. *Science* 124:228–29.

Ginsburg, Benson E. 1965. Coaction of genital and nongenital factors influencing sexual behavior. In *Sex and behavior*, ed. Frank A. Beach, pp. 53–75. New York: Wiley.

Golub, Sharon. 1975. The effect of premenstrual anxiety and depression on cognitive function. Paper read at 83rd annual convention of the American Psychological Association, Chicago.

Green, Richard. 1974. Children's quest for sexual identity. *Psychology today* 7 (February):44–47ff.

Hampson, John L. 1965. Determinants of psychosexual orientation. In *Sex and behavior*, ed. Frank A. Beach, pp. 108–32. New York: Wiley.

Hampson, John L., and Hampson, Joan G. 1961. The ontogenesis of sexual behavior in man. In *Sex and internal secretions,* vol. II, ed. William C. Young. 3rd ed. Baltimore: Williams and Wilkins.

Harlow, Harry F. 1962. The heterosexual affectional system in monkeys. *American psychologist* 17:1–9.

———. 1965. Sexual behavior in the rhesus monkey. In *Sex and Behavior,* ed. Frank A. Beach, pp. 234–65. New York: Wiley.

Hartlage, Lawrence C. 1970. Sex-linked inheritance of spatial ability. *Perceptual and motor skills* 31:610.

Hebb, Donald O. 1969. A conversation with D. O. Hebb, by Elizabeth Hall. *Psychology today* 3 (November):20–28.

Hediger, H. 1965. Environmental factors influencing the reproduction of zoo animals. In *Sex and behavior,* ed. Frank A. Beach, pp. 319–54. New York: Wiley.

Hyde, Janet S.; Rosenberg, B. G.; and Behrman, JoAnn. 1974. Tomboyism: implications for theories of female development. Paper read at annual convention of the Western Psychological Association, San Francisco.

Ivey, Melville E., and Bardwick, Judith M. 1968. Patterns of affective fluctuations in the menstrual cycle. *Psychosomatic medicine* 30:336–45.

Katchadourian, Herant A., and Lunde, Donald T. 1975. *Fundamentals of human sexuality.* 2nd ed. New York: Holt, Rinehart and Winston.

Kreuz, Leo E., and Rose, Robert M. 1972. Assessment of aggressive behavior and plasma testosterone in a young criminal population. *Psychosomatic medicine* 34:321–32.

Lancaster, Jane Beckman. 1973. In praise of the achieving female monkey. *Psychology today* 7 (September):30ff.

Levine, Seymour. 1966. Sex differences in the brain. *Scientific American* 214 (April):84–90.

MacArthur, Russell. 1967. Sex differences in field dependence for the Eskimo. *International journal of psychology* 2:139–40.

Meyer-Bahlburg, Heino F. L.; Boon, Donald A.; Sharma, Minoti; and Edwards, John A. 1974. Aggressiveness and testosterone measures in man. *Psychosomatic medicine* 36:269–74.

Mitchell, Gary; Redican, William K.; and Gomber, Jody. 1974. Lesson from a primate: males can raise babies. *Psychology today* 7 (April):63–68.

Money, John. n.d. Gender identity differentiation: change of stereotypes. Unpublished manuscript.

Money, John, and Ehrhardt, Anke A. 1972. *Man and woman, boy and girl.* Baltimore: The Johns Hopkins Press.

Moyer, Kenneth E. 1974. Sex differences in aggression. In *Sex differences in behavior,* eds. Richard C. Friedman, Ralph M. Richart, and Raymond L. Vande Wiele, pp. 335–72. New York: Wiley.

Neugarten, Bernice L. 1967. A new look at menopause. *Psychology today* 1 (December):42–45ff.

Nolen, William. 1975. *Healing: a doctor in search of a miracle.* New York: Random House.

O'Connor, Johnson. 1943. *Structural visualization.* Boston: Human Engineering Laboratory.

Paige, Karen E. 1971. The effects of oral contraceptives on affective fluctuations associated with the menstrual cycle. *Psychosomatic medicine* 33:515–37.

———. 1973. Women learn to sing the menstrual blues. *Psychology today* 7 (September):41–43ff.

———. In press. Sexual pollution: reproductive sex taboos in American society. *Journal of social issues.*

Paige, Karen E., and Paige, Jeffery M. In press. *Politics and reproductive rituals*. Berkeley: University of California Press.

Parlee, Mary Brown. 1973. The premenstrual syndrome. *Psychological bulletin* 80:454–65.

Pauly, Ira B. 1965. Male psychosexual inversion: transsexualism. *Archives of general psychiatry* 13:172–79.

Persky, Harold. 1974. Reproductive hormones, moods, and the menstrual cycle. In *Sex differences in behavior,* eds. Richard C. Friedman, Ralph M. Richart, and Raymond L. Vande Wiele, pp. 455–66. New York: Wiley.

Persky, Harold; Smith, Keith D.; and Basu, Gopal K. 1971. Relation of psychologic measures of aggression and hostility to testosterone production in man. *Psychosomatic medicine* 33:265–77.

Phoenix, Charles H.; Goy, Robert W.; Gerall, A. A.; and Young, William C. 1959. Organizing action of prenatally administered testosterone propionate on the tissues mediating mating behavior in the female guinea pig. *Endocrinology* 65:369–82.

Reuben, David. 1969. *Everything you always wanted to know about sex (but were afraid to ask)*. New York: D. McKay.

Rose, Robert M.; Gordon, Thomas P.; and Bernstein, Irwin S. 1972. Plasma testosterone levels in the male rhesus: influences of sexual and social stimuli. *Science* 178:643–45.

Rose, Robert M.; Holaday, John W.; and Bernstein, Irwin S. 1971. Plasma testosterone, dominance rank, and aggressive behavior in male rhesus monkeys. *Nature* 231:366–68.

Rosenblatt, Jay S. 1967. Nonhormonal basis of maternal behavior in the rat. *Science* 156:1512–14.

———. 1969. The development of maternal responsiveness in the rat. *American journal of orthopsychiatry* 39:36–56.

Schachter, Stanley, and Singer, Jerome E. 1962. Cognitive, social, and physiological determinants of emotional state. *Psychological review* 69:379–99.

Seaman, Barbara. 1972. *Free and female*. Greenwich, Connecticut: Fawcett Publications.

Sherman, Julia. 1971. *On the psychology of women: a survey of empirical studies*. Springfield, Illinois: Charles C. Thomas.

Shields, Stephanie A. 1975. Functionalism, Darwinism, and the psychology of women: a study in social myth. *American psychologist* 30:739–54.

Stafford, Richard E. 1961. Sex differences in spatial visualization as evidence of sex-linked inheritance. *Perceptual and motor skills* 13:428.

Stannard, Una. 1970. Adam's rib, or the woman within. *Trans-action* 8(1):24–25.

Stoller, Robert J. 1967. Etiological factors in male transsexualism. *Transactions of the New York academy of science* 29:431–34.

Strum, Shirley C. 1975. Life with the "Pumphouse Gang." *National geographic* 147:673–91.

Tavris, Carol. 1973. Who likes women's liberation and why: the case of the unliberated liberals. *Journal of social issues* 29(4):175–94.

Temerlin, Maurice Kahn. 1975. My daughter Lucy. *Psychology today* 9 (November):59–62ff.

Tiger, Lionel. 1969. *Men in groups*. New York: Random House.

———. 1970. Male dominance? Yes, alas. A sexist plot? No. *New York times magazine* (October 25, 1970):35–37ff.

Tiger, Lionel, and Fox, Robin. 1971. *The imperial animal*. New York: Holt, Rinehart and Winston.

Yen, Wendy M. 1973. Sex-linked major-gene influences on human spatial abilities. Unpublished doctoral dissertation, University of California, Berkeley.

Young, William C.; Goy, Robert W.; and Phoenix, Charles H. 1964. Hormones and sexual behavior. *Science* 143:212–18.

Chapter 5
Freud, Fantasy, and the Fear of
Woman: The Psychoanalytic
Perspective

Burton, Roger V., and Whiting, John W. M. 1961. The absent father and cross-sex identity. *Merrill-Palmer quarterly* 7:85–95.

Bettelheim, Bruno. 1962. *Symbolic wounds.* New York: Collier Books.

Figes, Eva. 1970. *Patriarchal attitudes.* New York: Stein & Day.

Freud, Sigmund. 1905a. Fragment of an analysis of a case of hysteria (the case of Dora). In *The Standard edition of the complete psychological works of Sigmund Freud,* rev. and ed. James Strachey, vol. IX. London: The Hogarth Press and the Institute of Psycho-Analysis (1964 edition).

———. 1905b. Three essays on the theory of sexuality. In *Standard edition,* vol. VII.

———. 1908. Civilized sexual morality and modern nervousness. In *Standard edition,* vol. IX.

———. 1918. The taboo of virginity. In *Standard edition,* vol. XI.

———. 1924a. The dissolution of the Oedipus complex. In *Standard edition,* vol. XIX.

———. 1924b. Some psychical consequences of the anatomical distinction between the sexes. In *Standard edition,* vol. XIX.

———. 1933. Femininity. In *Standard edition,* vol. XXII.

———. 1960. *A general introduction to psychoanalysis,* tr. Joan Riviere. New York: Washington Square Press.

———. 1961. *Letters of Sigmund Freud, 1873–1939,* ed. Ernst L. Freud. London: The Hogarth Press.

———. 1963. *Sexuality and the psychology of love,* ed. Philip Rieff. New York: Collier Books.

Horney, Karen. 1922. On the genesis of the castration complex in women. In *Psychoanalysis and women,* ed. Jean B. Miller, 1973. New York: Brunner/Mazel.

———. 1967. *Feminine psychology.* New York: Norton.

Lederer, Wolfgang. 1968. *The fear of women.* New York: Harcourt Brace Jovanovich.

Mahl, George F. 1971. *Psychological conflict and defense.* Irving L. Janis, ed. New York: Harcourt Brace Jovanovich.

Mead, Margaret. 1968. *Male and female.* New York: Dell (Laurel edition).

———. 1963. *Sex and temperament.* New York: Dell (Laurel edition).

Miller, Jean B., ed. 1973. *Psychoanalysis and women.* New York: Brunner/Mazel.

Mitchell, Juliet. 1974. *Psychoanalysis and feminism.* New York: Pantheon.

Parker, Seymour; Smith, Janet; and Ginat, Joseph. 1975. Father absence and cross-sex identity: the puberty rites controversy revisited. *American ethnologist* 2:687–707.

Sherman, Julia. 1971. *On the psychology of women: a survey of empirical studies.* Springfield, Illinois: Charles C. Thomas.

Chapter 6
Getting the Message: The
Learning Perspective

Almquist, Elizabeth M., and Angrist, Shirley S. 1971. Role model influences on college women's career aspirations. *Merrill-Palmer quarterly* 17:263–79.

Alper, Thelma G. 1974. Achievement motivation in college women: a now-you-see-it-now-you-don't phenomenon. *American psychologist* 29:194–203.

Atkinson, John W., ed. 1958. *Motives in fantasy, action, and society: a method of assessment and study.* Princeton, New Jersey: Van Nostrand.

Bandura, Albert. 1969. Social-learning theory of identificatory processes. In *Handbook of socialization theory and research,* ed. David A. Goslin, pp. 213–62. Chicago: Rand McNally.

———. 1960. Relationship of family patterns to child behavior disorders. Progress report, United States Public Health Research Grant M1734. Stanford University.

Bandura, Albert, and Huston, Aletha C. 1961. Identification as a process of incidental learning. *Journal of abnormal and social psychology* 63:311–18.

Bandura, Albert; Ross, Dorothea; and Ross, Sheila A. 1963a. A comparative test of the status envy, social power, and secondary reinforcement theories of identificatory learning. *Journal of abnormal and social psychology* 67:527–34.

Bandura, Albert; Ross, Dorothea; and Ross, Sheila A. 1963b. Imitation of film-mediated aggressive models. *Journal of abnormal and social psychology* 66:3–11.

Bandura, Albert, and Walters, Richard H. 1963. *Social learning and personality development.* New York: Holt, Rinehart and Winston.

Beauvoir, Simone de. 1953. *The second sex,* tr. and ed. H. M. Parshley. New York: Knopf.

Bem, Sandra Lipsitz. 1974. The measurement of psychological androgyny. *Journal of consulting and clinical psychology* 42:155–62.

———. 1975. Androgyny vs. the tight little lives of fluffy women and chesty men. *Psychology today* 9 (September):58–59ff.

Bem, Sandra L., and Bem, Daryl J. 1976. Case study of a nonconscious ideology: training the woman to know her place. In *Female psychology: the emerging self,* ed. Sue Cox, pp. 180–90. Chicago: Science Research Associates.

Bernard, Jessie. 1975. *Women, wives, mothers: values and options.* Chicago: Aldine.

Brown, Roger, and Ford, Marguerite. 1961. Address in American English. *Journal of abnormal and social psychology* 62:375–85.

Brown, Roger, and Gilman, Albert. 1960. The pronouns of power and solidarity. In *Style in language,* ed. Thomas A. Sebeok, Cambridge, Massachusetts: M.I.T. Press.

Burr, Elizabeth; Dunn, Susan; and Farquhar, Norma. 1972. Women and the language of inequality. *Social education* 36:841–45.

Chodorow, Nancy. 1974. Family structure and feminine personality. In *Woman, culture, and society,* eds. Michelle Zimbalist Rosaldo and Louise Lamphere, pp. 43–66. Stanford, California: Stanford University Press.

Condry, John, and Dyer, Sharon. 1976. Fear of success: attribution of cause to the victim. *Journal of social issues* 32(3):63–83.

Crandall, Virginia J. 1969. Sex differences in expectancy of intellectual and academic reinforcement. In *Achievement-related motives in children,* ed. Charles P. Smith, pp. 11–45. New York: Russell Sage Foundation.

Deaux, Kay. 1976. Ahhh, she was just lucky. *Psychology today* 10 (December):70ff.

Deaux, Kay; White, Leonard; and Farris, Elizabeth. 1975. Skill versus luck: field and laboratory studies of male and female preferences. *Journal of personality and social psychology* 32:629–36.

Epstein, Cynthia Fuchs. 1970. *Woman's Place.* Berkeley and Los Angeles: University of California Press.

Feather, N. T. 1968. Change in confidence following success or failure as a predictor of subsequent performance. *Journal of personality and social psychology* 9:38–46.

———. 1969. Attribution of responsibility and valence of success and failure in relation to initial confidence and task performance. *Journal of personality and social psychology* 13:129–44.

Frieze, Irene Hanson. 1975. Women's expectations for and causal attributions of success and failure. In *Women and achievement: social and motivational analyses,* eds. Martha T. Shuch Mednick, Sandra Schwartz Tangri, and Lois Wladis Hoffman, pp. 158–71. New York: Halsted Press.

Frieze, Irene; Parsons, Jacque; and Ruble, Diane. 1972. Some determinants of career aspirations in college women. Paper read at UCLA Symposium on Sex Roles and Sex Differences, Los Angeles.

Gerbner, George, and Gross, Larry. 1976. The scary world of TV's heavy viewer. *Psychology today* 9 (April):41–45ff.

Goldberg, Philip. 1968. Are women prejudiced against women? *Trans-action* 5 (April):28–30.

Hacker, Helen Mayer. 1951. Women as a minority group. *Social forces* 30 (October):60–69.

Henley, Nancy. 1970. The politics of touch. Paper read at 78th Annual Meeting of the American Psychological Association, Miami Beach, Florida.

Henley, Nancy, and Freeman, Jo. 1976. The sexual politics of interpersonal behavior. In *Female psychology: the emerging self,* ed. Sue Cox, pp. 171–79. Chicago: Science Research Associates.

Hess, Robert D., and Shipman, Virginia C. 1967. Cognitive elements in maternal behavior. In *Minnesota symposia on child psychology,* vol. 1, ed. John P. Hill, pp. 57–81. Minneapolis: University of Minnesota Press.

Hoffman, Lois Wladis. 1972. Early childhood experiences and women's achievement motives. *Journal of social issues* 28(2):129–55.

———. 1974. Fear of success in males and females: 1965 and 1971. *Journal of consulting and clinical psychology* 42:353–58.

Horner, Matina S. 1969. Fail: bright women. *Psychology today* 3 (November):36–38ff.

Joffe, Carole, 1971. Sex role socialization and the nursery school: as the twig is bent. *Journal of marriage and the family* 33:467–75.

Katz, M. L. 1973. *Female motive to avoid success: a psychological barrier or a response to deviancy?* Princeton, New Jersey: Educational Testing Service.

Kohlberg, Lawrence. 1966. A cognitive-developmental analysis of children's sex-role concepts and attitudes. In *The development of sex differences,* ed. Eleanor E. Maccoby, pp. 82–173. Stanford, California: Stanford University Press.

———. 1969. Stage and sequence: the cognitive-developmental approach to socialization. In *Handbook of socialization theory and research,* ed. David A. Goslin, pp. 347–480. Chicago: Rand McNally.

Kohlberg, Lawrence, and Zigler, Edward. 1967. The impact of cognitive maturity on the development of sex-role attitudes in the years 4 to 8. *Genetic psychology monographs* 75:89–165.

Lambert, W. E.; Yackley, A.; and Hein, R. N. 1971. Child training values of English Canadian and French Canadian parents. *Canadian journal of behavioural science* 3:217–36.

Lansky, Leonard M. 1967. The family structure also affects the model: sex-role attitudes in parents of preschool children. *Merrill-Palmer quarterly* 13:139–50.

Levenson, Hanna; Burford, Brent; Bonno, Bobbie; and Davis, Loren. 1975. Are women still prejudiced against women? a replication and extension of Goldberg's study. *Journal of psychology* 89:67–71.

Lynn, David B. 1966. The process of learning parental and sex-role identification. *Journal of marriage and the family* 28:466–70.

———. 1969. *Parental and sex-role identification: a theoretical formulation.* Berkeley, California: McCutchan.

McClelland, David C.; Atkinson, John W.; Clark, Russell A.; and Lowell, Edgar L. 1953. *The achievement motive.* New York: Appleton-Century-Crofts.

Maccoby, Eleanor Emmons, and Jacklin, Carol Nagy. 1974. *The psychology of sex differences.* Stanford, California: Stanford University Press.

Martyna, Wendy. In press. Beyond the he/man approach: a case for linguistic change. *SIGNS: Journal of women in culture and society.*

Milgram, Stanley. 1974. The frozen world of the familiar stranger. *Psychology today* 8 (June):70–73ff.

Milgram, Stanley, and Shotland, R. Lance. 1973. *Television and anti-social behavior: field experiments.* New York: Academic Press.

Mischel, Harriet. 1974. Sex bias in the evaluation of professional achievements. *Journal of educational psychology* 66:157–66.

Mischel, Walter. 1966. A social-learning view of sex differences in behavior. In *The development of sex differences,* ed. Eleanor E. Maccoby, pp. 56–81. Stanford, California: Stanford University Press.

———. 1970. Sex-typing and socialization. In *Carmichael's manual of child psychology,* vol. 2, ed. Paul H. Mussen, pp. 3–72. New York: Wiley.

Mischel, Walter, and Grusec, Joan. 1966. Determinants of the rehearsal and transmission of neutral and aversive behaviors. *Journal of personality and social psychology* 3:197–205.

Morris, M. B. 1970. Anti-feminism: some discordant data. Paper read at annual meeting of the Pacific Sociological Association.

Mussen, Paul H. 1962. Long-term consequents of masculinity of interests in adolescence. *Journal of consulting psychology* 26:435–40.

Mussen, Paul H., and Rutherford, Eldred. 1963. Parent-child relations and parental personality in relation to young children's sex-role preferences. *Child development* 34:589–607.

Ollison, Linda. 1975. Socialization: women, worth, and work. Unpublished paper, San Diego State University, San Diego.

Pheterson, Gail I.; Kiesler, Sara B.; and Goldberg, Philip A. 1971. Evaluation of the performance of women as a function of their sex, achievement, and personal history. *Journal of personality and social psychology* 19:114–18.

Robbins, Lillian, and Robbins, Edwin. 1973. Comment on "Toward an understanding of achievement-related conflicts in women." *Journal of social issues* 29(1):133–37.

Rotter, Julian B., and Hochreich, Dorothy J. 1973. Cited in Women's expectations for and causal attributions of success and failure, by Irene Hanson Frieze, in *Women and achievement: social and motivational analyses,* eds. Martha T. Shuch Mednick, Sandra Schwartz Tangri, and Lois Wladis Hoffman, pp. 158–71, 1975. New York: Halsted Press.

Rubin, Jeffrey Z.; Provenzano, Frank J.; and Luria, Zella. 1974. The eye of the beholder: parents' views on sex of newborns. *American journal of orthopsychiatry* 44:512–19.

Sears, Robert R.; Maccoby, Eleanor E.; and Levin, Harry. 1957. *Patterns of child rearing.* Evanston, Illinois: Row, Peterson.

Serbin, Lisa A., and O'Leary, K. Daniel. 1975. How nursery schools teach girls to shut up. *Psychology today* 9 (December):56–58ff.

Shaver, Phillip. 1976. Questions concerning fear of success and its conceptual relatives. *Sex roles* 2:305–20.

Simon, J. G., and Feather, N. T. 1973. Causal attributions for success and failure at university examinations. *Journal of educational psychology* 64:46–56.

Sternglanz, Sarah H., and Serbin, Lisa A. 1974. Sex role stereotyping in children's television programs. *Developmental psychology* 10:710–15.

Tangri, Sandra Schwartz. 1972. Determinants of occupational role innovation among college women. *Journal of social issues* 28(2):177–99.

Tidball, M. Elizabeth. 1973. Perspective on academic women and affirmative action. *Educational record* 54:130–35.

Tresemer, David. 1974. Fear of success: popular, but unproven. *Psychology today* 7 (March):82–85.

U'Ren, Marjorie B. 1971. The image of women in textbooks. In *Woman in sexist society: studies in power and powerlessness,* eds. Vivian Gornick and Barbara K. Moran, pp. 318–46. New York: New American Library.

Weitzman, Lenore J.; Eifler, Deborah; Hokada, Elizabeth; and Ross, Catherine. 1972. Sex role socialization in picture books for pre-school children. *American journal of sociology* 77:1125–50.

Weston, Peter J., and Mednick, Martha T. Shuch. 1970. Race, social class and the motive to avoid success in women. *Journal of cross-cultural psychology* 1:283–91.

Will, Jerrie; Self, Patricia; and Datan, Nancy. 1974. Unpublished paper presented at 82nd annual meeting of the American Psychological Association.

Women on Words and Images. 1972. Dick and Jane as victims: sex stereotyping in children's readers. Princeton, New Jersey.

———. 1975. Channeling children: sex stereotyping on prime time TV. Princeton, New Jersey.

Chapter 7
Earning the Bread vs. Baking It:
The Sociological Perspective

Adams, Margaret. 1971. The compassion trap. In *Woman in sexist society: studies in power and powerlessness,* eds. Vivian Gornick and Barbara K. Moran, pp. 555–75. New York: New American Library.

Bart, Pauline. 1971. Depression in middle-aged women. In *Woman in sexist society: studies in power and powerlessness,* eds. Vivian Gornick and Barbara K. Moran, pp. 163–86. New York: New American Library.

Bernard, Jessie. 1972. *The future of marriage.* New York: Bantam.

Birnbaum, Judith Abelew. 1975. Life patterns and self-esteem in gifted family-oriented and career-committed women. In *Women and achievement: social and motivational analyses,* eds. Martha T. Shuch Mednick, Sandra Schwartz Tangri, and Lois Wladis Hoffman, pp. 396–419. New York: Halsted Press.

Bunker, Barbara Benedict. 1976. Women in groups. Unpublished ms.

Campbell, Angus. 1975. The American way of mating: marriage sí, children only maybe. *Psychology today* 8 (May):37–43.

Clancy, Kevin, and Gove, Walter. 1975. Sex differences in mental illness: an analysis of response bias in self-reports. *American journal of sociology* 80:205–15.

Coser, Rose Laub, and Rokoff, Gerald. 1971. Women in the occupational world: social disruption and conflict. *Social problems* 18:535–54.

Crowley, Joan E.; Levitin, Teresa E.; and Quinn, Robert P. 1973. Seven deadly half-truths about women. *Psychology today* 6 (March):94–96.

Douvan, Elizabeth. n.d. Two careers and one family: potential pitfalls and certain complexity. Unpublished ms., Department of Psychology, University of Michigan, Ann Arbor.

Epstein, Cynthia Fuchs. 1970. *Woman's place.* Berkeley and Los Angeles: University of California Press.

Ferree, Myra Marx. 1976. The confused American housewife. *Psychology today* 10 (September):76–80.

Fidell, Linda S., and Prather, Jane E. 1976. The housewife syndrome: fact or fiction? Unpublished ms., California State College at Northridge.

Gillespie, Dair L. 1976. Who has the power? the marital struggle. In *Female psychology: the emerging self,* ed. Sue Cox, pp. 192–211. Chicago: Science Research Associates.

Glick, Paul C. 1975. A demographer looks at American families. *Journal of marriage and the family* 37:15–26.

Gove, Walter. 1972. The relationship between sex roles, mental illness, and marital status. *Social forces* 51:34–44.

Gove, Walter R., and Tudor, Jeannette F. 1973. Adult sex roles and mental illness. *American journal of sociology* 78:812–32.

Gurin, Gerald; Veroff, Joseph; and Feld, Sheila. 1960. *Americans view their mental health.* New York: Basic Books.

Hacker, Helen Mayer. 1951. Women as a minority group. *Social forces* 30:60–69.

Hennig, Margaret, and Jardim, Anne. 1977. *The managerial woman.* New York: Doubleday.

Hochschild, Arlie Russell. 1975. The sociology of feeling and emotion. In *Another voice,* eds. Marcia Millman and Rosabeth M. Kanter, pp. 280–308. Garden City, New York: Anchor/Doubleday.

Hughes, Everett C. 1958. *Men and their work.* Glencoe, Illinois: The Free Press.

Hunt, Janet G., and Hunt, Larry L. 1975. Dilemmas and contradictions of status: the case of the dual-career family. Paper read at annual convention of the Southern Sociological Society, April, Washington, D.C.

Johnson, Paula B. 1976. Women and power: towards a theory of effectiveness. *Journal of social issues* 32:99–110.

Johnson, Paula B., and Goodchilds, Jacqueline D. 1976. How women get their way. *Psychology today* 10 (October):69–70.

Kanter, Rosabeth Moss. 1975. Women and the structure of organizations: explorations in theory and behavior. In *Another voice,* eds. Marcia Millman and Rosabeth M. Kanter, pp. 34–75. Garden City, New York: Anchor/Doubleday.

———. 1976a. Why bosses turn bitchy. *Psychology today* 9 (May):56–59.

———. 1976b. Women in organizations: sex roles, group dynamics, and change strategies. In *Beyond sex roles,* ed. Alice Sargent, pp. 371–87. St. Paul, Minnesota: West Publishing.

Knupfer, Genevieve; Clark, Walter; and Room, Robin. 1966. The mental health of the unmarried. *American journal of psychiatry* 122 (February):842–44.

Kohn, Melvin, and Schooler, Carmi. 1973. Occupational experience and psychological functioning: an assessment of reciprocal effects. *American sociological review* 38:97–118.

Levitin, Teresa E.; Quinn, Robert P.; and Staines, Graham L. 1973. A woman is 58% of a man. *Psychology today* 6 (March):89–92.

Lieberman, Seymour. 1965. The effects of changes in roles on the attitudes of role occupants. In *Basic studies in social psychology,* eds. H. Proshansky and B. Seidenberg, pp. 485–94. New York: Holt, Rinehart and Winston.

Milgram, Stanley. 1974. The frozen world of the familiar stranger. A conversation with Stanley Milgram, by Carol Tavris. *Psychology today* 8 (June):70–80.

Myrdal, Gunnar. 1944. A parallel to the Negro problem (appendix 5), in *An American dilemma.* New York: Harper & Row.

Oppenheimer, Valerie Kincade. 1970. *The female labor force in the United States.* Population Monograph Series, no. 5. Berkeley: University of California Press.

———. 1975. The sex-labeling of jobs. In *Women and achievement: social and motivational analyses,* eds. Martha T. Shuch Mednick, Sandra Schwartz Tangri, and Lois Wladis Hoffman, pp. 307–25. New York: Halsted Press.

Osmond, Marie W., and Martin, Patricia Y. 1975. Sex and sexism: a comparison of male and female sex-role attitudes. *Journal of marriage and the family* 37:744–58.

Poloma, Margaret M. 1972. Role conflict and the married professional woman. In *Toward a sociology of women,* ed. Constantina Safilios-Rothschild, pp. 187–99. Lexington, Massachusetts: Xerox College Publishing.

Rapoport, Rhona, and Rapoport, Robert N. 1972. The dual-career family: a variant pattern and social change. In *Toward a sociology of women,* ed. Constantina Safilios-Rothschild, pp. 216–45. Lexington, Massachusetts: Xerox College Publishing.

Robertson, Wyndham. 1973. The ten highest-ranking women in big business. *Fortune* (April):81–89.

Robinson, Nancy H., and Robinson, John P. 1975. Sex roles and the territoriality of everyday behavior. Unpublished ms., Survey Research Center, University of Michigan, Ann Arbor.

Rossi, Alice S. 1965. Barriers to the career choice of engineering, medicine, or science among American women. In *Women and the scientific professions,* eds. J. A. Mattfeld and C. G. Van Aken, pp. 51–127. Cambridge, Massachusetts: M.I.T. Press.

―――. 1975. The future of the American family. Address delivered at Randolph-Macon Woman's College, November.

―――. n.d. The roots of ambivalence in American women. Unpublished ms.

Ruble, Diane N., and Higgins, E. Tory. 1976. Effects of group sex composition on self-presentation and sex-typing. *Journal of social issues* 32:725–31.

Selected symptoms of psychological distress. 1970. Series 11, no. 37. Washington, D.C.: National Center for Health Statistics, United States Department of Health, Education, and Welfare.

Shaver, Phillip, and Freedman, Jonathan. 1976. Your pursuit of happiness. *Psychology today* 10 (August):26–32.

Staines, Graham; Tavris, Carol; and Jayaratne, Toby Epstein. 1974. The queen bee syndrome. *Psychology today* 7 (January):55–60.

Stone, Philip J. 1972. Child care in twelve countries. In *The use of time,* ed. Alexander Szalai, pp. 249–64. The Hague, The Netherlands: Mouton.

Suter, Larry E., and Miller, Herman P. 1973. Income differences between men and career women. *American journal of sociology* 78:962–74.

Treiman, Donald J., and Terrell, Kermit. 1975. Sex and the process of status attainment: a comparison of working women and men. *American sociological review* 40:174–200.

United States Department of Labor. 1974. *Monthly labor review,* April.

Van Dusen, Roxann A., and Sheldon, Eleanor Bernert. 1976. The changing status of American women: a life cycle perspective. *American psychologist* 31:106–17.

Vanek, Joann. 1974. Time spent in housework. *Scientific American* 231 (November):14, 116–20.

Waller, Willard. 1938. *The family: a dynamic interpretation.* New York: Dryden.

Wolman, Carol, and Frank, Hal. 1975. The solo woman in a professional peer group. *American journal of orthopsychiatry* 45:164–71.

Chapter 8
The Origins of Roles and Rituals:
The Evolutionary Perspective

Bohannan, Laura, and Bohannan, Paul. 1953. *The Tiv of central Nigeria.* Ethnographic Survey of Africa: Western Africa, part 7. London: International African Institute.

Boserup, Ester. 1970. *Woman's role in economic development.* New York: St. Martin's Press.

Brown, Judith K. 1970. Economic organization and the position of women among the Iroquois. *Ethnohistory* 17:151–67.

―――. 1975. Iroquois women: an ethnohistoric note. In *Toward an anthropology of women,* ed. Rayna R. Reiter, pp. 235–51. New York and London: Monthly Review Press.

Campbell, Donald. 1975a. The experimenting society. A conversation with Donald Campbell, by Carol Tavris. *Psychology today* 9 (September):46–56.

———. 1975b. On the conflicts between biological and social evolution and between psychology and moral tradition. *American psychologist* 30:1103–26.

Chagnon, Napoleon A. 1968. *Yanomamo: the fierce people.* New York: Holt, Rinehart and Winston.

Collier, Jane Fishburne. 1974. Women in politics. In *Woman, culture, and society,* eds. Michelle Zimbalist Rosaldo and Louise Lamphere, pp. 89–97. Stanford, California: Stanford University Press.

Divale, William Tulio, and Harris, Marvin. 1976. Population, warfare, and the male supremacist complex. *American anthropologist* 78:521–39.

Draper, Patricia. 1975. !Kung women: contrasts in sexual egalitarianism in foraging and sedentary contexts. In *Toward an anthropology of women,* ed. Rayna R. Reiter, pp. 77–110. New York and London: Monthly Review Press.

Engels, Friedrich. 1973. *The origin of the family, private property and the state,* ed. Eleanor Burke Leacock. New York: International Publishers.

Friedl, Ernestine. 1975. *Women and men: an anthropologist's view.* New York: Holt, Rinehart and Winston.

Gouldner, Alvin W. 1970. *The coming crisis of Western sociology.* New York and London: Basic Books.

Harding, Susan. 1975. Women and words in a Spanish village. In *Toward an anthropology of women,* ed. Rayna R. Reiter, pp. 283–309. New York and London: Monthly Review Press.

Harris, Marvin. 1968. *The rise of anthropological theory.* New York: Thomas Y. Crowell.

———. 1974. *Cows, pigs, wars, and witches: the riddles of culture.* New York: Random House.

———. 1975. Male supremacy is on the way out. It was just a phase in the evolution of culture. A conversation with Marvin Harris, by Carol Tavris. *Psychology today* 8 (January):61–69.

Hayes, Rose Oldfield. 1975. Female genital mutilation, fertility control, women's roles, and the patrilineage in modern Sudan: a functional analysis. *American ethnologist* 2:617–34.

Johnson, Orna R., and Johnson, Allen. 1975. Male/female relations and the organization of work in a Machiguenga community. *American ethnologist* 2:634–48.

Lamphere, Louise. 1974. Strategies, cooperation, and conflict among women in domestic groups. In *Woman, culture, and society,* eds. Michelle Zimbalist Rosaldo and Louise Lamphere, pp. 97–113. Stanford, California: Stanford University Press.

Lancaster, C. S. 1976. Women, horticulture, and society in sub-Saharan Africa. *American anthropologist* 78:539–65.

Leis, Nancy B. 1974. Women in groups: Ijaw women's associations. In *Woman, culture, and society,* eds. Michelle Zimbalist Rosaldo and Louise Lamphere, pp. 223–43. Stanford, California: Stanford University Press.

Martin, M. Kay, and Voorhies, Barbara. 1975. *Female of the species.* New York and London: Columbia University Press.

Marx, Karl. 1964. *Selected writings in sociology and social philosophy,* tr. T. B. Bottomore. New York: McGraw-Hill.

Naroll, Raoul, and Divale, William Tulio. 1976. Natural selection in cultural evolution: warfare versus peaceful diffusion. *American ethnologist* 3:97–128.

Ortner, Sherry B. 1974. Is female to male as nature is to culture? In *Woman, culture, and society,* eds. Michelle Zimbalist Rosaldo and Louise Lamphere. Stanford, California: Stanford University Press.

Paige, Karen E. In press. Sexual pollution: reproductive sex taboos in American society. *Journal of social issues.*

Paige, Karen E., and Paige, Jeffery M. 1973. The politics of birth practices: a strategic analysis. *American sociological review* 38:663–76.

Paige, Karen E., and Paige, Jeffery M. In press. *Politics and reproductive rituals.* Berkeley: University of California Press.

Reed, Evelyn. 1975. *Women's evolution.* New York: Pathfinder.

Reiter, Rayna R., ed. 1975. *Toward an anthropology of women.* New York and London: Monthly Review Press.

Rogers, Susan Carol. 1975. Female forms of power and the myth of male dominance. *American ethnologist* 2:727–55.

Rosaldo, Michelle Zimbalist. 1974. Woman, culture, and society: a theoretical overview. In *Woman, culture, and society,* eds. Michelle Zimbalist Rosaldo and Louise Lamphere, pp. 17–43. Stanford, California: Stanford University Press.

Rubin, Gayle. 1975. The traffic in women. In *Toward an anthropology of women,* ed. Rayna R. Reiter, pp. 157–211. New York and London: Monthly Review Press.

Sacks, Karen. 1974. Engels revisited: women, the organization of production, and private property. In *Woman, culture, and society,* eds. Michelle Zimbalist Rosaldo and Louise Lamphere, pp. 211–35. Stanford, California: Stanford University Press.

———. 1976. State bias and women's status. *American anthropologist* 78:565–70.

Sanday, Peggy R. 1973. Toward a theory of the status of women. *American anthropologist* 75:1682–1700.

———. 1974. Female status in the public domain. In *Woman, culture, and society,* eds. Michelle Zimbalist Rosaldo and Louise Lamphere, pp. 189–207. Stanford, California: Stanford University Press.

Sherfey, Mary Jane. 1973. *The nature and evolution of female sexuality.* New York: Vintage.

Turner, Victor W. 1962. Three symbols of passage in Ndembu circumcision ritual: an interpretation. In *Essays on the ritual of social relations,* ed. Max Gluckman, pp. 124–73. Manchester, England: Manchester University Press.

Whiting, John W. M.; Kluckhohn, Richard; and Anthony, Albert. 1958. The function of male initiation ceremonies at puberty. In *Readings in social psychology,* eds. E. Maccoby, T. M. Newcomb, and E. L. Hartley, pp. 359–70. New York: Holt.

Wispé, Lauren G., and Thompson, James N., Jr. 1976. The war between the words: biological versus social evolution and some related issues. *American psychologist* 31:341–47.

Chapter 9
Conclusion: The Age of Alliance?

Bernard, Jessie. 1976. Maternal deprivation: a new twist. *Contemporary psychology* 21:172–74.

Campbell, Colin. 1976. What happens when we get the manchild pill? *Psychology today* 10 (August):86–91.

Committee of Concerned Asian Scholars. 1972. *China! Inside the People's Republic.* New York: Bantam.

Curtin, Katie. 1975. *Women in China.* New York and Toronto: Pathfinder Press.

Diamond, Norma. 1975. Collectivization, kinship, and status of women in rural China. In *Toward an anthropology of women,* ed. Rayna R. Reiter, pp. 372–96. New York and London: Monthly Review Press.

Dodge, Norton T. 1966. *Women in the Soviet economy: their role in economic, scientific, and technical development.* Baltimore: Johns Hopkins Press.

Engels, Friedrich. 1973. *The origin of the family, private property and the state,* ed. Eleanor Burke Leacock. New York: International Publishers.

Field, Mark G., and Flynn, Karin I. 1970. Worker, mother, housewife: Soviet woman today. In *Sex roles in changing society,* eds. Georgene H. Seward and Robert C. Williamson, pp. 257–84. New York: Random House.

Galbraith, John Kenneth. 1973. The economics of the American housewife. *Atlantic* (August):78–83.

Gerson, Menachem. 1971. Women in the kibbutz. *American journal of orthopsychiatry* 41:566–73.

Guttentag, Marcia, and Bray, Helen. 1976. *Undoing sex stereotypes.* New York: McGraw-Hill.

Haavio-Mannila, Elina. 1975. Convergences between east and west: tradition and modernity in sex roles in Sweden, Finland, and the Soviet Union. In *Women and achievement: social and motivational analyses,* eds. Martha T. Shuch Mednick, Sandra Schwartz Tangri, and Lois Wladis Hoffman, pp. 71–84. New York: Halsted Press.

Harris, Marvin. 1975. Male supremacy is on the way out. It was just a phase in the evolution of culture. A conversation with Marvin Harris, by Carol Tavris. *Psychology today* 8 (January):61–69.

Mandel, William M. 1975. *Soviet women.* Garden City, New York: Anchor Books.

Martin, M. Kay, and Voorhies, Barbara. 1975. *Female of the species.* New York and London: Columbia University Press.

Marx, Karl. 1964. *Selected writings in sociology and social philosophy,* tr. T. B. Bottomore. New York: McGraw-Hill.

Mednick, Martha T. Shuch. 1975. Social change and sex-role inertia: the case of the kibbutz. In *Women and achievement: social and motivational analyses,* eds. Martha T. Shuch Mednick, Sandra Schwartz Tangri, and Lois Wladis Hoffman, pp. 85–103. New York: Halsted Press.

Myrdal, Alva, and Klein, Viola. 1956. *Women's two roles: home and work.* London: Routledge and Kegan Paul.

Rosner, Menahem. 1967. Women in the kibbutz: changing status and concepts. *Asian and African studies* 3:35–68.

Safilios-Rothschild, Constantina. 1975. A cross-cultural examination of women's marital, educational, and occupational options. In *Women and achievement: social and motivational analyses,* eds. Martha T. Shuch Mednick, Sandra Schwartz Tangri, and Lois Wladis Hoffman, pp. 48–70. New York: Halsted Press.

Scott, Hilda. 1974. *Does socialism liberate women? Experiences from eastern Europe.* Boston: Beacon Press.

Talmon, Yonina. 1972. *Family and community in the kibbutz.* Cambridge, Massachusetts: Harvard University Press.

Tavris, Carol. 1974. Women in China: the speak-bitterness revolution. *Psychology today* 7 (May):43–47ff.

Tiger, Lionel, and Shepher, Joseph. 1975. *Women in the kibbutz.* New York: Harcourt Brace Jovanovich.

Trotsky, Leon. 1970. *Women and the family.* Introduction by Caroline Lund. New York: Pathfinder Press.

Index

baboons: nurturance of, 125; sex differences in, 95, 98, 99

Bachofen, Johann Jakob: *Mutterrecht, Das,* 16–17

Bacon, Margaret K., 16

Baker, Susan, 107 *n.*

Bamberger, Joan, 17

Bandura, Albert, 165, 166 *n.*, 170, 182

Bardwick, Judith M., 44, 67, 107, 114, 115, 117

Barry, H., 16

Bart, Pauline, 77–78 and *n.*, 121, 223

Beatrice, 2

Beauvoir, Simone de, 156, 183–84

Bedouin, 246, 264

behavior: biologically determined, 45, 94–99, 104 and *n.*, 105–16, 118, 121–24, 125, 126, 127–28, 140, 141, 163, 202, 251–52, 259, 288–89; culturally conditioned, 11, 53, 87–89 and *n.*, 90, 94, 95, 98, 103, 107 *n.*, 108, 109–10, 116, 118, 124–26, 127–28, 162–86, 195, 202–14, 232, 239–69, 288, 289; feminine, 16, 47, 139, 141, 142–43, 148, 150–52, 156, 162–88, 191–92, 194 *n.*, 195, 202, 210–11, 213–14, 219, 225, 231–32, 233–34, 288, 289–92; masculine, 16, 141, 148, 150–51, 156, 162–88, 191, 195, 211, 213–14, 219, 231, 233–34, 282, 291, 292; media stereotypes of, 182–83; rules for, 7–9, 15, 25, 98, 171, 202, 203, 239; *see also* men; women

behaviorist school, 164–66 and *n.*, 168–69, 202

Behrman, JoAnn, 107 *n.*

Belgium, 230 *n.*

Bell, Robert R., 65

Bem, Daryl, 176, 195

Bem, Sandra, 47, 53, 176, 194–95, 211

Bemba, 262

Benedek, Thérèse, 112–13, 117

Benjamin, Harry, 108

Bergler, Edmund: *Kinsey's Myth of Female Sexuality* (with Kroger), 78

Berman, Edgar F., 118

Berman, Phyllis, 52

Bernard, Jessie, 197–98, 289–90; *Future of Marriage, The,* 219, 220–21, 222, 224, 225, 226

Bernays, Martha, 132–33

Bernstein, Irwin, 122

Bernstein, R. C., 44

Berry, John W., 103

Bettelheim, Bruno: *Symbolic Wounds,* 145–48

Bible, 6, 9, 17, 248

biological perspective, 94–128; animal research into, 94–99, 105, 121–22, 124–26; behavior determined by, 14, 45, 86–87, 88, 94–99, 104 and *n.*, 105–16, 118, 121–24, 125, 126, 127–28, 140, 141, 163, 202, 251–52, 259, 288–89; biogram and, 288–89; evaluation of, 127–28; and evolution, 48, 94–98, 240, 268, 288–89; prenatal factors in, 99–111; *see also* genetics, hormones; reproduction

Birnbaum, Judith, 228–30

birth-control pill, 216 *n.*; and menstrual anxiety, 115; *see also* population control

blacks, 63, 214; and achievement motive, 194 *n.*; and job segregation, 217; and premarital sex, 65, 66; self-esteem of, 188, 233–34; status of, 172, 233–34; and tokenism, 211, 213; as working wives, 218 *n.*

Bock, R.D., 102

Bohannan, Laura, 255

books for children, sex typing in, 162, 177 and *n.*, 178–80

Boserup, Ester, 254, 266 *n.*

Boston, Massachusetts, 20, 291

boys: abilities of, 35–36, 175; adult attention to, 175–76; bond to mother of, 173, 247; creativity of, 37–38; energy level of, 55; erections of, 87; hormonal imbalance in, 105–06, 107 *n.*; infantile sexuality of, 136–37, 155; Mangaian, 89–90; masturbation of, 75, 87–88, 137; multiple orgasms of, 81; and Oedipus complex, 137–38, 140, 148, 155–56, 168, 245; and parental disapproval, 173–74; personality traits of, 44–45, 49, 50, 51–52, 54–55, 97, 162, 163, 172, 173–76, 197; physical abilities of, 42; role playing of, 24; sex determination of, 99–100 and *n.*, 103–04, 108–10; sex-typing of, 162–88, 239, 247, 291–92; sexuality of, 87–88, 137, 155, 254; training of, 16, 24, 88; in tribal societies, 145, 147–48, 246–48; *see also* children; teenagers brain: and hormones, 104, 106–07, 108; and theory of inferiority of women, 13 and n., 14, 30

breast-feeding, 18, 95 n., 124, 260–61; male envy of, 143, 144

breasts: development of, 110; during menopause, 120

Brecher, Edward: *Sex Researchers, The,* 61–62

Broverman, Donald, 38–39 and n.

Broverman, Inge K., 21, 22–23

Brown, Judith K., 17, 238, 262

Brown, Roger, 184, 185

Browning, Robert and Elizabeth Barrett, 2

Brownmiller, Susan: *Against Our Will,* 8–9, 20

Brunswick, Ruth, 133

Bulgaria, 230 n.

Bullough, Vern L., 6, 7, 10

Bunker, Barbara, 218

Burr, Elizabeth, 184

Burton, Roger V., 148

Bushman, 259, 260; Dobe, 18

Campbell, Angus, 222, 223 and n., 228

Campbell, Colin, 280 n.

Canada, 284

cancer, 42, 119; and synthetic estrogen, 119 n.

capitalism, 256, 277, 282, 285, 290, 294; in Soviet Union, 281; and subjection of women, 256

castration complex: of men, 137–38, 143–44, 153–54, 155, 245; of women, 138, 142, 154

Cato, 10

cervix, during arousal and orgasm, 80, 82

Chagnon, Napoleon, 238, 240–41

Chaskes, Jay B., 65

Chiang Kai-Shek, 278 n.

Child, I. I., 16

childbirth, 139, 140, 260–61; male envy of, 143, 144, 146–48; natural, 147 n.; *see also* couvade

children: abuse of, 126; communal care of, 273, 275, 276, 278, 279, 282, 284, 285–86, 288, 289, 290, 295; illegitimate, 126 n., 255 n.; and nurturance, 51–53, 137, 146 n., 165, 170, 186, 232, 234, 290; personality set in, 162, 163, 195; and pleasure vs.

reality principles, 135, 136, 155, 163; sacrifice of, 149; *see also* boys; girls

chimpanzees: and incest taboo, 98; maternal behavior of, 125; sex differences of, 97; sexuality of, 251–52

China, ancient, 9, 18, 194

China, People's Republic of, 42; Communist Party of, 278 and n., 279, 280; continuing revolution in, 281; division of labor in, 279–81; equality experiment in, 25, 272, 277–81, 290, 293–94; feminist movements in, 277–78, 280, 294; repression in, 277; and sexual liberation, 279

chivalric rules, 8

Chodorow, Nancy, 166, 173

Christensen, Harold T., 64, 67

chromosomes, 99–103, 104

circumcision, 145, 239, 240; and castration anxiety, 245; and father–son rivalry, 245; as manhood ritual, 247; as tribal loyalty symbol, 246–48, 251

Clancy, Kevin, 222 n.

Cleopatra, 2, 5, 18

clitoris, 83 n., 88, 89, 105, 109; during arousal, 80, 83; and infantile sexuality, 137, 138; and intercourse, 76; and masturbation, 75, 76, 137, 139; and orgasm, 82–85 and n.

cognitive ability, 38–41

cognitive-developmental theory, 166–68, 169–71

Cohen, Arthur, 206

Committee of Concerned Asian Scholars, 280

communication: and evolution, 268; language and; 164, 184 and n., 185; nonverbal, 47–48, 185; subliminal, 183–86, 291–92

communism: in China, 278 and n., 279–81; and equality, 256–57, 273–75, 278–81, 290–91; in Soviet Union, 274–75; and status differences, 275

Comnena, Anna, 4 n.

competition, 191, 193, 285; and job segregation, 217; and men, 191, 193; and women, 191, 193–94, 214

conception, 144, 146, 157, 253

Condry, John, 192–93

conscience, and superego, 134, 137

contraception, 135, 216 n., 276

Cook, M., 56 n.

80–81, 87, 252 n.; physiological responses to, 78–80, 83–84; therapy to induce, 76 n.; time to reach, 76–77; vaginal, 82–85 and n.; in Victorian era, 62

orgasms, male, 77, 90; and ejaculation, 80, 81–82; and ejaculation, premature, 90; frequency of, 64, 87; in masturbation, 79; multiple, 80, 81–82; physiological responses to, 78–80, 82; time to reach, 76

Ortner, Sherry, 265 n.

Osmond, Marie W., 232

ovaries, 103–04, 105, 110, 112; during menopause, 119

ovulation, 112, 114, 117, 119, 254, 260

ovum, 99

Paige, Jeffery M., 116, 245–46 and n., 247–51

Paige, Karen, 111, 113, 115–16, 121, 245–46 and n., 247–51

Paliyans, 258

Pan Chao, 4 n.

parent, 21; and disapproval of children, 173–75; -infant exchanges, 173 n.; nurturance by, 124–26, 165; and sex-typing, 162, 163–66 and n., 168, 169–70, 171–74, 194, 198; see also fathers; mothers

Parke, Ross, 53

Parker, Seymour, 148

Parlee, Mary Brown, 39 n., 113

Parsons, Jacque, 169, 170

passivity, 139 and n., 140, 143, 144, 151, 242, 244

patriarchy, 17, 143, 150, 256, 291; and Freud, 132–33, 136, 140

Pauly, L., 108

pedestal-gutter syndrome, 3, 7, 61, 150, 185, 239

penis, 83 n., 105; during arousal and orgasm, 80, 83; construction of, 108; erection of, 108, 144; erections of, in boys, 87; in infantile sexuality, 137; and Oedipus complex, 137–39; in refractory period, 80; in rites, 146–47, 240

penis envy concept: criticism of, 142–44, 150–52, 153, 154; of Freud, 134, 138–42, 155, 289; interpretation of, 155

Pensa, U.S.S.R., 282–83

Peplau, Anne, 46

People's Republic of China, see China, People's Republic of

Persky, Harold, 113–14, 118, 122

personality: changes in, 195, 197; and hormones, 107, 110; and Oedipus complex, 137, 138–39, 141–43; as set in childhood, 162, 163, 195; traits, 13–16, 20–24, 32, 33, 37, 43–56, 136, 140–41, 168–69, 172, 173–76, 187–88, 195–98, 202–03, 234, 239; and work, 206–07; see also behavior; men; women

Peru, 230 and n.

Peterson, Candida C. and James L., 21

phallic: stage, 137; symbols, 153 n.

Pheterson, Gail I., 189

Philippines, 16, 51

philosophes, 9, 10

Phoenix, Charles H., 104 n.

physiology: and belief in inferiority of women, 13 and n., 14, 24; of men, 13 and n., 14, 60, 73–74, 78–80; of sexual arousal, 60, 73–74, 77, 78–84, 88; of women, 13 and n., 14, 24, 60, 73–74, 77, 78–84

Piaget, Jean, 167

Pilagá, 146

pituitary gland, 104, 112, 119

Plato, 9, 12, 14

Playboy Foundation survey, see Hunt, Morton

Pliny, 6

Plutarch, 3

Poland, 281, 284

politics, 8, 10, 14, 18, 19, 24, 187, 208 n., 234; and equality experiments, 272, 274–75, 280–81, 285, 286, 287–88, 292

Poloma, Margaret, 227–28

polyandry, 15, 244, 251 and n., 255

polygamy, 278

polygyny, 15, 244, 251 and n., 254–55

Polynesian societies, 254 and n.

Pomeroy, Sarah, 3, 7, 10, 12, 16

Pomeroy, Wardell B., 64, 81

population control: and abortion, 275–76 and n., 279; and birth-control pill, 216 n.; and Catholics, 254; and freedom of women, 272, 279; and infanticide, 241–43, 255; and polyandry, 255; and sexual customs, 253 and n., 254, 255; and status of women, 266 n.; and warfare, 242–44, 253 n.

255; in Victorian era, 61, 62; and women, 60, 75–76, 139, 150; *see also* orgasm, female; orgasm, male

sexuality, 60–90; biologically determined, 86–87, 88, 94, 104 and n., 106, 251–52; conditioned by masturbation, 87; culturally conditioned, 87–89 and n., 90, 252 n.; and education, 65, 73; equality in, 24, 96, 150–51, 286; infantile, 136–37; of men, 6–7, 24, 60, 64, 67–81, 85–90, 135, 139 n., 251; problems in, 67–68; and sexual peaks, 88–89, 90; of women, 4–8, 24, 60, 64–89 and n., 90, 116, 120, 139 and n., 149, 208, 251–53; of women, men and, 4–8, 85–86, 252

sexual liberation, 90, 254, 279, 286; anxiety about, 85–86, 252 n.

sexual "perversions," 64, 141, 147

sexual repression, 61, 252 n., 254; in marriage, 135–36; and psychoanalysis, 135 n.; in Victorian era, 11, 60–62, 141

sexual taboos, 6, 144, 245, 250, 254, 260

Shainess, Natalie, 84

Shaver, Phillip, 45, 86, 192, 222, 224, 225

Shaw, George Bernard, 11 and n.

Sheldon, Eleanor Bernert, 216

Shepher, Joseph, 286, 288–89

Sherfey, Mary Jane, 87, 251–52 and n., 253

Sherman, Julia, 41, 42, 44, 117, 155

Shields, Stephanie, 13–14

Shipman, Virginia C., 175

Shorter, Edward, 62

Shotland, R. Lance, 182

Siberians, early, 5

Sigusch, Volkmar, 73

Simbiti, 249 n.

Simon, J. G., 189

Simon, William, 87–88

Singer, Jerome, 127

Singer, Josephine and Irving, 84 n.

Smith, Janet, 148

sociability, 32, 43–46, 197, 264; housewives' need for, 224

socialism, 256, 273; *see also* China; Israeli kibbutz; Soviet Union

socialization: consequences of, 186–94, 197–98, 203, 290–92; pleasure vs. reality principles in, 135 and n., 136, 155, 163;

and sex-typing, 162–88; sources of, 171–83, 194, 197; theories of, 164–71

social-learning theory, 164–66 and n., 170–71, 195 n.; modeling in, 165–66 and n., 168, 170, 178 n.; reinforcement in, 164–66 and n., 167–68, 171, 174, 186 n., 194, 195, 202, 294

social roles, 203–04; in marriage, 218–32; perpetuating inequality, 204, 232–34, 289, 290–93; role playing and, 24, 43; selfishness as requirement of, 226–27; and work, 204–18

Social Security Administration, 292

societies, 256; aging in, 120; behavior conditioned by, 11, 53, 87–89 and n., 90, 94, 95, 98, 103, 107 n., 108, 109–11, 116, 118, 124–26, 127–28, 162–86, 195, 202–14, 232, 239–69, 288, 289; change in, 204, 233, 268–69, 290–91, 293; drawing universal principles from specific, 152; equality experiments in, 25, 269, 272–95; and evolution, 94, 239–69; industrialized, 272, 277; regulations in, 6, 7–9, 15, 25, 98, 171, 202, 203, 239, 245 n., 246 n., 250; traditions in, 268–69; values in, 4 n., 15–19, 21, 24–25, 61, 171, 257, 290, 292–94

societies, tribal: customs of, 239–45 and n., 246 n., 253–55, 259, 260–66; division of labor in, 242, 256, 258–66; economic systems of, 244, 246, 248, 251, 253, 254–55, 262, 265; and fission, 242, 247, 248; horticultural, 246, 252, 255, 261–65; hunting and gathering, 18, 241–42, 246, 252, 256, 258–61, 265 n.; loyalty in, 245–48, 251; marriage in, 249, 254; myths of, 116, 148–50, 253; paternity rights in, 249 and n., 250–51, 255; power in, 240, 241–44, 246–47, 249, 255, 258, 261; rituals of, 145–46 and n.; 147–48, 239–40, 245–46 and n., 247–51, 253, 266; sexual taboos of, 245; status in, 262, 266 n.

sociological perspective, 202–34; evaluation of, 232–34; and marriage, 218–32; and work, 204–18; *see also* marriage; social roles; work

Solomon, Neil, 86

Somali, 264, 265

Sorensen, Robert, 66

FRANK A. BEACH for **Figure 3,** p. 96. Reprinted by permission.

SANDRA L. BEM for **Table 7,** p. 196. Reprinted by permission.

INGE K. BROVERMAN for **Table 1,** pp. 22–23. Reprinted by permission.

COLUMBIA UNIVERSITY PRESS for the table in footnote 10, p. 259, from *Female of the Species,* by M. Kay Martin and Barbara Voorhies. New York: Columbia University Press, 1975, p. 181. By permission of the publisher.

WILLIAM T. DIVALE for **Table 11,** p. 243. Reprinted by permission.

GERALD DUCKWORTH AND COMPANY LTD. for "General Review of the Sexual Situation," by Dorothy Parker, from *The Portable Dorothy Parker.* Reprinted by permission.

SIGMUND FREUD COPYRIGHTS LTD. for permission to quote from *The Letters of Sigmund Freud,* edited by Ernst L. Freud, 1961.

SIGMUND FREUD COPYRIGHTS LTD., THE INSTITUTE OF PSYCHO-ANALYSIS, AND THE HOGARTH PRESS LTD. for permission to quote from *The Standard Edition of the Complete Psychological Works of Sigmund Freud,* revised and edited by James Strachey.

HARPER & ROW, PUBLISHERS, INC., for **Figure 2,** p. 40, drawn from photo of "Rod-and-Frame Test" in *Personality Through Perception: An Experimental and Clinical Study,* by H. A. Witkin et al. Copyright 1954 by Harper & Row, Publishers, Inc. Reprinted by permission of the publisher.

HEMISPHERE PUBLISHING CORPORATION for **Table 10,** p. 229, from Judith Birnbaum, "Life Patterns and Self-Esteem," in *Women and Achievement,* eds. Martha Mednick, Sandra Tangri, and Lois Hoffman (Halsted, 1975). Reprinted by permission.

HOGARTH PRESS LTD. for permission to quote from *The Letters of Sigmund Freud,* edited by Ernst L. Freud, 1961.

HUMANITIES PRESS INC. for **Figure 1,** p. 39, from W. D. Ellis, ed., *A Source Book of Gestalt Psychology.* Reprinted by permission of Humanities Press Inc., New Jersey.

GENEVIEVE KNUPFER for **Table 9,** p. 221. Used by permission.

KAREN E. PAIGE for **Table 12,** p. 250. Used by permission.

PLAYBOY PRESS for **Table 3,** p. 66, from Morton Hunt, *Sexual Behavior in the 1970s.* Copyright © 1974 by Morton Hunt. Reprinted with permission of Playboy Press.

ROUTLEDGE & KEGAN PAUL LTD. for **Figure 1,** p. 39, from W. D. Ellis, ed., *A Source Book of Gestalt Psychology* (New Jersey: Humanities Press Inc., 1950). Reprinted by permission.

SOCIETY FOR THE PSYCHOLOGICAL STUDY OF SOCIAL ISSUES for **Table 1,** pp. 22–23, from Inge K. Broverman et al., "Sex Role Stereotypes: A Current Appraisal," *The Journal of Social Issues,* Vol. 28, no. 2 (1972). Reprinted by permission.

STANFORD UNIVERSITY PRESS for **Table 13,** p. 263, and **Figure 5,** p. 264, adapted from *Woman, Culture, and Society,* edited by Michelle Zimbalist Rosaldo and Louise Lamphere, with the permission of the publishers, Stanford University Press. © 1974 by the Board of Trustees of the Leland Stanford Junior University.

VIKING PRESS for "General Review of the Sexual Situation," from *The Portable Dorothy Parker.* Copyright 1926, 1954 by Dorothy Parker. Reprinted by permission of The Viking Press.

WOMEN ON WORDS & IMAGES for the table on p. 177, and **Table 6,** pp. 179–80, from *Dick and Jane as Victims: Sex Stereotyping in Children's Readers* (1972, 1975). Reprinted by permission of Women on Words & Images, Box 2163, Princeton, N.J. 08540. $2.00 ppd.

B 7
C 8
D 9
E 0
F 1
G 2
H 3
I 4
J 5